Community Policing
and Peacekeeping

Community Policing and Peacekeeping

Edited by
Peter Grabosky

with the assistance of Christine Nam

CRC Press
Taylor & Francis Group
Boca Raton London New York

CRC Press is an imprint of the
Taylor & Francis Group, an **informa** business

Cover photo courtesy of David Hegarty, 2001 leader of the International Peace Monitoring Team in the Solomon Islands. The community policing of weapons disposal in the Solomon Islands.

CRC Press
Taylor & Francis Group
6000 Broken Sound Parkway NW, Suite 300
Boca Raton, FL 33487-2742

First issued in paperback 2019

© 2009 by Taylor and Francis Group, LLC
CRC Press is an imprint of Taylor & Francis Group, an Informa business

No claim to original U.S. Government works

ISBN-13: 978-1-4200-9973-7 (hbk)
ISBN-13: 978-0-367-86427-9 (pbk)

Library of Congress Cataloging-in-Publication Data

Community policing and peacekeeping / Peter Grabosky, editor.
    p. cm. -- (Advances in police theory and practice series)
  Includes bibliographical references and index.
  ISBN 978-1-4200-9973-7 (hardcover : alk. paper)
    1. Community policing. 2. Police-community relations. 3. Peacekeeping forces. I. Grabosky, Peter N., 1945- II. Title.

HV7936.C83C6633 2009
363.2'3--dc22
    2009016172

Visit the Taylor & Francis Web site at
http://www.taylorandfrancis.com

and the CRC Press Web site at
http://www.crcpress.com

Table of Contents

Series Preface

While the literature on police and allied subjects is growing exponentially, its impact upon day-to-day policing remains small. The two worlds of research and practice of policing remain disconnected even though cooperation between the two is growing. A major reason is that the two groups speak in different languages. The research work is published in hard-to-access journals and presented in a manner that is difficult to comprehend for a lay person. On the other hand, the police practitioners tend not to mix with researchers and remain secretive about their work. Consequently, there is little dialogue between the two and almost no attempt to learn from one another. Dialogue across the globe, amongst researchers and practitioners situated in different continents, is, of course, even more limited.

I attempted to address this problem by starting the IPES, www.ipes.info, where a common platform has brought the two together. IPES is now in its 15th year. The annual meetings, which constitute most major annual events of the organization, have been hosted in all parts of the world. Several publications have come out of these deliberations and a new collaborative community of scholars and police officers has been created whose membership runs into several hundreds.

Another attempt was to begin a new journal, aptly called *Police Practice and Research: An International Journal* (PPR), which has opened the gate to practitioners to share their work and experiences. The journal has attempted to focus upon issues that help bring the two on a single platform. *PPR* is completing its 10th year in 2009. It is certainly evidence of growing collaboration between police research and practice that *PPR*, which began with 4 issues a year, expanded to 5 issues in its fourth year and now, it is issued 6 times a year.

Clearly, these attempts, despite their successes, remain limited. Conferences and journal publications do help create a body of knowledge and an association of police activists but cannot address substantial issues in depth. The limitations of time and space preclude larger discussions and more authoritative expositions that can provide stronger and broader linkages between the two worlds.

It is this realization of the increasing dialogue between police research and practice that has encouraged many of us — my close colleagues and I connected closely with IPES and *PPR* across the world — to conceive and implement a new attempt in this direction. I am now embarking on a book series, Advances in Police Theory and Practice, which seeks to attract writers from all parts of the world. Further, the attempt is to find practitioner contributors. The objective is to make the series a serious contribution to our knowledge of the police as well as to improve police practices. The focus is not only in work that describes the best and successful police practices but also one that challenges current paradigms and breaks new ground to prepare police for the twenty-first century. The series seeks comparative analysis that highlights achievements in distant parts of the world as well as one that encourages an in-depth examination of specific problems confronting a particular police force.

This ever-increasing search is illustrated by Peter Grabosky's *Community Policing and Peacekeeping,* which comprises a collection of essays focusing on two themes central to policing in the twenty-first century — developments in contemporary community policing and peacekeeping. It will make a valuable contribution to the literature on police partnerships with civil society and with other government agencies in western democratic societies. It provides comparative perspectives from China, South Africa, and Papua New Guinea. The book will also break important ground in the emerging field of police as peacekeepers — the delivery of policing services in weak and failing states and in post-conflict situations. This is particularly significant given the fragility of many states in the developing world, and the increasing demand for policing assistance. The collection contains contributions from world class scholars, including Anthony Braga, Harvard University; John Braithwaite, Australian National University; Martin Innes, Cardiff University; Tracey Meares, Yale University; David Thacher, University of Michigan; and Clifford Shearing, University of Cape Town. Among the book's many insights is the importance of cultural and political contexts in the delivery of police work, whether in advanced industrial societies or in poorer countries.

It is hoped that through this series it will be possible to accelerate the process of building knowledge about policing and help bridge the gap between the two worlds — the world of police research and police practice. This is an invitation to police scholars and practitioners across the world to come and join in this venture.

Dilip K. Das Ph.D.

Founding President,
International Police Executive Symposium, IPES, www.ipes.info

Founding Editor-in-Chief, *Police Practice and Research:*
An International Journal, PPR, www.tandf.co.uk/journals

Preface

This collection brings together two important themes in contemporary policing: community policing and peacekeeping. The two are not unrelated. Some (but not all) peacekeeping missions will entail elements of community policing. And wherever they are attempted, both community policing and peacekeeping are more easily said than done. To be accomplished properly, each entails considerable expense and requires extraordinary attention to local context and culture.

The significance of these themes is underscored by two contemporary trends that show no signs of abating. In modern industrial societies, the demand for policing services far exceeds the current and foreseeable availability of public policing resources. One needs look no further than the burgeoning private security industry for evidence of this. Consequently, public police must seek to engage with other institutions of civil society in order to get the most out of their own limited capacities. Community policing, despite its cost, is one way of doing this.

The second major theme is the weakening of states in many parts of the developing world. The inability of some states to provide a basic level of security for their citizens may bring about a request for law enforcement assistance; in extreme cases, it may instigate humanitarian intervention. Of course, donor nations may have their own geopolitical or economic reasons for embarking on peacekeeping missions. Whatever the case, the setting for peacekeeping may vary from modest development assistance to outright civil war. How police should deal with these different contingencies is beginning to receive important scholarly attention.

Sincere thanks are due to all the contributors to this volume for their exemplary cooperation throughout the life of the project. The superb editorial assistance of Christine Nam is gratefully acknowledged, as is the support of the Australian Research Council (LP0346987), the Australian Federal Police (ACT Policing), and the ARC Centre of Excellence in Policing and Security. Thanks are also due to the Regulatory Institutions Network of the Australian National University and the Berkeley Center for Criminal Justice for their institutional support, the editors at CRC Press for their guidance, and Professor Dilip Das for proposing this contribution to his series.

Peter Grabosky

Australian Research Council Centre of Excellence in Policing and Security
Regulatory Institutions Network
Research School of Pacific and Asian Studies
Australian National University
Canberra

The Editor

Peter Grabosky is a professor in the Regulatory Institutions Network, Research School of Pacific and Asian Studies, Australian National University, and is Deputy Director of the Australian Research Council Centre of Excellence in Policing and Security. He holds a PhD in political science from Northwestern University, and has written extensively on criminal justice and public policy. He is a Fellow of the Academy of the Social Sciences in Australia, and was the 2006 winner of the Sellin-Glueck Award of the American Society of Criminology for contributions to comparative and international criminology.

Contributors

Laurence Abbott
Universities' Police Science Institute
Cardiff University School of Social Sciences
Cardiff, United Kingdom
Email: abbottl@cardiff.ac.uk

Thierry Bouhours
Faculty of Law
Queensland University of Technology
Brisbane, Australia
Email: t-bouhours@qut.edu.au

David Bradley
Victoria Police
Melbourne, Australia
and
Adjunct Professor
Department of Psychology and Social
    Sciences
Edith Cowan University
Joondalup, Australia
Email: david.bradley@police.vic.gov.au

Anthony A. Braga
Program in Criminal Justice Policy and
    Management
Kennedy School of Government
Harvard University
Cambridge, Massachusetts
and
Berkeley Center for Criminal Justice
School of Law
University of California, Berkeley
Berkeley, California
Email: anthony_braga@harvard.edu

John Braithwaite
Regulatory Institutions Network
Australian National University
Canberra, Australia
Email: John.Braithwaite@anu.edu.au

Rod Broadhurst
ARC Centre of Excellence in Policing and
    Security
Regulatory Institutions Network
Research School of Pacific and Asian
    Studies
Australian National University
Canberra, Australia
Email: r.broadhurst@griffith.edu.au

Sinclair Dinnen
SSGM Program
College of Asia and the Pacific
Australian National University
Canberra, Australia
Email: sinclair.dinnen@anu.edu.au

Benoît Dupont
International Centre for Comparative
    Criminology
University of Montreal
Montreal, Quebec, Canada
Email: benoit.dupont@umontreal.ca

Mark Findlay
Law Faculty
University of Sydney
Sydney, Australia
Email: mark.findlay@usyd.edu.au

Jenny Fleming
Tasmanian Institute of Law Enforcement
    Studies
University of Tasmania
Hobart, Australia
Email: jenny.fleming@utas.edu.au

Andrew Goldsmith
Law and Criminal Justice
Flinders University
Adelaide, Australia
and
Centre for Transnational Crime Prevention
University of Wollongong
Belair, SA
Email: andrew.goldsmith@flinders.edu.au

Peter Grabosky
ARC Centre of Excellence in Policing and
    Security
Regulatory Institutions Network
Research School of Pacific and Asian
    Studies
Australian National University
Canberra, Australia
Email: peter.grabosky@anu.edu.au

B. K. Greener
International Relations
Massey University
Palmerston North, New Zealand
Email: B.Greener@Massey.AC.NZ

Steve Herbert
Department of Geography/Law, Societies
    and Justice Program
University of Washington
Seattle, Washington
Email: skherb@.u.washington.edu

Martin Innes
Universities' Police Science Institute
Cardiff University School of Social Sciences
Cardiff, United Kingdom
Email: innesm@Cardiff.ac.uk

Trudy Lowe
Universities' Police Science Institute
Cardiff University School of Social Sciences
Cardiff, United Kingdom
Email: Lowet@cardiff.ac.uk

Monique Marks
Sociology Programme
University of KwaZulu-Natal
Howard College
Durban, South Africa
Email: marks@ukzn.ac.za

John McFarlane
Strategic and Defence Studies Centre
Australian National University
and
School of Humanities and Social Sciences
University of New South Wales
Australian Defence Force Academy
Canberra, Australia
Email: j.mcfarlane@adfa.edu.au

Abby McLeod
Australian Federal Police
International Deployment Group
Canberra, Australia
Email: abby.mcleod@afp.gov.au

Tracey Meares
Yale Law School
New Haven, Connecticut
and
Berkeley Center for Criminal Justice
School of Law
University of California, Berkeley
Berkeley, California
Email: tracey.meares@yale.edu

Tony Murney
Australian Federal Police
Canberra, Australia
Email: tony.murney@afp.gov.au

David Onek
Berkeley Center for Criminal Justice
School of Law
University of California, Berkeley
Berkeley, California
Email: donek@law.berkeley.edu

Juani O'Reilly
Policy and Future Strategies
Australian Federal Police
Canberra, Australia
Email: juani.o'reilly@afp.gov.au

Liliokanaio Peaslee
Department of Political Science
James Madison University
Harrisonburg, Virginia
Email: peaslelx@jmu.edu

Colin Roberts
Universities' Police Science Institute
Cardiff University School of Social
    Sciences
Cardiff, United Kingdom
Email: colin.roberts@esi-research.co.uk

Clifford Shearing
Faculty of Law
Centre of Criminology
Durban, South Africa
Email: clifford.shearing@uct.ac.za

Samuel Tanner
International Centre for Comparative
    Criminology
University of Montreal
Montreal, Quebec, Canada
Email: samuel.tanner@umontreal.ca

David Thacher
Public Policy and Urban Planning
University of Michigan
Ann Arbor, Michigan
Email: dthacher@umich.edu

Lee King Wa
Department of Sociology
University of Hong Kong
Shatin, Hong Kong
Email: kentlkw@cuhk.edu.hk

Jennifer Wood
Department of Criminal Justice
Temple University
Philadelphia, Pennsylvania
Email: woodj@temple.edu

Lena Y. Zhong
Department of Applied Social Studies
City University of Hong Kong
Kowloon, Hong Kong
Email: ylzhong@cityu.edu.hk

Community Policing, East and West, North and South

1

PETER GRABOSKY

Contents

Part 1: Community Policing in Democratic Societies

The term *community policing* has become something like *motherhood*. It has a wonderful connotation. Who could be against it? Indeed, there are probably not too many police executives in the Western world who would admit that they are *not* practicing community policing. Those who do make such admissions have probably succumbed to the imperatives of innovation and refer to what they are now doing as a "higher form" of community policing.

Of course, the term *community policing* means many things to many people. The dominant paradigm of policing today is community policing, which combines *consultation* with community members, *responsiveness* to their security needs, collective *problem solving* to identify the most appropriate means of meeting these needs, and *mobilization* of the public to make all this happen (Bayley, 2006). Although the virtues of community policing are widely extolled (at least in Western democracies), it is not always practiced; even more rarely is it done well.

Ideally, police should be able to anticipate what the community's security preferences are, that is, what they, the public, are looking for. Equipped with comprehensive criminal statutes and an implicit understanding of what "respectable" people wanted from their police, law enforcement officers simply did what came naturally. Unfortunately, police understanding of citizens' expectations has not always kept pace with citizen preferences. In English-speaking democracies of a half-century ago, conservative, masculine, homophobic, and racist attitudes tended to be overrepresented in the ranks of police. Violence against women was traditionally regarded as private, and "not a police matter." It took concerted effort on the part of the

Adapted from Grabosky, P. Community policing: East and West, North and South. *Police Practice and Research*, 10(2), forthcoming and Grabosky, P. Police as international peacekeepers. *Policing and Society*, 19(10), forthcoming.

feminist movement to place violence against women on the public agenda. Fortunately, police are becoming more diverse and more representative of the communities they serve (Sklansky, 2008).

Where the security preferences of the public may not be immediately apparent, it may be possible to actively consult in order to determine what their real needs might be. This too may be problematic, as processes of consultation may privilege the better-resourced and more articulate members of the community, at the expense of the disadvantaged and marginalized.

Co-production entails actually working *with* the community to identify problems and craft solutions, or allowing sectors of the community to manage their own security needs. Absent careful attention, however, this too can work to the advantage of better-resourced interests, and to the disadvantage of the poor.

One can begin to see that community policing is extremely difficult to implement. The impediments to community policing are numerous and varied.

Traditionally, many were drawn to the police profession because of the excitement and adventure that it offered. Public perceptions of policing were colored by media depictions, fictional or factual, which were crafted in order to excite the reader, viewer, or listener.

By contrast, a great deal of policing is routine and mundane. This paradox is represented in the title of a classic essay by Egon Bittner (1974), "Florence Nightingale in Pursuit of Willie Sutton." In the traditional culture of policing, certain police tasks were dismissed as "social work." The real stuff of policing was "catching crooks." Resistance on the part of rank-and-file officers to what they regard as demeaning, "touchy-feely" work can be a significant impediment to community policing. One notes the continued attractiveness of police careers to those who equate policing with "fast cars and locking up bad guys."

In contrast to the police officer's traditional presentation of self as dominant, community policing requires the officer to deal with citizens more as equals, a transition that some have found difficult to make. The egalitarian, problem-solving ethos that is an essential requisite of community policing has yet to fully displace the authoritarian, risk-aversive, and change-resistant nature of traditional police culture. To the extent that this new ethos has begun to emerge, it has come under challenge from the new managerialism that has begun to characterize 21st-century policing.

Another challenge to community policing is the difficulty in mobilizing the public. In some tranquil settings, crime is simply not perceived as a problem. In other locations, disadvantaged and otherwise marginalized segments of the community may harbor a certain mistrust of police, or they may simply lack the skills to engage with them.

In addition, community policing is resource intensive; contrast the time and human resources required for consultations with the less costly strategy of reactive patrol.

Chapter 1 of this volume by Peter Grabosky is devoted to selected approaches to community policing from all points of the compass. It begins with an exploration of some interesting ideas about community policing that are being developed in the United Kingdom, Australia, and the United States, and concludes with some observations from South Africa and China.

Innes et al.'s chapter, arising from extensive field research on reassurance policing in the United Kingdom, confirms that police tend to view the world through their own lenses, and that their perceptions of reality may diverge from those of the citizens they serve. They discuss the "signal crimes" perspective, where specific prominent incidents tend to galvanize public attention. When these incidents are atypical, they can contribute to a public mindset that may diverge from reality. A further irony of life in some locations today is that police may not see it as their business to address many issues that are in fact the drivers of public insecurity. Innes sees a need for a more structured approach to strategic analysis and community engagement that will form the basis for an appropriate distribution of problem solving between police and community.

Grabosky's chapter looks at community policing through the lens of democratic theory. It identifies a number of methods by which the policy preferences of the community may be assessed, but notes that all of these are flawed to some extent. The chronic problem is that the most vocal members of a community tend to overshadow the least articulate. Moreover, individual or sectional preferences may not always be consistent with the wider public interest. Assessing, aggregating, and evaluating policy preferences, and delivering policing services to diverse communities remain immense challenges.

Thacher's contribution discusses informal social control as a means of managing forms of disorder, such as street harassment of women, excessive noise, and obstruction of public thoroughfares. He questions whether community policing of disorderly behavior can be achieved *without* the police, by such individuals as building attendants, transit workers, food vendors, and other "place managers." Although police in the United States and elsewhere have been historically heavy-handed in dealing with vagrants and public inebriates, Thacher notes that informal agents of social control remain less accountable and less well positioned to manage public disorder in a legitimate manner. Police, if they are up to the task, are the ultimate guarantors of fairness and equity.

Fleming and O'Reilly note that community policing, rather than core business, is often regarded as an add-on to traditional police practice. They discuss the formidable obstacle to the wider implementation of community policing that is posed by a resistant occupational culture, and by continued preoccupation with reactive emergency response and conventional performance measurement. In a climate of fiscal restraint, the costly, labor-intensive nature of community policing represents a further impediment to its serious adoption.

Herbert reinforces this skeptical interpretation, maintaining that the traditional insularity of police constitutes a formidable impediment to the effective realization of community policing. Police have historically resisted change in general and external oversight in particular, both essential elements of community policing as we know it. Detachment and aloofness characterized the police role in the latter half of the 20th century. This, combined with a masculinist "John Wayne" ethos, still dominates police culture in many places, where community policing tends to be scorned as "not real police work."

Despite these relatively pessimistic assessments of community policing, there have been promising developments. Skogan's (2006) review of Chicago's Alternative Policing Strategy (CAPS) program showed that community policing can work well in some communities. Another promising dimension of community policing is based on partnerships between police and other social service agencies. Such connections are significant, since a great deal of police work arises from the functioning (or malfunctioning) of other agencies of government. Police partnerships with social service agencies are an important part of community policing but don't receive as much attention in the community policing literature as issues such as citizen engagement and "broken windows."

Peaslee's contribution provides an interesting perspective on youth-based partnerships in four New England cities, and suggests ways that police leadership can overcome barriers to working with social service agencies. She identifies such exemplary partnerships as those between the police of New Haven, Connecticut, and the Yale Child Development Center, and the Boston, Massachusetts, police and a network of youth service providers. Peaslee concludes that, much like community policing reform, adoption of social service partnerships will require a shift in police culture. Departments must pay attention to agency structure, the role of police leadership, education and training, and the measures used to evaluate officer performance. Although Peaslee presents a generally positive view of police partnerships, she warns against giving the police too large a role in collaborations.

Wood and Bradley describe developments in partnership policing in the Australian state of Victoria. The subject of their essay is Nexus policing, a program designed to transform the way the second largest police service in Australia, with upwards of 12,000 sworn officers, does business. The key to Nexus policing is for individual officers to identify and leverage diverse forms of knowledge and capacity that reside outside of police ranks, elsewhere in government, in civil society and in the private sector. Transforming a large, rule-bound organization into one comprised of innovative and entrepreneurial officers is certainly a challenge, but one that can be addressed through the creative application of other management tools, such as COMPSTAT, and the artful use of incentives. By pushing the boundaries of partnership thinking and practice, Nexus policing has the potential to enhance the capacity of Victoria police to an extent previously unimagined.

Braga, Onek, and Meares review the concept of "pulling levers" policing, a strategy that addresses a specific crime problem by convening a special interagency working group of police social service, community, and academic partners. They describe a pilot project aimed at reducing the level of firearms violence in the city of San Francisco. Based on previous work in Boston and Chicago, it entails community forums involving high-risk offenders, community groups, and representatives of criminal justice agencies. Like Wood and Bradley, they see enormous potential in collaboration between academics and practitioners.

The three subsequent chapters provide perspectives on community policing from a non-Western perspective. The contribution by Marks, Shearing, and Wood looks at South Africa, a country with massive crime problems and limited state capacity to control them. As a consequence, people in South Africa have sought alternatives to the conventional solution of more police, or increasing the ambit of policing functions. The private security sector is massive, and for the affluent, gated communities abound. Those less fortunate are also left to their own devices, since the public police in South Africa have more business than they can handle. The authors seek alternatives to simply transplanting the Western model of police as generalized problem solvers within communities. In essence, they advocate the development of nongovernmental institutions of social control, which might include, *inter alia*, street committees, traditional courts, and neighbourhood patrols. They suggest that current public police constraints (and indeed broader state service delivery constraints and deficits) should be accounted for when thinking about the broad policing landscape. With these in mind, they advocate that a minimalist approach to understanding the role and function of the public police should be seriously considered. They provide a possible model for what African nodal policing could look like if this minimalist view is adopted. Issues of accountability, networked arrangements, and decentralization are then discussed in their presentation of a potential alternative model for policing in places like South Africa.

Zhong's contribution provides an insight on community policing in China, where 20% of the world's population resides, a country in the midst of dramatic social and economic change. After a brief history of crime control in China since 1949, Zhong describes the diverse apparatus of contemporary social control that includes not only public police, but also neighborhood committees that undertake surveillance and provide conflict resolution services. Larger workplaces have social order joint protection teams that work in close liaison with police. The provision of direct professional guidance by police to grassroots institutions is an important feature of public security in China. In a very real sense, the array of policing institutions described by

Zhong resembles a pluralistic system envisaged by Marks and her co-authors. Readers hardly need reminding that culturally and politically, China is a very different place from South Africa, as well as from Western English-speaking democracies. Just as models of community policing developed in Chicago may not lend themselves to implementation in South Africa, so too may the elaborate system of social control in China defy transplantation. And indeed, the breathtaking changes currently occurring in China, from unprecedented affluence to unprecedented population mobility, are likely to be accompanied by further developments in institutions of social control, both public and private.

Lee's chapter describes contemporary community policing in the former British Colony of Hong Kong, now a Special Administrative Region of the People's Republic of China. Citing survey evidence of widespread satisfaction with police performance, he concludes that community policing has been successfully implemented, and goes on to note that close relations between the police and the public are important for the effective control of organized crime.

Part 2: Police as International Peacekeepers

Policing is a challenging task at the best of times. The practice of community policing becomes even more difficult in situations where the "community" in question has recently experienced civil war, communal violence, or the erosion or collapse of effective government. The term *peacekeeping* is used to refer to intervention in such situations. Increasingly, it has become recognized that the appropriate role of military organizations in such situations is finite, and after an initial period of stabilization, responsibility for the assurance of domestic security should fall to the police. Over time, the police peacekeeping role becomes one of peace *building*—the implementation of community policing practices as the host society gradually strengthens.

But we must not get too far ahead of ourselves. In many weak and failing states, and in other postconflict situations, there may be no functioning police agency. Alternatively, the police in the host location may be corrupt, incompetent, abusive, or some combination of the three. Thus, there is often a need for external assistance in building or rebuilding an indigenous police service.

Whatever the challenges of community policing in stable Western democracies, they are that much greater in settings where political, social, and economic circumstances are often drastically different, where the population may be traumatized, desperately poor, and divided among itself.

The best blueprint for the role of police in peacekeeping is that of David Bayley (2006). Although directed primarily at a U.S. readership, the general principles he articulates that relate to planning, recruitment, organization, and evaluation of international policing operations in furtherance of peacekeeping are appropriate for any nation or group of nations that would proffer law enforcement assistance abroad, whether under the UN banner or otherwise.

One important consideration for peacekeeping is the cultural distance between the public and the police. In English-speaking democracies, at any rate, it has become received wisdom that the police should be, to the greatest possible extent, culturally and demographically representative of the public that they serve (Sklansky, 2008). The reasons for this are pragmatic, as well as symbolic. It is usually easier to trust someone who bears some resemblance to oneself. This in turn is more conducive to support for, and cooperation with, police, and can make it much easier for them to do their job.

However, in situations of peacekeeping a demographic mirror of the host community is not always possible. In the absence of demographically representative peacekeepers, a significant degree of preparation is required. Suitable candidates must be identified, recruited, and trained. It is important that peacekeepers have at least a modicum of familiarity with the language and culture of those to whom they are providing police services. Unfortunately, where urgency dictates that peacekeeping missions be executed quickly, this is not always feasible.

Community policing usually requires a degree of continuity of interface between the police and the public. This is the foundation for mutual trust—an essential ingredient of good policing. Ideally, at the microlevel, the police officer will get to know his or her community, and the community will get to know their police officer. In the real world of peacekeeping, this may be an elusive goal. For better or worse, many modern police careers are moveable feasts, with frequent transfers and reassignments more common than not. In the setting of international peacekeeping, one can appreciate the difficulties of sustaining continuity of service in surroundings that may be extremely arduous and distant from home and family.

Another consideration relates to the personality and suitability of the prospective peacekeeper. Many individuals are drawn to policing as a career because they are attracted by the prospect of excitement and adventure. In addition to paperwork, police officers have traditionally resented those aspects of the job that they dismiss as the business of social workers.

Those police who are attracted to peacekeeping work may have additional motives of their own. For some, it might entail a bigger paycheck. It often involves travel to exotic locations, and the prospect of adventure that was absent from the drudgery of paperwork and social work at home. For others, it may entail breathing space (if not the beginning of a definitive escape) from a difficult domestic relationship. The needs of the individual peacekeeper may be very different from those of the host community.

States almost always act in their own national interest (or what they think is their national interest). It is not surprising, therefore, that there is an element of self-interest in the world of international law enforcement assistance. Many donor countries (and members of their peacekeeping contingents) are themselves very poor, and derive significant economic advantage from peacekeeping work. As one of the contributions in this collection suggests, the prospect of financial benefit can also be attractive to the police officers and the police services of affluent nations.

Bayley (2006) suggests that law enforcement assistance bestowed by the United States is likely to reflect that nation's concerns over terrorism, drugs, money laundering, and people smuggling, even if the recipient nation may have other priorities. Bowling (2006) suggests that these divergent national interests can serve to distort resource allocation in some poorer countries. Although violence against women may be considered a more urgent priority than money laundering, funds may be available for the latter but not the former.

One can see that the task of international peacekeeping entails a great deal of compromise on the part of donor police agencies. The chapters in the next part of this book illustrate some of these paradoxes as they address different facets of peacekeeping.

Murney and McFarlane's chapter provides an overview of the peacekeeping challenge. They note that the role of police in nation building is varied, and that the setting for peacekeeping activity can differ widely, depending on local culture and state capacity. Each police peacekeeping mission is unique, and policy options, such as the relative contribution of police and military assets, must be carefully weighed. The authors provide a guidance model for international police engagement.

Greener's contribution focuses upon the role of the United Nations in mobilizing peacekeepers. She observes that the UN has begun to devote increasing emphasis to civilian police, as opposed to military forces, in both peacekeeping operations and the peace building operations that succeed them. The challenge of coordination is formidable, given the number of nations who are willing to contribute to policing under UN auspices, and the number of locations where peacekeeping services are required. The rise of the peace building agenda has brought further challenges for UN policing specialists, as peace building requires a more comprehensive and multifaceted approach. Greener outlines some of these challenges, including the lack of common standards across participating donors, and issues relating to recruitment and predeployment training. She notes the wide variation in quality of personnel offering themselves for international service, and the different skill sets required in the policing of vulnerable publics from other cultures. Greener also observes some interesting developments designed to reach out more broadly to the community, referring to the female police unit from India posted to Liberia 2007.

Goldsmith's chapter, based on interviews with Australian police personnel who served as peacekeepers and capacity builders in Timor-Leste, illustrates the challenge of adapting to a very different set of problems and a very different culture from those prevailing at home. Gangs of violent youth, and outbreaks of arson, looting, and civil disorder greeted those Australian police who were deployed to the former Indonesian province (and previously, Portuguese colony) in 2006. Goldsmith observes that the best technical preparation is not always sufficient to adequately police such complex situations. Tried and true tactics can fail to achieve their objectives. Orders to disperse would often be ignored by groups of young males; however, young people would scatter whenever they perceived that they were about to be photographed. Goldsmith emphasizes that enhanced cultural awareness on the part of police is a *sine qua non* of effective peacekeeping.

Dupont and Tanner's contribution, based on interviews with Canadian peacekeepers, addresses the "flip side" of international deployment: the reintegration of former peacekeepers into their home police service. The authors call attention to the paradox of considerable investment in the recruitment and training of peacekeepers, and the relative neglect of returnees by their home police force. Some police services fail to exploit the newly acquired skills of their returnees, and could do more to further their professional development. Dupont and Tanner also note the risk that the physical and mental health of returned peacekeepers may also be neglected. They take the view that unlike health issues, which are amenable to individual interventions, the reintegration problem will be more difficult to remedy, as it requires organizational changes.

Findlay's chapter notes the difficulties faced by Papua New Guinea (PNG) today, in particular the inverse relationship between crime and economic development. Based on findings from a business crime victimization survey, he concludes that business proprietors tend largely to look after their own security needs, engaging private security services and passing the costs of crime and security onto consumers. They do not engage in community initiatives, and do not rely on the police. The degree of disillusionment with state policing services illustrates the formidable challenge faced by those who would provide law enforcement assistance to PNG. In the meantime, Findlay suggests that better engagement by businesses with the community might be a fruitful strategy.

McLeod's chapter, based on extensive interviews with local police in PNG, addresses policing assistance from the point of view of the recipient. Over the past two decades, Australia has given substantial assistance, in cash and in kind, to the Royal Papua New Guinea Constabulary (RPNGC). It is not surprising that the RPNGC have certain values and expectations regarding the assistance that they receive. PNG police officers are acutely aware that their society differs from that of their Australian guests. They are likely to resent a visitor who assumes that he or she has learned all one needs to know by having patrolled the suburbs of a major Australian metropolis. Members of the RPNGC want to be respected, and would appreciate Australian police advisors to have knowledge of PNG culture, language, and local nuances. Age, for example, is highly esteemed in PNG. Young Australian police officers on law enforcement assistance assignments, regardless of their competence, are less likely to be well received than a counterpart with grey hair. Moreover, significant differences in law enforcement practices between donor and recipient may be seen in attitudes toward the use of force. Here, RPNGC members see violence as an important tool of law enforcement. Encouraging host police officers to abandon such practices, while avoiding an outward show of cultural superiority on the part of the donor, is a significant challenge.

The contribution by Dinnen and Braithwaite recalls an earlier era of policing in frontier societies, when the police officer was often the only representative of government at the frontier. As such, he (and in those days, it was always a he) provided a range of services to the public that has been lost in the modern era of specialization of policing and the growth of the private security industry. The focus of the chapter then moves to Papua New Guinea, a vastly diverse society that became a nation-state in 1975. During its colonial era, most of Papua New Guinea was policed by district officers, called *kiaps*. These too had widespread governmental responsibilities. The authors suggest that such holistic service provisions can play a constructive role in contemporary settings where the state may be weak. With more than a touch of irony, they also suggest that such a model may have something to contribute to the policing of remote indigenous communities in Australia.

Broadhurst and Bouhours look at the challenges of police assistance from the standpoint of a host country. Their chapter focuses on Cambodia, a country ravaged by catastrophic violence during the 1970s and 1980s. They observe that in recent years, both property crime and violent crime have decreased, the latter especially so. The authors interpret this as good news, suggesting that the traumas of the genocide are giving way to the correlates of affluence. The authors demonstrate the use of survey research, specifically the International Crime Victims Survey, as a complement to official police statistics, and as a means of measuring public perceptions of police corruption. Despite the useful assistance provided in recent years by Australia and other international donors, the authors' prognosis remains guarded; low salaries, poor training, a political system characterized by patron-style leadership, and a lack of legislative oversight do not bode well for the quality of Cambodian policing in the short term.

One can be confident that the problem of weak and failing states will only become more acute in the years ahead. These chapters should provide some guidance on how policing arrangements in these settings may best be addressed.

References

Bayley, D. H. (2006). *Changing the guard: Developing democratic police abroad.* New York: Oxford University Press.

Bittner, E. (1974). Florence Nightingale in pursuit of Willie Sutton: A theory of the police. In H. Jacob (Ed.), *The potential for reform of criminal justice* (pp. 17–43). Beverly Hills: SAGE Publications.

Bowling, B. (2006). Sovereignty vs. security: Transnational policing in the contemporary Caribbean. *Caribbean Journal of Criminology and Social Psychology,* 1–21. Retrieved March 4, 2009 from http://www.kcl.ac.uk/content/1/c6/01/84/31/sovereigntyvssecurity.pdf

Sklansky, D. (2008). *Democracy and the police.* Stanford, CA: Stanford University Press.

Skogan, W. (2006). *Community policing in Chicago: A tale of three cities.* New York: Oxford University Press.

Seeing Like a Citizen
Field Experiments in Community Intelligence-Led Policing

2

MARTIN INNES
LAURENCE ABBOTT
TRUDY LOWE
COLIN ROBERTS

Contents

Permutations of community policing theory and practice have, for over three decades now, been implemented in different contexts and under varied conditions in pursuit of an array of social benefits. But with a few notable exceptions, the longer-term transformations predicted by advocates of such reforms have failed to be realized (Herbert, 2006; Weisburd & Eck, 2004; Mastrofski, 2006). As such, it would seem the criticism that the transformative capacity of community policing functions more effectively at the level of rhetoric than reality would seem to have some validity (Weatheritt, 1988).

Part of the problem with engaging community policing (CP) as an agent of social change is that for all the talk of consulting and engaging with communities, such programs have ultimately failed to find ways to "see like a citizen." Police organizations have, with a few notable exceptions, largely resisted adopting an appreciative stance to understanding how and why issues of neighborhood security are influenced and shaped by a range of problems, including incivilities and physical disorder. Rather, police have tended to retain the power to define which situations and incidents are deserving of policing action, for the most part selectively focusing their attention upon

Adapted from Innes, M., Abbott, L., Lowe, T., and Roberts, C. (2008). Seeing like a citizen: Field experiments in community intelligence-led policing. *Police Practice and Research*, http://dx.doi.org/10.1080/15614260802264545

volume and major crime (Herbert, 2006). In the process, they have worked to refute the salience of certain types of problems and concerns routinely brought to them by the public, dismissing them as falling outside a police remit, or as not involving a determinable harm to an individual, and thus insufficiently serious to warrant much attention. It is an organizational optic, powerfully shaped by the disciplinary apparatus of centrally set performance indicators, functioning to articulate and animate what the focus of police work on the ground really is (Fielding & Innes, 2006). However, viewing the world through this lens means that the police simply fail to understand why a range of problematic situations, additional to those clearly involving a criminal act, might function as signifiers of trouble and thereby be influential in shaping levels of neighborhood security.

In this chapter we report on the findings of a number of field experiments conducted over the last three years in the UK, designed to try to better attune the delivery of community policing to the needs, wants, and expectations of communities. Based upon a systematic methodology of structured engagement performed by police officers, the process enacted has sought to develop a "community intelligence" feed that provides valid and reliable insights into the principal "drivers" of insecurity across different neighborhoods and communities. The chapter starts by outlining the conceptual and methodological apparatus underpinning the approach to be discussed, following which, we report findings from a field trial conducted with Lancashire police in the town of Morecombe in 2007. These data help to illuminate the nuanced and complex ways in which different communities react to the presence of criminal and antisocial behaviors, and how such matters are folded into the ways they symbolically construct notions of social space, and consequently self-define a sense of collective identity. Extending and developing the implications of this analysis, in the subsequent section we move on to consider how this community intelligence-led policing style can inform and improve the delivery of policing services in respect to other facets of the modern police mission. The article concludes with some conceptual and more pragmatic reflections upon the use of community intelligence.

Engaging Communities

One of the principal criticisms often leveled at CP is that it tends to lack specificity in terms of what systems and practices are integral to its conduct (Manning, 1997). In effect, the community policing concept has been reduced to a free-floating signifier that can be, and indeed has been, applied to such a wide diversity of policing circumstances that its unique signature has been obliterated. While criticisms of this tenor are undoubtedly true, it is equally the case that most practitioners and commentators would agree that some form of community engagement activity is a core ingredient of any approach seeking to self-define as CP. Indeed, part of the fundamental philosophical rationale for CP is the belief that there are various beneficial outcomes to be derived from reducing the social distance between the police and those policed (Skogan, 2007). In practice, though, a wide variety of consultative mechanisms have been employed under a CP rubric, and overall, the question "What are the requirements for the conduct of effective community-police engagement interactions?" remains comparatively neglected (Mastrofski, 2006).*

Currently in the UK, under the auspices of the Neighbourhood Policing Programme (discussed in more detail below), which included a government commitment to ensure that by 2008 all neighborhoods would have a dedicated policing team, there is a particular emphasis upon the importance of engaging communities (cf. Quinton & Morris, 2008). While individual police forces have experimented with a variety of different techniques for engaging across neighborhoods and communities, the principal vehicle for doing so has, more or less by default, become the "Police and Communities Together" meeting (often dubbed a PACT meeting). While many officers appreciate that these are problematic undertakings, the continued reliance upon meetings convened by police that members of the public can attend has three supports: (1) Historically there is precedent for them, in that many police agencies introduced them following the publication of the Scarman report in the early 1980s; (2) more recently, they have been comparatively successfully enacted as part of the Chicago's Alternative Policing Strategy (CAPS) program in Chicago (Skogan, 2007); and (3) pragmatically they are relatively easy to manage compared with other techniques.

As intimated above, though, meetings as a tactic for public engagement are mired in problems. The principal concerns that can be identified with them are:

- There is a lack of clarity over what function such meetings should perform within the context of a wider and more elaborated policing process. Is their purpose to (1) encourage members of the public to report crime and disorder concerns to the police, (2) enable community members to help police define local priorities, or (3) establish a forum in which police can report on their activities to their "customers"?
- Typically they fail to provide a genuine democratic input into policing because only certain groups tend to attend on a regular basis. Moreover, given that this is the case, the agenda of the groups is susceptible to "capture" by individuals and small cliques seeking to operationalize single-issue campaigns.

---

* Some of the more popular engagement techniques include community meetings, "street briefings," telephone surveys, letter drops, and mass media advertising.

- From the police point of view, this aspect of CP work tends to become ritualized fairly quickly. That is, rather than seen as performing a genuine operational function, these meetings are something that has to be got out of the way. Consequently, such aspects of community policing work are not valued by front-line officers, and as a result, they do not invest effort in organizing engagement activities.

The accent upon community engagement within the current rollout of neighborhood policing in the UK is directly derived from the research evidence from its smaller-scale, more experimentally oriented predecessor, the National Reassurance Policing Programme (NRPP). The NRPP was launched in April 2003 in 16 wards across eight police forces throughout England. Its purpose was to test a particular formulation of CP theory and its capacity to reduce fear of crime and improve public trust and confidence in the police. The evaluation of the NRPP conducted by the Home Office found strong evidence that an appropriately calibrated form of community policing could indeed deliver the predicted outcomes. Compared with control sites elsewhere, the 16 sites trialing the NRPP approach were found to have performed better across a number of key performance indicators (Tuffin et al., 2006). The evaluators concluded that a key determinant of the success of the program had been its use of a structured approach to community engagement directed toward identifying what citizens' neighborhood priorities for policing were (Quinton & Morris, 2008). But as with so much in life, the devil is in the detail in terms of understanding what insights this engagement afforded the police and why it was so important in achieving particular outcomes.

Within the conduct of the NRPP there was a particular conceptual innovation providing the theoretical engine for the approach to community engagement developed that was crucial in securing the predicted benefits. This was the signal crimes perspective (SCP). The SCP provides a theoretical framework for understanding social reactions to crime and disorder and, in particular, the ways in which certain incidents tend to trigger change in how people think, feel, or act in relation to their individual and collective security (Innes, 2004).

Situated within the context of a reassurance policing process, the SCP approach afforded police several important insights. First, it provided a framework and method for systematically diagnosing which crime and disorder incidents were impacting upon local perceptions and experiences, thus setting out a mechanism for targeting resources and effort to those signal events on the basis that by dealing effectively and visibly with those issues that really matter in neighborhoods, police can minimize the impact of these incidents upon both the subjective and objective dimensions of a local social order. Second, it introduced a non-negotiable requirement for the police to engage with communities in order to identify what the signals were and where they were occurring. The early research conducted using the SCP clearly identified that the profile of neighborhood signal concerns varied widely across the different trial sites. Concomitantly, it was important to engage at a local level in order to capture and reflect these variations in neighborhood signal profiles. Consequently, as part of the NRPP, a stream of work was initiated to develop a locally oriented engagement methodology that could be used by police to generate intelligence about the presence of signal crimes and signal disorders.

A crucial aspect of reassurance policing's delivery mechanisms was its use of community engagement to identify community intelligence on the signal crimes and signal disorders shaping local perceptions of security, and using this intelligence to bring focused problem-solving approaches to bear upon such matters. In effect, the SCP widened the scope of the police's intelligence radar to collect intelligence about a wide variety of issues, stretching from volume crime through to disorder, while simultaneously sharpening the level of precision in focusing police efforts upon the signal events that really drive insecurity.

Signal Crimes as Community Intelligence

Community intelligence (COMMTEL) is a term that has entered the UK policing vernacular despite lacking an agreed definition. This lack of definition means that it tends to operate as something of a dust-bin concept, used whenever police want to refer to a form of information that does not fit into their more firmly established conceptions of crime or criminal intelligence. As with all forms of intelligence, COMMTEL is information that, when analyzed, provides foresight into some future condition or episode. But whereas police practitioners typically invoke it as a generic term for more or less any form of open source information, herein we will define it more narrowly. COMMTEL can thus be understood as information that when analyzed provides insight into the risks posed by or to a group sharing some common conception of self-identity.*

On this basis, it can be seen how diagnosing the presence of signal crimes and signal disorders can function as a form of community intelligence. The products of the analytic work conducted present a collective view of the knowledge that exists within a community setting about what troublesome incidents are occurring and the impacts these are having upon a local social order. To understand the value of this intelligence, we need to look in more detail at the method of diagnosing signals.

* This definition was arrived at following research funded by the Association of Chief Police Officers into processes and systems of managing community intelligence (Innes, Roberts, & Maltby, 2005).

Rather than relying upon community meetings as the engagement interface between the police and public, the NRPP utilized a system of face-to-face interviews. The design of the interview schedule incorporated several of the key principles of cognitive interviewing on the basis that rather than collecting attitudinal data, for example, through more established surveys (such as the British Crime Survey), the new approach was intended to capture information and knowledge about actual local events, together with data on the dynamics of social reaction to these events. Originally these interviews were conducted by a team of academic researchers using a paper-based system for the NRPP, but as the process has been refined, the interviews have been conducted by front-line police staff using a bespoke Computer-Assisted Personal Interviewing (CAPI) software program written to guide the process.

Much of the interview format is organized around a map of the respondent's neighborhood and surrounding areas. The map is used to encourage the interviewee to plot the geographic locations of where they think any troubling incidents are located. This geo-coded data can be recorded in three formats:

- Point data—Denotes where a specific problem occurs at a particular location, for example, the vandalism of a particular telephone box.
- Line data—Used where a problem occurs between two points, such as speeding cars on a road.
- Area data—Used where an area or public space is designated as a problematic locale, as occurs with regards to drug dealing in the local park.

There is a subtle filter built into the process here, in that if the interviewee cannot assign the problem to a particular location, then it may not constitute reliable data, so the interview does not capture it.

A number of interviewer prompts are built into the interview interaction so as to subtly guide the respondent to talk about certain things, but overall the idea is that it should be a fairly free-flowing conversation about any issues or problems that have occurred in the locality and what effects these have provoked in terms of shaping how the individual or his or her associates thought, felt, or acted in relation to their security. As the respondent talks about the area, the interviewer, who has been trained to locate signal crimes and disorders in peoples' crime talk, has a number of tick boxes available on the computer laptop screen to capture when the respondent states particular things pertaining to the presence of a signal event. Over the course of the interview interaction this can build up to provide quite a complex picture of how an individual views his or her neighborhood and surrounding area. The questions asked by the interviewer seek to progressively build up a textured and layered picture about:

- What incidents are shaping how people think, feel, or act in relation to their security
- Why they are doing this, in terms of what kinds of reactions these problems are generating
- Where these troublesome incidents are located
- When they are taking place (i.e., are they one-offs, or are they repeating on certain days of the week or at certain times of the year?)
- Who is thought to be causing the signal event
- How important the different issues are relative to each other within a particular neighborhood setting and that are being attributed the status of causes and symptoms

In terms of the interview process, it constitutes something of a hybrid methodology. The interview interaction is conducted in the style of a qualitative semistructured interview, while the data generated from the interaction are recorded in a format more akin to a structured questionnaire.

The purpose of collecting the data generated by the interview interaction in this way is that it enables individual-, neighborhood-, and community-level analyses. At the individual level, it is comparatively easy for an analyst to look at the content of the interview to see what kinds of behaviors, and the physical traces of these, are generating concern for that respondent. More important, though, is the collective level of analysis that this procedure affords. By aggregating the data from a number of interviewees in an area, it is possible to comparatively easily build up a localized picture of what incidents are occurring that are impacting upon how people think, feel, and act in relation to their security. Importantly, by layering the outputs from the individual interview accounts on top of each other and examining the points of correspondence between them, an analyst can quickly build up a picture of what issues are triggering collective perceptions of risk and threat. This form of data triangulation also affords a reliability and validity check on the grounds that if multiple respondents are identifying similar problems at similar locations, we can have greater confidence that an actual event has transpired there.

Case Study: West End Ward, Morecombe, Lancashire

Having outlined some of the key considerations that have informed the approach to community intelligence that has been developed, and in order to illustrate the insights that can be obtained from such a process, we will now draw upon a project conducted with Lancashire Constabulary in the town of Morecombe in northwest England during 2007. In the process of discussing the analysis and findings, we will also elaborate upon some of the key aspects of the methodology.

At the start of the project the ward in question was divided into its constitutive output areas (OAs), and a sociodemographic profile for each of the OAs was constructed based upon UK 2001 census data.* These profiles were then provided to the local policing teams, who were tasked to locate "neighborhood sentinels" in each of the OAs coherent with the sociodemographic profile for the ward as a whole. *Neighborhood sentinel* is a label used to describe individuals who are especially sensitive and well attuned to the biography of the neighborhood and the occurrence of any problems therein. For example, mothers with children, postal delivery workers, and people who are engaged in local groups have often been found to possess neighborhood sentinel traits. Of course, in practice, the capacity to always identify neighborhood sentinels in all target areas is constrained, but the attempt to do so nevertheless constitutes an important principle in terms of how the approach is operationalized in the context of neighborhood policing.

The decision to structure the methodology so as to purposively engage with neighborhood sentinels was informed by research evidence from the NRPP that clearly demonstrated a marked difference in the quality and quantity of information captured through the interview interactions with different individuals. Some were effortlessly able to provide thickly descriptive accounts of their neighborhood and its problems, while others were able to provide very little data of this kind. Upon further investigation, it appeared that there were structured differences between these high-knowledge individuals and the lower-knowledge ones. The former group either tended to have highly developed and densely populated social networks, or spent comparatively large amounts of time in public spaces—lifestyle effects that cast them in a neighborhood sentinel role. Such people are, by virtue of their routine activities, especially well attuned to detecting any potential signals of risk in their environments. Interestingly, precedents for thinking in this way are to be found in the works of Gresham Sykes (1951) and Donald Campbell (1955).

The move from a sampling frame that provides a representative sample to one based upon a logic of neighborhood sentinels reflects some of the difficulties associated with small area sampling. To achieve a representative sample that provides for statistically significant findings at a neighborhood level would be prohibitively expensive and operationally unsustainable. By targeting key individuals who are most likely to know what is going on in each neighborhood, the aim is to establish a practical tool that can be used regularly. Certainly when this approach was tested against a far larger randomly selected telephone sample as part of the NRPP, it identified a broadly similar profile of collective concerns in most neighborhoods. Moreover, it is

---

* Output areas are constructed by the UK Office for National Statistics and are the smallest unit at which they output census data. Each OA is made up of 350 residents.

an approach coherent with police methodologies for identifying and using intelligence more generally. An additional virtue of using OAs to structure engagement activities is that it forces police to engage systematically across a territory and across all major community groups therein. It stops the phenomenon encountered several times in the fieldwork, where although police organizations verbally report that they are actively engaging with communities, when mapping in detail who they are in contact with and where, it often transpires that there are significant gaps in their coverage.

In West End Ward in Morecombe a total of 56 neighborhood sentinels were identified and interviewed using the i-NSI software.* The analysis revealed that across the ward as a whole, from the residents' point of view, the five most important signal events were:

1. Youth-related disorder
2. Fly tipping
3. Litter
4. Dog mess
5. Speeding cars and inconsiderate parking

It is notable that within this list, only youth-related disorder and traffic issues are problems that the police might usually attend to. Importantly though, and in keeping with the notion that this approach should generate usable community intelligence data for the police, the data collected can offer a more detailed view about where these key signal events are actually occurring. For example, Table 2.1 lists the particular locations where these specific issues are especially generative of community concern.

The particular strength of how the data are captured is that they can be quickly aggregated and disaggregated in different ways so as to illuminate understandings of different problems. For example, taking the most prominent signal in the West End Ward of youth-related disorder, it is possible to construct a visual representation of the locations where local people are identifying the occurrence of these types of problems as shaping their perceptions of safety.

In Figure 2.1, the black dots, lines, and shaded areas illustrate signal events relating to the activities of young people, which are not uniformly distributed throughout the ward, but rather clustered in particular micro-locations within it. This indicates how such data function as a form of intelligence

---

* Twenty-nine respondents were female, 20 male, and for 7 respondents this information was not recorded. The majority (52) described their ethnicity as White British. Of the remainder, 2 described themselves as White Irish, 1 as Asian/Asian British from an Indian background, and 1 as another, unspecified ethnicity. Forty-one respondents were residents, and the remaining 15 worked in the cell in which they were interviewed. Of those who were residents, 9 also worked in the area.

Table 2.1   Significant Locations in West End Ward

Signal Theme/Type	Most Coherent Locations
All signals	Euston Road
Drugs related	Westminster Road
Environmental signals	Euston Road
Fear and avoidance	Chatsworth Road
Road safety	West End Road
Groups of youths	Poulton Road
Fly tipping	Chatsworth Road
Litter	Euston Road
Dog mess	Albert Road
Speeding	West End Road
Inconsiderate parking	Clark Street

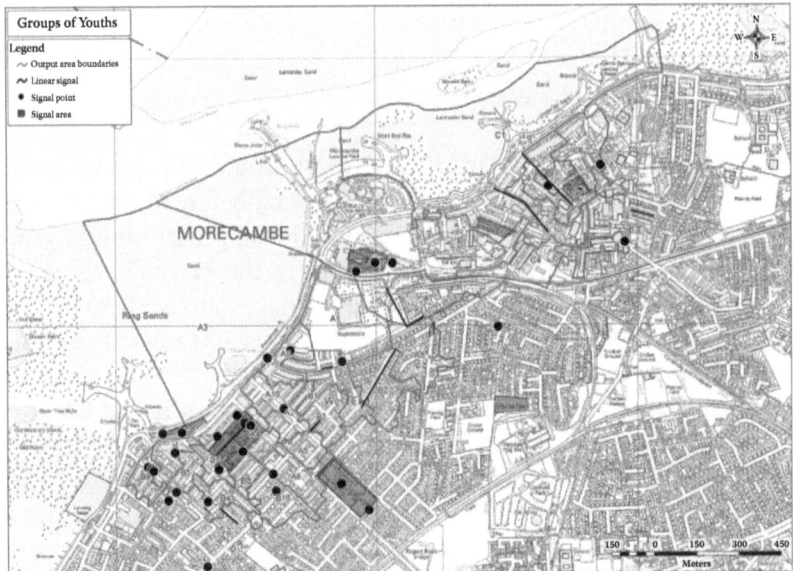

Figure 2.1 Signals of youth-related disorder.

in that they afford insight into where Lancashire police should focus their resources and efforts to deal with these types of issues. In this particular case, and indeed in other areas where we have conducted field trials with the software, it is clear that public perceptions identify different locations as being associated with different signal events.

During the interviews, respondents were also asked to plot on the maps the boundaries of what they consider to be their neighborhood, together with any other distinct territories they are aware of. By layering these data from across the interviews, it is possible to construct a form of COMMTEL that is very

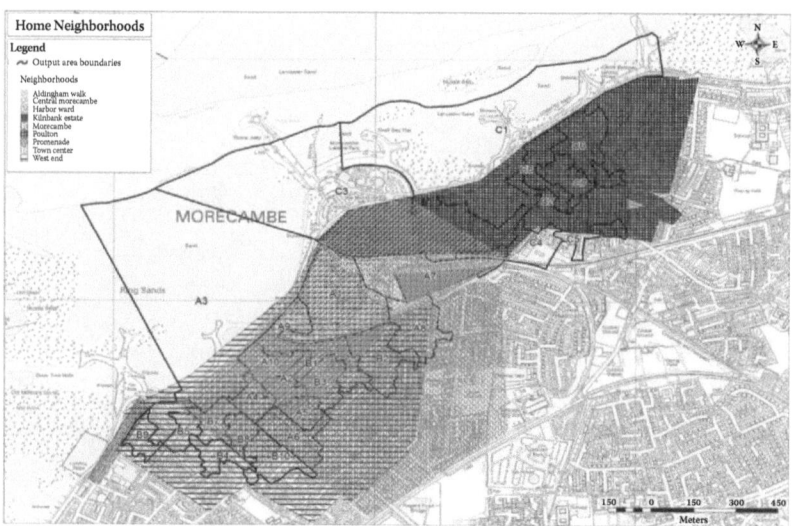

Figure 2.2 Self-defined neighborhoods.

useful in guiding community engagement strategies. Identifying self-defined neighborhoods where people conceive of the residents having a shared identity and interests is likely to be a more successful basis for engaging people than if this is attempted across areas where people possess no sense of mutual belonging. As will be discussed in due course, such data are also valuable for mapping community tensions. Figure 2.2 is a map of the West End Ward, on to which are superimposed the respondent data identifying the mosaic of neighborhoods that are involved in how local people symbolically construct local spaces. Each of these areas has a specific name and sense of identity imputed to it.

Extending this notion of understanding the symbolic construction of social spaces, and reflecting the emphasis within the SCP on processes of social reaction, the data can also be used to map what amounts to risk perception hot spots. For example, Figure 2.3 depicts all the locations where more than one of the people interviewed in the West End Ward stated they "feared to go" or "actively avoided." This analysis revealed two particular roads in this part of Morecombe where public anxieties were especially pronounced: Regent Road and Chatsworth Road. As police intelligence, such information offers the possibility of targeting high-visibility patrols to those areas, where they might genuinely make a difference to public perceptions, rather than using such a tactic in an undirected form.

Overall though, perhaps the most useful intelligence product derived from this approach to community engagement is the area signal profile. This provides the basis of a targeting mechanism for the police, enabling them to focus their resources upon the specific problems in particular locations that are functioning as the key drivers of neighborhood insecurity. The map

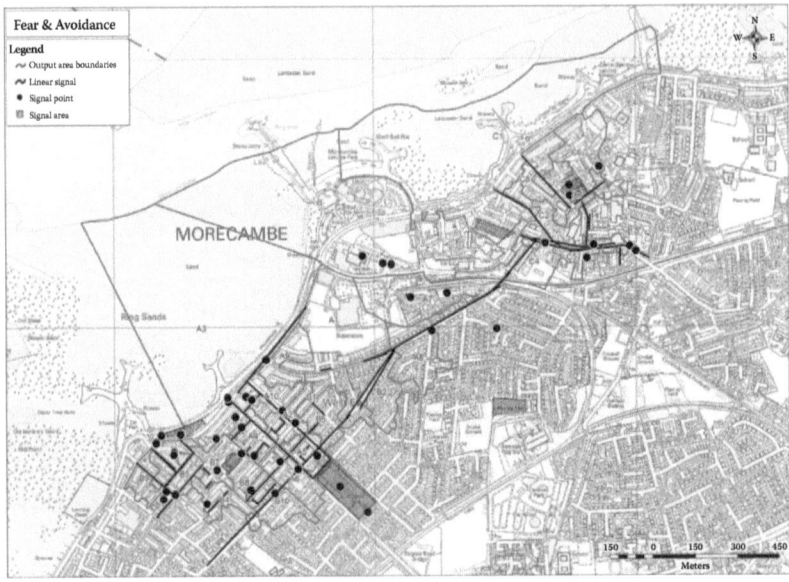

Figure 2.3 Fear and avoidance hot spots.

displayed in Figure 2.4 visually represents the concentration of signals in each OA. The cells are shaded to connote the relative strength of the signals in the cell compared to the other cells in the ward. The darker shaded areas indicate where the strongest signals were located (hot cells), followed by medium grey, and then finally light grey, denoting the presence of very weak signals. The accompanying table highlights the key locations and signals associated with them for the 15 OAs where the signals were strongest and most coherent.

As can be seen, the various analytic products provide a rich community intelligence picture that was used to help Lancashire police to understand different aspects of the neighborhood settings in which they are working. The level of granularity achievable through this data and the fact that the process is conducted in a structured and systematic fashion distinguish it from the PACT meetings, where the process and its outputs are ultimately dependent upon who turns up.

The face-to-face contact between local policing staff and members of the public built into the process (rather than outsourcing the conduct of the interviews to an agency who will conduct a telephone survey) also seems to be important. There have been a significant number of occasions in our field experiments with this approach where, in the process of building rapport and trust, police interviewers have been provided high-quality criminal intelligence by the ordinary members of the public they are talking to. It seems that the structured interview approach provided by the software helps officers to interact with members of the public in a way more likely to elicit detailed and useful intelligence.

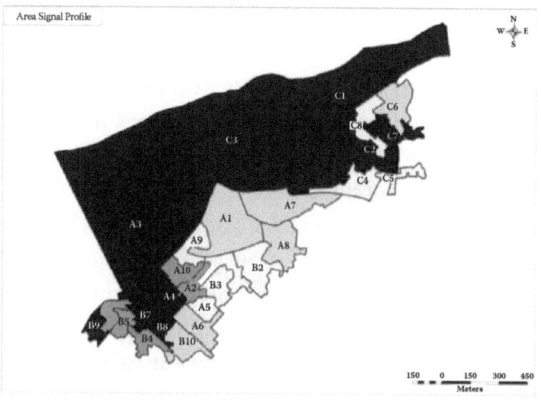

Rank	Temp	Cell ID	Location	Signals
1	■	A3	West End, Marine Road West, Yorkshire Street	Public drinking, Litter, Groups of youths
2	■	C1	Poulton, Euston Road, Town Centre	Litter, Verbal abuse, Public violence
3	■	C2	Poulton, Euston Road, Town Centre	Litter, Broken glass, Dirty / unclean
4	■	C7	Poulton, Poulton Road, Green Street	Groups of youths, Public drinking, People shouting
5	■	C3	Central Drive, Town Centre, Euston Road	Groups of youths, Litter, Theft (commercial)
6	■	A6	West End, Regent Road, Regent Park	Undesirable groups, People shouting, Verbal abuse
7	■	B7	West End, Alexandra Road, Grafton Road	Litter, People shouting, Damage to buildings
8	■	A4	West End, Regent Road, Parliament Street	Litter, Threatening behavior, Public drinking
9	■	A2	West End, Albert Road, Clarendon Road	Dog mess, Signs of drug use, Undesirable groups
10	■	C4	Poulton, Euston Road, Town Centre	Litter, Broken glass, Verbal abuse
11	■	C8	Poulton, Town Centre, Green Street	Inconsiderate parking, Road traffic, Speeding
12	■	C6	Poulton, Poulton Road, Rose Street	Inconsiderate parking, Litter, Damage to vehicles
13	■	A10	West End, Albert Road, Marine Road West	Verbal abuse, People shouting, Public drinking
14	■	B8	West End, Clarendon Road, Balmoral Road	Litter, Graffiti, Broken glass
15	□	B4	West End, Grafton Road, Balmoral Road	Signs of drug use, People shouting, Litter

Figure 2.4 Area signal profile.

By way of summary, the field trials of this method conducted in the context of reassurance and neighborhood policing processes have suggested it delivers a number of benefits:

- New information—It overcomes the underreporting associated with police recorded crime data and the even more significant difficulties with capturing data on the prevalence of physical and social disorder.
- Priority identification—It affords police an understanding of what issues are driving local communities' concerns.
- Hard intelligence—Building trust with individuals has resulted in criminal and crime intelligence being passed to police during the interviews.
- Organizational memory—The formal nature of the process allows organizations to build information about each neighborhood that does not move on when the local officers assigned to that area do.

Connecting Community Policing 1: Impact Assessment

Having established a community intelligence and engagement methodology capable of generating detailed insights into the issues and locations neighborhood officers should focus upon, in several recent field trials conducted in collaboration with the police, we have been conducting exploratory research into how this approach might connect to and inform other dimensions of police work. The aim is to understand how the kinds of connectivity into communities afforded by a neighborhood or community policing system might potentially underpin and be utilized by officers engaged in other roles. For example, a project funded by the Association of Chief Police Officers (ACPO) has been investigating how the instrument and apparatus developed might provide a tool for measuring the impact of major crimes and critical incidents upon communities.

The first case where this approach was trialed was the murder of a wealthy financier named John Monckton, who lived in an affluent neighborhood in Kensington and Chelsea in London. He was murdered in his home by two strangers who targeted him for a robbery. In the attack his wife was also severely injured, and the case received a very high national media profile. For this pilot study, a team of police officers were tasked to conduct interviews in the local area 3 months after the attack, and these respondents were subsequently reinterviewed 12 months later, shortly after a jury found the suspects guilty of the crime.*

Based upon a signal crimes analysis, two key findings emerged from the empirical fieldwork. First, homicide registered as the strongest and most coherent signal crime in the area. This was not something that had happened in any of the 16 NRPP trial sites, or indeed any of the other areas we have worked in England. The significance of this is that it confirms the commonsense supposition that major crimes can have a profound impact upon community perceptions of risk and threat. Intriguingly though, despite widespread media coverage, the incident resonated as a signal crime only among the more affluent residents in the ward, for whom it had a marked impact upon their sense of security. For those living about one kilometer from the crime scene in a comparatively deprived council estate, it was a tragic incident but did not function as a signal for them. It seems that because it was widely reported in the media that the victims were targeted for their wealth, the risk was not perceived as being shared by the council estate residents. The latter group, however, were far more concerned by a murder that had happened outside a nearby pub that had received little media interest.

---

* A more detailed account of the crime and the subsequent research is available in Lowe et al. (2007).

The second key finding related to how members of the community living close to the scene were disaffected by the police response. For the residents, the murder represented an escalation of a growing street crime menace in the area that the police had failed to tackle. In effect, the residents had a collective memory of a series of incidents over the past decade that they interpreted as markers of a growing threat. The local police did not share this framing of the area, nor its problems, because few of them had been working in the area for more than two years and were consequently not sensitized to any longer-term trends.

Such findings are suggestive of how the kinds of insecurity that are triggered by signal crimes travel through space and time. They also point to the ways that the presence of ostensibly less serious and harmful types of crime can "prime" a neighborhood for a more profound social reaction should a major incident occur. As such, while police will attend to a particular incident and organize their response around dealing with that, the dynamics of a community's reaction may not be a function of the incident alone, having been framed by a situated history of prior occurrences and tensions. As such, these findings have significant implications for the effective management of the impacts of major crimes upon communities. But they also help to map out how and why an appropriately configured style of neighborhood policing might be useful in providing intelligence on communities helping police to comprehend where and when the occurrence of an incident might assume particular salience.

Connecting Community Policing 2: Tensions and Cohesion

In a second program of work, again funded by ACPO, we have been looking at how a systematic community engagement strategy used to generate community intelligence might have utility for understanding inter- and intracommunity tensions. The initial research on this topic was conducted in Oldham in 2004 looking at tensions between a white working-class neighborhood and a Pakistani-Asian area, where infamous race riots took place in 2001. The first thing that was obvious when conducting the interviews, and it was not something observed anywhere else, was that respondents from both communities held shared beliefs that there were distinct White and Asian territories. During the interviews people explained, "I will walk down this side of the street, but not that side." When we went to conduct some field observations in these areas, it became clear that there were a number of physical signal disorders—such as racist graffiti and George Cross flags—used to physically demarcate the frontiers of the respective territories. A visual representation of the tensions and the signal crimes driving them in the area is provided in Figure 2.5.

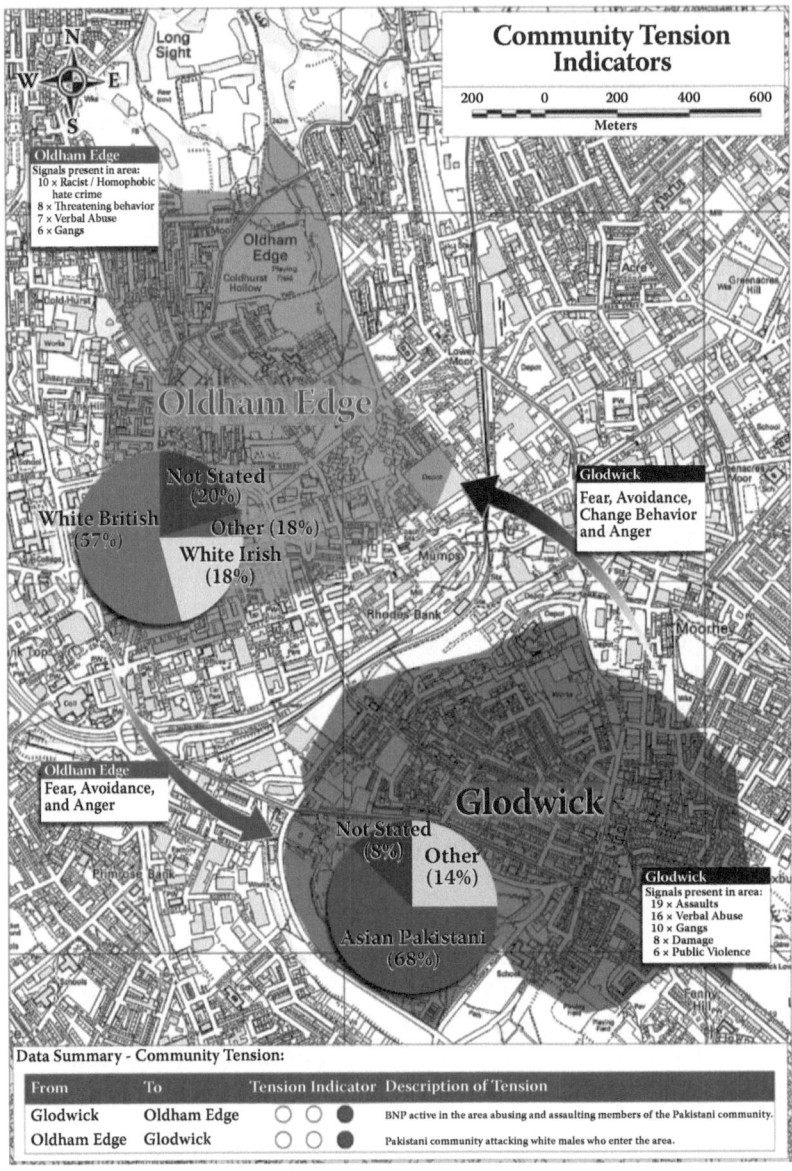

Figure 2.5 Community tension indicator in Oldham.

Using survey measures for collective efficacy it was identified that the Pakistani residents exhibited far higher levels of collective efficacy than were present in the White areas, and this inflected how various signal crimes and disorders impacted upon them. In effect, the Pakistani residents felt safe in their own area, but there were a number of signal crimes that made them fearful of the White area. In contrast, the White residents were talking about signal crimes in both their neighborhood and the Asian neighborhood. But what was especially striking was that, in this situation, a number of incidents that elsewhere might have been afforded little significance, were construed as potent signals of risk and threat. Set against a backdrop of ongoing tension and anxiety, even comparatively trivial events assumed the significance of major signals that reheated extant concerns and anxieties. The dynamics of such processes seemed to be forcing the communities to turn inwards, constructing increasingly well-defined insider/outsider identities for themselves and "the others." Results such as these afford important insights into the dynamics of how crime and disorder play into the corrosion of community cohesion.

The purpose of briefly discussing these last two examples has been to start to think through the ways in which CP approaches might connect to and shape the capacity of police organizations to deliver other elements of their mission, as community policing is often treated as being slightly removed from mainstream policing activity. In both the examples discussed, there are intimations of how the connectivity with communities afforded by a properly organized and directed community policing approach can have an important role in shaping the capability of the police to deliver various aspects of their social function.

Conclusion: Community Intelligence-Led Policing

In this chapter we have described some of the principal components of a community intelligence methodology enabling police organizations to align their service delivery in ways more likely to meet the complex needs of the communities and neighborhoods they serve. By capturing intelligence data that more accurately and precisely articulate how individuals and groups are viewing their situated environments, the aspiration would be to achieve policing interventions that are more effective. This responds to a real need in current police practice, where, despite the impetus for establishing a national neighborhood policing system in the UK (aside from in a few localities), there is a general failure to grasp the importance of a professional and structured approach to community engagement. There remains a continued reliance upon poorly attended and conducted PACT meetings that suffer from a lack of definition as to what role they are performing for the wider neighborhood management process.

One of the most prominent discourses on police reform in recent years has been concerned with configuring policing in an intelligence-led form (Innes & Sheptycki, 2004). In many ways, the conceptual framing of intelligence-led policing has served to cast it as the antithesis of community policing. Proponents of this position have argued that by improving the analysis of data within police information systems, and by enhancing their closed and open source intelligence assets, police organizations can significantly improve their effectiveness and efficiency in managing crime. By utilizing a disciplined and structured approach that explicitly targets prolific offenders, crime clusters and series, and criminogenic situations, it is maintained that policing can have an important role in preventing criminality and suppressing crime rates. There is some research evidence to support such claims (Weisburd & Braga, 2006), although others have implicated such intelligence-led methodologies in promoting recourse to disruption of crime as a measure of performance, rather than securing detections in the courts (Innes & Sheptycki, 2004).

In contrast to the sense of tension that exists between the two pure formulations of these respective positions, the approach that has been outlined herein effectively seeks to establish a synthesis between them to construct what might be dubbed community intelligence-led policing. The structured and systematic approach to community engagement described above affords police the opportunity to appropriate and reconfigure the kinds of disciplined approaches to intelligence collection and processing already familiar to them, but in a manner that is coherent with the philosophical tenets and desired practical outcomes of CP. In effect, it extends the paradigm of intelligent policing in a way that makes it coherent with providing reassurance and increased neighborhood security in an era of globalized insecurity.

Creating conceptual bridges of this kind is important in reshaping the delivery of policing in a way that enables it to gain traction in responding to an increasingly prevalent and pervasive sense of insecurity that many leading social commentators identify as one of the defining social problems of our age.* From national security issues to perceptions of unsafe and vulnerable neighborhoods, there is a growing appreciation that if people perceive themselves to be at risk, this can be sufficient to induce social reactions that seriously degrade the quality of their lives. Providing services that help people to better manage both the objective and subjective vagaries of their security in conditions of "liquid modernity" may be emerging as a pivotal challenge for policing.

---

* The arguments here have been nicely summarized by Judt (2007, p. 26): "Fear is re-emerging as an active ingredient of political life in Western democracies.... And, perhaps above all, fear that it is not just we who can no longer shape our lives but that those in authority have lost control as well, to forces beyond their reach."

References

Campbell, D. (1955). The informant in quantitative research. *American Journal of Sociology, 60*, 339–42.

Fielding, N., & M. Innes. (2006). Reassurance policing, community policing and measuring police performance. *Policing and Society, 16*, 127–45.

Herbert, S. (2006). *Citizens, cops and power.* Chicago: Chicago University Press.

Innes, M. (2004). Signal crimes and signal disorders: Notes on deviance as communicative action. *British Journal of Sociology, 55*, 335–55.

Innes, M., C. Roberts, & S. Maltby. (2005). *Community intelligence: A report to the National Community Tensions Team.* London: ACPO.

Innes, M., & J. Sheptycki. (2004). From detection to disruption: Some consequences of intelligence-led crime control in the UK. *International Criminal Justice Review, 14*, 1–14.

Judt, T. (2007). The wrecking ball of innovation. *New York Review of Books, LIV,* 22–27.

Lowe, T., M. Innes, & C. Roberts. (2007). The impact of homicide on community reassurance. *The Journal of Homicide and Major Incident Investigation, 3*(1), 67–84.

Manning, P. (1997). *Police work: The social organization of policing* (2nd ed.). Prospect Heights, IL: Waveland Press.

Mastrofski, S. (2006). Community policing: A sceptical view. In D. Weisburd & A. Braga (Eds.), *Police innovation: Contrasting perspectives* (pp. 44–76). Cambridge: Cambridge University Press.

Quinton, P., & J. Morris (2008). *Neighbourhood policing: The impact of piloting and early national implementation.* London: Home Office.

Skogan, W. (2007). *Police and community in Chicago.* New York: Oxford University Press.

Sykes, G. (1951). The differential distribution of community knowledge. *Social Forces, 29*, 376–82.

Tuffin, R., et al. (2006). *The National Reassurance Policing Programme: A six site evaluation.* London: Home Office.

Weatheritt, M. (1988). Community policing: Rhetoric or Reality? In J. R. Greene & S. D. Mastrofski (Eds.), *Community policing: Rhetoric or reality?* (pp. 153–75). New York: Praeger.

Weisburd, D., & A. Braga (2006). Hot spots policing as a model for police innovation. In D. Weisburd & A. Braga (Eds.), *Police innovation: Contrasting perspectives* (pp. 225–244). Cambridge: Cambridge University Press.

Weisburd, D., & J. Eck. (2004). What can police do to reduce crime, disorder, and fear? *Annals of the American Academy of Political and Social Science, 593*, 42–65.

Democratic Policing

PETER GRABOSKY

3

Contents

Previously published and translated into Chinese in Grabosky, P. (2008). Democratic policing. *Crime and Criminal Justice International*, 11, 1–25.

The challenge of policing a democratic society is to design a means by which public preferences are converted into policing outputs. This is less easy than it sounds, for reasons well known to democratic theorists. Moreover, it may not always be desirable. Foremost among the concerns is the fundamental risk of majority tyranny. The public may well prefer solutions that are exclusionary, or indeed, draconian, to the great disadvantage of the marginalized minorities against whom they are directed. Compounding this is the fact that people from disadvantaged backgrounds are less likely to participate in any political process, even those through which they might further their own interests. The flip side of this is the risk of *minority* tyranny, where a shrill minority would prevail over an apathetic majority (Thacher, 2001).

This chapter will discuss a variety of mechanisms for converting citizen preferences into policing practice. The traditional model of police exercising their independent professional judgment will be noted, but the pages that follow will be primarily devoted to the various mechanisms of community consultation, including representative government on the Westminster model, policing boards, survey research, and community meetings.

Particular attention will be accorded to mechanisms designed to ensure that the preferences of the disadvantaged and inarticulate are not ignored, and that the most disadvantaged citizens are neither neglected nor persecuted. The ideal mechanism (or combination of mechanisms) will be one that empowers all citizens, including the disadvantaged, to identify and to address their own security problems to the greatest extent possible.

The questions of scale, and the level at which community consultation might optimally be undertaken will also be discussed, as will the question of the cultural resonance of the various mechanisms of consultation that have been proposed.

Why Democratic Policing?

In his book *Strong Democracy* (1984) Benjamin Barber suggests that the general principle of an active, engaged citizenry is inherently good, for the participant as well as for society. According to Barber, when an individual sees herself as a citizen, and not merely as a subject, her support for the political system, and ultimately the stability of that system, is enhanced.

Participation can also be an educative process. The exchange of information among citizens, and between the police and the public, can increase awareness about the strengths and limitations of various policy options. It can also serve to broaden the outlook of the citizen, and to enhance an individual's community-mindedness (Pateman, 1970, pp. 42–43; Sklansky, 2008, pp. 62–65).

Beyond this, active citizen involvement in the process of government may instill in members of the public a sense of competence and efficacy that in turn may facilitate the development of higher moral and ethical standards. Civic engagement thus serves to improve both the government and the citizen. Ideally, the citizen becomes more knowledgeable and tolerant, more sensitive to others' interests, and more introspective (Dryzek, 2000; Warren, 1992). But Dahl (1989, p. 92) suggests that this may be wishful thinking.

If what Barber says can be generalized to policing, citizen involvement has a number of potential benefits. Democratic policing is more likely to be perceived as legitimate by the public than is a system of policing imposed from above. All else equal, it is likely to lead to a greater degree of compliance (Sunshine & Tyler, 2003).

Lord Scarman's observations in the aftermath of the Brixton riots suggest that policing an alienated public is fraught with risk. Policing by an institution perceived as less than legitimate is less likely to be effective, or worse. His concerns were fundamentally instrumental, when he observed that a police service that failed to consult locally would fail to be efficient.

Problems of Democracy

Democratic theorists will differentiate between the aggregate of individual private interests, and the public interest or the common good (Dahl, 1989, p. 71). Most law-abiding citizens, if asked, would prefer to see a greater police presence in their own neighborhood than in somebody else's across town. Conversely, proposals to close down police stations tend to be greeted with considerable dismay by local residents. It may not matter much to the self-interested citizen that his preferred outcomes might entail an inefficient or ineffective allocation of police resources. "Looking after number one" is a familiar mindset in our individualistic society. Citizens are usually competent judges of their own interest, but less so of the interests of others or of the public in general.

Whether the opportunity to exchange information with other than like-minded citizens can lead to a higher level of consciousness is by no means certain. As Dahl (1989, p. 61) notes, "Most people seem unwilling to give the interests of a stranger, or anyone unknown to them, anything like equal weight in comparison with their own." He further notes that democracy may not be a panacea for individual or collective shortcomings. "The conjecture that political participation tends to create a stronger sense of self worth, greater tolerance, and more public spiritedness is only weakly supported by systematic observation, if at all" (Dahl, 1989, p. 92).

Dimensions of Democratic Policing

Skogan (1998) observes a continuum of public involvement in policing. At one extreme, policing is done by a specialized elite, on behalf of the public. In *The Republic*, Plato entrusted rulership to a minority of people with superior knowledge and virtue. Like Plato's Guardians, police in the English-speaking world have relied for most of the modern era on their own professional judgment to determine public security needs. Until relatively recently, they enjoyed a quasi-judicial independence from political control. Unfortunately, for most of the modern era, police have fallen short of this Platonic ideal. Disclosures of corruption and abuse of power, combined with evidence of inferior service (or worse) to the disadvantaged and inarticulate, suggest that police have not always been able to claim monopolies on virtue or wisdom (Westley, 1970; Sherman, 1978; Mollen, 1994; Queensland, 1989; Wood, 1997). As a result, their independence and autonomy are now much less than they once were, and the "playing field" of policing policy is now very crowded.*

Toward the middle of the continuum, the public serves as the eyes and ears of the police. They provide a degree of surveillance and intelligence data, but have no input as to where and how police resources are used.

At the other end of the continuum, the public are actively involved in the identification of policing needs, and in the development of policing policy. Moreover, they are fully involved in the co-production of policing, through such activities as neighborhood surveillance, dispute resolution, and target hardening to reduce criminal opportunities.

In the 1960s, interest in participatory democracy began to emerge in the United States (Sklansky, 2008, pp. 61–70). The suggestion that members of the public (especially members of minority groups) knew better than the police what their security needs were, met with initial resistance from law enforcement. But the public was not content to remain passive. Support grew for civilian review of police misconduct. Arguably even more significant was the rise of the feminist movement, accompanied by trenchant criticism of the traditional manner in which police handled victims of sexual assault and domestic violence.

This pattern was repeated in the United Kingdom, Canada, and Australia. In the 1980s police services in these countries became more attentive to public preferences, and most began to establish mechanisms of community consultation.

---

* Jones, Newburn, and Smith (1994) refer to such players in the British political system as the Home Office, Her Majesty's Inspectorate of Constabulary, the communications media, and various community groups, *inter alia*. One might also mention police unions, who, for better or worse, have sometimes constrained the decision making of police executives.

The Machinery of Democratic Policing

What is the optimal mechanism for identifying public preferences, reconciling them with community security needs, and translating them into public policy (or security outcomes delivered by public, private, or hybrid institutions)? For reasons that will become clear in the following discussion, there is no single ideal solution. Each mechanism has its strengths and limitations. The appropriate combination of mechanisms will vary depending on the relative capacities of the citizenry, the public police service, and the private sector.

The administrative or other means by which public preferences are registered may take diverse forms. Media of transmission can vary from institutions of direct democracy, such as town meetings, to mechanisms of representative democracy, such as elections and representative government. They may be broad in scope, or targeted in a manner designed to identify the needs of special minorities.

Elections

In Western democracies, elections are the basic institution of political participation. Elected governments with constitutional responsibility for policing may implement those policies that have been endorsed by the electorate. Electoral systems vary widely, but in most instances, elections are contested on a broad spectrum of issues. To the extent that parties or candidates have different policies on policing and criminal justice, they tend to be inextricably packaged with policies on many issues, ranging from health and education to roads and refuse removal. Ultimately, the elected government is responsible for determining the composition and deployment of policing services, including such complementary services as health, education, recreation, and welfare. The presentation of these policy packages, moreover, is done in a manner that does not encourage thoughtful deliberation on the part of the public; the "seven-second grab" has replaced meaningful discourse.

Electoral systems, however, are very imperfect instruments for the transmission of policy preferences. In places where the franchise is restricted or where voting is optional, significant segments of the population may not be heard. Moreover, minority groups may be too small to make a difference in terms of electoral outcome. For example, with citizens of indigenous background comprising less than 3% of the Australian population, their ability to influence the outcome of elections is limited indeed.

Initiatives and Referenda

Some political systems provide for citizen initiatives or referenda, enabling the electorate to vote for or against a specific policy proposal (Bowler,

Donovan, & Tolbert, 1998). Depending upon the constitutional arrangements of the jurisdiction in question, a particular proposition that receives a requisite number of signatures may be placed on the ballot for ratification or rejection by the electorate. Alternatively, it may be referred to the electorate by the legislature. For example, California's "three strikes" legislation arose as a citizen initiative (Zimring, Hawkins, & Kamin, 2001).

These instruments of direct democracy also have significant downside risks. Most prominent among these is, again, the risk of majority tyranny. It has been suggested that initiatives and referenda facilitate the targeting and indeed the stigmatization of vulnerable minorities (Wenzel, Donovan, & Bowler, 1998). California's three strikes initiative, passed by a 72% majority, sought permanently to banish repeat offenders; an earlier initiative in that state sought to deny health care, education, and social services to illegal immigrants and their children.

Like elections generally, referenda may not facilitate thoughtful deliberation by voters. Even where explanatory materials setting out arguments for or against a proposal are distributed prior to a referendum vote, they may be ignored. The result is a vote that may reflect knee-jerk reaction rather than thoughtful consideration of an issue.

Sample Surveys of Public Opinion

One of the more rigorous ways of gauging public opinion, including public preferences relating to policing services, is the sample survey. A well-designed survey administered to a carefully selected sample will provide a very accurate assessment of public attitudes toward police, security concerns, fear of crime, and so forth.

In a society that includes one or more small minority groups, however, it may be difficult, if not impossible, to achieve reliable estimates from the smallest group or groups. A statewide survey with a sample size of 2,000, for example, would yield very few indigenous or transsexual respondents, too few from which to base meaningful generalizations.

There may be other sources of bias in sample surveys. Normally respondents are limited to persons aged 18 and over, thereby excluding children.

Oversampling and weighting may compensate for some of these sources of bias.

But there are others that may be less tractable. For example, persons who are linguistically challenged may be underrepresented in telephone or face-to-face surveys. Those who are illiterate are also less likely to complete paper-and-pencil questionnaires unless they receive special assistance.

Surveys conducted by telephone will exclude respondents who, by choice or circumstance, do not have a telephone. Surveys based on samples of residential premises may miss the homeless or transient, as well as tourists generally. Special surveys may be conducted of such subgroups where appropriate (Sudman, Sirken, & Cowan, 1998; Thompson & Seber, 1996).

And then there is the risk that the respondent, rather than thoughtfully consider her response, will respond in an instinctive or intolerant manner.

Community Forums

Assuming that they are well publicized and held at a convenient time and place, community forums provide an opportunity for interested citizens to express their security preferences. Such forums, however, are vulnerable to the intensity problem. They may amplify the voices of the intense, and mute those of the apathetic (Thurman & Resig, 1996). As with most forms of participation, the economically disadvantaged and socially marginalized will be disinclined to participate.

Beat Meetings

These entail regular periodic meetings of residents within a prescribed geographic area. That is, they are "turf based." Beat meetings are the core of the system of community policing that was introduced in Chicago in 1993 (Skogan & Hartnett, 1997; Skogan, 2006; Fung, 2004). They serve as forums for identifying and prioritizing local problems. In Chicago, they suffer from the same kind of bias as most citizen-initiated contributions to policy decision making: a degree of middle-class bias. As Skogan (2003, p. 59) observes, "Beat meetings are composed of those who happen to hear about them, and those who choose to attend." Once again, the relatively disadvantaged are underrepresented. However, at least in Chicago, complementary surveys of neighborhood residents reveal a convergence of views between beat meeting participants and nonparticipants in terms of priorities (Skogan, 1998).

Consultative Boards and Advisory Committees

These usually take the form of standing committees that meet periodically and are designed to be broadly representative of community interests. In some jurisdictions, they may be required by law. In the United Kingdom, the Police and Criminal Evidence Act imposed a statutory duty on police authorities to set up consultative arrangements (Jones, Newburn, & Smith, 1994, p. 22). Their effectiveness will depend on the degree to which board members are in fact representative of significant community interests, and the capacity of these representatives to articulate the needs of their constituents (Goldstein, 1977, p. 146).

Focus Groups

Focus groups are another means of determining public attitudes. The challenge here is to recruit a focus group that is representative of the larger population to which one seeks to generalize. Focus groups are a particularly useful means of tapping into segments of the population (i.e., high school students) who might not be reached by a general sample survey. They are also means of determining the preferences of small minorities such as transsexuals, whose representation in a general survey is likely to be extremely small, and whose attitudes may not be amenable to measurement through community surveys.

Deliberation

Given the inherently selfish perspective adopted by many citizens, it has been suggested that democratic processes entail a degree of deliberation, where proponents of a particular course of action will meet face-to-face with those who may be skeptical or opposed to the idea (Fishkin, 1991; Dryzek, 2000; Fishkin & Laslett, 2003). Theoretically, this will better enable citizens to empathize with their fellow citizens, improve the quality of decision making, and reduce the likelihood of tyrannous outcomes.

It is not very comforting to note that face-to-face deliberation is the very basis of the legislative process, which all too often deteriorates into a dialogue of the deaf and is hardly a recipe for empathetic understanding, even when the playing field is level. We know, of course, that the playing field is rarely, if ever, level, and that the better-resourced interests in a community are also likely to command advocacy skills that are superior to those of the marginalized. To overcome this potential source of bias, Goodin (2003) encourages what he describes as "reflective democracy," where citizens are encouraged to reflect on their preferences and internalize the perspectives of others. He encourages this even when the other might not be physically present.

Groucho Marx is reputed once to have commented, "Why should I worry about future generations? What have they done for me?" Goodin nevertheless suggests that it should be possible to give consideration to future generations, and other so-called mute interests. "Conversation is useful, but imagination is essential" (Goodin, 2003, p. 228). He uses the phrase "democratic deliberation within" to refer to such a process.

One of the more ambitious expositions of deliberation in furtherance of democratic policing (and criminal justice more broadly) is the work of Loader and Walker (2007). They seek to restore security as a public good and, in so doing, to use reflexive deliberation to enriching the democratic process. Even these authors recognize the inequalities on which such a project can founder; they acknowledge a need to provide participatory capacity and compensatory protection for the most disadvantaged.

Specific Targeting of Peak Bodies

Most societies are rich in organizational life. Even the marginalized, who themselves are not organized, may have advocates able to speak on their behalf. Strategic consultation with these organizations or advocates can help identify the security needs of special interests who would not otherwise have a voice.

Many groups, by definition, lack political and moral competence, that is, the ability to engage in reasoned decision making and to know what is right or just. Young children and some mentally ill and developmentally disabled citizens come immediately to mind. Members of these groups still have very real security needs. For obvious reasons, they will be unable to articulate these needs, and therefore usually need an advocate.

Foot Patrol

Police officers on foot gather information in their day-to-day contact with members of the public (Hornick, Burrows, Phillips, & Leighton, 1993). Absent a clearly defined data collection protocol (which is not what foot patrol is about), they are an unsystematic means of collecting information, as they depend on those who would approach (or those who would be approached by) police officers. Nevertheless, observant and inquisitive patrol officers are able to form an impressionistic assessment of security preferences on their beat.

Kobans and Shop-Front Offices

The police box or mini-station has long been a feature of Japanese policing (Bayley, 1976). The size and location of such a facility (usually in well-traversed public places) place it on a human scale, enhancing its physical and psychological accessibility to members of the public. Its apparent success in Japan led to its adaptation in Singapore in the mid-1980s, and in various other locations over the succeeding years. Like foot patrol, kobans permit at best an impressionistic assessment of security preferences.

Emergency Response Calls

Over the past two decades, the dominant mechanism for mobilizing the police, at least in English-speaking democracies, had been the telephone. Emergency numbers such as 000 in Australia or 911 in North America provide a medium through which the public can communicate its preferences for police attendance directly to police themselves. This will give some indication about the demand for police services on a day-to-day basis, but are only indirectly indicative of policy preferences.

Diversity Within the Police Organization

Sklansky (2008) has observed that members of a police organization that is demographically representative of the public it serves are potentially more capable of empathetic understanding than the "overwhelmingly white, virtually all-male, pervasively homophobic police forces of thirty or forty years ago" in the United States. A diverse police organization is also likely to have greater interpersonal skills in dealing with a diverse community, and is likely to be perceived as more legitimate as a result.

Market Solutions

There are those who will seek to meet their own security needs by purchasing goods and services from the private sector. This may entail the purchase of security hardware or of other security services, such as guards. Such resort to the market may indicate (justifiably or otherwise) dissatisfaction with publicly funded policing. Issues of equity arise given the inability of financially disadvantaged citizens to afford private services. Whether the existence of a market in private security frees up public resources to better attend to the security needs of disadvantaged citizens is an empirical question (Sklansky, 2008, pp. 127–131).

Regardless of the nature of the medium, one should be wary of models that amplify the voices of those who are already disproportionately vocal. In many settings, a few of the people will do most of the talking. These may not be representative of the general community, nor of the public interest.

There are those who are less likely to avail themselves of basic services, even when such services may be available. Truants and early school leavers, those who do not seek medical and dental treatment (even when such services are publicly available), individuals who shun available public housing and prefer to live on the street, and those victims of crime who will not notify the police, all illustrate the difficulty of aggregating preferences for security in the wider public interest.

Scale and Scope of Machinery

The capacity for meaningful individual political participation varies directly with the size of the collectivity. The prospects for direct democracy where policy issues can be canvassed in the course of an extended moral argument are limited.

It is much easier to have one's voice heard in a community of 500 than in a city of 3 million. Even then, Dahl (1998, p. 105) reminds us that if every one of the 500 citizens were given 10 minutes in which to express their views, the meeting would last 83 hours.

Dahl (1998, p. 109) refers to "the law of time and numbers: The more citizens a democratic unit contains, the less that citizens can participate directly in government decisions and the more they must delegate authority to others." Dahl (1998, p. 110) also reminds us that there may also be trade-offs between citizen participation and system effectiveness. "The larger the unit, the greater its capacity for dealing with problems important to its citizens, and the greater the need for citizens to delegate decisions to representatives."

Other structural properties of a collectivity that will bear upon the appropriate consultative mechanisms are area, homogeneity, and stratification. The wider the spatial boundaries, and the more heterogeneous and more stratified the community, the greater the diversity of views one may expect. Capturing and reconciling these views will be challenging, regardless of what medium of assessment one might choose. All else equal, the greater the diversity, the less the solidarity and the greater the suspicion among diverse members of the community. This will pose formidable challenges to identifying common interests, and to reconciling them when they are in conflict.

Policy questions vary in terms of scope and the scale of consultative mechanisms appropriate to address them. At the most micro-level, there may be a problem of graffiti in a particular location, or a question of whether to install a stoplight at the intersection of Smith Street and Jones Avenue. Assuming the problem is confined to a specific location, so too is the solution, subject, perhaps, only to resource issues that may have wider applications. Problems on this scale are arguably amenable to identification at the local level. The degree of devolution will depend on the scope of the issue. Issues that are everybody's business can be addressed at higher levels, while those that are micro-concerns can be addressed at the grass roots.

At the intermediate level, problems will impact upon a wider cross section of the community, for example, the level of resources devoted to traffic enforcement.

Macro-level issues deal with fundamental matters affecting the entire police service, for example, whether police should be armed at all, or be equipped with more powerful weapons. Sample surveys are perhaps the most accurate means of determining public attitudes on matters of this nature.

As a general principle, it has been suggested that democratic solutions be based on the principle of subsidiary. The keystone of Hirst's theory of associative democracy (Hirst, 1994, 2002), the principle states that "as many social activities as possible should be devolved to self-governing voluntary associations" (Bader, 2001, p. 1). In other words, the ends and means of policing should be determined at the lowest possible level, and by nonstate interests to the greatest extent feasible. Nevertheless, there are obvious economies of scale that militate against extreme decentralization. Moreover, size varies inversely with exclusivity. The smaller the group, the less likely its members will reflect a diversity of views. Devolution may well be accompanied by parochial thinking.

Another general principle holds that regardless of their level, decisions made about policing should be made through deliberative processes. Translating this principle into practice is no mean feat, because citizens vary in both their interest in and their capacity for deliberation. Those individuals or groups unwilling to articulate their own interests should arguably not be required to do so. Those incapable of stating their own case may require encouragement or assistance. In the end, a proxy may be required in both instances (Loader & Walker, 2007, chap. 8).

Problems of Democratic Policing

Police Resistance

Throughout most of the modern era, police in many jurisdictions were regarded as the living embodiment of the law, and enjoyed a kind of quasi-judicial autonomy. Although this has changed over the past three decades, many police will still cling to their traditional role as contemporary equivalents of Plato's Guardians, monopolists of wisdom and virtue (Dahl, 1989, p. 52). To the extent that they do, they will be resistant to the idea of letting citizens set the police agenda. In this regard, police are no different from members of other professions, who have usually had little time for laypeople claiming a degree of knowledge or expertise. Few professionals like to be told how to do their job.

The Problem of Conflicting or Divergent Preferences

In a diverse community, there are bound to be differences of opinion regarding the desirability of certain policy alternatives. These options may be mutually exclusive, or differences may be irreconcilable. Consider the case of injecting drug use. There are those citizens who would advocate the provision of hygienic premises that injecting users may visit with impunity, and indeed, some who would advocate providing heroin on prescription to users who are certifiably dependent. Other citizens, however, would favor the automatic arrest of any injecting drug user. Even within minority communities, there may be intense differences of opinion, not to mention internal conflict, which would make a consensus difficult, if not impossible, to achieve.

Short of solutions that are mutually exclusive, there are some issues that might be described as zero-sum in nature. These often involve questions of resource allocation. That is, one person's gain comes at the expense of another. The decision to locate a police station in neighborhood A and not across town in neighborhood B is one such example. So too would be the decision to double the size of the drug squad at the expense of traffic enforcement.

Fortunately, the apparently irreconcilable may lend itself to compromise. Enforcement strategies keyed to time, place, and manner might be illustrative. Police may turn a blind eye to discreet marijuana consumption in places like concert venues, but may choose to mobilize the law when such activity occurs on or near school premises.

The Problem of Unrealistic Expectations

Elsewhere, we have discussed the notion of an expectations gap—the fact that police cannot be everywhere and do everything the public might expect of them. The extent to which police have succeeded in portraying themselves as omnipresent and omniscient means that public expectations will occasionally exceed the capacity of police to fulfill them (Sklansky, 2008, chap. 6). The challenge of consultation processes is to train the public in what police are legally capable of delivering, what they can reasonably deliver with the finite resources available to them, and what the public can constructively contribute to meeting their own needs.

The Problem of Imperfect Information

The capacity of the public to make reasoned assessments may be limited by the quantity and quality of information to which they have access.

Police services may have good operational reasons for not disclosing certain types of information. Obviously, one does not wish to alert prospective offenders to potential criminal opportunities. Needless to say, premature disclosure of some information can jeopardize ongoing investigations. And too much information might serve to instill a level of fear in the public that is largely unwarranted.

But even when information might not be inherently criminogenic, there may be barriers to an informed public.

Moreover, neither police nor their political masters like to be the bearers of bad news. As we have seen, police have traditionally been very successful at exploiting the myth of their omniscience and omnipresence. Elected officials often remain in power because of their ability to reassure the public that theirs is the best of all possible worlds. Sir Humphrey would describe as courageous any police commissioner who would contradict his or her minister.

The Problem of Things Better Left Unsaid

Even the most energetic proponents of transparency in policing would concede that some matters are best excluded from public discourse. A full and frank discussion of the overrepresentation of certain ethnic groups among identified offenders, and the pros and cons of restoring capital punishment in jurisdictions that have abolished it, are but two examples. As Gutman and Thompson (1996, p. 42) observe, greater deliberation may serve to intensify conflict. Heclo (1999) sees a risk in "hyperdemocracy," where issues can be overpoliticized. There are some issues best treated with benign neglect, lest they awaken darker impulses within the citizenry.

It is hardly surprising, therefore, that information flowing to the public from police or politicians tends to be selectively filtered.

Impediments to Democracy

Apathy

One of the basic facts of life in democratic societies is political indifference. Whether born of perceived inefficacy, resignation, alienation, or other preference, this attitude of "preferring not to get involved" may well be increasingly common in modern society, where those who are employed tend to be working longer than ever. Or, as Oscar Wilde is reported to have commented, "The problem with socialism is that it would take too many evenings."

Apathy may also arise from the fact that many citizens have become dependent on the state for a wide range of benefits and services, and have grown out of the habit of looking after themselves. And others are simply time-poor. Entire industries exist today to serve people who simply don't have the time to do the things, from food preparation to housecleaning, that people did for themselves a generation ago. It may also be slightly presumptuous to assume that low-income people, who cannot always afford child-minding and other timesaving services, have an abundance of time to devote to civic engagement (Skolnick, 1971).

There is, of course, more to a passive citizenry than laziness and dependence. This is reinforced in the realm of criminal justice by very significant legal constraints on what one can do in self-defense. Disproportionate response to an actual or threatened criminal act may find the original victim facing criminal charges more serious than those to which the original offender was liable. Indeed, the modern professional criminal justice system evolved to preclude private revenge.

Whatever the causes, it is instructive to note Grinc's (1994) observation that "despite the apparent popularity of the community policing approach, community residents may not want closer interaction with the police nor the responsibility for maintaining social control."

Fear of Retaliation

Buerger's (1994) report of an evaluation of innovative neighborhood policing programs (INOPs) in the United States noted that fear of retaliation from drug dealers was the primary inhibitor of public participation. Such fears may be realistic. In 1952 a New York man named Arnold Schuster provided police with information regarding the whereabouts of the notorious armed robber Willie Sutton. Schuster's identity and his role in assisting police became public knowledge, and he was shot to death not long thereafter (Gutterman, 1967).

Distrust of Police

Buerger (1994) also noted that estrangement between police and public can also inhibit citizen participation. Then, there are those who, for whatever reason, simply do not wish to have contact with the police. Perhaps they themselves have something for which they would not wish to draw the attention of the authorities. Perhaps they immigrated from societies where police were repressive. Perhaps if they are not fluent in the official language of their place of residence, they may feel self-conscious. Perhaps they simply do not like symbols of authority. Perhaps mobility and turnover in police ranks preclude the formation of bonds with communities or neighborhood residents.

In a study of a multiethnic New York neighborhood, Davis (2000) concluded that members of ethnic groups that perceived themselves as politically disempowered were less likely to regard the police favorably, and less likely to report crimes. These cultural influences were found to be more important than individuals' personal experiences in shaping their attitudes toward police.

This suggests that, while important, the general demeanor of police may not be sufficient to improve police community relations. According to Davis, what is required is close dialogue with the communities in question, and encouragement of these communities to set priorities and develop strategies.

Differential Capacity

Elitism theorists of the 20th century, such as Michels (1949) and Mosca (1939), remind us that every society develops a ruling class. In any society there will be some variation in citizen competence. Access to information, or at the very least the ability to process it, is by no means uniform.

There are those groups who may lack organizational skills, financial means, or other political resources, such as knowledge and social status. And there are others who will be both knowledgeable and articulate. There are those individuals who may lack sufficient knowledge to state an informed preference. Simplistic and demagogic solutions are not uncommon in criminal justice. As Dahl (1989, p. 182) put it, "We cannot assume that citizens are invariably guided by an enlightened understanding of their interests."

Differential Moral Competence

Not every citizen has an equally legitimate moral claim—knowledge of what is virtuous and in furtherance of the common good (Dahl, 1989, p. 58). In matters of criminal justice, there are those who would like to view the world as a morality play, a struggle between good and evil. This may be true, but only to a limited extent. Not all moral claims should have equal weight. Recidivist armed robbers have some moral claims, but arguably fewer than law-abiding widows who live alone.

Paternalistic authority may still have a place in public security. Consider the mentally ill or developmentally disabled person who threatens passersby. Or, take the 10-year-old who thinks it in his interests to hang out on street corners and smoke cigarettes. There are few people today who would regard the criminal sanction as an appropriate means of dealing with either of these matters. Nevertheless, when other institutions in either the public or private sectors are unavailable to deal with such matters, the preferences of the individuals in question may have to yield.

The Problem of Intensity

On almost any issue of public policy, preferences will vary in intensity. There are those individuals who feel deeply, indeed passionately, about an issue, those whose opinions are more moderate, and those who couldn't care less.

The risk that a passionate and shrill minority might prevail over a more apathetic majority cannot be ignored (Shapiro, 2003). Elsewhere, Grabosky (1992) has speculated on the risks of a "hyperactive citizenry" (see also Jones et al., 1994, p. 40).

Lucia Zedner (2003) has queried whether there can be such a thing as "too much security." This is hardly a far-fetched question. In recent Australian political history, the issue of capital punishment was traditionally kept off the political agenda by all major political parties, despite the fact that survey data reveal a majority in support of reintroducing the death penalty.

Zimring et al. (2001) argue that because of their tendency to inflame public opinion, issues of punishment should be insulated from direct democracy. Just as interest rates are best set by central banks, so too should criminal sentences be determined in a manner apart from the democratic process.

The monetary inflation that is likely to occur as a result of public preferences for low interest rates would be mirrored by the inflation in rates of imprisonment likely to arise from direct translation of public preferences into criminal sentencing. This, after all, is the role that judges are supposed to perform.

Paradoxes

Ironies abound in criminal justice. Indigenous Australians suffer disproportionately as victims of crime, mostly at the hands of other indigenous Australians. Objectively, their security needs are much greater than those of the general nonindigenous population. At the same time, they express concerns that they are overpoliced and that indigenous people are overrepresented as clients of the criminal justice system. To be sure, the circumstances of indigenous criminality lie beyond the capacity of police alone to control. But reconciling their policy preferences and security needs is a real challenge. Sklansky (2008, p. 133) has observed similar ironies in U.S. minority communities.

The Challenge of Guardianship

Until only recently, the role of the police was that of guardians or trustees of the common good or public interest. The criminal law as enacted by legislatures provided general guidance, and public input was not encouraged. Much of the criminal law on the books served an expressive rather than instrumental purpose. That is, it was enacted to send a message rather than to provide the basis for response to undesirable behavior. Or at the very least, it was retained on the books rather than repealed, in order not to send the wrong message. As a result, the statute books were cluttered with archaic laws of embarrassing scope. The author once lived in a jurisdiction that made it a crime to have sexual intercourse with anyone other than a lawfully wedded spouse. Fortunately, he managed to avoid official notice.

Although police would often recite the mantra that they were only enforcing the law, without fear or favor, in fact they exercised considerable discretion. This discretion was not always exercised in an even-handed manner. The annals of policing contain many examples of bias and discrimination in the enforcement of law and in the provision of service, as well as police misconduct as troubling as it has been diverse.

The Blessings of Apathy

On the other hand, some observers suggest that apathy is a blessing. Consider the problem of excessive demands on limited resources. If every victim of crime were to report his or her misfortune to the police, law enforcement agencies would be hopelessly overloaded. Indeed, even with the substantial dark figure of unreported crime that prevails today, police have more business than they can handle. A hyperactive citizenry may not always be a good thing (Jones et al., 1994, p. 40).

Moreover, Pateman (1970) observed that "non-democratic attitudes are relatively more common among the inactive," and suggests that apathy and disinterest may contribute to stability.

Conclusion

At the end of the day, it is the elected government that is accountable for the provision of public safety. To the extent that they can afford to ignore minorities, they sometimes do. This will be easier when the minorities are quiescent. When they are not, the government faces the challenge of placating the intense minority without antagonizing the mainstream public.

Alternatively, there are those minorities that are singled out for stigmatization and persecution. Some political cultures actually encourage the demonization of minorities.

Police should beware of models that amplify the voice of those who are already disproportionately vocal, and guard against instinctively according less moral weight to claims made by those people from disadvantaged minorities.

Pure democracy is likely to lead to some fairly brutal outcomes. Three strikes legislation, publicly accessible sex offender registries,* and, indeed, capital punishment are among the policies introduced in jurisdictions where there is an efficient and unbuffered transformation of public preferences into public policy.

Indeed, many years ago a very senior judge mentioned to the author, "The role of the judge is to stand between the man in the dock and the angry public."

There is no one recipe for democratic policing. Democracies differ dramatically, and the mechanisms of consultation that prevail in Norway may be inappropriate in South Africa. As Sherman (2000, p. 17) observes, "Diverse democracies require diverse means to achieve compliance among diverse peoples."

---

* Retrieved March 4, 2004 from http://sex-offender.vsp.state.va.us/Static/Search.htm

We know that preferences differ. There are those who feel overpoliced, and those who see themselves (or at least their immediate environment) in need of more police attention. Of course, it should be patently obvious that all security needs are not equal. There are those who, by choice or circumstance, are at much greater risk of suffering criminal predation than are others. Weighing these needs and devising policing solutions that provide an optimal level of freedom and security in society will require a variety of means of public consultation as well as the exercise of professional judgment. Providing widespread opportunity for input may require that the most marginalized members of the public be sought out.

Ironically, nondemocratic means may be required to address specific failures resulting from the democratic process (Dahl, 1989, p. 177). Plato's Guardians and participatory democracy can coexist, and probably should.

As Bayley and Shearing (1996, 2001) have observed, the current era has seen a pluralization of who *authorizes* policing and who actually *implements* it. In addition to public police as we know them, there are a variety of private sector and public-private hybrid auspices for policing. This pluralization may make for more democracy, or for less (Sklansky, 2008, chap. 6).

In conclusion, there will be no perfect mechanism for translating public preferences into policing practice. What is required is some institution that will receive input from as wide a cross section of the public as possible, and reach beyond them to identify those groups who may lack the capacity to articulate their own needs. The challenge is to select a combination of consultative mechanisms that will compensate for the inherent defects of each, and that will be sufficiently responsive as to maintain legitimacy, but not so responsive as to produce irresponsible outcomes.

A fundamental question remains: What or who is best situated to broker and distill the articulated and unarticulated needs of the public, and who is best situated to deliver a policing package that meets the most essential of those needs. In other words, who or what will command the requisite wisdom and virtue, and political entrepreneurship, essential to this task? The question is more than academic, for the legitimacy of the legal order may be at stake.

The answer, of course, will vary from location to location, depending on the local political structure and culture. Some would argue that in the ideal world, the public police themselves are best suited to this task, especially if their diversity reflects that of the community they serve. Others would argue that because public police have been less than successful in adapting to a rapidly changing policy environment, they have been displaced by private and other public sector providers of security (broadly defined). As a result, some form of cabinet government is the appropriate mechanism. And there are those who would invent entirely new institutions, such as policing boards, to broker security (Shearing, 2001). Suffice it to say that if the public police of today are unable or unwilling to undertake a more comprehensive management of public security with a view toward delivering a responsive and responsible product, there are other players waiting in the wings.

Acknowledgments

The research reported herein was supported in part by a grant from the Australian Research Council (LP0346987). Earlier versions of this chapter were presented at the International Francophone Conference on Police and Citizens, Nicolet, Quebec, May 2005; the Annual Meeting of the Law and Society Association, Las Vegas, Nevada, June 2005; and the American Society of Criminology, Toronto, November 2005. The author thanks Jenny Fleming, Michael Kempa, Al Klovdahl, and Wesley Skogan for comments on earlier versions.

References

Bader, V. (2001). Introduction. In P. Hirst & V. Bader (Eds.), *Associative democracy: The real third way*. London: Frank Cass.

Barber, B. (1984). *Strong Democracy: Participatory Politics for a New Age*. Berkeley: University of California Press.

Bayley, D. (1976). *Forces of order: Police behavior in Japan and the United States*. Berkeley: University of California Press.

Bayley, D., & Shearing, C. (1996). The future of policing. *Law and Society Review, 30*, 585–606.

Bayley, D., & Shearing, C. (2001). *The new structure of policing: Description, conceptualization and research agenda*. Washington, DC: National Institute of Justice.

Bowler, S., Donovan, T., & Tolbert, C. (1998). *Citizens as legislators: Direct democracy in the United States*. Columbus: Ohio State University Press.

Dahl, R. A. (1989). *Democracy and its critics*. New Haven, CT: Yale University Press.

Dahl, R. A. (1998). *On democracy*. New Haven, CT: Yale University Press.

Davis, R. C. (2000). *The use of citizen surveys as a tool for police reform*. New York: Vera Institute of Justice. Retrieved January 2, 2008, from http://www.vera.org/publication_pdf/citizenssurveys.pdf

Dryzek, J. (2000). *Deliberative democracy and beyond*. New York: Oxford University Press.

Fishkin, J. (1991). *Democracy and deliberation: New directions for democratic reform*. New Haven, CT: Yale University Press.

Fishkin, J., & Laslett, P. (Eds.). (2003). *Debating deliberative democracy*. Malden: Blackwell Publishing.

Fung, A. (2004). *Empowered participation: Reinventing urban democracy*. Princeton, NJ: Princeton University Press.

Goldstein, H. (1977). *Policing a free society*. Cambridge, MA: Ballinger Publishing.

Grabosky, P. (1992). Law enforcement and the citizen: Non-governmental participants in crime prevention and control. *Policing and Society, 2*, 249–271.

Grinc, R. (1994). Angels in marble: Problems in stimulating community involvement in community policing. *Crime and Delinquency, 40*, 437–468.

Gutterman, M. (1967). The informer privilege. *Journal of Criminal Law, Criminology, and Police Science, 58,* 32–64.

Heclo, H. (1999). Hyperdemocracy. *Wilson Quarterly, 23,* 62–71.

Hirst, P. (1994). *Associative democracy.* Cambridge: Polity Press.

Hirst, P. (2002). Renewing democracy through associations. *Political Quarterly,* 409–421.

Hornick, J., Burrows, B., Phillips, D. M., & Leighton, B. (1991). An impact evaluation of the Edmonton neighbourhood foot patrol program. *Canadian Journal of Program Evaluation, 6,* 47–70.

Jones, T., Newburn, T., & Smith, D. (1994). *Democracy and policing.* London: Policy Studies Institute.

Loader, I., & Walker, N. (2007). *Civilizing security.* Cambridge: Cambridge University Press.

Michels, R. (1949). *Political parties: A sociological study of the oligarchical tendencies of modern democracy* (E. Paul & C. Paul, Trans.). Glencoe, IL: Free Press.

Mollen, M. (1994). *Commission to investigate allegations of police corruption and the anti-corruption procedures of the police department* (Mollen report). New York: Mollen Commission.

Mosca, G. (1939). *The ruling class* (H. D. Kahn, Trans.). New York: McGraw Hill.

Pateman, C. (1970). *Participation and democratic theory.* Cambridge: Cambridge University Press.

Queensland. (1989). *Report of a commission of inquiry pursuant to orders in council: Dated 26 May 1987, 24 June 1987, 25 August 1988, 29 June 1989* (Fitzgerald report). Brisbane: S. R. Hampson, Govertment Printer.

Shapiro, I. (2003). Optimal deliberation? In J. Fishkin & P. Laslett (Eds.), *Debating deliberative democracy* (pp. 121–137). Malden, MA: Blackwell Publishing.

Shearing, C. (2001). A nodal conception of governance: Thoughts on a police commission. *Policing and Society, 11,* 259–272.

Sherman, L. W. (1978). *Scandal and reform: Controlling police corruption.* Berkeley: University of California Press.

Sherman, L. W. (2000). Consent of the governed: Police democracy and diversity. In S. Einstein & M. Amir (Eds.), *Police, security and democracy* (pp. 17–33). Hampshire: Ashgate Publishing Co.

Sklansky, D. A. (2008). *Democracy and the police.* Stanford, CA: Stanford University Press.

Skogan, W. G. (1998). Community participation and community policing. In J. P. Brodeur (Ed.), *How to recognize good policing* (pp. 88–106). Thousand Oaks, CA: Sage Publications.

Skogan, W. G. (2003). Representing the community in community policing. In W. Skogan (Ed.), *Community policing: Can it work?* (pp. 57–75). Belmont, CA: Wadsworth Publishing.

Skogan, W. G. (2006). *Police and community in Chicago: A tale of three cities.* New York: Oxford University Press.

Skogan, W. G., & Hartnett, S. M. (1997). *Community policing, Chicago Style.* New York: Oxford University Press.

Skolnick, J. (1971). Neighborhood police. *The Nation,* March 22, pp. 372–373.

Sudman, S., Sirken, M., & Cowan, C. (1988). Sampling rare and elusive populations. *Science, 240,* 991–996.

Sunshine, J., & Tyler, T. (2003). The role of procedural justice and legitimacy in shaping public support for policing. *Law and Society Review, 37,* 513–548.

Thacher, D. (2001). Equity and community policing: A new view of community partnerships. *Criminal Justice Ethics, 20,* 3–16.

Thompson, S., & Seber, G. (1996). *Adaptive sampling.* New York: Wiley.

Thurman, Q. C., & Resig, M. D. (1996). Community–oriented research in an era of community oriented policing. *American Behavioral Scientist, 39,* 570–586.

Warren, M. (1992). Democratic theory and self-transformation. *American Political Science Review, 86,* 8–23.

Wenzel, J., Donovan, T., & Bowler, S. (1998). Direct democracy and minorities: Changing attitudes about minorities targeted by initiatives. In Bowler, S., Donovan, T., and Tolbert, C. (Eds.), *Citizens as legislators: Direct democracy in the United States* (pp. 228–248). Columbus: Ohio State University Press.

Westley, W. A. (1970). *Violence and the police: A sociological study of law, custom, and morality.* Cambridge, MA: MIT Press.

Wood, J. R. T. (1997). *Royal commission into the New South Wales police service.* Retrieved January 2, 2008, from http://www.pic.nsw.gov.au/RoyalCommissionReports.aspx

Zedner, L. (2003). Too much security? *International Journal of the Sociology of Law, 31,* 155–184.

Zimring, F., Hawkins, G., & Kamin, S. (2001). *Punishment and democracy: Three strikes and you're out in California.* New York: Oxford University Press.

Community Policing Without the Police? The Limits of Order Maintenance by the Community

4

DAVID THACHER

Contents

The proper role for the police in combating disorder has sparked controversy for as long as the police have existed. Recently much of this debate has been about whether "public order" is a worthwhile goal at all,* but the debate also raises a different question: If we want our public spaces to be orderly, who should have the responsibility for maintaining that order? In principle, the police are not the only possible answer to this question, since a variety of other community institutions might take responsibility for order maintenance. It is in that context that I mean to examine the wisdom of community policing without the police.

This question may appear unimportant simply because much of the recent criminological literature has been skeptical about the importance of public order. If order is not an important goal, there is no point in asking who should have responsibility for it. In the end, however, this skeptical position is untenable. Disorderly behavior such as verbal harassment of women, obstruction of busy thoroughfares, noise pollution, flagrant public urination, and deliberate intimidation make unfair use of public spaces. Even if it turned out that these actions do not contribute to a feeling of lawlessness

---

* Most of that debate, in turn, has focused on the question of whether order maintenance prevents serious crime down the road. I have criticized this preoccupation elsewhere (Thacher, 2004; Harcourt & Thacher, 2005).

that emboldens more serious criminals (Wilson & Kelling, 1982),* they are still wrong, and our public spaces would be better off without them. Without any attempt to regulate disorder, the very existence of shared public spaces becomes precarious, as city dwellers disengage from the world around them and retreat into segregated environments where they will not encounter conflict in the first place (Milgram, 1970; Lynch, 1984, p. 214).

Despite appearances to the contrary, even the most radical critics of police order maintenance concede that disorder should be regulated. Richard Sennett's *Uses of Disorder*, for example, is not really a defense of disorder. It is an argument that neighborhood residents rather than government officials ought to regulate it. Sennett worried that modern society insulates us too well from the need to deal with conflict, so that personality development remains stuck in a self-centered adolescence in which we ignore the concrete demands made by other people. As treatment for this modern personality disease, Sennett did prescribe more exposure to a "challenging social matrix," and this is the sense in which he "wants more disorder" (Skogan, 1990, p. 8). Simply experiencing disorder, however, was not enough for Sennett; he believed that true personality development requires actual engagement with conflict through attempts to resolve it. Thus, what was needed was "not simply ... places where the inhabitants encountered dissimilar people; the critical need is for men to have to deal with the dissimilarities" (1970, p. 138). To accomplish that goal, Sennett believed that state regulatory bodies (including police but also other agencies, like land use authorities) should step aside to allow neighborhood residents to cope with conflicts themselves:

> If the kids were playing records loudly, late at night, no cop would come to make them turn the record player off—the police would no longer see to that kind of thing. If a bar down the street were too noisy for the children of the neighborhood to sleep, the parents would have to squeeze the bar owner themselves, by picketing or informal pressure, for no zoning laws would apply throughout the city. (Sennett, 1970, p. 144)

Sennett sought to ensure that "men and women must deal with each other as people" in order to block "the flight into abstraction" that allows personality development to stall in adolescence (1970, p. 154).

Less elaborate considerations have led other critics to support some form of community-based order maintenance. In keeping with his "left realist" emphasis on the importance of public safety to the urban poor, Roger

---

* In putting the point this way, I do not mean to concede the criminological criticisms of the broken windows hypothesis (which I discuss in Harcourt & Thacher, 2005). I simply find that way of analyzing order maintenance policing unpromising—even irrelevant (Thacher, 2004).

Matthews acknowledges that public order is important, but he insists that the ambiguity surrounding the proper meaning of disorder makes it unwise for police to play a role in regulating it, since the task will draw them into conflicts among different community factions and thereby risk "alienating sections of the community" (Matthews, 1992, p. 35). More simply, police order maintenance is like swatting flies with heavy armor: Mobilizing a "heavy handed, truncheon-wielding army of police officers" to regulate disorder is simply an overreaction (Matthews, 1992, p. 37). In place of the heavy hand of the police, Matthews advocates a larger role for community institutions in order maintenance, pointing to recent disorder reduction initiatives where police played a subordinate role or no role at all (Matthews, 1992, p. 38).*

Community as Police

It is not always clear what alternative to police order maintenance these critics have in mind. Sennett apparently envisions an anarchistic form of self-help—a world in which neighbors resolve their own disputes (in unspecified ways) rather than invoking the police or land use authorities.† Urbanologist William Whyte similarly advocates self-policing by the users of public space, who may, for example, admonish a pedestrian who throws trash on the ground (1990, pp. 158–159). Others advocate for more formal interventions. Matthews, for example, points to a recent resurgence of "various 'intermediary' agencies in regulating social (mis)behaviour," including "park-keepers, station guards ... working mens' clubs, trade union associations, church organizations" (1992, p. 39); he goes on to mention unemployed adults enlisted as "transport officers" in a Dutch transit system (p. 39) and "concierges or receptionists" in British council estates (p. 40). Bernard Harcourt similarly highlights the role that social workers, transit workers, and even publicly hired mimes can play in combating disorderly conduct (2001, pp. 221–224; Harcourt & Thacher, 2005), and Whyte emphasizes the importance of the informal "mayors" who occupy many public spaces—people like newsstand operators, building guards, and food vendors who have a long-term presence in a space that gives them the contextual knowledge and sense of ownership that order maintenance requires (Whyte, 1990, p. 160). Grabosky

---

* Other critics who ultimately concede the importance of public order but argue that someone other than the police ought to take responsibility for it include Whyte (1990, pp. 158–162) and Harcourt (2001, pp. 221–224).
† It is hard to understand why the result would be tolerable. Sennett asserts with little argument that these confrontations will not erupt into violence (1970, p. 147), and his suggestion that the unregulated city would attract racial and economic diversity (1970, p. 143) flies in the face of his own observations about the temptation to retreat to the safety of segregation when confronted by conflict (Sennett, 1970, 1976).

(1992, p. 255) mentions civilian "wardens" in New Zealand who respond to public drunkenness and other forms of disorderly conduct (though he does not necessarily advocate this model).

The advocates for these alternative forms of order maintenance often emphasize the role these actors can play in preventing disorder, rather than their role in responding to it once it has it occurred (especially Harcourt, 2001; Matthews, 1992). In general these proposals are uncontroversial: If it is possible to prevent subway fare beating through better turnstile design (Harcourt & Thacher, 2005), few would oppose that strategy; indeed, leading advocates for a robust police role in order maintenance have endorsed it (e.g., Kelling & Coles, 1996, p. 136).* But the question remains: What should be done when unacceptable disorder occurs despite society's best efforts to prevent it? Should the police play a role in regulating it? Should the task be left to other community institutions, or to no one at all? The real debate about the responsibility for order maintenance is primarily a debate about who, if anyone, should respond to various kinds of disorder when they actually occur—as they inevitably will, despite the vigorous preventative efforts that almost everyone endorses.

Disorder and the Function of the Police

The question of who should respond to disorder cannot be separated from the question of what types of response would be legitimate. Outright physical coercion is almost entirely the province of the police.† If a man continually accosts passing women with epithets like "You're just a piece of meat to me, bitch" (Bowman, 1993, p. 523) and refuses to stop when passers-by or Whyte's informal mayors scold him, the passers-by and the mayors have no legal authority to force him to stop. If anyone does (q.v. Bowman, 1993), it is presumably the police, who largely monopolize the legitimate use of coercive force in our society. If we conclude that it is legitimate to physically

---

* Though Whyte (1990, pp. 157–158) notes how prevention through physical design can make public spaces uninviting to regular users, and Carr, Mark, Rivlin, and Stone (1992, p. 267) argue that preventative design sometimes comes at the cost of segregation; truly integrated spaces (which are not only socially valuable but also efficient users of scarce land) require a commitment to managing the conflicts that inevitably arise in them.

† This account of the police role is of course Egon Bittner's. "Like everybody else patrolmen want to succeed in what they undertake. But unlike everybody else, they never retreat. Once a policeman has defined a situation as properly his business and undertakes to do something about it, he will not desist till he prevails. That policemen are uniquely empowered and required to carry out their decisions in the 'then and there' of emergent problems is the structurally central feature of police work" (1990, p. 254). Thus, "the policeman, and the policeman alone, is equipped, entitled, and required to deal with every exigency in which force may have to be used" (1990, p. 256).

restrain a man who behaves in this way after he defies less authoritative interventions, then the police are the only institutional vehicle available.

The question of whether the police ought to play a role in regulating disorder, then, is equivalent to the question of whether there are any types of disorder that fall into the category of things that it would be legitimate to put a stop to by resorting to coercive authority after other interventions have failed (Bittner, 1990, pp. 249, 256).* To conclude that there are does not imply that police should always arrest the disorderly. It simply means that if less authoritative intervention fails, coercive action would be justified (Bittner, 1990, pp. 242, 252, 256).† The police are society's "or else" (Bittner, 1990, p. 10), and if there is any form of disorder that justifies such a threat, then it is properly the business of police. (Bittner himself apparently believed that there was [Bittner, 1967].)

Managing Disorder

Police and community members alike may try to regulate disorder without forcibly restraining the perpetrators—for example, by cajoling or shaming the disorderly (Harcourt's publicly hired mimes who mock jaywalkers are one illustration) or by trying to persuade them to desist (Whyte's mayors typically seem to rely on this sort of remonstration). Again, community members ultimately have no legitimate recourse other than these informal interventions. Despite their arrest powers, however, even police often do not use them to maintain order (Thacher, 2004, pp. 392–393; Kelling, 1999, p. 50).‡

The noncoercive interventions that police and community members alike use to maintain order can take many forms. At the informal extreme, Erving Goffman has described the social sanctions that all of us apply in everyday life to people who violate norms of public decorum (such as the ironic sanction of staring down someone who rudely stares) (Goffman, 1966,

---

* Bittner's examples of this category deserve repeating because they clearly have little to do with serious crime: "I have seen policemen helping a tenant in arrears gain access to medication which a landlord held together with other possessions in apparently legal bailment, I have seen policemen settling disputes between parents as to whether an ill child should receive medical treatment, I have seen a patrolman adjudicating a quarrel between a priest and an organist concerning the latter's access to the church" (1990, p. 250).

† "I am *not* saying that police work consists of using force to solve problems, but only that police work consists of coping with problems in which force *may have to be used*" (Bittner, 1990, p. 256).

‡ Compare Bittner's observation that "the police were developed as a distinct institution with a monopoly over coercive force precisely in order to minimize and regulate the use of such force.... The skill involved in police work, therefore, consists of retaining recourse to force while seeking to avoid its use, and using it only in minimal amounts" (1990, pp. 257–258, 262).

p. 88). In practice, however, these least formal social sanctions are not really viable tools for order maintenance because much of the disorderly behavior at the center of recent debates about public order would not occur in the first place if the person who engaged in it were sensitive to normal social pressure. (Goffman [1972, p. 141] mentions "the drunk and the costumed" as illustrations of the idea that insulation from social pressure facilitates disorderly conduct.) If disorder arises precisely when the ordinary sanctions that underwrite everyday social interactions have broken down, some other means of controlling it will be necessary.

One possibility is the more deliberate efforts to exert social pressure that authors like Matthews, Whyte, and Harcourt have emphasized—the sustained and overt reprimands of disorderly conduct by food vendors, shopkeepers, security guards, and even mimes. These interventions are not authoritative in the way that police interventions are: If the person harassing women, blocking pedestrians, or flagrantly urinating refuses to stop, the vendor or shopkeeper cannot force him to. All the same, the forms of social pressure available to people other than the police can certainly be powerful.

They are most powerful, however, when they are backed up by the implicit threat of calling the police. During the 1970s and 1980s a large body of research examined the possibility of community-based crime prevention. A major conclusion of that literature was that informal social control works best when the threat of invoking formal authority backs it up. When that threat is perceived to be idle, informal control breaks down (Foster, 1995; Hope, 1995; Yin, Vogel, Chaiken, & Both, 1976). It is precisely because the police would be authorized to take definitive coercive action (and because everyone involved knows they would) that many informal sanctions succeed. One study that reached this conclusion focused on the Priority Estates Project in Britain, which Matthews cites as a model of community-based order maintenance (Matthews, 1992, p. 40). One of ethnographer Janet Foster's interviewees in that research put the matter succinctly: "Community works in a lot of cases but obviously in some circumstances ... [tenants] like to put the onus on the council or some legal authority" (Foster, 1995, p. 580). In this respect, community-based order maintenance is not an alternative to police order maintenance but a complement to it.

Regulating the Regulators

All of this said, it remains true that a variety of community institutions might be effective at maintaining order to some important degree. They lack the "or else" power of the police, but the informal sanctions they do control can be powerful. Should we encourage them to use those sanctions more vigorously? The possibility seems attractive because it provides an alternative to state authority, which should always be used reluctantly.

We should be wary of governmental coercion, but we should be equally wary of the less authoritative forms of coercion wielded outside of government. One early warning about the apparently gentle control exercised by actors in civil society came from John Stuart Mill:

> When society is itself the tyrant—society collectively, over the separate individuals who compose it—its means of tyrannizing are not restricted to the acts which it may do by the hands of its political functionaries. Society can and does execute its own mandates: and if it issues wrong mandates instead of right, or any mandates at all in things with which it ought not to meddle, it practices a social tyranny more formidable than many kinds of political oppression, since, though not usually upheld by such extreme penalties, it leaves fewer means of escape, penetrating much more deeply into the details of life, and enslaving the soul itself. (1978, p. 4)*

For this reason, Mill insisted that defenders of liberty should worry about community-based control as well as governmental coercion. "Protection ... against the tyranny of the magistrate is not enough: there needs protection also against the tyranny of the prevailing opinion and feeling; against the tendency of society to impose, by other means than civil penalties, its own ideas and practices as rules of conduct on those who dissent from them" (1978, p. 4).

This analysis shaped the task that Mill set himself in *On Liberty*. Mill concluded that the defense of freedom could not be accomplished by relocating the *locus* of social control from "rulers" to "the people." It could only be accomplished by defining and enforcing clear limits to all forms of social control, regardless of who exercised them. "There is a limit to the legitimate interference of collective opinion with individual independence," he wrote, "and to find that limit, and maintain it against encroachment, is as indispensable to a good condition of human affairs as protection against political despotism" (1978, p. 5).

All of this is to say that what ultimately matters is the *what* of social control rather than the *who*—what kinds of conduct can legitimately be regulated, not who should do the regulating. The order maintenance function raises this question as sharply as any, since the line between legitimate order maintenance and intolerant fussiness about the bustle of city life is clearly a delicate one. Among the many actions sometimes viewed as disorderly, which of them really qualify as wrongful conduct that society has the right to

---

* Since Mill wrote these lines, Michel Foucault and others have elaborated this basic insight at length, describing the many mechanisms of community-based social control and analyzing the danger they pose to personal liberty (e.g., Foucault, 1977).

control? This question cannot be answered once and for all with simple intuitive principles. It requires a continuing effort to refine our understanding of disorder as we encounter new kinds of social conflict in our public spaces (Thacher, 2004, pp. 397–398).*

Although what to control ultimately matters more than who should do the controlling, the *who* still matters indirectly. It matters because the *who* has implications for the *what*. Not all institutions have the same capacity for defining and enforcing the type of complex moral boundary that separates legitimate order maintenance from illegitimate harassment.

The professionalization of social control has gotten a bad name, but it has important advantages. Duties assigned to formal roles (such as the role of accountant, doctor, or police officer) can be far more complex and demanding than duties assigned to laypeople who do not specialize in the task. We can only expect laypeople and nonspecialists to be familiar with a few broad and intuitively understandable principles of common morality. By contrast, we can expect much more from the occupants of clearly defined roles: It is easier to educate them about the subtle distinctions contained in detailed codes of ethics, and it is easier to establish oversight structures that can monitor their compliance with those duties. None of this means that professionals are more moral than laypeople. It just means that the kinds of moral duties that society can fairly assign to professionals are different from the kinds of duties it can fairly assign to nonspecialists operating outside of the support structures provided by organizations and professions (for example, to people operating as private individuals in civil society). This idea is a core principle underlying the enterprise of professional ethics, and it is echoed in the civil law, which regularly assigns more stringent duties to people acting on behalf of an institution than to private individuals acting alone.

These considerations suggest a major advantage of police order maintenance. As a formal institution, the police potentially have the capacity to develop and enforce a relatively complex moral framework defining the scope and limits of order maintenance. No comparable capacity is available to nonspecialists in civil society. How will William Whyte's food vendors and shopkeepers develop an appropriate understanding of the distinction between legitimate order maintenance and illegitimate control of merely eccentric behavior? Who will enforce that line when one of them crosses it?

I am not claiming that the institutional context in which the police operate guarantees that they will carry out tasks like order maintenance

---

* In this essay I cannot fully consider how Mill's own analysis of the limits of legitimate state action might apply to order maintenance. One important principle underlying "disorderly conduct" statutes is the so-called "offense principle" (Thacher, 2004, pp. 404–408), which Mill apparently endorsed (Feinberg, 1985). I have come to believe that the fundamental idea underlying the concept of disorder is not *offense* but *unfair use of public spaces*. That, however, is a subject for another essay.

honorably. That would be an absurd claim. Individual police officers, despite the formal training and oversight that surrounds them, continually overstep their legitimate authority. Indeed, their own history of abuses best illustrates the dangers posed by the order maintenance role.

Caleb Foote called attention to those abuses more than 50 years ago in his ethnography of the administration of vagrancy-type law in Philadelphia magistrates' courts. Foote himself framed his research as a case study of the administration of justice in a context where meaningful procedural and constitutional safeguards did not exist (Foote, 1956, p. 604). At the time, defendants in disorderly conduct cases generally lacked the right to counsel, and the courts had developed almost no case law defining the legitimate scope of the order maintenance function. Five decades later, legal and administrative guidelines regulating order maintenance have proliferated, but in the meantime, Foote's research illustrated the kinds of abuses that order maintenance can lead to in the absence of structured guidance and formal oversight.

Here is one sample of what Foote observed:

A number of defendants were discharged with orders to get out of Philadelphia or to get out of the particular section of Philadelphia where they were arrested. "What are you doing in Philadelphia?" the magistrate asked one of these. "Just passing through." "You get back to Norristown. We've got enough bums here without you." Another defendant whose defense was that he was passing through town added, "I was in the bus station when they arrested me." "Let me see your bus ticket," the magistrate said. "The only thing that's going to save you this morning is if you have that bus ticket. Otherwise you're going to Correction for sure." After considerable fumbling the defendant produced a Philadelphia to New York ticket. "You better get on that bus quick," said the magistrate, "because if you're picked up between here and the bus station, you're a dead duck."

In discharging defendants with out-of-the-central-city addresses, the magistrate made comments such as the following:

"You stay out in West Philadelphia."
"Stay up in the fifteenth ward; I'll take care of you up there."
"What are you doing in this part of town? You stay where you belong; we've
    got enough bums down here without you."

Near the end of the line the magistrate called a name, and after taking a quick look said, "You're too clean to be here. You're discharged." (Foote, 1956, pp. 605–606)

Today many attacks on order maintenance seem to be motivated by a concern that it amounts to a systematic campaign to eject undesirable people—particularly the homeless—from parks and sidewalks in desirable neighborhoods. Foote's case study illustrates that concern as vividly as any I am aware of. In the exchanges he documented, it becomes clear that police

and the courts used the vagrancy and disorderly conduct laws to keep unde-
sirables in their places. In Foote's own words, "unwanted drunkards, pan-
handlers, gamblers, peddlers, or paupers are committed or banished" (1956,
p. 614). Even among the acquitted, a common defense was "I have a bus ticket
out of Philadelphia," or at least a promise to stay out of the central business district. The cases that reached the magistrates' courts—decided by the
dozens every 15 minutes—show no evidence of any serious inquiry into the
specifics of the defendants' conduct. There is no evidence that police or the
magistrates drew any distinction at all between conduct that could legitimately be prohibited and conduct that could not. Indeed, most of the "disorderly conduct" and "vagrancy" statutes at the time cast a remarkably broad
net, and many of the cases Foote observed involved the "offense" of being a
certain type of person (such as a vagrant or a habitual drunk) rather than
behaving in a specific manner.

Partly because of exposés like Foote's, and partly because of abusive use
of public order laws to harass civil rights and antiwar demonstrators during
the 1960s, the courts have substantially restricted order maintenance authority in the half century since he wrote. The resulting case law has, for example,
stressed that police must tread cautiously in regulating even offensive public
speech, that they may not arrest anyone simply because of his status (e.g.,
because he was a habitual drunk or vagrant), and that disorderly conduct
statutes must be specific enough to provide fair notice of what is prohibited (Amsterdam, 1967; Livingston, 1997, pp. 595–608). At the same time, the
American Law Institute developed a detailed disorderly conduct statute in
its Model Penal Code that took these legal developments into account, and
many jurisdictions adopted the proposal. All of these newly articulated legal
constraints and guidance sought to define *disorder* more precisely in order
to guard against the danger that police would exercise their authority capri-
ciously and overzealously.

These legal reforms have fundamentally changed the landscape of police
order maintenance. Most obviously, they have dramatically reduced police
arrests under the major order maintenance statutes. (According to the
Uniform Crime Reports, the share of all arrests associated with the charges
of drunkenness, disorderly conduct, and vagrancy fell from 44% in 1965 to
9% in 2005.) The arrests that remain are made within the more tailored public order statutes that survived the reforms of the 1960s and 1970s, which
exclude (at least as a matter of law) the most serious abuses documented in
studies like Foote's. For example, today it is simply illegal to arrest a man for
the status of being homeless.

Despite these reforms, there clearly remains considerable potential for
abusive order maintenance, as there is in all areas of law enforcement. (Despite
decades of legal reform focused on criminal interrogation, abuses continue
to occur, but no one argues that police should stop questioning suspects.)

Today the frontier for improving police practice in this area is administrative rather than legal. There are limitations to the guidance and constraints that the law can provide, since so many order maintenance judgments require a level of detail and attention to context that the law cannot provide. The value of additional legal controls was much larger in Foote's time, when order maintenance practice was so crude that even the blunt tools available to the courts could play a useful role in reshaping it. Today, however, the best hope for improving order maintenance practice generally involves the development of administrative guidelines and training by police themselves, in dialogue with local government officials and community members. The possibility of this kind of development is illustrated in the most progressive police departments that have already developed nuanced guidelines for order maintenance practice (Livingston, 1997; Kelling, 1999; Thacher, 2004).

Very few police departments have given this task the attention it deserves, so their practice undoubtedly remains imperfect in many respects. Proponents of police order maintenance should view further progress in regulating street-level practice in this manner as the most important priority. In most departments the call should be for higher-quality order maintenance rather than higher quantity.

Nevertheless, the substantial legal evolution I have described—as well as the visible possibility of further progress based on the capacity for institutional learning that any complex organization potentially has—already highlights a central advantage of formal institutions like the police for cultivating the kind of nuanced practice that order maintenance requires. The resources embodied in a continuing institutional system (such as the body of case law that courts collect and enforce or the body of guidelines and training practices developed by the most progressive police departments) make it possible to develop a more refined understanding of a normative concept like disorder over time. At any moment in time any institution will fall short of ideal practice, but healthy institutions have the capacity to make continual improvements.

To defend the possibility of community-based order maintenance, its advocates must show either that the kind of institutional structures that surround the police can be developed in the community or that these structures are not a necessary precondition for the legitimate exercise of the order maintenance function. I find both possibilities dubious. Informality and freedom from institutional routine are precisely the advantages of community over bureaucracy (McKnight, 1988). Those features impart immense advantages to community-based action in many contexts, but they raise serious concerns in this one. If the relatively unregulated police in Caleb Foote's time engaged in such a crude form of order maintenance, why should we expect better performance from actors in the community who are even less regulated? The idea that society should entrust one of its most delicate social control functions to unregulated nonprofessional community actors is at best counterintuitive.

There is so little documented experience with true community-based order maintenance that it is impossible to say whether these concerns have been realized in practice. One extended example, however, suggests reason for pessimism.

In the 1970s New York City began to award height bonuses to developers who agreed to provide publicly accessible spaces on their property. These spaces include some of the most well-known public plazas in Manhattan. The zoning law that encouraged them generally required that these spaces allow unrestricted access and free use by the public,* but it assigned responsibility for maintaining these spaces to the property owner. That responsibility typically encompassed order maintenance as well as physical maintenance. In this respect, New York City's privately owned public spaces provide the most sustained example of community-based order maintenance that I am aware of.

Lawyer Jerold Kayden has provided by far the most extensive analysis of how these spaces have functioned in practice. Based on a comprehensive review of all 503 spaces developed over a 39-year period, Kayden concluded that a very large share of these spaces have violated both the law and the spirit of the zoning act that created them—particularly by restricting public access and infringing on free use of the spaces (Kayden, 2000, p. 55). It is, of course, very difficult to document the essentially invisible day-to-day order maintenance performed by building representatives, but some of Kayden's observations are suggestive:

> Building superintendents and guards incorrectly inform users that a public space is not "public", or impose unreasonable rules that lessen public enjoyment.... Plaques intended to identify the space as "public" are strategically located behind fast-growing vines or trees, or are not installed at all.... A doorman, security guard, or superintendent informs the user, incorrectly, that the space is not a public space and that the user may not enter, or must vacate, the space. When the management representative is a security guard accompanied by a large dog, the warning becomes all the more compelling. Sometimes, management tells the user that the space is private, but that the user may stay as a guest of the building. In several instances during field surveys, after being told that the space was private, the surveyor would inform the buildings representative that the space was on an "official" public space list. The building representative would then reverse himself and confide that his supervisor had instructed him to inform the public that the space was private.... Amenities are rendered dysfunctional through an intentionally disabling act. Ledges and

---

* There are minor exceptions. For example, a property owner may apply to the city planning commission for permission to close its public space at night.

benches become useless when they are decorated with the spiked railings and small fences that have proliferated in the city over the past 20 or so years. (2000, pp. 56–59)

Some of these exclusionary tactics cross over into physical design rather than direct regulation of behavior. In other cases space managers post explicit behavioral rules prohibiting activities like loitering and sitting on benches for an extended period that police could not legally enforce (Kayden, 2000, p. 315). As Kayden notes (p. 38), it is unclear whether it is legal for private space managers to enforce these rules because

> the Zoning Resolution is silent … when it comes to the owner's "management" of use by members of the public.… To what extent may an owner craft and apply its own rules of conduct for members of the public?… The Zoning Resolution requires privately owned spaces to host "public use", but never expressly defines what limits, if any, an owner may impose upon such public use. (2000, p. 38)

Perhaps this experience is unique. The New York public spaces are certainly idiosyncratic, particularly since private landowners have the responsibility for maintaining order in them with little input from the spaces' *users*. In other words, only a narrow slice of "the community" managed the spaces, so it isn't surprising that order maintenance took discriminatory forms. As Kayden puts it: "Privately owned public space introduces an axiomatic tension between private and public interests. After the euphoria of receiving the floor area bonus has faded, the owner is left with a space whose public operation may not necessarily please the building's occupants or otherwise serve profit-oriented interests" (2000, p. 55). From this perspective, the narrow interests of the specific "community actors" who manage these public spaces distort the way they perform the order maintenance role.

Undoubtedly this objection contains an element of truth, and more broadly diffused order maintenance responsibility would respond to a broader range of community interests. At the same time, it must be acknowledged that insofar as any community actors are likely to take responsibility for order maintenance, property owners and their agents are among the most probable candidates. (Indeed, Whyte and Matthews pay special attention to shopkeepers, property managers, groundskeepers, and security guards as possible community-based place managers.)

More important, although any particular example of community-based order maintenance may be criticized on the grounds that it is not truly responsive to the *whole* community, there are reasons to believe that the ideal itself is problematic. Urban designer Kevin Lynch has written lucidly about the relevant limitations of community-based place management. Lynch begins by defining the principle of *congruence*, which is "the extent to which the actual users or inhabitants of a space control it, in proportion to the degree or permanence of their stake in it" (Lynch, 1984, p. 208). To a point, this principle captures an important ideal for the management of spaces. But Lynch immediately notes its complications:

> In the first place, it should somehow be expanded to take account of future and potential users, as well as actual ones. User control must not deny others the basic opportunities that the owners themselves enjoy. Regulation by present users often entails the exclusion of those who are elsewhere, but who may have a legitimate interest in the use of the place or of some similar space. (1984, p. 208)

This concern is very salient in the present context, since this kind of exclusion lies at the heart of the concerns that have actually been raised about order maintenance. The trouble, as Lynch's analysis suggests, is that the "entire public" whose interests ought to be taken into account in place management is not a tangible group of people at all. "The public" is an abstraction, not an identifiable group of people whose involvement we could enlist if we only invited their participation more energetically. For that reason, when the interests of absent and future publics need to be taken into account, we typically assign that responsibility to government officials charged with promoting the public interest. Thus, Lynch himself writes that "some external authority representing potential users must determine how outsiders may have access to a place, and how they may join in its use and control," and he goes on to repeat the sentiment with respect to future users (1984, pp. 208–209).

These considerations suggest why the laudable desire to ensure that policing authority is exercised in the public interest cannot be accomplished entirely through direct community control of the order maintenance function. At some point the ability to directly involve the relevant community members gives out, and public officials must themselves represent the necessary commitment to the unavoidably amorphous concept of the "public interest" (Thacher, 2001). That commitment, in turn, is safeguarded by dual oversight from elected representatives and the judiciary, as well as the ideals of public service embraced by civil service professions.

Conclusion

When pressed, no one really denies that public order is important, though many people do disagree about what disorder is. Those disagreements themselves may be the most important argument for a large police role in maintaining order. As compared with informal actors in civil society, ongoing public institutions like the police can potentially develop the kind of complex, continually evolving, and democratically accountable conception of disorder that defensible order maintenance demands. No institution is perfect, but the police are usually far better positioned than food vendors, shopkeepers, mimes, groundskeepers, and passers-by to safeguard the legitimacy of this delicate regulatory function. Moreover, they have a unique responsibility in our society for the legitimate exercise of coercive force, and that capacity provides an indispensable foundation for the success of whatever level of supplementary informal social control society ought to encourage.

References

Amsterdam, A. (1967). Federal constitutional restrictions on the punishment of crimes of status, crimes of general obnoxiousness, crimes of displeasing police officers, and the like. *Criminal Law Bulletin, 3*, 205–241.

Bittner, E. (1967). The police on skid row: A study in peacekeeping. *American Sociological Review, 32*, 699–715.

Bittner, E. (1990). *Aspects of police work*. Boston: Northeastern University Press.

Bowman, C. G. (1993). Street harassment and the informal ghettoization of women. *Harvard Law Review, 106*, 517–580.

Carr, S., Mark, F., Rivlin, L., & Stone, A. (1992). *Public space*. New York: Cambridge University Press.

Feinberg, J. (1985). *Offense to others*. New York: Oxford University Press.

Foote, C. (1956). Vagrancy-type law and its administration. *University of Pennsylvania Law Review, 104*, 603–650.

Foster, J. (1995). Informal social control and community crime prevention. *British Journal of Criminology, 35*, 563–583.

Foucault, M. (1977). *Discipline and punish*. New York: Vintage.

Goffman, E. (1966). *Behavior in public places*. New York: Free Press.

Goffman, E. (1972). *Relations in public*. New York: Harper and Row.

Grabosky, P. (1992). Law enforcement and the citizen: Non-governmental participants in crime prevention and control. *Policing and Society, 2*, 249–271.

Harcourt, B. (2001). *Illusion of order*. Cambridge, MA: Harvard University Press.

Harcourt, B., & Thacher, D. (2005). Is broken windows policing broken? *Legal Affairs Debate Club*. Retrieved from www.legalaffairs.org/webexclusive/debateclub_brokenwindows1005.msp

Hope, T. (1995). Community crime prevention. In M. Tonry & N. Morris (Eds.), *Crime and justice* (p. 19). Chicago: University of Chicago Press.

Kayden, J. (2000). *Privately-owned public space: The New York City experience*. New York: Wiley.

Kelling, G. (1999). *Broken windows and police discretion* (National Institute of Justice Research Report). Washington, DC: USGPO.

Kelling, G., & Coles, C. (1996). *Fixing broken windows*. New York: Simon & Schuster.

Livingston, D. (1997). Police discretion and the quality of life in public places: Courts, communities, and the new policing. *Columbia Law Review, 97*, 551–672.

Lynch, K. (1984). *Good city form*. Cambridge, MA: MIT Press.

Matthews, R. (1992). Replacing broken windows. In R. Matthews & J. Young (Eds.), *Issues in realist criminology* (pp. 19–50). London: Sage.

McKnight, J. (1988). Regenerating community. *Social Policy, 17*, 54–58.

Milgram, S. (1970). The experience of living in cities. *Science, 167*, 1461–1468.

Mill, J. S. (1978). *On liberty*. Indianapolis: Hackett.

Sennett, R. (1970). *The uses of disorder*. New York: Knopf.

Sennett, R. (1976). *The fall of public man*. New York: W.W. Norton.

Skogan, W. (1990). *Disorder and decline*. Berkeley: University of California Press.

Thacher, D. (2001). Equity and community policing: A new view of community partnerships. *Criminal Justice Ethics, 20*, 1–16.

Thacher, D. (2004). Order maintenance reconsidered: Moving beyond strong causal reasoning. *Journal of Criminal Law and Criminology, 94*, 381–414.

Whyte, W. (1990). *City: Rediscovering the center*. New York: Anchor Books.

Wilson, J. Q., & Kelling, G. L. (1982). Police and neighborhood safety: Broken windows. *The Atlantic Monthly*, March, pp. 29–38.

Yin, R. K., Vogel, M., Chaiken, J., & Both, D. (1976). *Patrolling the neighborhood beat*. Santa Monica, CA: RAND.

The Small-Scale Initiative
The Rhetoric and the Reality of Community Policing in Australia

5

JENNY FLEMING
JUANI O'REILLY

Contents

Australia, like many Western democratic countries, has embraced the concept of community policing. Through their individual annual reports and strategic plans, eight Australian police jurisdictions pledge their commitment to community policing. Police commissioners emphasis the importance of being in partnership with the community and publicly commit themselves to actively involving the community in preventing and reducing crime. Police ministers talk about engaging the community and establishing partnerships to achieve a safer, more secure community (APMC, 2005).

In examining community policing in Australia, this chapter suggests that notwithstanding the rhetoric, community policing in Australia is not a fully developed concept, and its approach is essentially what Beyer (1991) would call small scale, that is, a local approach designed to bring police into nonconfrontational contact with the community in some way. Despite the proliferation of local (and in some cases award-winning) community policing initiatives across Australian states and territories, community policing as an organizing concept has not been factored into the organizational structures and management initiatives of police organizations. According to Beyer (1991,

Previously published in Fleming, J. and O'Reilly, J. (2007). The small-scale initiative: The rhetoric and reality of community policing in Australia. *Policing: A Journal of Policy and Practice*, 1(2), 214–222.

p. 89), a more "wholistic"[1] model would see police organizational structures and management "organized around what police actually do and around what the community wants them to do." Such an approach would see "community policing affecting every aspect of the police organization, including being reflected in the informal corporate culture." To date this approach has not been adopted in Australia. It is argued here that unless police organizations adapt more fully to accommodate new ways of doing business, community policing in Australia will remain an add-on to traditional police practice rather than the claimed new paradigm it is held to be. The chapter briefly examines community policing practice in Australia and considers the challenges of developing a comprehensive community policing model.

Australian Police

Australia comprises six states—Queensland, New South Wales, Victoria, Tasmania, South Australia, and Western Australia—and for the purposes of policing, two territories: the Australian Capital Territory (ACT) and the Northern Territory. Each jurisdiction has its own government-administered police agency. The Australian Federal Police is Australia's federal law enforcement agency. It provides a community policing service to the ACT government. With a national total of 52,000 officers, the eight police forces range in size from New South Wales with almost 15,000 officers to the ACT with approximately 621.

Funding for policing is a matter for individual states and territories. Much of this funding is calculated through benchmarking and other ways of measuring police performance and productivity (see below). There is no national legislation concerning policing standards, practice, or policy, nor is there any federal control of state police (Edwards, 2005, pp. 31–33), although there are a number of national forums in which police commissioners, police ministers, and others come together to discuss policing and security issues of national importance.

Policing in Australia is distinctive. A single jurisdiction will police the diverse needs of urban cities, regional centers, and rural and remote bush communities. In addition, some jurisdictions have indigenous communities and vast geographical areas. To illustrate this last point, the Queensland Police Service is responsible for policing a geographical area of 1,852,642 square kilometers and providing a policing service to a population of 4 million. It has a total of 9,631 police officers.[2]

Community policing initiatives take a variety of forms and reflect differences in organizational structures, management strategies, resource availability, and geographical scope (Gianakis & Davis, 1998). We acknowledge there are significant operational differences across jurisdictions, and that what we offer here is a broad overview of community policing in Australia.

Community-Based Activity

Community-based crime prevention strategies include Neighbourhood Watch, Safety House, Police Beat Shopfront Schemes, and Home Assist Services. Most police organizations would include these in their community program services, and they are usually administered by crime prevention units in the organization. The extent of police involvement in these programs varies considerably (Fleming, 2005).

The federal government supports community partnerships through national funding initiatives that encourage community safety and crime prevention practice. Despite the challenges associated with police working with other organizations generally (Fleming, 2006), police in Australian jurisdictions have become more involved in community preventative problem solving and have implemented a number of local programs in an attempt to reduce crime and address social disorder issues. An example of such an initiative is the Homelands Partnership Initiative in Queensland.

Initiated in February 2004, the Homelands Partnership[3] is a multiagency program comprising police, government agencies, community organizations, and businesses addressing homelessness in Cairns. The homeless in this region are predominantly indigenous people from throughout the state who have become displaced after arriving in Cairns for medical treatment or release from custody and have then found they no longer have the means or the motivation to return home. The project was a response to people's concerns that police and government were failing to address crime, drunkenness, and general public disorder in a city where tourism represents 47% of the entire gross domestic product for the region.

The program offers itinerants the voluntary (but state-supported) choice of returning home, access to alternate housing, or undertaking rehabilitation programs. The program includes various strategies and smaller initiatives (such as saturation foot patrol at specific times) and promotes associated project development to address homelessness as the core problem of alcohol abuse. Police entered into voluntary management plans with local liquor stores where proprietors agreed not to sell wine casks before 4 p.m. Such a strategy provided a specific opportunity for agencies to consult with the homeless to discuss their various personal issues. Apart from the central objectives of returning displaced people to their homes and the provision of housing or rehabilitation, objectives of the project included a reduction in antisocial behavior and incidents of violence, reduced levels of crime, and improved perceptions of safety in the community. The program has been formally evaluated and is deemed to be successful (for more information, see Fleming & O'Reilly, 2008). The project was the recipient of an Australian Crime and Violence Prevention Award in 2006.[4]

In Australia, visible policing, what Bayley (1989) calls "nonemergency patrol deployment," is an important way of building good relations with the public. To this end a number of local nonemergency interactive programs have been piloted, and in some cases adopted. Examples include bicycle patrols (South Australia), shop fronts (Taylor & Charlton, 2005), country town policing (Halstead, 1994), and beat policing (Mazerolle, Adams, Budz, Cockerill, & Vance, 2003). As well as providing a visible presence through these programs, most Australian police services have in place mechanisms to improve communication between various community groups. Examples include multicultural liaison officers in Tasmania; lesbian, gay, bisexual, transgender, and intersex liaison officers in Queensland; aboriginal liaison officers in Western Australia; youth liaison officers in New South Wales; and business liaison officers in the ACT. Police ethnic advisory groups and community policing branches have been implemented in most Australian police jurisdictions. They provide feedback to police services on numerous issues, including strategies for effective communication in culturally diverse communities. The difficulties are numerous. Edwards (2005, p. 105) points to the example in Perth, Western Australia, where a scheme to appoint a community policing liaison officer in 1995 identified over 20 immigrant groups with a significant number of members, few of whom were native speakers.

Commenting on community policing in Australia in 1990, Bayley argued that it was a secondary policing activity rather than part of core police business, and that it was principally an add-on crime prevention program. In many ways little has changed. Australia has not adopted the wholistic approach that Beyer (1991) refers to. Despite the community activity, these initiatives, programs, and projects are established on an *ad hoc* basis, and many are pilot projects where funds and in kind support are provided for a single initiative. However successful these initiatives might be, what we don't see is a level of institutional support that embraces community policing as a way of doing business on a regular basis.

Working Together: The Challenges of Community Policing

In this section we focus on the organizational and managerial constraints that hinder the development of strong community policing models in Australia. The argument is not new. Such arguments have been discussed often in the United States and the United Kingdom (for example, see Fielding, 2004; Vito, Walsh, & Kunselman, 2005; Rosenbaum, 1994). In Australia, these constraints include conflicting management styles around service provision, the lack of any sustained legislative or policy basis for community policing initiatives, and a high-performance culture that is not structured around the philosophy or practice of community policing. This list of organizational deficits is not exhaustive, but it identifies significant barriers to implementing a wholistic approach to community policing in Australia. Also, such barriers are reinforced when they interact with other well-known and established features of the police, such as an occupational culture that is resistant to change (Chan, 1996) and risk adverse (O'Malley, 1997).

The move to reconstruct police services as corporate entities has seen the introduction of such managerial practices as strategic planning, performance management, and decentralized authority for budgetary and resource allocation with an emphasis on local accountability. Despite the subsequent restructuring of police services, which has seen some Australian police organizations flatten their structures primarily by reducing the rank structures, all the organizations retain strong elements of authoritarian, hierarchical governing structures, featuring command and control management systems, regulated through strict organizational rules and legislation. Such a governing structure does not complement the nonauthoritarian and problem-solving culture usually associated with community policing (Fleming & Rhodes, 2005).

If a wholistic approach to community policing were to be embraced, the allocation of resources would need to be reconsidered. Community policing is labor intensive and costly (Edwards, 2005, p. 121). How such resources are sustained, particularly in a country that, regardless of state or territory responsibilities, is expected to contribute to offshore policing activities in the Pacific and elsewhere (Burgess, 2007), is a managerial dilemma. To avoid disappointment for those who see policing as fast cars and locking up bad guys, recruitment strategies would need to be defined more specifically to outline to potential applicants what is required of police engaged with the community. The training curricula would need to be reconsidered, with more emphasis on proactive work, problem solving, and networking generally. As well, internal reward systems should emphasize the importance of interpersonal skills, working with the community, prioritizing problem solving over citizen-generated calls for service (Vito et al., 2005, p. 506), and increasingly, the political pressure to demonstrate a safe and secure environment (Fleming, 2004).

Performance Management

Australian police organizations are committed to corporate governance and the culture of managerialism. They are output focused, and their operational practice relies on hierarchies of objectives, targets, and a high-performance culture. There is a preoccupation with measurement for both individuals and the organization. A significant component of the measurement process is the level of community satisfaction with police services and their feelings of safety and security. Satisfaction levels are gauged through monthly telephone national surveys (Fleming & O'Reilly, 2008). Community expectations are a decisive factor in the allocation of resources. As Edwards (2005, pp. 123–125) has pointed out, community expectations are largely concerned with prompt responses to calls for service and visibility. As a result, scarce resources are often directed into what the public wants and, perhaps more importantly, what can be measured.

Internally, a high-performance culture is unlikely to encourage activity and innovative practice (Scott, 1998). If community policing and proactive problem solving are not an integral part of an organization's performance structure, then tensions arise over resource allocation. Resources will not be committed to an activity that has no intrinsic measurement value (Fleming, 2006). The use of statistics-driven management approaches such as COMPSTAT compounds this dilemma.

Imported from the United States, COMPSTAT focuses on mission clarification, internal accountability, geographic organisation of command, data driven problem identification and innovative problem solving (Mazerolle, Rombouts, & McBroom, 2006). Problem-solving activities are measured regularly at a divisional level. While such forums encourage the development of strategies to work with the community and reduce crime, invariably time constraints are imposed on such activities. So, the proactive (and often long-term) activity essential to the success of community policing is weakened because measurement invariably focuses on short-term gains. As Edwards notes (2005, p. 310):

> The Compstat process is antithetical to any long term approach to police planning … if police agencies adopt the approach of working with the community and building partnerships to reduce crime, as police agencies in Britain do, then this can only take place if short-term variations in the crime rate are ignored.

In Australia, while a demonstrated commitment to community policing is useful when applying for promotion, such activity is not considered a priority. Proactive work is applauded when results can demonstrate an unequivocal numeric result, but is not prioritized against those strategies or activities that have produced results for management before.[5] As Fleming has argued (2006, p. 109), if police organizations are serious about their public commitment to community policing and associated practices, then a "more sympathetic set of [performance] measures than exist at present" are required. "It makes no sense to articulate one set of standards and develop policy for another."

Funding and Policy

In the US and the UK, specific legislation and government funding promote the concept of community policing and consultation. In the UK, working with communities is formally encouraged through policy initiatives and legislation. In 1998, the Crime and Disorder Act made working through partnerships a statutory requirement for police and local authorities. Police in the UK are required to collaborate with public agencies and other bodies to establish and promote community safety strategies (Fleming, 2006).

No funding source or policy imperative will necessarily ensure the success of community policing, nor mandate the organizational changes that would be required for such success. However, some formal resource commitment would encourage the application of community policing principles on a more serious basis than small-scale initiatives primarily driven by individuals or local crime prevention departments. Despite the various commitments to working and engaging with communities in pursuit of reduced crime and enhanced relationship objectives, unlike the UK and the US, there are no formal policy parameters or legislation that compel Australian police organizations to undertake a committed wholistic approach to working with communities. There is no official mandate in Australia for police to work through partnerships and legislation that, for example, would enhance the ability of organizations to exchange information and would arguably progress the functionalism of partnerships. There is no extra funding for collaborative activity, and where organizations have sought to work through networks and partnerships, they have done so within existing funding arrangements (Fleming, 2006).

Conclusion

Australian police jurisdictions engage in several forms of community policing. Numerous initiatives in all states and territories are delivered through a range of programs. Common to these programs is a commitment to community involvement and participation. The ability of police to form networks across professional groups, other public sector agencies, and a variety of communities to address common issues, the obvious expansion of servicing, particularly in rural and indigenous areas, coupled with the creation of mechanisms to ensure feedback opportunities from communities and other interested parties, suggests that the idea of community policing has led to a more proactive understanding of the role of communities in police practice.

However, it is clear that a wholistic approach to community policing in Australia is largely constrained by organizational and management factors and arguably compounded by what many see as a resistant occupational culture and risk-adverse management strategies. In Gianakis and Davis's (1998, p. 494) terms, Australia can be categorized as a "minimal implementer"—one that adopts a philosophy but provides minimal resources to the existing service delivery structure (1998, p. 49). However, as this chapter has suggested, there are a number of factors that constrain Australia from becoming a "maximum implementer" (one that seeks to restructure an organization with a view to institutionalizing community policing as the dominant policing paradigm).

In 2007, Australian police jurisdictions were primarily concerned with their reactive emergency response service function—not only because it is the way "they do business," but also because community expectations demand such a focus. Conflicting governing structures (such as the bureaucratic processes and administrative systems that potentially conflict with the values of decentralization and the enhancement of rank-and-file autonomy), the absence of state legislative and policy support, an emphasis on performance management in a highly politicized environment, and the expectations and opinions of a community whose support is imperative to the legitimacy of the police institution are the primary constraining factors. Recruitment and training practices are also not consistent with community policing practice. To add community policing to law enforcement duties, conflict resolution, and general service would expand an organization's functions considerably. As Gianakis and Davis (1998, p. 86) have noted, the "maintenance of a dual proactive/reactive patrol capacity would certainly strain the resources of most agencies." Given the organizational environment in which police organizations operate, such a dual capacity is not an option.

The above observations should not necessarily be seen as criticisms. Police organizations have always struggled to meet the expectations of their stakeholders in terms of what communities expect of them and what can realistically be delivered. This is made more challenging when we consider that performance measurement and productivity are central to perceptions of legitimacy and government funding. While the community and its opinions feature heavily in an organization's performance mandate, a community's expectations of its police will shape and determine the way that organization conducts its business. Anything that may constrain a community's satisfaction levels with police would need to be seriously considered, and a campaign conducted to re-educate the public as to what constitutes police work. As David Moore's discussions with senior police officers suggest (1994, p. 202), for community policing to become an organization's priority, it would require:

> [communities and governments to] confer full authorization on police for achieving outcomes beyond those traditional outcomes of arresting offenders … [until that time, community policing] is not seen as a strategy for the police organization per se.

That time has not yet arrived. While communities are still wedded to arrival times, the arrest of offenders, and their own sense of safety and security as the determinants as to whether police are doing the job, Australian police organizations will have no choice but to pursue small-scale community policing initiatives, leaving them sufficient resources to pursue the more reactive calls for service approach the community expects.

References

APMC. (2005, November). *Directions in Australasian policing: 2005–2008.* Canberra: Australian Police Minister's Council. Retrieved March 17, 2009, from http://www.acpr.gov.au/pdf/Directions05-08.pdf

Bayley, D. H. (1989). Community policing in Australia: An appraisal. In D. Chappell & P. Wilson (Eds.), *Australian policing contemporary issues* (pp. 63–82). Sydney, Australia: Butterworths.

Bayley, D. H. (1990). *Towards policing 2000: Final report* (Report Series 103). Australasian Centre for Policing Research. Retrieved May 21, 2007, from http://www.acpr.gov.au/pdf/ACPR103.pdf

Beyer, L. (1991). The logic and the possibilities of 'wholistic' community policing. In J. Vernon & S. McKillop (Eds.), *The police and the community* (pp. 89–106). Canberra: Australian Institute of Criminology.

Burgess, M. (2007). High tempo of international deployments stretches police resources. *Association News, 11,* 18–19.

Chan, J. (1996). Changing police culture. *British Journal of Criminology, 36,* 109–133.

Edwards, C. (2005). *Changing policing theories for 21st century societies* (2nd ed.). Leichhardt, Australia: Federation Press.

Fielding, N. (1994). The organisational and occupational troubles of community police. *Policing and Society, 4,* 305–322.

Fleming, J. (2004). Les liaisons dangereuses: Relations between police commissioners and their political masters. *Australian Journal of Public Administration, 63,* 60–74.

Fleming, J. (2005, September). *Working together: Neighbourhood watch, reassurance policing and the potential of partnerships* (Trends and Issues in Crime and Criminal Justice 303). Canberra: Australian Institute of Criminology.

Fleming, J. (2006). Working through networks: The challenge of partnership policing. In J. Fleming & J. Wood (Eds.), *Fighting crime together: The challenges of policing and security networks* (pp. 87–115). Sydney: University of New South Wales Press.

Fleming, J., & O'Reilly, J. (2008). In search of a process: Community policing in Australia. In T. Williamson (Ed.), *The handbook of knowledge based policing: Current conceptions and future directions* (pp. 139–156). Chichester, Sussex: John Wiley.

Fleming, J., & Rhodes, R. (2005). Bureaucracy, contracts and networks: The unholy trinity and the police. *Australian and New Zealand Journal of Criminology, 38,* 192–205.

Gianakis, A. G., & Davis, G. J. (1998). Reinventing or repackaging public services? The case of community-orientated policing. *Public Administration Review, 58,* 485–498.

Halstead, B. (1994, September). *Country town policing—A community policing initiative: Literature review*. Canberra: Australian Institute of Criminology.

Mazerolle, L., Rombouts, S., & McBroom, J. (2006, May). *The impact of operational performance reviews on reported crime in Queensland* (Trends and Issues in Crime and Criminal Justice 313). Canberra: Australian Institute of Criminology.

Mazerolle, P., Adams, K., Budz, D., Cockerill, C., & Vance, M. (2003). *On the beat: An evaluation of beat policing in Queensland* (Crime and Misconduct Commission Research Report). Brisbane: Crime and Misconduct Commission.

Moore, D. (1994). Views at the top, down under: Australian police managers on Australian policing. *Policing and Society, 4*, 191–217.

O'Malley, P. (1997). Policing, politics and postmodernity. *Social & Legal Studies, 6*, 363–381.

Rosenbaum, D. P. (1994). *The challenge of community policing: Testing the promises*. Thousand Oaks, CA: Sage Publications.

Scott, J. (1998). Performance culture: The return of reactive policing. *Policing and Society, 8*, 269–288.

Taylor, N., & Charlton, K. (2005, March). *Police shopfronts and reporting to police by retailers* (Trends and Issues in Crime and Criminal Justice 295). Canberra: Australian Institute of Criminology.

Vito, G., Walsh, W., & Kunselman, J. (2005). Community policing: The middle manager's perspective. *Police Quarterly, 8*, 490–511.

Endnotes

1. This is the spelling that Beyer uses in her article. For consistency we have adopted this spelling for the article.
2. Retrieved March 17, 2009 from http://www.police.qld.gov.au/Resources/ Internet/services/reportsPublications/statisticalReview/0506/documents/13_ personnel.pdf
3. The authors appreciate the support of Superintendent Mike Keating and the Queensland Police Service (2006) for providing us with the documentation and evaluation of the Homelands Project. The discussion about the Homelands Project is drawn from this documentation.
4. Retrieved March 17, 2009 from http://www.aic.gov.au/acvpa/2006.html#1
5. Various personal emails and phone calls from officers in South Australia, Queensland, New South Wales, Victoria, Western Australia, Tasmania, and the ACT.

Community Policing and Accountability

6

STEVE HERBERT

Contents

The Seattle Police Department (SPD), the evidence suggests, enforces drug delivery law in a racially disparate manner (see Beckett, Nyrop, & Pfingst, 2006; Beckett, Nyrop, Pfingst, & Bowen, 2005). Minorities in the city, and especially African Americans, are far more likely to be arrested for an alleged instance of drug dealing than their white counterparts. Although such disparities are not uncommon in American cities, their extent in Seattle is dramatic.

Disparities such as these obviously conflict with the goal of fair, neutral law enforcement. Presumably, all are equal in the eyes of the law. Any time race unduly influences law enforcement practice, closely held liberal ideals are violated. When such violations occur and are brought to public attention, police departments in liberal societies should change their practices. This is especially true in the U.S. context, where tensions between the police and minorities are longstanding and sometimes volatile (Kennedy, 1998; Walker, Spohn, & DeLone, 2003; Weitzer & Tuch, 2006).

Yet no attempts to remedy racial disparities are occurring in Seattle. Instead, the SPD and Mayor Greg Nickels (who possesses the authority to hire and fire the police chief) are presently working ardently to contest the possibility that racial disparities exist. Even though high-ranking officials in both the SPD and the mayor's office are aware of the extent of selective enforcement of drug delivery laws, their stance is entirely adversarial. The strength of their resistance is no better illustrated than the uninvited intrusion of a policy analyst in the mayor's office into the editorial review process for a prestigious criminology journal. This analyst received a prepublication copy of a paper demonstrating racially disparate drug law enforcement practices that successfully journeyed through that journal's review process. He received the paper in a meeting where the mayor's office and the SPD were urged to consider policies to remedy the situation. Instead of a constructive response to the evidence of disparities, the mayor's analyst sent a long and misleading letter to the journal editor accusing the lead author of the paper of bias and academic misconduct (see Beckett, 2008).

Such actions do not constitute a constructive response to inequitable policing. Given an opportunity to acknowledge the value of academic assessment of police practice and to demonstrate a willingness to be held accountable, the police and the mayor's office chose a more combative approach. Instead of hearing the message of potential inequities, and thereby allowing police power to be held open to scrutiny, they worked instead to condemn the messenger. Police accountability in Seattle thereby suffered.

The recent history of policing is Seattle is notable, as well, for one of the more ambitious efforts to enact community policing as a thoroughgoing reform. This occurred in the 1990s, when Norm Stamper came from San Diego to become the city's police chief. Stamper sought to restructure the SPD's culture and practices around community policing, to make the police the lynchpin for efforts to make neighborhoods more safe and livable. The police were to be the key point of contact for citizens with any of a wide range of complaints, including issues that were not directly related to crime.

Stamper knew that success in such an effort would require the support of the rank and file. To secure this, he began sponsoring daylong seminars on community policing to which select officers were invited. These seminars introduced the philosophy of the then wildly popular reform movement and explained the planned reorientation of police practice. The hope was that so-informed officers would spread the word to their brethren.

It did not work. Instead, officers who were summoned downtown were strongly advised by their colleagues not to "drink the Kool-Aid" (see Herbert, 2006a). The reference was to the cyanide-laced drink that imperiled the Jonestown colony in Guyana in 1978. To embrace police reform, in other words, was seen as akin to organizational suicide. The resistance worked so well that Stamper's successor, Gil Kerlikowske, penned a widely circulated piece for the national police community that was structured as an obituary for community policing (Kerlikowske, 2003). As analysts such as myself (Herbert, 2006a), Lyons (1999), and Reed (1999) learned in examining the SPD, community policing transformed the department only little (see also Maguire & King, 2004).

Community Policing and Police Accountability

Each of these stories is instructive, and each deserves to be considered alongside the other. Each is about the politics of policing, and the too-common resistance of police departments to change and oversight. A police department that can resist opening itself up to close consultation with citizen groups is not surprisingly the same department that can spurn a close examination of its race-inflected practices.

Police departments, of course, are long notorious for such resistance to outside interference, for constructing an "us versus them" relationship to the citizenry (Niederhoffer, 1967; Skolnick, 1966). They are also prone to celebrate their muscular responses to crime (Herbert, 1997), symbolized most potently in the contemporary era by the widespread embrace of zero tolerance (Fyfe, 2004; McArdle & Erzen, 2001; Silverman, 1999). Any suggestions that such aggressiveness should be questioned (perhaps in the context of drug enforcement practices) and subject to review by nonsworn civilians are typically resisted. For this reason, citizen oversight of the police is a halting and frequently frustrated political project (Walker, 2000, 2005).

Yet the stories of racial disparities from Seattle fuel the continued need for such a project, and demonstrate the inadequacy of community policing as a central prong of any such effort. Despite initial hopes for it as a means to increase police legitimacy through greater police-citizen cooperation, community policing largely withers as meaningful reform. I use this essay to offer an explanation for this pattern, and to suggest alternate paths forward.

I move through three main sections. First, I briefly review the historical antecedents of community policing and revisit early hopes for its ability to foster partnerships between cops and citizens. The subsequent section explains why resistance to community policing was typically robust, and thus why efforts at partnering largely foundered. A key consequence of this failure is that improved citizen oversight of the police was rarely a consequence of efforts to embrace community policing. The third section explores alternate (and potentially superior) means to improve police accountability.

In short, the failure of community policing is one component of a wider resistance to citizen oversight. For this reason, it is best jettisoned in any strategy to increase police accountability.

The History and Founding Myths of Community Policing

Like many social programs, community policing arose in response to social unrest in the 1960s. Several cities witnessed uprisings during the period, many of which were touched off by an encounter with the police. This gave credence to concerns that relations with the police were needlessly tense in disadvantaged, minority-dominated urban neighborhoods. The then-prevailing model for organizing police departments, focused upon professionalism, was commonly viewed as part of the problem (Fogelson, 1977). As professionals, the police worked to become more detached and aloof from the citizens they patrolled. This left them less prone to corruption and also more beholden to generalized standards of efficient and impartial practice.

Yet such aloofness was seen as detrimental to smooth community relations. Community policing, it was hoped, could help reduce this social distance and thereby temper police-community tensions. Rather than adopting a posture as removed from the citizens, the police were to be become "partners" who engaged in "co-production" of crime reduction strategies (Cordner, 1998; Moore, 1992; Skolnick & Bayley, 1986; Trojanowicz & Bucqueroux, 1994). Any meaningful crime reduction strategy, the argument went, could only work if both the police and the citizenry worked together. This understanding of mutual need was to be the base upon which cooperative relations could be built. These relations would flourish in a range of different projects: neighborhood watch groups, graffiti paint-outs and other cleanup efforts, collective problem solving, and other forms of collaboration.

The police were to earn several benefits from such efforts at partnership. One was that they would get better information from the "eyes and ears" provided by the citizens (Saunders, 1999). A second, and more profound, benefit was improved legitimacy (Skogan, 2006). Greater responsiveness to input from citizens, and greater willingness to work alongside them, would help the police improve their social standing, particularly among those communities who feared them.

Citizens, it was hoped, would also benefit. Close and ongoing relations with the police would improve their senses of empowerment and efficacy. They would possess greater information about crime dynamics in their neighborhoods, and more opportunities to work constructively to address them. They would also possess regular forums in which they could voice concerns about police practice. Through such participation, community members could more directly influence local dynamics and thereby feel a stronger sense of civic engagement. No longer "bowling alone" (Putnam, 2001), urban residents could experience the sort of localized democracy idealized by New England town meetings (Bryan, 2004).

For this reason, it was reasonable to view community policing as an important potential mechanism for improving police legitimacy, in no small part through an increase in police accountability. As Walker (2005, p. 141) puts it: "The historic closed and secretive nature of American police organizations has been a combination of two factors: the inherent nature of all bureaucracies to be self-protective in the face of outside inquiry, and the unique tradition of the police subculture. Community policing, it should be noted, is designed to overcome this problem."

Ideally, then, community policing practices would generate encounters with citizens that would force the police to explain and justify their practices. A recognition of the need for partnerships would require officers to understand citizen concerns. To place the police on the same plane as citizens (as the language of partnering necessarily implies) was to suggest that they could listen closely and respond constructively. The police would, in short, be accountable to citizen input.

The Limits of Community Policing, the Limits of Accountability

Yet the partnership never quite forged in this ideal fashion. As Roth (2000, p. 239) summarized matters: "True community partnerships, involving sharing power and decision making, are rare" (see also Moore, Thacher, Hartman, Coles, & Sheingold, 1999). Because of this, it becomes necessary to adopt a skeptical attitude toward community policing as a vehicle for improved police accountability.

One cannot blame the police entirely for this failure at partnership. For various reasons, urban communities are difficult to organize. Despite evidence that community-based informal social control is central to crime reduction (Sampson, Raudenbush, & Earls, 1977), and despite ongoing public concern about crime, urban citizens often prove unwilling or unable to maintain political momentum behind neighborhood security efforts (Grinc, 1994; Herbert, 2006a). Neighborhood residents are often too busy to provide ongoing energy to communal crime reduction efforts, and neighborhood groups are often too fractured or short-lived to accomplish long-term transformations.

Yet it is essential to recognize that the police resist efforts by citizen groups to engage in extensive oversight of their activities. I draw upon fieldwork conducted with both the Los Angeles (Herbert, 1997) and Seattle (Herbert, 2006a) Police Departments to help explain this reluctance to embrace full-fledged partnerships. These extensive ethnographic observations led me to conclude that several cultural and organizational features of contemporary police departments leave them ill-disposed to engage too deeply with citizens, as community policing demands they must, and to possess an abiding recalcitrance to public oversight.

Cultural Factors

One key component of police culture stems from the requirement that officers occasionally visit scenes of potential danger and violence. In response to this reality, officers frequently celebrate each other's courage. Indeed, many seek to distinguish themselves in precisely this way—as those willing to handle the most fraught scenarios. These officers quickly volunteer to handle calls that represent risks; they seek opportunities to turn on lights and siren in pursuit of a particularly notorious perpetrator. These are officers said to fall victim to the John Wayne syndrome, to be unusually interested in demonstrating their strength and bravery. Even if this masculinist ethos is not embraced by all officers, it permeates the culture in potent ways, not the least of which is to help fuel the admonition not to drink the Kool-Aid. For instance, many officers disparage the slow-paced, interactive work of communicating with the citizenry. There is scant drama in citizen meetings, little adrenalin needed to contact another city agency to help clean up a drainage ditch. These components of community policing are widely scorned as social work, and are thereby feminized as such (see Herbert, 2001). From here, it is easy for many police to critique their brethren who are involved in community policing as less than full-fledged officers; they are frequently dismissed as seeking to "work banker's hours," to avoid doing "real police work."

A second consequence of this love of masculinist adventurousness is its implicit condoning of brusque behavior, particularly toward those considered dangerous and potentially antipolice. Not surprisingly, officers are most likely to characterize minority-dominated neighborhoods as hostile, and to see those dressed in "gang attire" as most deserving of suspicion. Yet tools for isolating those in need of such displays of power are crude, and thus the police sometimes assert their superiority against those who do not, in fact, represent a credible threat. In this way, the possibility that community policing might decrease tensions in minority-dominated neighborhoods is undercut by officers who wish to insert themselves aggressively into areas they consider fraught with hostility and danger.

Related to this endorsement of the rough and tumble associated with confronting potentially dangerous citizens is the police's central concern for safety. Given that their coercive capacity forces the police to enter dangerous situations, it is understandable that they work to protect themselves. The need for such protection is reinforced via both formal training and informal suggestions to "stay safe out there." These sensible practices can produce unintended consequences, some of which are arguably unwanted. These stem primarily from the way officers treat those they consider suspects. Officers will typically conduct pat-down searches when interacting with individuals they presume to be dangerous, citing a concern for their own safety as their justification. Yet most citizens do not possess weapons, and most bristle when forced to endure the embarrassing public spectacle of a search. When the subject of unfounded suspicion, a citizen may well lose respect for the police and view them as something other than partners.

Officers' concerns for their safety help reinforce an additional cultural emphasis on their felt need for deference to their authority. Encounters that are chaotic are often the ones that officers fear most; in such situations, they do not know what to expect. The best means to reduce such chaos is to attempt to take charge as quickly and effectively as possible. This is rendered difficult if citizens do not defer immediately to officer directives. This expectation of deference becomes ingrained more widely, and carries over to situations that are less turbulent, such as community meetings. In these forums, the police consistently dictate the terms of their interactions with citizens, and effectively limit the range of discourse (Herbert, 2006a; Skogan & Hartnett, 1997). Encouraged by cultural norms to value their own authority, officers struggle to accept fully the notion that citizens are their co-equal partners.

This reluctance to embrace partnering is reinforced, in part, by the dominant narrative officers employ to explain crime, as a plague delivered unto neighborhoods by "bad apples." This individualistic explanation for crime divides citizens into two basic camps: the criminally minded and the criminally victimized. The latter are seen in primarily passive terms, as the unwitting potential targets of the bad guys who might strike. The police are simultaneously constructed as the protectors of those who might be so targeted. Here, again, the police implicitly set themselves apart from the citizenry, as the well-trained and highly capable crime fighters to whom the citizens should defer. Otherwise, public safety will wither.

In short, various currents within the subcultural world of the police work collectively to minimize the extent to which officers see citizens as true partners, and thereby to accomplish one of the principal goals of community policing. Because these partnerships are rarely forged, the possibility that community policing can meaningfully increase police accountability is frustrated. Other organizational dynamics are also impediments here.

Organizational Dynamics

As long noted by police researchers, officers in the field possess considerable discretion about how best to handle the situations before them (Banton, 1964; Bittner, 1967; Brown, 1981; LaFave, 1965). This discretion is enabled by the extent of unsupervised time officers spend in the field, and by the variability of incidents they are called to handle. These factors lead officers to develop working styles that conform to their own personalities (Muir, 1977) and to the requirements of the areas they patrol (Rubinstein, 1973). Such discretion is generally considered endemic to policing, particularly in the United States.

Beyond being unavoidable, discretion is understood as a fact of organizational life within police departments. In fact, individual officers earn praise for the extent to which they exercise initiative and self-reliance. They also endure scorn if they seem too dependent on others. A community police officer in Seattle learned this lesson shortly after assuming his new post. In his first weeks, he sent a memo to the detective unit seeking information about individuals he suspected of criminal activity. He received no response. He drew a lesson that he needed to "take ownership" of the problems on his beat rather than to signal the possibility that he was trying to get other units to do his work for him.

By contrast, another police officer worked largely by himself to understand the dynamics at a house where he suspected drug sales were occurring. He developed relationships with many of the people who lived there, and communicated regularly with the building's landlord. He said that he enjoyed working by himself, and that he was reluctant to share any information he gathered with any of his colleagues. He did not want to appear to be "passing the buck." This neglect of collective organizational efforts is reinforced, in part, by the functional division of labor within police departments. The reality of specialized units means that an officer's range of focus is determined significantly by his or her bureaucratic location. Further, the prestige accorded any one of these units is often contingent upon their demonstrated successes. This may require the unit to demonstrate that it solved some crime problem or other organizational challenge deploying its idiosyncratic base of knowledge. For this reason, units may possess disincentives to work closely with each other, for fear that they will not acquire sufficient credit for their work. As one Seattle officer noted, "Around here, one hand does not know what the other is doing."

Community policing suffers as a consequence. As noted, officers in other units disparage the alleged avoidance of "real" police work that community policing implies. Beyond this, they largely eschew any close working relationships with community police officers. Some patrol officers in Seattle could not even name the community policing officer assigned to their beat. Others admitted to using the community police unit as a "garbage can" into which they tossed low-level problems, like graffiti, that they did not want to address. In this way, community police units can remain isolated within departments. Thus, even if community police officers are receptive to messages delivered by citizens, they will often find it difficult to influence their brethren to be responsive.

In short, the police often define authority and competence in largely individualist terms, and seek to protect their own range of authority against incursions from both citizens and other officers. The cultural emphasis on bravery and authority coupled with the organizational emphasis on specialization combine to push community groups aside, and to render community policing a suspect enterprise. Any hope for meaningful interaction with citizen groups on anything resembling equal footing lies largely unrealized in the face of internal police dynamics.

Police Accountability: Alternative Approaches

In liberal, democratic societies, it is unacceptable for police departments not to be accountable, in some fashion, to the citizenry. Because of their tools of coercion, the police represent the potential excesses of government, the possibility of force to stretch beyond legitimate bounds. If unchecked, the police may abuse their powers in ways that threaten the principle of citizen sovereignty. No component of liberal government deserves greater oversight than the police.

Given this central precept of liberal democracy, it is indeed unfortunate that police departments so resist meaningful cooperation with citizen groups. For this reason, the lack of partnerships through community policing must be seen as more than just an unfortunate failure at institutional reform. It should, instead, be seen as an opportunity to recognize the need for alternate and effective mechanisms for ensuring police accountability.

The police's capacity to resist community policing makes clear that more informal means to ensure accountability are not ones upon which we should rely. This does not mean that forums for police-community relations should be dropped, or that efforts at informal cooperative relations should be abandoned. It does mean that such efforts cannot be expected to result in the police changing their practices in response to public concern. Police officers are quite effective at controlling the discussions at most public forums (Skogan & Hartnett, 1977), part of their general reluctance to see politics enter into policing (Herbert, 2006a). Officers respect their own expertise, desire to succeed on their own, and fear incursions of public groups into their operations. This embrace of professional prestige is understandable. Indeed, the police are hardly unique in their embrace of occupational status (Abbott, 1988). Yet the police, as noted, are different: They are the coercive arm of the state. For this reason, their pleas for professional autonomy, while understandable, cannot stand uncontested. Instead, police practice must undergo constant and effective oversight.

Indeed, one can argue that it is the police that will benefit the most from such oversight, if it works to improve their legitimacy. Police officers rely upon citizen consent to work effectively. Without such cooperation, the police will find all aspects of their job more difficult. Yet citizens are more likely to comply with state institutions that they view as legitimate. Such legitimacy, however, is dependent on citizen perceptions that those institutions are fair and impartial (Tyler, 1990; Tyler & Huo, 2002). So, if accountability mechanisms help ensure fair police practice, legitimacy will improve, and public consent to police requests will increase. Police resistance to robust public oversight is thus functionally counterproductive.

But the history of community policing reminds us that such police resistance is, at least at present, an organizational fact of life. For this reason, less formal means to ensure accountability cannot help much. The only path forward, then, requires an embrace of more formal mechanisms to shed light on police practices. It is regrettable that this choice is necessary, because invoking formal procedures can, at least initially, magnify tensions between the police and the citizenry. Yet officer resistance to community policing—the unwillingness to drink the Kool-Aid—makes clear that democratic liberal societies must pursue this course.

It is not my intention here to survey the various efforts to formalize citizen oversight of the police (for this, see Walker, 2000, 2005), nor to articulate the precise mechanisms by which such oversight should best be pursued. However, I would urge the foregrounding of four general principles to help shape the form of oversight.

First, citizens must be well aware of any avenues they possess to comment on police practice. This includes, of course, being able to register complaints easily when they perceive themselves victims of an abuse of force. Police departments need to make the complaint process smooth and obstruction-free. Beyond this, ideally, police departments will make available an avenue to comment more generally on police practices that are not as obvious or as seemingly egregious as a use of force.

Second, as Walker (2005) argues convincingly, it is quite useful for a citizen oversight structure to include a role for an auditor who does more than just review the investigation process for complaints. Such an auditor, he suggests, can perform an even more significant function if he or she is able to assess a given department's practices more widely. This way, the oversight role includes attending to matters that might help prevent abuses of force from occurring in the first place. If the auditor can isolate patterns, policies, or informal norms that contribute in some way to subpar policing, then officer conduct can improve before a visible public problem emerges. If Seattle possessed an auditor with this wide an ambit, for instance, the SPD might face needed pressure to take the patterns of racially disparate drug law enforcement more seriously.

Third, citizen oversight should be constructed to help maximize the degree of mutual understanding between city residents and the police. Police and citizens each frequently complain that neither understands the other very effectively (Herbert, 2006a). No better way to address this issue than to provide forums for mediated interaction. Walker (2000) notes that, in many instances, complaining citizens are not looking to see an allegedly offending officer punished. Rather, they simply want a sense that their complaint can be heard and that some steps might be taken to address the issue they are raising. It may also be the case that citizens can be helped to understand the pressures the police face and the reasons why they made choices that seem inexplicable. Certainly, the police possess an enormous degree of support from much of the population, and so should not necessarily assume that those who complain are resolutely antipolice. Police hostility to oversight will not readily be overcome, but forums that aim at mutual understanding (and are not controlled by the police) could help officers realize that citizen oversight is not an inherently illegitimate project.

Finally, citizen oversight should always be seen as an incomplete, ongoing, and ever-changing process. The politics of police oversight will always remain fraught. Part of this is due to the likelihood that the police will continue to resist it, to some degree or another. But part of this also stems from contradictory desires within the body politic (see Herbert, 2006b). Just as there are citizens who fear the police and their potential to abuse their discretionary and coercive power, others idolize them as the key protectors against urban chaos. As a consequence, the police will typically find support from significant members of the citizenry, and thus of elected officials, for protection against outside interference. These turbulent politics are endemic to efforts to create more broad oversight mechanisms, and need to be accepted as endemic to the enterprise.

Conclusion

I told this story through a primary focus on Seattle, the city about which I know most. One could argue that I might tell a different story were I located somewhere else. Take Chicago, for instance. It is, after all, the U.S. city with arguably the most successful community policing effort. As Skogan (2006; see also Skogan & Hartnett, 1997) extensively catalogs, Chicago's political establishment instituted a quite thorough-going community policing effort, one that mandated regular police-citizen gatherings and that forced close cooperation between city government agencies. Because of this, citizen involvement in "beat meetings" was high, and satisfaction with the police increased, especially with African Americans. (Chicago's Latinos displayed a different pattern, a reality that Skogan attributes to the high number of recent immigrants. Many of these, he speculates, lack facility with English and may fear law enforcement, because either they or their close associates are undocumented migrants.) Were I in Chicago, might I tell a more optimistic story about community policing and accountability?

Perhaps. But very recently a controversy developed in Chicago over allegations of excessive use of force. A recent study overseen by a University of Chicago law professor Craig Futterman asserts that only 19 of more than 10,000 complaints of police abuse between 2002 and 2004 resulted in any disciplinary action. The study's results were reported during ongoing turbulence from a scandal that emerged when video cameras recorded instances of off-duty police officers physically abusing citizens. The scandal led to the resignation of Chicago's chief, Philip Cline. Not surprisingly, the combined effects of these developments led many citizen groups to call for more effective accountability mechanisms. Said Fullerman, "The way in which the Chicago Police Department investigates police abuse is a joke. If the

CPD investigated civilian crime in the same way it investigates police abuse, they'd never solve a case" (Gallagher, 2007).

Granted, my distance from Chicago renders me unable to monitor these developments closely, and to sift more discriminately among various claims and counterclaims. Yet the recent controversies there demonstrate the political volatility that necessarily attends to police practice, given the possibilities that coercive force might exceed its bounds. These controversies also suggest that, whatever the impact of community policing there, recent reforms do not dampen the persistent need for robust forms of police accountability.

The promise of community policing, as Skogan (2006) rightly notes, rested primarily on the hope that it would improve the legitimacy of the police. Greater attentiveness and responsiveness by the police to citizen concerns would help ensure a more positive assessment of their practices, and thereby diffuse unhelpful tensions. These tensions, it is important to remember, hamper the police as much as anyone, because they make officers' jobs all the more difficult. A dissatisfied citizenry is often a noncompliant one, and a noncompliant one is difficult to manage. More than any other social group, the police stand to gain the most from increasing their legitimacy.

In most cities, however, the promise of community policing lies unrealized. In Seattle, the current police chief now dismisses it (Kerlikowske, 2003). In some respects, this is not so completely hard to understand. As Walker (2005, p. 162) notes:

> The simple fact of the matter is that changing a police organization is an extremely difficult task. In addition to the inherent inertia of all bureaucracies, policing is heavily shaped by informal officer norms at the street level. Eliminating deeply ingrained practices and habits of mind throughout a police bureaucracy is an enormous challenge.

Given this, perhaps it is not too surprising that monthly beat meetings are not foolproof mechanisms for ensuring police accountability. As long as the police can control the conversation (as they typically do in such venues), they can reinforce their longstanding practice of minimizing the force of citizen input.

Unfortunately, just as Chief Kerlikowske pronounces a perhaps understandable obituary for community policing, he also dismisses the need to take seriously patterns of racial disparities in drug law enforcement. These two realities are not isolated from one another. Because of this, efforts should continue to increase the manner and extent of citizen oversight of the police. Such oversight of the state's coercive capacities is a core principle in liberal democracies, and must remain robust if police legitimacy is ever to prosper.

References

Abbott, M. (1988). *The system of professions*. Chicago: University of Chicago Press.

Banton, M. (1964). *The police man in the community*. London: Tavistock.

Beckett, K. (2008). Drugs, data, race and reaction: A field report. *Antipode, 40*, 442–447.

Beckett, K., Nyrop, K., & Pfingst, L. (2006). Race, drugs and policing: Understanding disparities in drug delivery arrests. *Criminology, 44*, 105–138.

Beckett, K., Nyrop, K., Pfingst, L., & Bowen, M. (2005). Drug use, drug arrests, and the question of race: Lessons from Seattle. *Social Problems, 52*, 419–441.

Bittner, E. (1967). The police on skid row: A study in peace keeping. *American Sociological Review, 32*, 699–715.

Brown, M. (1981). *Working the street: Police discretion and the dilemmas of reform*. New York: Russell Sage.

Bryan, F. (2004). *Real democracy: The New England town meeting and how it works*. Chicago: University of Chicago Press.

Cordner, G. (1998). Community policing: Evidence and effects. In G. Alpert & A. Piquero (Eds.), *Community policing: Contemporary readings* (pp. 45–62). Prospect Heights, IL: Waveland Press.

Fogelson, R. (1977). *Big-city police*. Cambridge, MA: Harvard University Press.

Fyfe, N. (2004). Zero tolerance, maximum surveillance? Deviance, difference and crime control in the late modern city. In L. Lees (Ed.), *The emancipatory city?* (pp. 40–56). London: Sage.

Gallagher, R. (2007). Study: Police abuse goes unpunished. *Medill reports: Chicago*. Retrieved March 3, 2009 from http://news.medill.northwestern.edu/chicago/news.aspx.id=6125

Grinc, R. (1994). Angels in marble: Problems in stimulating community involvement in community policing. *Crime & Delinquency, 40*, 437–468.

Herbert, S. (1997). *Policing space: Territoriality and the Los Angeles Police Department*. Minneapolis: University of Minnesota Press.

Herbert, S. (2001). Hard charger or station queen? Policing and the masculinist state. *Gender, Place and Culture, 8*, 55–71.

Herbert, S. (2006a). *Citizens, cops and power: Recognizing the limits of community*. Chicago: University of Chicago Press.

Herbert, S. (2006b). Tangled up in blue: Conflicting paths to police legitimacy. *Theoretical Criminology, 10*, 481–504.

Kennedy, R. (1998). *Race, crime and the law*. New York: Vintage.

Kerlikowske, G. (2003). *The end of community policing*. Speech delivered to National Community Policing Organizing Conference, Washington DC. Retrieved from http://www.seattle.gov/police/Leadership/COPStatements/06_18_03.htm

LaFave, W. (1965). *Arrest: The decision to take a suspect into custody*. Boston: Little, Brown.

Lyons, W. (1999). *The politics of community policing: Rearranging the power to punish*. Ann Arbor: University of Michigan Press.

Maguire, E., & King, W. (2004). Trends in the policing industry. *Annals of AAPSS, 593*, 15–41.

McArdle, A., & Erzen, T. (2001). *Zero tolerance: Quality of life and the new police brutality in New York City*. New York: New York University Press.

Moore, M. (1992). Problem-solving and community policing. In M. Tonry & N. Morris (Eds.), *Modern policing* (pp. 99–158). Chicago: University of Chicago Press.

Moore, M., Thacher, D., Hartman, F., Coles, C., & Sheingold, P. (1999). *Case studies of the transformation of police departments: A cross-site analysis* (Working Paper 99-05-16). Cambridge, MA: Harvard University.

Muir, W. (1977). *Police: Streetcorner politicians.* Chicago: University of Chicago Press.

Niederhoffer, A. (1967). *Behind the shield: The police in urban society.* Garden City, NJ: Doubleday.

Putnam, R. (2001). *Bowling alone: The collapse and revival of American community.* New York: Simon & Schuster.

Reed, W. (1999). *The politics of community policing: The case of Seattle.* New York: Garland Publishing.

Roth, J. (2000). *National evaluation of the COPS Program: Title I of the 1994 Crime Act.* Washington, DC: National Institute of Justice.

Rubinstein, J. (1973). *City police.* New York: Farrar, Strauss and Giroux.

Sampson, R., Raudenbush, S., & Earls, F. (1997). Neighborhoods and violent crime: A multilevel study of collective efficacy. *Science, 277,* 918–924.

Saunders, R. (1999). The space community policing makes and the body that makes it. *Professional Geographer, 51,*135–146.

Silverman, E. (1999). *NYPD battles crime: Innovative strategies in policing.* Boston: Northeastern University Press.

Skogan, W. (2006). *Police and community in Chicago: A tale of three cities.* New York: Oxford University Press.

Skogan, W., & Hartnett, S. (1997). *Community policing, Chicago style.* New York: Oxford University Press.

Skolnick, J. (1966). *Justice without trial: Law enforcement in democratic society.* New York: John Wiley & Sons.

Skolnick, J., & Bayley, D. (1986). *The new blue line: Police innovation in six cities.* New York: Free Press.

Trojanowicz, R., & Bucqueroux, B. (1994). *Community policing: How to get started.* Cincinnati: Anderson.

Tyler, T. (1990). *Why people obey the law.* New Haven, CT: Yale University Press.

Tyler, T., & Huo, Y. (2002). *Trust in the law: Encouraging public cooperation with the police and courts.* New York: Russell Sage Foundation.

Walker, S. (2000). *Police accountability: The role of citizen oversight.* Belmont, CA: Wadsworth Publishing.

Walker, S. (2005). *The new world of police accountability.* Thousand Oaks, CA: Sage Publications.

Walker, S., Spohn, C., & DeLone, M. (2003). *The color of justice: Race, ethnicity and crime in America.* Belmont, CA: Wadsworth Publishing.

Weitzer, R., & Tuch, S. (2006). *Race and policing in America: Conflict and reform.* Cambridge: Cambridge University Press.

Police–Social Service Collaboration
Creating Effective Partnerships

7

LILIOKANAIO PEASLEE

Contents

The late 1980s and early 1990s marked a shift in police practices away from a professional, bureaucratic model to the employment of community and problem-oriented policing.* This new paradigm has expanded the police mandate from traditional goals of arrest and deterrence to include a responsibility for crime prevention, problem solving, community engagement, and the formation of community and interagency partnerships (Roth et al., 2000; Braga, 2002; U.S. Department of Justice, 2003; Skogan & Frydl, 2004). In some cities, police work with municipal agencies, community-based organizations, and other social actors to improve community relationships, enhance their institutional legitimacy, control crime, and achieve other policy goals. This

Adapted from Peaslee, L. (2008). Community policing and social service partnerships: Lessons from New England. *Police Practice and Research,* http://dx.doi.org/10.1080/15614260802264578

---

* The traditional, or professional, model became dominant in the 1940s, 1950s, and 1960s, before beginning to erode in the 1970s. It emphasizes hierarchical command, professional standards, organizational autonomy, and the adoption of technology. Under this rubric police came to rely primarily on three crime-fighting strategies: preventative patrol to maximize police visibility, rapid response through 911 and radio dispatches, and retrospective investigation (Fogelson, 1977; Sparrow, 1988; Sparrow et al., 1990).

transformation has the potential to increase police involvement in the social policy arena, situating police as change agents rather than simply enforcers of the status quo.*

Yet while most police departments are now involved in some form of problem-oriented and community policing, interagency and community partnerships continue to pose a challenge for many departments. A national evaluation of the Community Oriented Policing Services found that while "problem-solving partnerships for coordinating the appropriate application of ... resources are commonplace in many ... agencies ... all too often, partnerships are in name only, or simply standard, temporary working arrangements" (Roth et al., 2000, p. 20). Furthermore, while police collaboration with social service agencies is an important element of community and problem-oriented policing, such partnerships have not received systematic research attention.† The growing body of literature on community and problem-oriented policing tends to focus on the challenges of citizen engagement (for example, Fung, 2004; Herbert, 2006; Skogan, 2006; Wycoff, 1994) and the decentralization of police bureaucracies (Greene, Bergman, & McLaughlin, 1994; Weisel & Eck, 1994; Wilkinson & Rosenbaum, 1994; Wilson, 1989). While the scholarship developed from Wilson and Kelling's (1982) well-known broken windows thesis is replete with examples of interagency partnerships, the emphasis is largely on physical changes to the urban environment, such as graffiti, trash removal, or housing code enforcement (see Fung, 2004; Moore, 1999; Skogan, 2006; Skogan & Hartnett, 1997; Sparrow, Moore, & Kennedy, 1990).‡ The dominance of these approaches in community policing—both in research and

---

* While there is some disagreement within the discipline, this study uses the term *social services* or *social policy* to mean policies, organizations, and programs aimed at improving individual and social well-being, particularly for meeting the basic needs of vulnerable populations. This typically includes access to health and behavioral health care services, education, housing, income maintenance, job training, and employment. Because my focus is on juveniles, I also include youth intervention and prevention programs, such as out-of-schooltime programs, mentoring, and other youth development programs.

† Although sometimes used interchangeably, a distinction can be made between community and problem-oriented policing. In the latter, police identify the underlying, immediate causes of criminal activity. Community policing, on the other hand, emphasizes strong police-community partnerships to reduce crime and increase community safety (Braga, 2002, p. 12). Therefore, while community policing always entails problem-oriented policing, problem-solving activities could be limited to law enforcement rather than community partners (see, for example, Capowich and Roehl's 1994 analysis of problem solving in San Diego).

‡ Wilson and Kelling (1982) argue that neighborhood disorder and decay give rise to more serious crimes by signaling to would-be criminals that the area lacks informal social control. While broken windows policing is sometimes confused with zero tolerance, I use it here to mean situational crime prevention (e.g., providing better lighting in a park to discourage drug dealing) and initiatives geared toward neighborhood revitalization (e.g., rehabbing dilapidated housing or cleaning up graffiti). Sparrow et al. (1990) do point to Baltimore's COPE program as an example of how police referral of elderly and shut-in residents to municipal agencies can help citizens access social services, but their analysis is limited to a single page.

in practice—has resulted in a tendency to focus on tangible, visible results, rather than long-term solutions through social service provision.

The relatively limited research on police–social service partnerships is striking considering the important role that youth development programs and social services play in juvenile delinquency and crime prevention (Bownes & Ingersoll, 1997; Carnegie Council on Adolescent Development, 1995; Chaiken, 1998; Leslie, 2007; Wald & Martinez, 2003). Building "meaningful partnerships to improve public safety" is "arguably the core ideal" of community policing (Thacher, 2001, p. 765). Yet Skogan and Hartnett (1997, p. 14) assert that "interorganizational cooperation turns out to be one of the most difficult problems for innovative departments." Because social service collaboration can pose unique challenges for police organization and practice, it is important for police researchers to better address the organizational forms and processes of interagency collaboration.

This chapter identifies some of the benefits, challenges, and strategies for creating robust police partnerships with social service agencies. I begin by identifying how partnerships can enhance the work of police and social service agencies and lay out a framework for how police departments can better engage social service partners. I then examine the challenges involved in trying to transform police culture and practice to include collaboration with other social actors, and offer recommendations to police departments looking to build or strengthen such partnerships. I demonstrate that many of the same causal variables that have been addressed in the broader literature on community policing—organizational restructuring, strong leadership, improved education and training, and creating opportunities and incentives for collaboration—can lead to stronger police–social service partnerships.

In addition to a review of the literature, I use case studies of four urban police departments located in the United States to draw lessons about police–social service partnerships. Cases include Boston and Springfield, Massachusetts, and New Haven and Hartford, Connecticut. Findings are drawn from more than 100 semistructured interviews that I conducted with police, elected officials, clergy, and social service providers. The different degrees of success with social service collaboration illustrated by these cases provide a good lens through which to assess police–social service partnerships.

Police departments in both Boston and New Haven emerged in the 1990s as leaders in innovative police–social service collaboration. In Boston, a strategy to prevent youth violence was heralded as a model of crime fighting, with collaboration between law enforcement, social services, clergy, business, and community members leading to a record reduction in crime.* Representatives

---

* While the partnerships that developed in Boston over the course of the 1990s are sometimes referred to as the Boston Strategy to Prevent Youth Violence, Anthony Braga explains that this is largely "a term of convenience that actually has little meaning." The "network of capacity ... developed at the grass roots.... There was not a coherent planned strategy from the outset; it was more of an evolution" (personal communication, April 21, 2008).

from hundreds of cities have come to Boston to learn from the Boston Police Department's experiences. Similarly, the New Haven Police Department boasts a substantial youth-oriented policing initiative, and has won national recognition from the New England Community-Police Partnership, the International Association of Chiefs of Police, and the National League of Cities for excellence in community policing and police partnerships.

In contrast, police in Springfield, Massachusetts, and Hartford, Connecticut, have had lower levels of social service collaboration than Boston and New Haven. While some partnership activity occurred in Springfield and Hartford in the 1990s, most failed to outlast external funding or to take root department-wide. Although both departments show some signs of moving toward a more community-oriented model, social service collaboration continues to lag. On the other hand, some of the initiatives that developed in Boston during that time period have been difficult to sustain, and both Boston and New Haven are trying to strengthen crime prevention partnerships in the face of rising rates of youth violence.

The Potential Value of Interagency Collaboration

Police partnerships with municipal and community-based agencies can improve police practice and enhance social service provision. Conversations with police, government officials, and a variety of social service agencies in each of the study cities point to the benefits of police–social service partnerships. Interagency collaborations can *create value* by enabling independent organizations to work toward a common goal (Moore, 1990; Bardach, 1998). Together, their "collaborative capacity" gives partners the ability "to conceptualize problems more holistically than each ... is capable of doing alone and to mass resources necessary to solve them" (Bardach, 1998, p. 306).

Although crime is influenced by many factors outside of law enforcement, including family, community, and economic characteristics, police are often held responsible for managing behavior that, under traditional law enforcement, is beyond their control. As Plotkin and Narr point out, "Police are expected to be problem solvers, social workers, employment counselors, order maintenance workers, fear-reduction experts, and mediators. Yet they often lack the community resources and direction to adequately assume these roles" (1993, p. 58). Similarly, Boston Police Superintendent Paul Joyce explains that youth violence is

> too complex a problem for just the police. We often inherit kids with a lot of damage very late in the game. And the whole idea of working with ... social service agencies is [to] intervene earlier to make a difference so they don't make it to us. (Personal communication, February 20, 2006)

Many of the police interviewed for this project explain that under a traditional model, officers were often frustrated with the tools available to them for crime prevention. They could issue a warning or an arrest but neither seemed to get at the underlying causes of criminal activity, and neither seemed effective at deterrence, especially for juvenile crime. Connecting with social service resources and professionals expands police ability to address the root causes of crime and delinquency.

Moreover, collaboration with community actors outside law enforcement can increase police legitimacy in poor and minority neighborhoods where mistrust and hostility often run deep (Tyler, 2001, 2004). Police work will always entail responding to calls, investigating crime, and arresting criminals. Still, shifting some attention to prevention and intervention initiatives helps to humanize police officers and signals to residents that the police care about what happens to youth and their communities. As trust increases, so too can citizens' willingness to be the eyes and ears of law enforcement—to cooperate with the police and share information that will help solve crime. This intelligence can help police prioritize arrests by distinguishing impact players from those at the periphery of criminal activity, who might be better served by social service agencies (Berrien & Winship, 2002; Braga & Winship, 2005).

Police-community and interagency partnerships also have important implications for social welfare policy. Police are not typically included in the range of actors pursuing social policy reform, but they are positioned to make a significant impact. Work by Winship and Berrien (1999) has highlighted the way that police can act as "neutral conveners" and enhance civic capacity by bringing together antagonistic community groups to work toward mutual problem solving. Echoing Wilson and Kelling (1982), Moore (1999) asserts that police play a vital role in promoting social welfare because order and security are paramount to stimulating investment in poor communities.

While cleaning up abandoned lots and keeping drug dealers off the corner are certainly important endeavors, police capacity in supporting neighborhood revitalization and community-building initiatives need not be limited to crime control and order maintenance. Police partnerships can also have a more direct impact on social service delivery. As one of the most ubiquitous public agencies, police departments can be a bridge between the communities they serve and other parts of government. Their position in municipal government offers the potential to leverage resources to which poor communities might not otherwise have access. As first responders—and one of the few agencies that operates 24 hours a day, 7 days a week—police have a greater capacity than other government agencies for intervening in communities and are in a unique position to reach families in crisis. Partnerships with social service agencies enhance police capacity to refer individuals to available resources and help social service agencies reach clients in need. Coordination of this kind has become increasingly important given recent revenue shortfalls in many states and localities. Creating partnerships can enable state, local, and community-based agencies to use resources more efficiently.

A Framework for Collaboration

Before the push for police professionalization, police played a larger role in strengthening the health and welfare of the communities they served. Monkkonen (1981) explains that police provided overnight housing for the homeless and were responsible for returning home lost children, and Schulz (1995) argues that prison matrons functioned more as social workers than crime fighters, since they largely concerned themselves with the custodial care of women and children. In the early 20th century, however, progressive administrative reformers trying to curb corruption and the influence of urban political machines set their sights on police departments. They initiated a series of reforms to insulate police not only from politicians but also from ordinary citizens. As a result, law enforcement and social service provision were compartmentalized into distinct professional agencies (Fogelson, 1977; Monkkonen, 1981; Sparrow et al., 1990). The contemporary shift from traditional to community policing is once again blurring the boundaries between law enforcement, crime prevention, and social service provision.

Goldstein, whose 1979 article on problem-oriented policing helped usher in this most recent period of reform, points to the ways that police problem solving can draw departments out of traditional law enforcement and into the social policy arena. Police, he argues, must recognize that solutions to crime-related problems go "beyond ways in which to affect the environment or 'situational' factors ... it includes ... *anything* that might be done to deal with the problems the community looks to the police to handle" (1990, pp. 103–104). Since police have neither the expertise nor the resources to handle all the problems that come their way, Goldstein offers three possible strategies for action: (1) refer residents to available community resources, (2) coordinate policing activities with other government or community-based agencies in order to better address the problem at hand, or (3) actively press state or municipal political actors to expand or create new programs when services are inadequate (Goldstein, 1990, p. 106). I offer examples of each of these strategies below, though it will be clear that none are mutually exclusive; robust partnerships and programs contain elements of each.

Referrals

The primary means by which police can engage social service agencies is through referrals to government and community-based services. Rather than expecting police to *solve* citizens' problems, this type of social service collaboration expands police capacity to refer residents to those with more expertise. As one officer in Boston explained, police "are a bridge, not an answer." This bridge might lead to general case management, mental health counseling, afterschool and educational opportunities, or material resources like heating and emergency food assistance. It is important for police to know what resources are available in their community and to be able either to provide contact information to individuals or to provide social service staff with a way to reach individuals in need. This referral capacity can be greatly enhanced though the co-location of police and agency staff.

In Boston, the Youth Service Providers Network (YSPN) stations full-time, licensed clinical social workers in police precinct houses to connect children and families in trouble with the resources provided by partnering agencies. The YSPN gives police an in-house referral source to Boston's youth service agencies to address teenage runaways, dropout prevention, mentoring, job training and placement, tutoring, and leadership skills (Office of Juvenile Justice and Delinquency Prevention [OJJDP], 1999). Referrals to social workers come either directly from police officers or from social workers' access to internal police reports.

According to Jeff Butts, the program's executive director, there are many benefits to the partnership. First, police officers have a referral source with whom they are personally acquainted and who they can be confident will provide follow-up. Second, officers, who function as outreach workers, work 24 hours a day, 7 days a week and are in touch with the most at-risk. Third, social workers are stationed in district substations. They see young people as they are arrested and read police reports every morning, increasing their access to information about clients and potential clients. Lastly, through their work with the police, many social workers have become more familiar with other aspects of the criminal justice system, such as probation, parole, the district attorney, and the courts, allowing them to better understand multiple points of advocacy for the people they serve (personal communication, March 21, 2006).

In New Haven the Child Development–Community Policing (CD-CP) partnership between police and mental health clinicians at the Yale Child Study Program is the cornerstone of the department's Youth Oriented Policing Initiative. The program's consultation service, which is made up of mental health clinicians and police supervisors, gives police the ability to call mental health practitioners 24 hours a day when they encounter children exposed to trauma (victims of crime, witnesses of domestic violence, etc.). Early intervention is geared toward breaking cycles of violence, and partnership with police gives clinicians access to populations that may never seek out mental health services (Marans & Berkman, 1997). As first responders, police are in a unique position to reach children in crisis *before* the effects of trauma set in. Immediate referral allows clinicians to provide services when acute intervention can make the most impact (Marans et al., 1995). CD-CP clinician Miriam Berkman explains:

> If you sit in a traditional clinic ... you don't see these kids; we tend to see them many months and years later when they've established much more entrenched kinds of symptoms—they're doing badly in school, they're acting out, they're arrested, [or] they show up in the juvenile justice system. (Personal communication, May 17, 2006)

All New Haven officers receive program training and carry the beeper numbers and schedules of on-call staff. Police administration further facilitates the referral process by incorporating program referrals into routine police paperwork. In addition to the CD-CP program, this also includes referral to three other community-based agencies: the Coordinating Council for Children in Crisis, Clifford Beers Child Guidance Clinic, and Community Mediation. At the station, copies of the reports are separated for pickup by the appropriate referral agencies, which often have staff working out of the neighborhood substations (S. Reading, personal communication, November 20, 2006).*

In the case of Hartford, simplifying the referral process has helped police to overcome officer resistance to social service collaboration. For example, Hartford's Juvenile Review Board is designed to divert youth from court involvement by providing them with alternative sanctions. When officers encounter a minor youth offense, they simply have to check a box on the summons and a copy goes to Catholic Charities (a local social service agency) rather than to the court. The Crisis Intervention Team—a partnership between Hartford police and the Capital Region Mental Health Center (CRMHC)—teaches officers how to identify and better respond to mental illness. Lieutenant Brian Foley points out that one of the reasons officers have been so accepting of the program is that work with crisis teams actually *reduces* the amount of paperwork that officers have to complete (personal communication, November 14, 2006).

Interagency Collaboration

While patrol officers in New Haven are primarily engaged in the CD-CP program through the referral process, a number of sergeants and lieutenants are engaged in a much higher level of program collaboration. Police supervisors take part in weekly case conferences with clinicians to review

---

* The Coordinating Council for Children in Crisis is a local agency that conducts home visiting and outreach, parenting education, family strengthening activities, counseling, and advocacy. Clifford Beers provides child mental and behavior health counseling. Community mediation facilitates community conflict resolution.

the referral program and better address their respective strategies. The case conferences are primarily conducted by police and mental health providers but have broadened to include representatives from the Department of Children and Families, the New Haven Public Schools, and juvenile probation. Unlike partnerships in Boston that often take a wide approach to public safety by involving multiple actors in the process, the CD-CP program does not try to include all community stakeholders in case conferences. Clinicians do, however, take a broad view of what constitutes clinical interventions, and they engage other partners as needed. Three outreach advocates who are not clinicians help connect families with services to address financial problems, legal issues, education, and food security (M. Berkman, personal communication, May 17, 2006).

In Boston, activity that initially occurred independently among police, probation officers, community outreach workers, and clergy in the early 1990s laid the groundwork for a multifaceted, community-wide approach to youth violence prevention (Braga, Kennedy, Piehl, & Waring, 2001; Braga & Winship, 2006; Pruitt, 2001). The Comprehensive Community Safety Initiative (CCSI) is one of the most recent initiatives. Under the direction of the police department, CCSI has convened local, county, and state social service agencies to identify individuals and extended families, who together account for the majority of criminal activity in Boston's highest crime neighborhood. While many of the targeted families already were involved with at least one social service agency, coordination of multiple agencies is aimed at devising a systems-wide approach that allows partners to address multiple points of intervention, including health and mental health, housing, substance abuse, and unemployment (A. Braga, personal communication, January 27, 2007; J. Maconochie, personal communication, April 20, 2006; National League of Cities, 2007).

Advocacy

Over the past decade, police in Boston and New Haven have been active in advocating for expanded services and positive opportunities for young people. Police leadership in both cities have worked closely with their respective mayors in order to devise strategies for reducing youth violence. In Boston, this has included expansion of the city's street outreach worker and city-sponsored summer jobs programs (P. Joyce, personal communication, February 20, 2006).

Similarly, in New Haven, police have also pushed the city to expand summer jobs for teens, and worked with the school system to increase summer and afterschool programming (S. Reading, personal communication, November 20, 2006).

This advocacy role has also extended to the private sector. For example, in response to increased community-based activity around youth violence,

John Hancock Mutual Life Insurance Company in 1994 sought the advice of the police department on how they could best impact public safety. The police recommended that the organization increase opportunities for inner city youth. Together, they created the Summer of Opportunity program, a partnership between the Boston Police Department, John Hancock, and Northeastern University. The program provides youth participants (who are recommended by local social service agencies) with a summer workshop program, weekly stipends, mentors, computer and life skill training, team-building, conflict resolution workshops, and a year-round internship program (P. Joyce, personal communication, February 20, 2006).

Transforming Police Culture

The expansion of a police department's goals and activities to include social service collaboration is a significant shift from the way police departments operated for nearly a century. Even within the trend toward community policing, partnerships with social service agencies, particularly those that involve the allocation of agency resources, are not widespread. Collaboration with social service providers—much like community policing itself—necessitates a substantial culture change inside police agencies. Interagency collaborations challenge traditional organizational boundaries. Likewise, concerns about turf, autonomy, resources, and perceived incompatibility of missions and funding sources can make it difficult to establish working relationships (Bar-On, 1995; Skogan et al., 1999; Tapper, Kleinman, & Nakashian, 1998; Wilson, 1989).

Police departments have been characterized as "coping agencies," where officers are largely driven by the situational imperatives that they encounter on a daily basis. The realities of police work often make it difficult to observe officer activities and to link those activities to departmental outcomes, such as crime prevention (Wilson, 1989). To increase the likelihood that police officers would adhere to formal expectations, police professionalism emphasized the formalization of rules and procedures so that police would follow agreed-upon goals. Traditional police practices that used rapid response, scientific investigation, and extensive record keeping were an attempt to formalize officers' activities in order to diminish discretion (and thus the possibility of corruption) (Wilson, 1989).

The renewed emphasis on crime prevention, problem solving, and community policing has shifted some attention from these activities toward increased officer discretion and processes that are difficult to formalize (Brooks, 2005; Mastrofski, 1994). While decentralization and expanded officer discretion can facilitate innovative partnerships on the ground (Rogers, 2003), changes in police organizational structure, strong leadership, enhanced education and training, and the creation of opportunities and incentives for collaboration are necessary to ensure that officers work toward furthering the goal of interagency collaboration. Recommendations for each of these strategies are outlined below.

Organizational Structure

Institutions shape the skills, preferences, and goals of actors, and influence the strategies they pursue to achieve these ends (Hall, 1990; Steinmo & Thelen, 1992; Wilson, 1989).

Attention to organizational structure is a fundamental part of institutionalizing the practical and behavioral changes necessary to orient a department toward social service collaboration (Greene et al., 1994; O'Keefe, 2004; Walker, 1993; Williams, 2003). The strategies that allow community policing to take root and flourish—department-wide adoption of community policing, fixed geographic accountability, and decentralized decision making (U.S. Department of Justice, 2003; Zhao, 1996)—are important antecedents to creating sustainable police–social service partnerships.

The importance of the breadth of reform is evident in Boston and New Haven, where community policing was viewed as a philosophy that would be driven by a problem-oriented approach to police work and adopted department-wide. This approach drew in a greater number of officers and better facilitated a shift in the departments' organizational culture, opening the door to other forms of community-centered collaboration. Resistance to community policing in the Springfield and Hartford Police Departments, on the other hand, coupled with the federal incentives for reform, resulted in a tiered system in which a small number of officers were doing community-based work, but first responders and investigative units continued to do traditional police work. The fragmentation between community police officers and the rest of the department made innovation unstable and unsustainable (W. Fitchet, personal communication, October 17, 2006; J. Lopez, personal communication, August 23, 2006).

All bureaucracies exhibit some degree of hierarchy and centralized authority. However, those departments that have adopted community and problem-oriented policing have begun a structural evolution from top-down to bottom-up decision making (Skogan et al., 1999). Although some aspects of policing may continue to be centralized (or pushed to mid-level managers), problem-oriented policing tends to empower lower-level operators in fashioning solutions and directing police activities. Community policing devolves some decision making not only to street-level actors but also to external stakeholders (Lipsky, 1980; Moore, 1999). While centralization enhances executive power and increases authority to mandate top-down changes, it decreases the likelihood that innovations will be generated by other actors within an organization, and makes it difficult to cultivate the buy-in that is necessary for implementation (Williams, 2003). In Boston and New Haven, officers were given autonomy to experiment with problem-oriented approaches and to find innovative solutions, resulting in more substantial police–social service partnerships than the approach taken by Springfield and Hartford.

Similarly, regular connection with a geographic area also allows officers to better understand neighborhood problems and to develop more constructive relationships with their communities (Mastrofski, 1981). Police deployment in Boston and New Haven combined decentralization with consistent beat assignments. Neighborhood policing not only allowed officers to develop a better sense of problems on their beat, but also provided them with multiple opportunities to interact with local community organizations and other social actors. Because barriers to collaboration come not only from police resistance to change but also from other agencies' reluctance to working with authorities, the decentralization of police into neighborhood precincts can help nurture the informal social networks and capital that are essential in facilitating more formal collaboration with social service partners (Patterson, 2007). The Hartford Police Department did not adopt a comparable neighborhood policing strategy until 2001, and at the time of this study, the Springfield Police Department had not yet implemented plans to permanently assign officers by district.

Early attempts at interagency and community collaboration can lead to the development of "networks of capacity" (Moore, 1999) and lay the groundwork for more intensive social policy work as actors recognize common goals and develop trust and strong working relationships (Goldstein, 1990). Collaboration between Boston police, probation, clergy, and street outreach workers (Streetworkers) provides a good example of the iterative nature of relationships. Once community policing had given the gang unit more visibility at the neighborhood level, informal encounters between probation, Streetworkers, and clergy led each group to recognize their shared interests and common goals. They realized they could be more effective if working together rather than in isolation. Partnerships began to grow in the neighborhoods from the ground up. Early collaborations created positive feedback and drew in other partners (Braga & Winship, 2006; Pruitt, 2001; Winship & Berrien, 1999).

Police Leadership

The establishment and maintenance of partnerships between police and social service agencies necessitates strong and consistent police leadership from both the police chief and mid-level supervisors. Collaborative departments require police executives with different skills than do those that are insulated. Unlike traditional command and control models, community-based work brings with it the need to give front-line officers more discretion (Brooks, 2005; Mastrofski, 1994; Wilson, 1989). For police leadership to be effective, they must be able to connect with officers and lead by example (Engle, 2005). Police leadership in Boston and New Haven played a key role in implementing a department-wide community policing philosophy and encouraging problem-solving and police–social service collaboration in middle management and on the front lines. Police partnerships in Springfield and Hartford, on the other hand, were limited by high executive turnover and leadership that enforced either the status quo or the perception of officers as weak (A. DiChiara, personal communication, September 19, 2006).

Evidence from the four case studies indicates that outsiders have been more successful in challenging traditional police practices and creating the organizational structures necessary for police-community partnerships. On the other hand, while leadership capacity ultimately rests on the abilities of individual police executives, internal promotions seem to better illicit the loyalty of officers. The pattern that seems most effective is when internally promoted chiefs follow on the heels of an externally appointed executive. Although turnover in police leadership tends to precede institutional change, continuity is important for durability. High turnover—particularly when police executives are brought in from the outside—can destabilize reform efforts. Constant experimentation reduces buy-in by officers, who may doubt leadership's commitment to follow through. However, if a reform-oriented chief has been able to make high-level promotions based on his or her vision of policing, internal executive appointments can provide consistency even with the appointment of a new chief.

In addition to providing leadership *within* the department, police executives also need to manage their relationship with city hall. Yates (1977) has argued that citizens look to the mayor to solve public problems, regardless of his formal powers to institute reform. In Boston and New Haven, mayoral leadership has been essential to strengthening interagency cooperation. Police–social service partnerships were enhanced by good working relationships between innovative police chiefs and the mayor, who in each case marshaled city resources to support police partnerships and facilitate greater interagency collaboration within municipal government. In Springfield and Hartford, the high turnover among mayors and vacillation between support for community policing and law and order policing have hindered reform efforts.

Education and Training

A lack of officer buy-in is a significant barrier to top-down reform (Lipsky, 1980; Sadd & Grinc, 1994). In each case study respondents noted some initial resistance to community policing by front-line officers. The bigger challenge, however, was posed by mid-level management and command staffs. This point is particularly evident when examining the implementation of community policing in Boston and Springfield. In the former, Commissioner Evans had the support of top commanders. In the latter, Chief Meara had to rely primarily on officers and sergeants to carry out community policing. The support of mid- and upper-level officers in Boston is no accident but the result of purposive strategic planning that gave them a voice in the process and a stake in the outcome of reform efforts.

The willingness of officers to work with social service agencies can be facilitated by intentional efforts to transform police culture and make collaboration synonymous with real policing. As O'Keefe (2004, p. 28) explains, "the best way to actually align individual police officer behavior with a broader, more philosophical political vision is through effective education and training of that vision." Training must clearly lay out the roles and responsibilities of police and other agencies. If orders are not explained effectively to officers, they are likely to be negatively received. Even if officers embrace social service partnerships *in theory*, the tasks and skills required for collaboration may make them wary of change. For example, officers must learn to be culturally competent, develop analytic skills for problem identification and analysis, and hone the ability to propose and articulate solutions (O'Keefe, 2004). Academy and ongoing in-service training must help officers develop the new skill sets needed by collaborative problem solving. Training in problem solving, mediation, and leadership can help officers be more accepting of and confident in new approaches to police work (Moore, 1999).

Education and training have been crucial in displacing traditional organizational culture and making room for alternative conceptions of real police work in Boston and New Haven. All officers were trained in community and problem-oriented policing strategies and were expected to interact with residents in new ways. In New Haven, new recruits were trained in a restructured academy, geared toward community and problem-oriented policing. Chief Nicholas Pastore appointed a civilian with a background in radical theater to head the academy. This represented a sharp departure from prevailing departmental norms. In Boston, the police department partnered with the Boston Management Consortium to conduct an intensive training program for all police personnel. In both cases, the curriculum included training by diverse organizations and emphasized the importance of police referrals to community-based resources. In Springfield and Hartford, on the other hand, recruits learned about community policing at their respective academies, but there was little effort to orient officers with a conception of social service collaboration as part of that strategy. Moreover, the bifurcated structure of community service officers and regular officers meant that few police were actually using community policing concepts in their daily work. Hartford's district chief Neil Dryfe explains that police leadership did a poor job communicating to officers their role in social service partnerships. Officers assumed that they would be expected to provide services directly rather than refer citizens to those with more expertise. As a result, many officers resisted proposals to collaborate (personal communication, November 14, 2006).

The turnover of street-level actors can pose problems for program execution and sustainability (Bardach, 1998; Wilson, 1989). Creative and dedicated front-line officers initiated many innovations in Boston. Over the years, those officers have been promoted to higher levels of police leadership and the department has struggled with maintaining the intensity of programs that were grounded in personal relationships (E. Rivers, personal communication, May 6, 2006). Training can provide a good venue for relationship building not only between police and other agency staff, but also between new recruits and seasoned veterans. As Cordner (2005, p. 413) explains, "Young employees need mentoring from managers, supervisors, and/or peers—not just to learn how to do the job right but also to learn what constitutes the right job … to learn about ethics and values and what it means to be a good police officer."

Creating Opportunities and Incentives for Collaboration

Community-oriented police work requires a shift in operational tasks as well as in officers' general orientation toward community partners. Strong leadership and good training can help induce behavioral changes, but they may not ensure officer compliance. Wilson, for example, points to the ability of "street-corner socialization" to undo academy training, as officers are often driven by the situational imperatives of the encounter in the field (1989, p. 37). In order to encourage partnerships, departments need to create buy-in from officers with a more traditional orientation toward policing and to institute rewards for officers engaging in problem solving and social service collaboration. Accountability mechanisms, such as Compstat, have the potential to link officer behavior and promotions, but police must find better ways to measure social service collaboration (E. Flynn, personal communication).* Referrals and other forms of collaboration can also be made routine by incorporating them into officers' paperwork.

Police departments must also provide formal opportunities for networking and the development of social capital. The success of police–social service partnerships relies in large part on informal, personal relationships between front-line officers and street-level social service staff. As discussed earlier, the decentralization of police into neighborhood precincts can help nurture these

---

* As a goal-oriented, strategic management process, the introduction of Compstat in police departments has helped to institutionalize agency priorities, including crime rates and quality of life measures (e.g., citations for public drinking or urination) (Walsh, 2001/2005).

connections. In Boston and New Haven, police have been able to strengthen partnerships through the co-location of police and service staff. Informal connections are essential to maintaining collaboration over time, but require institutionalized mechanisms for police and service providers to get to know one another and work together. Without such a vehicle, turnover or promotion of agency staff will make collaboration more difficult.

Because police and social service providers have distinct missions, particular attention needs to be paid to how collaborations respect organizational boundaries. A number of police and social service providers point to the problem of confidentiality in trying to coordinate agency activities. While HIPAA has complicated information sharing among the police, schools, and other entities in recent years, the barrier is not insurmountable.* Memoranda of understanding (MOU) and other formal agreements between agencies can help partners have a clearer understanding of their roles. Mental health clinicians in the CD-CP program have been given consultant status with the police department so that they may access police reports (this access does not extend to ongoing investigations). Police, on the other hand, are limited by counselor-patient confidentiality. Police have similar boundaries worked out with social workers in the Youth Service Providers Network.

Conclusion

The models provided by Boston's strategy to prevent youth violence and the New Haven Youth Oriented Policing Initiative indicate that police capacity to facilitate community problem solving need not be limited to fixing broken windows. Police also play an important role in social service delivery. Officers can be a source of referral to community resources. They can also effectively coordinate prevention strategies with social service providers, and successfully advocate for the expansion of youth services. As first responders, police engagement in social policy issues can help target resources to those in need of service, and their position in city government can provide police with unique access to the mayor and other municipal resources.

While it is clear that police can be valuable players in social policy coalitions, reformers must pay adequate attention to transforming traditional police culture if collaboration is to expand access to social service provision rather than simply expand the power of law enforcement. As one source in Boston observed, "You need to be cautious when two partners are unequal in resources and in power. There is always a danger that human services will lose their identity" (anonymous). Unless police departments and police

---

* The 1996 Health Insurance Portability and Accountability Act (HIPAA) created national standards to ensure the confidentiality of patients' health care information.

officers truly embrace partnerships as a way to enhance prevention and inter-vention, a number of unintended consequences are likely to follow.

First, police–social service collaboration not only opens up police departments to outside actors, but also extends police surveillance to the activities of partnering agencies and their clients. Part of the rationale is that such partnerships will divert juveniles from the criminal justice system and provide them alternatives to incarceration. Yet ironically, "instead of reduc-ing the number of youth formally processed through the juvenile justice system, [many] prevention and early intervention policies actually subject more youths to formal justice system intervention" (Macallair, 2002). Hector Glynn, executive director of the Connecticut Juvenile Justice Alliance, points out that while there is a presumption that nontraditional policing is better for youth outcomes, New Haven's juvenile arrest rate is higher than that of Hartford (personal communication, October 20, 2006). This finding is par-ticularly troubling for the logic of police–social service partnerships that emphasize prevention and intervention.

Second, although framing police–social service initiatives around crime prevention may help garner more political support, it may also reduce the sustainability of collaboration. Social policy collaboration, when sold as crime prevention, is inherently reactive. Visibility—and therefore attention by police and other stakeholders—will be greatest when crime statistics rise. When they decline, members are likely to reduce their diligence. This was the case in Boston after the city's unprecedented drop in violent crime. While specific programs such as the Youth Services Providers Network have per-sisted, larger city-wide collaboration has waned. Moreover, the link between social service interventions and crime prevention is tenuous. It takes more time for interventions to show results than public officials afford to their decision making. If the benchmark for successful partnerships is measured by reductions in crime, when rates go up, the police or other actors can con-clude that the community-based model is ineffective.

Finally, the collaborations in each of these cases center on issues of youth violence. When partnerships are framed in response to crime prevention, young people are viewed as problems, not as assets to their communities. If ownership for community collaboration was institutionalized outside police departments, it might be easier to facilitate a positive youth develop-ment or a public health approach to youth violence.* For example, the City of New Haven recently created a youth department to better coordinate youth

---

* Youth development focuses on youths' assets and strengths and not just their deficits, through programs and policies that provide young people with opportunities to master a wide range of competencies (Catalano, Berglund, Ryan, Lonczak, & Hawkins, 2004; Pittman, 1991). Public health also focuses on primary prevention, but does so by identi-fying and creating programs to address the behavioral, biological, and community risk factors associated with violence (Dahlberg, 1998; Rosenberg & Fenley, 1991).

services. While the police will continue to play a vital role, they will be just one group of stakeholders setting the youth agenda.

Police, government officials, community-based agencies, and citizens have realized that safe neighborhoods necessitate a shared responsibility for crime prevention. The police–social service partnerships that have grown out of community policing and collaborative problem solving have demonstrated that police are important actors outside of law enforcement; they can also play a critical role in more effective social service delivery and in creating healthier communities. Although best practices can provide models for police reform, it is unlikely that programs can be replicated in their entirety. This is particularly true of community-based partnerships that build on individual relationships. Instead, police and their partners need to map out and draw on the strengths and capacities of local resources.

Acknowledgment

The author thanks the Horowitz Foundation for Social Policy for research support.

References

Bardach, E. (1998). *Getting agencies to work together: The practice and theory of managerial craftsmanship*. Washington, DC: Brookings Institution Press.

Bar-On, A. (1995). They have their job, we have ours: Reassessing the feasibility of police social work cooperation. *Policing and Society, 5*, 35–51.

Bownes, D., & Ingersoll, S. (1997). Mobilizing communities to prevent juvenile crime. *OJJDP Juvenile Justice Bulletin*. Retrieved February 25, 2008, from http://www.ncjrs.org/pdffiles1/165928.pdf

Braga, A.A. (2002). *Problem-oriented policing and crime prevention*. New York: Criminal Justice Press.

Braga, A. A., Kennedy, D. M., Piehl, A. M., & Waring, E. J. (2001). *Reducing gun violence: The Boston gun project's Operation Ceasefire*. Washington, DC: National Institute of Justice.

Braga, A. A., & Winship, C. (2006). Partnership, accountability, and innovation: Clarifying Boston's experience with pulling levers. In D. Weisburd & A.A. Braga (Eds.), *Police innovation: Contrasting perspectives* (pp. 171–187). New York: Cambridge University Press.

Brooks, L. W. (2005). Police discretionary behavior: A study of style. In R. G. Dunham & G. P. Alpert (Eds.), *Critical issues in policing: Contemporary readings* (5th ed., pp. 89–105). Long Grove, IL: Waveland Press.

Capowich, G., & Roehl, J. (1994). Problem-oriented policing: Actions and effectiveness in San Diego. In D. Rosenbaum (Ed.), *The challenge of community policing: Testing the promises* (pp. 127–146). Thousand Oaks, CA: Sage.

Carnegie Council on Adolescent Development. (1995). *Great transitions: Preparing adolescents for a new century*. New York: Carnegie Corporation of New York.

Catalano, R. F., Berglund, M. L., Ryan, J. A. M., Lonczak, H. S., & Hawkins, J. D. (2004). Positive youth development in the United States: Research findings on evaluations of positive youth development programs. *Annals of the American Academy of Political and Social Science, 591,* 98–124.

Chaiken, M. R. (1998). *Kids, cops, and communities.* Washington, DC: National Institute of Justice.

Cordner, G. W. (2005). Community policing: Elements and effects. In R. G. Dunham & G. P. Alpert (Eds.), *Critical issues in policing: Contemporary readings* (5th ed., pp. 451–468). Long Grove, IL: Waveland Press.

Dahlberg, L. (1998). Youth violence in the United States: Major trends, risk factors, and prevention approaches. *American Journal of Preventive Medicine, 14,* 259–272.

Engle, R. S. (2005). How police supervisory styles influence patrol officer behavior. In R. G. Dunham & G. P. Alpert (Eds.), *Critical issues in policing: Contemporary readings* (5th ed., pp. 131–140). Long Grove, IL: Waveland Press.

Fogelson, R. M. (1977). *Big-city police.* Cambridge, MA: Harvard University Press.

Fung, A. (2004). *Empowered participation: Reinventing urban democracy.* Princeton, NJ: Princeton University Press.

Goldstein, H. (1979). Improving policing: A problem-oriented approach. *Crime and Delinquency, 24,* 236–258.

Goldstein, H. (1990). *Problem-oriented policing.* Philadelphia: Temple University Press.

Greene, J. R., Bergman, W. T., & McLaughlin, E. J. (1994). Implementing community policing: Cultural and structural change in police organizations. In D. P. Rosenbaum (Ed.), *The challenge of community policing: Testing the promises* (pp. 92–109). Thousand Oaks, CA: Sage.

Hall, P. (1990). *Governing the economy.* New York: Oxford University Press.

Herbert, S. (2006). *Citizens, cops, and power: Recognizing the limits of community.* Chicago: University of Chicago Press.

Leslie, A. (2007). *YouthBuild USA youthful offender project year 1.* Retrieved September 14, 2007, from http://www.youthbuild.org/atf/cf/%7B22B5F680-2AF9-4ED2-B948-40C4B32E6198%7D/YouthfulOffenderProject1.pdf

Lipsky, M. (1980). *Street-level bureaucracy: Dilemmas of the individual in public services.* New York: Russell Sage Foundation.

Macallair, D. (2002). *Widening the net in juvenile justice and the dangers of prevention and early intervention.* Center on Juvenile and Criminal Justice. Retrieved February 2, 2008, from http://www. cjcj.org/pubs/net/netwid.html

Marans, S., Adnopoz J., Berkman, M., Esserman, D., MacDonald, D., Nagler, S., et al. (1995). *The police-mental health partnership: A community-based response to urban violence.* New Haven, CT: Yale University Press.

Marans, S., & Berkman, M. (1997). *Child development–community policing: Partnership in a climate of violence.* Office of Juvenile Justice and Delinquency Prevention. Retrieved February 18, 2006, from http://www.ncjrs.gov/txtfiles/164380.txt

Mastrofski, S. (1981). Policing the beat: The impact of organizational scale on patrol behavior in urban residential neighborhoods. *Journal of Criminal Justice, 9,* 343–358.

Mastrofski, S. (1994). Community policing: A cautionary tale. In J. R. Greene & S. D. Mastrofski (Eds.), *Community policing: Rhetoric or reality* (pp. 47–67). New York: Praeger.

Monkkonen, E. (1981). *Police in urban America, 1860–1920.* Cambridge: Cambridge University Press.

Moore, M. (1999). Security and community development. In R. Ferguson & W. T. Dickens (Eds.), *Urban problems and community development* (pp. 293–338). Washington, DC: Brookings Institution Press.

Moore, M. H. (1990). *Creating public value.* Cambridge, MA: Harvard University Press.

National League of Cities. (2007). *Beyond city limits: Cross-system collaboration to reengage disconnected youth.* Washington, DC: Author.

Office of Juvenile Justice and Delinquency Prevention (OJJDP). (1999). *Promising strategies to reduce gun violence.* Washington, DC: U.S. Department of Justice. Retrieved July 15, 2006, from http://ojjdp.ncjrs.gov/pubs/gun_violence/profile02.html.

O'Keefe, J. (2004). *Protecting the republic: The education and training of American police officers.* Upper Saddle River, NJ: Pearson.

Patterson, G. T. (2007). The role of police officers in elementary and secondary schools: Implications for police–school social work collaboration. *School Social Work Journal, 31,* 82–99.

Pittman, K. (1991). *Promoting youth development: Strengthening the role of youth serving and community organizations.* Washington, DC: Center for Youth Development and Policy Research, Academy for Educational Development.

Plotkin, M. R., & Narr, T. (1993). *Police response to the homeless: A status report.* Washington, DC: Police Executive Research Forum.

Pruitt, B. (2001). *The Boston strategy: A story of unlikely alliances.* Retrieved August 10, 2005, from http://www.bostonstrategy.com/story.html

Rogers, E. M. (2003). *Diffusion of innovations* (5th ed.). New York: Simon & Schuster.

Rosenberg, M. L., & Fenley, M. A. (1991). *Violence in America: A public health approach.* New York: Oxford University Press.

Roth, J. A., Ryan, J. F., Gaffigan, S. J., Koper, C. S., Moore, M. H., Roehl, J. A., et al. (2000). *National evaluation of the COPS program: Title 1 of the 1994 Crime Act.* U.S. Department of Justice, Office of Justice Programs. Retrieved from http://www.urban.org/pdfs/COPS_fullreport.pdf

Sadd, S., & Grinc, R. (1994). Innovative neighborhood oriented policing: An evaluation of community policing programs in eight cities. In D. P. Rosenbaum (Ed.), *The challenge of community policing: Testing the promises* (pp. 27–52). Thousand Oaks, CA: Sage.

Schulz, D. M. (1995). *From social worker to crime fighter: Women in United States municipal policing.* Westport, CT: Praeger.

Skogan, W. (2006). *Police and community in Chicago: A tale of three cities.* New York: Oxford University Press.

Skogan, W., & Frydl, K. (Eds.). (2004). *Fairness and effectiveness in policing: The evidence.* Washington, DC: National Academies Press.

Skogan, W. G., & Hartnett, S. M. (1997). *Community policing, Chicago style.* New York: Oxford University Press.

Skogan, W. G., Hartnett, S. M., DuBois, J., Comey, J. T., Kaiser, M., & Lovig, J. H. (1999). *On the beat: Police and community problem solving.* Boulder, CO: Westview Press.

Sparrow, M. (1988). *Implementing community policing.* Washington, DC: National Institute of Justice.

Sparrow, M., Moore, M., & Kennedy, D. (1990). *Beyond 911: A new era for policing.* New York: Basic Books.

Steinmo, S., & Thelen, K. (1992). Historical institutionalism in comparative politics. In S. Steinmo, K. Thelen, & F. Longstreth (Eds.), *Structuring politics: Historical institutionalism in comparative analysis.* New York: Cambridge University Press.

Tapper, D., Kleinman, P., & Nakashian, M. (1998). An interagency collaboration strategy for linking schools with social and criminal justice services. In P. Ewalt, E. M. Freemen, & D. L. Poole (Eds.), *Community building: Renewal, well-being and shared responsibility.* Washington, DC: NASW Press.

Thacher, D. (2001). Conflicting values in community policing. *Law & Society Review, 35,* 765–798.

Tyler, T. R. (2001). Trust and law abiding behavior: Building better relationships between the police, the courts, and the minority community. *Boston University Law Review, 81,* 361–406.

Tyler, T. R. (2004). Enhancing police legitimacy. *Annals of the American Academy of Political and Social Science, 593,* 84–99.

U.S. Department of Justice Office of Community-Oriented Policing Services. (2003). *What is community policing?* Retrieved February 27, 2008, from http://www.cops.usdoj.gov/Default.asp?Item=36

Wald, M., & Martinez, T. (2003). *Connected by 25: Improving the life chances of the country's most vulnerable 14–24 year olds.* Retrieved July 26, 2007, from http://www.hewlett.org/Archives/Publications/connectedBy25.htm

Walker, S. (1993). Does anyone remember team policing? Lessons of the team policing experience for community policing. *American Journal of Police, 12,* 33–55.

Walsh, W. (2005). Compstat: An analysis of an emerging police managerial paradigm. Reprinted in R. G. Dunham & G. P. Alpert (Eds.), *Critical issues in policing: Contemporary readings* (5th ed., pp. 201–216). Long Grove, IL: Waveland Press. (Original work published 2001)

Weisel, D. L., & Eck, J. E. (1994). Toward a practical approach to organizational change: Community policing initiatives in six cities. In D. P. Rosenbaum (Ed.), *The challenge of community policing: Testing the promises* (pp. 53–72). Thousand Oaks, CA: Sage.

Wilkinson, D. L., & Rosenbaum, D. R. (1994). The effects of organizational structure on community policing: A comparison of two cities. In D. P. Rosenbaum (Ed.), *The challenge of community policing: Testing the promises* (pp. 110–126). Thousand Oaks, CA: Sage.

Williams, E. J. (2003). Structuring in community policing: Institutionalizing innovative change. *Police Practice and Research, 4,* 119–129.

Wilson, J. Q. (1989). *Bureaucracy: What government agencies do and why they do it.* New York: Basic Books.

Wilson, J. Q., & Kelling, G. L. (1982). Police and neighborhood safety: Broken windows. *Atlantic Monthly, 249,* 29–38.

Winship, C., & Berrien, J. (1999). Boston cops and black churches. *The Public Interest, 136.*

Wycoff, M. A. (1994). The benefits of community policing: Evidence and conjecture. In J. R. Greene & S. D. Mastrofski (Eds.), *Community policing: Rhetoric or reality?* (pp. 103–120). New York: Praeger.

Yates, D. (1977). *The ungovernable city: The politics of urban problems and policy making*. Cambridge, MA: MIT Press.

Zhao, J. (1996). *Why police organizations change: A study of community-oriented policing*. Washington, DC: Police Executive Research Forum.

Embedding Partnership Policing

What We've Learned From the Nexus Policing Project

8

JENNIFER WOOD
DAVID BRADLEY

Contents

In a recent public lecture, Sir Ian Blair (commissioner of the London Metropolitan Police) urged British citizens to engage deeply with the question, "What kind of police do we want?" (2005). This question is more than just an existential one for Blair, who is known for his intellectual engagement in conferences and other public forums. He has his finger on the pulse of developments shaping the field of policing and security that are begging for a renewed vision of what the police do, and what they must stand for. Sir Ian speaks about the "expanding mission" of police who, especially in the wake of September 11, 2001, and the London bombings of 2005, are required to effectively manage every issue ranging from "truancy to terror, from graffiti to gunmen" (Blair, 2005). In all of this, partnerships matter.

In the American context, William Bratton—a former commissioner of the New York Police Department and now chief of the Los Angeles Police Department—similarly speaks of the "ever increasing list of organizational priorities" (2007, p. 24) faced by his and other (especially urban) police agencies across the country. Both Blair and Bratton suggest that now, more than ever, previous emphases on neighborhood and problem-oriented policing achieved through partnerships must not be lost (Blair, 2005; Bratton, 2007). Blair states:

Adapted from Wood, J. and Bradley, D. (2009). Embedding partnership policing: What we've learned from the Nexus Policing Project, *Police Practice and Research*, 9(6), forthcoming.

> What we should seek to avoid, at all costs, is a separation of local, neighbour-
> hood policing from either serious criminal investigation or counter terrorist
> investigation. Every lesson of every police inquiry is that, not only the issues
> that give rise to anti-social behaviour, but also those that give rise to criminal
> activity and to terrorism begin at the most local level. (2005)

The language of "partnerships" and "networks" cuts across discourses of neighborhood/community policing, serious criminal investigations, and counterterrorism, and as such is an uncontroversial language—at least as a policing strategy. The capacity to link knowledge, capabilities, and resources across police organizational units and outward to other state security agencies, the private sector, and various community groupings (defined by space, interests, ethnicity, or other variables) is essential. Networking, or what we also describe as Nexus policing (creating specific forms of connectivity that serve to leverage multiple forms of knowledge and capability), is central to the "intelligence-led" (Ratcliffe, 2008) management of problems ranging from the most trivial to the most damaging.

The importance of partnerships is thus a rather unoriginal proposition, no less in Australia than elsewhere. Notwithstanding, efforts to sustain meaningful and innovative partnerships remain profoundly challenging for police organizations. In the next section, we will outline the vision that Victoria Police, a state police agency in Australia, has for itself. We will then examine our experience with the Nexus Policing Project, an exploratory program designed to create new methods and habits that can assist officers of all ranks in imagining what partnerships could mean, what they could look like, and how they could be institutionalized. We argue that the sustainability of Nexus hinges on organizational commitment to three key dimensions of change: (1) building capabilities across all police ranks, (2) changing culture in tiny increments by nurturing and spreading the creativity of each individual change agent, and (3) restructuring accountability processes to include those that require and reward "plural policing" solutions (Loader, 2000).

Imagining Partnership Policing in Victoria

The challenges facing policing in Australia are no different from those facing police organizations in the United Kingdom, United States, and others dealing with the expanding mission associated with governing security in democratic societies. Like other police leaders from around the world, Chief Commissioner of Victoria Christine Nixon recognizes the increasingly complex and sophisticated set of capacities required of her police agency. In facing this imperative, she (along with many others who have helped shape her thinking) has endeavored to articulate a coherent vision for her organization.

Central to this vision (which is expressed in *The Way Ahead: Strategic Plan 2003–2008*) is an understanding of Victoria Police as a networking agency that possesses the appropriate knowledge and capabilities to resolve problems effectively. As stated in *The Way Ahead*, "Often, the solutions lie within the capacity and capability of other agencies, community groups and individuals to participate in and contribute to crime prevention and community safety strategies. Sometimes, by influencing others' behaviour, the need for police intervention can be avoided altogether" (Victoria Police, 2003, p. 16).

Following a recent review of its structures, procedures, and practices, Victoria Police now emphasizes a principles-based approach, as opposed to a programmatic approach to service delivery. The first principle is: "All members of Victoria Police will deliver our services in a fair, responsive and client-focused manner" (Victoria Police, 2006, p. 58). Being fair and responsive to communities requires a tremendous sensitivity to difference and to diversity in priorities and perspectives. Often such differences are shaped along geographic, demographic, social, and cultural lines.

The second principle is: "Any person who makes a reasonable decision in pursuit of the aims of *The Way Ahead* that is lawful, ethical and within organizational boundaries, will be supported" (Victoria Police, 2006, p. 62). This principle reflects Victoria Police's commitment to nurturing the creative capacity of its membership in pursuit of the value of confident policing.

The third principle is: "The setting of priorities in the delivery of our services will be achieved through appropriate internal and external collaboration, partnerships, and networks, in order to strengthen communities and make them safer" (Victoria Police, 2006, p. 65). This principle reinforces the partnership policing vision of the organization.

The fourth principle is: "We will create an environment in which people are able to use their capabilities and the resources available to them to achieve the objectives of the organisation in the most efficient, effective and fair manner" (Victoria Police, 2006, p. 69). This principle equally stresses the importance of creativity, supported by critical thinking and research, in the tasking and allocation of police resources.

The Nexus Policing Project

Nexus began in late 2003 as a four-year project, jointly coordinated by Victoria Police and the Australian National University (ANU). It received financial support from the Australian Research Council (ARC) through its Linkage Program, a funding stream designed to encourage applied collaborative research between university academics and industry partners. Nexus is 1 of 17 ARC-Linkage projects between Victoria Police and a range of academic partners. For each of these projects, Victoria Police has invested substantial amounts of direct financial contributions as well as in-kind support through human and other organizational resources.

Nexus aims to explore both the conceptual and practical potential of partnerships. By working in several pilot areas and topics—ranging from youth safety to transit safety to the management of sex offenders postrelease—it has sought to both test and challenge current thinking about what partnerships mean and how they might be institutionalized. This applies to police-academic relationships as much as it does to security-producing relationships on the ground. The overall management of Nexus was set up in the beginning as an equal relationship between ANU and Victoria Police in the collaborative process of knowledge generation, application, and diffusion. Through the process of working together (co-coordinating the project), and in the spirit of mutual trust, reciprocity, and engagement, Nexus has tried to break down some of the symbolic and practical barriers that tend to reinforce the insider/outsider dichotomy separating practitioners and researchers. It has sought to do so according to an approach described in the literature as participatory action research (PAR) (for more detail on this, see Wood & Marks, 2007).

Nexus has not been designed to impose yet another one-size-fits-all structure to partnership arrangements. Rather, it has been concerned with fostering a new "thinking process"* and accompanying set of habits on the part of police members to see themselves as part of a broader safety delivery system, and to identify and critique the relationships between themselves and others as security-producing actors in the system. It is a thinking process designed to prompt reflection on the big questions of what police should do (roles) and who they should be. We have operated on the assumption that such questions can only be meaningfully explored in site/topic-specific contexts rather than in general terms.

We knew that over the course of the project we would need to develop, in an experimental fashion, a set of tools to guide and structure this process of nodal analysis—tools to be developed jointly and in an iterative fashion by project coordinators and pilot site-level team members. We were clear that there was a need to have an overall phased structure to the thinking process. At the outset of each Nexus pilot, police members would need to participate in identifying existing nodes and networks of safety delivery. We refer to this process as a mapping of knowledge, capabilities, and resources—an identification of organizations and groupings that contribute to the promotion of safety in the specified area.

We do not refer to maps in the literal sense, but rather to a mental schema or framework that acknowledges diverse safety partners or actors and their relationships to one another in the system. In exploring such

---

* We are grateful to Clifford Shearing for highlighting the importance of "best thinking" as well as "best practice."

relationships—for example, mental health services, correctional services, police, nonprofit organizations, schools, and young people—it is important to develop an understanding of the particular worldviews and perspectives that each organization or group expresses around the problem, or aspects of the problem at hand (e.g., youth safety or recidivism of sexual offenders). Such worldviews and perspectives are informed by special sources of knowledge and experience, what one might refer to as "situated knowledge" (Nygren, 1999), or knowledge that is grounded in groups' particular forms of education, vocation, circumstances, and life experiences. An important principle of Nexus is that formal "professional" forms of knowledge cannot be allowed to trump the views of those who are most affected by the ways in which safety issues are currently addressed in society. To achieve this, it is necessary to draw out understandings and perspectives that otherwise remain implicit or hidden.

Such research involves both formal and informal agencies—usually in the form of in-depth conversations, interviews, and focus groups. While the discourses of professional agency workers can be generally gleaned from formal policies and other texts, conversations with them provide a nuanced account of the struggles they face in striving to meet their organizational objectives. Additionally, research examining the views of people (particularly those belonging to traditionally marginalized groupings) forms an important part of the Nexus research process.

In the project on youth safety, we knew, for example, that mental health agencies approached the issue of youth safety from a health perspective, that the city promoted a broader community development and well-being focus, and that the local police were primarily concerned with safety from a lawbreaking perspective. What was missing in these official stories was any in-depth understanding of what young people (students) in the area felt about the very notion of safety and what their priorities were. Accordingly, two Nexus team members (a postdoctoral fellow from ANU and a youth worker from the city council) conducted focus groups over several months in both a primary and a middle school. What we discovered was that this cohort of students was particularly concerned with what might be more generally understood as issues of human security. While we were not surprised to hear that bullying was a systemic issue for young people, other concerns about issues such as eating disorders, self-mutilation, sexuality and sexual behavior, discrimination, and family violence emerged very clearly and consistently throughout the focus group discussions.

The process of mapping can be a protracted one, leading to new discoveries, similar to those found in the snowballing approach of social science research. In regards to the Nexus transit safety pilot, for example, the team had moved from the traditional set of contacts and networks (such as safety committees) toward radically different thinking about those who deliver the end result of transit passenger safety. During this process they encountered how difficult it can be for some groups to make a contribution, and have taken it upon themselves to try to make it easier for groups to contribute. For example, the volunteer organization Keep Australia Beautiful has adopted a number of railway stations that they work on to make them more visually attractive, and hence more conducive to "capable guardianship" (Cohen & Felson, 1979). However, the team discovered that due to existing legal and contractual arrangements between owners and operators of services on the Melbourne metropolitan transit system, it could take volunteer groups up to seven months to go through the formal authorizing process before being able to start working on a railway station—a very off-putting and high transaction cost for volunteers. The identification of this blockage thus prompted the transit team to explore, and successfully advocate for, a new standardized set of procedures that had reduced that period to only four weeks.

Mapping can be seen as a two-level process, starting with an emphasis on the nature and role of individual safety partners, seeing how partners interface (or not) with one another (nodal assessment), and understanding how these connections might be strengthened. Depending on the specific operational area at issue, the findings of such an analysis can be very different. Illustrative of this were two projects with Victoria Police that, while not falling formally under the Nexus project banner, were strongly inspired by Nexus thinking. These projects involved reviews of existing police approaches to organized crime and road safety, respectively. It was found that the existing police approach to organized crime had excellent internal networks within the police organization, but poor external ones. The opposite turned out to be the case with road policing. Over the past 35 years, Victoria Police has developed an extensive and effective partnership with a range of other sectoral bodies, including, among others, the insurance industry and the Transport Accident Commission. Internally, however, while a central and regional road safety capability had been developed, these nodes had not been effectively linked, and the authority to develop such linkages had not been used. Consequently, policy and practice were ineffectually linked.

The nodal mapping and assessment process then leads to another key thinking phase that involves the design of a new Nexus arrangement that addresses, in whole or in part, the issues identified. For example, through negotiations with project partners involved in the youth safety pilot, it was decided that establishing stronger links between young people and the professional community of agency workers that served them (including, but far from limited to, the police) would be where efforts were devoted. It was also decided that efforts would be invested in mobilizing and further building the capacity of young people to participate more actively in the governance of the problems that affected them the most. The model proposed was a de-centered one. The police were to be seen as one among many resources to be enrolled by young people engaged in their own problem-solving efforts.

The transit passenger safety pilot devoted itself to strengthening and adding to the various ties that bound different nodes involved in the provision of capable guardianship in selected sites of the Melbourne metropolitan transit system. In this pilot, the capable guardianship achieved through environmental planning, aesthetics, lighting, maintenance, and electronic surveillance (CCTV) was seen as equally important to the visible reassurance provided by police and other forms of security patrolling and presence. Not unlike the youth safety example, the resources and capabilities of the police were located (seen to exist) on a horizontal plane, along with other auspices and providers of security. Going through a mapping process, police transit team members came to see capable guardianship from a broader perspective than had been the case in the past.

The Challenges of Embedding Partnership Policing

In this section we comment on what we argue to be the essential conditions that need to exist for Nexus to become a habit of mind and a way of doing business, rather than simply a brief experiment or a mere organizational add-on. We will discuss such conditions around three key headings—capability, culture, and accountability—and suggest that each on its own is insufficient; instead, all three must be interlocked and mutually supporting.

Capability

Change, whether it is in the form of Nexus thinking or some other organization-wide mentality shift, is most effectively achieved when the need for it is acknowledged and embraced. At the level of capacity building, there are at least three approaches to such intellectual and practical ownership that should be considered. To begin with, police recruits need to be educated and trained as reflective practitioners, people willing and able to identify and test the basic assumptions and most profound beliefs upon which their professional lives are based and, if they find these faulty, to initiate making the repairs themselves (Bradley, Nixon, & Marks, 2006). This reflection needs to occur at both the workplace and the "reflective space" of the classroom (Bradley et al., 2006; Wood & Marks, 2007).

In the classroom, trainers should draw strongly upon the tacit knowledge of junior police officers. In pedagogical terms, this requires active teaching that encourages police to spend more time articulating their experiences and, through group exercises and role-plays, to engage in criticism of these and think up improvements and solutions. This approach does not treat the student as ignorant, as in the dark, blind, and needing superior people from outside to guide them into the sunshine (Bradley, 1992). It respects their tacit knowledge and skills, and encourages them to articulate these and then reflect upon progressive moves forward.

This micro-reform approach, however, can only hope to achieve marginal results, trickling police students back into their individual police organizations with perhaps the willingness to advance change, but without possessing either the power or authority to make much of a difference. This is the classic reentry issue confronted by practitioner trainers everywhere.

The reentry problem requires complementing at the macro-level with research-based approaches such as Nexus policing, approaches that provide opportunities to marry big ideas with those in positions of authority and leadership: the organizationally powerful. To that end, Nexus now forms part of a large, well-funded, and long-term applied and collaborative research program (consisting of 17 projects and involving more than 10 universities) that hopefully will open up many new and effective intellectual pathways for Victoria Police.

However, such partnerships present a series of challenges, including a move away from an organizational culture that manages through rules and procedures to one that fosters a culture of creative problem solving by espousing a plural policing view of the world. While it is important for the police to maintain a command and control capability for operational purposes, they must also develop an organizational capability that encourages creativity. This shift to a reflective and creative organization cannot be realized by simply removing the prescriptions that members are so used to. Rather, what is required is a process that embeds the Nexus thinking process into the daily workings of officers.

To this end, the Nexus team is finalizing a package of mapping and related tools that officers can use in approaching new problems from a Nexus perspective. The tools are guides that prompt officers to ask certain questions of the landscape that they are examining. They also provide methods for answering the questions. A key assumption upon which Nexus is based is that officers themselves must learn to function as researchers in their own right. Historically, they have been trained to look for answers to particular questions, especially questions tied to tactical-level issues such as investigations of particular cases. Nexus works to shift investigative capabilities to a strategic problem-oriented level. In this regard, Nexus extends what is already being advanced by supporters of intelligence-led policing (Ratcliffe, 2008). The difference with Nexus is that it more explicitly advocates a nodal or plural perspective of security governance and, as such, looks to different forms of knowledge and capability beyond those traditionally associated with criminal intelligence gathering and analysis.

Culture

Wood and colleagues advance a cautiously optimistic view of the potential for cultural change within police organizations by adopting what they term a "micro-cultural" framework (Wood & Marks, 2007; Wood, Fleming, & Marks, 2008). The optimism stems from what they have seen in Nexus: that cultural change takes place one person at a time. Individual actors are single embodiments of organizational culture, and as such constitute the indispensable units of cultural transformation. Changes in the ways of thinking and acting occur through one person at a time, and then, cumulatively, more can build up in the form of larger "waves" when organizational conditions allow for reflective, innovative actors to direct and shape the mentalities and practices of their peers.

In this macro-reform process, officers of all ranks must be seen as the potential seeds of cultural change. Power structures do matter, of course, and as such, those in key managerial or leadership positions must serve as important "seeds." However, it is operational police officers who deliver police services. To be receptive to change, they must feel valued by their organization and be provided with opportunities to acquire professional satisfaction from their work—to participate in and own change. At the same time, middle managers (who run teams, units, or divisions) constitute vital conduits of culture. They have a capacity to transmit organizational vision to operational police and to provide opportunities for innovation to "bubble up" (Braithwaite, 2006) in small experimental pockets. As well, middle managers are well placed to communicate the nature of effective innovations to others located beside and above themselves within the organizational hierarchy.

This kind of cultural change was evident as Nexus thinking led to a series of incremental but significant impacts upon the ways in which Victoria Police approached its management of serious and organized crime. At the beginning of Nexus, the head of the crime department at the time approached ANU team members to work collaboratively in reviewing Victoria Police's current organized crime strategy. Historically it has been unusual, if not unheard of, for Victoria Police to call upon an external group in this way. The request led to the deployment of an inspector to join the ANU research team in an examination of Victoria Police's approach to organized crime. He worked with ANU researchers on a review of the literature on organized crime, developed discussion papers, and identified an international group of leading researchers and expert practitioners in the field. Victoria Police's conventional approach to organized crime was revealed to be locked in to an outdated conceptual model of the problem. A new draft policy centered on the nodal and networked characteristics of contemporary organized criminal activity was developed and circulated to a range of internal and external experts, and in 2004, a two-day closed conference was held in Melbourne to review, revise, and endorse the new policy.

The new policy ideas shaped by this research helped form the conceptual foundation for a larger review of Victoria Police's organization and management of its response to serious crime. An evidence-based application to the state government led to the funding of a larger review by a consultancy group. What followed was a policy on serious crime that radically reshaped the way the crime department is organized, managed, and held to account, and how it interfaces with the rest of the service. Later, the same inspector who had been tasked with the organized crime analysis subsequently moved to a different domain of policing practice, where he played a key role in undertaking a nodal analysis of road safety practices. This kind of "seeding" must be acknowledged and built upon if Nexus thinking is to be diffused as well as owned across all parts of the organization. This is because characteristically, there is significant turnover or horizontal rotation of police members. This can frustrate the dissemination of new practices and innovations. It must also be recognized that new thinking is difficult to propagate if established accountability and rewards mechanisms discourage reflective behaviors and innovative practices.

Accountability

In the case of Victoria Police, Commissioner Nixon strongly believes that policing can and should make a difference to the communities it serves, and that this difference can be measured (though not completely, perfectly, or always directly) sufficiently for us not to be frightened by attempts at such measures.

Nixon acknowledges that much of what police do has yet to be sufficiently evaluated and tested by robust research and experimentation, and she appreciates that many, if not all, of the outcomes police strive for are caught up by forces, circumstances, and the actions of others over which police may have little control. However, that police work is complex, intertwined, and embedded in the lives and actions of others only means that more thought and invention need to be put into what we do and how we do it with others.

Upon taking office in 2001, Nixon was keen to get her government to think about police success in terms of valuable social outcomes, such as measurable increases in community safety, reductions in numbers of road deaths and serious trauma cases, reductions in residential burglaries, reductions in numbers of cars stolen, increases in people's perception of safety, and increases in people's trust and satisfaction with their police. The government subsequently agreed to change the performance measures and hold Victoria Police accountable for the differences in community well-being it had promised to deliver. What was actually achieved greatly exceeded the official government targets. For example, within five years the overall official crime rate fell by 21.5%. Reported robberies fell by 36.8%. Residential burglaries dropped by 39%. And theft of automobiles, which had had a rate soaring upwards, reaching a peak of 48,000 per annum and nearly 1,000 a week in 2001, fell to 21,000 within five years.

A powerful enabling tool for these kinds of reforms has been the development of a strong internal accounting framework within Victoria Police. An important element of this is COMPSTAT, which Victoria Police adopted and tailored from the version in New York. The Victoria version holds managers accountable not just for results, but for how they achieve these results and, in particular, how they treat and support their officers. To that end, police managers are held accountable for the ways in which they deal with a range of human resource issues and problems, such as work-based accidents, public complaints, and unplanned leave rates. If there is a rise in these or other indices of working conditions, Victoria Police leadership wants to know the magnitude of such rises and the reasons for them. When public complaints spike in a division or area, relevant police managers must offer a thorough explanation considering the reasons for the rise. When spectacular results are achieved, it is important not simply to know how these were achieved, and to offer congratulations, but also to share good practices across the organization. The COMPSTAT process fully recognizes that effective policing outcomes require the police to work with others. Victoria Police measures managerial success in terms of the generation of partnerships and networks and the power of "third-party policing" (Mazerolle & Ransley, 2005).

Victoria's version of COMPSTAT is still developing. As a means of embedding problem-oriented thinking and practice, it is beginning to be applied to emerging problems and themes *across* the organization rather than simply structuring analyses around specific and spatially defined police service areas. Themes have included youth issues, human resource management, and most recently, what could be the beginning of an interesting but worrisome rise in assaults—not just of young males but also against women in public places. This themed approach to COMPSTAT has the potential to advance and embed Nexus thinking by requiring managers to think through what mix of partners and solutions could be deployed to solve problems. It is a tool that will require managers to think nodally.

Outcome-based performance measurement is essential in promoting public value for money and in requiring smarter tasking and allocation practices on the part of police managers. It also places requirements on managers to consider evidence about what works or what could potentially be tried and tested. At the same time, COMPSTAT can be shaped to deepen a police organization's commitment to partnership policing. This is particularly the case when a third-party approach to partnerships is in order; police managers can explore means to enroll external partners in police-defined outcomes. However, it has to be recognized that accountability becomes more difficult to achieve within a de-centered partnership framework, where outcomes outside of those defined by police are being negotiated and prioritized by others. In a de-centered model, where a particular agenda is subject to a protracted process of negotiation, police-defined outcomes may not be accorded more weight than others. In such cases, while police are seen by others as important players and bearers of knowledge and capability, there is a potential for police to disinvest from a process they do not see as serving their own institutional interests. Put simply, some partnerships may not matter to police, or at least matter as much, when they do not fully tie in with police organizational interests. This predicament, of course, is entirely understandable.

The clearest expression of this problem emerged in the context of the youth safety project. A youth problem-solving model had been developed in selected schools in the rural border town mentioned previously. The model has been taken up and successfully applied in another part of Victoria as a result of the kinds of peer-to-peer conversations we identified previously with regards to cultural change. However, with respect to the original youth model devised, although police participation was important, it was not central. The main auspices for this project were the local municipality and schools, whose interests fell more squarely on the human security focus articulated by the schoolchildren. Because the project did not involve working with high-risk youth or youth necessarily involved in criminal behavior, local police found it difficult to see the relevance of school-based problem solving and conflict resolution that resonated with a broader shift in Victorian schools toward restorative justice practices. Without having a direct operational involvement in the pilot and without the project having a direct impact upon operational outcomes, police in the original pilot location found it easy to discount the relevance of the project to them.

Discussions as to the best way to diffuse the learning gained from this particular project and other police-de-centric ones like it continue as we write this chapter. We are currently forging a way ahead with the measurement problem. How do we define whether this project is beneficial if we are not looking at reductions in crime? How, if at all, should Victoria Police actively assist in the diffusion of the model to other state government departments? The answer may well rest with a new multiagency form of COMPSTAT to have been introduced by police initiative in 2008 in Victoria. This will bring together representatives from all of the major government departments with an operational concern for youth safety and crime, including schools, social work, health, and corrections.

We are also now in the process of exploring outcome-level and process-level measures, and associated mechanisms of accountability, which suit both police and their external partners. Our view is that process-level measures matter when it comes to partnerships, notwithstanding the importance of achieving specific outcomes. For instance, a commitment to policing through partnerships firmly expresses a commitment to engaging in new, more meaningful, and more democratic forms of interface with others. As well, a commitment to partnerships is surely a commitment to continuous learning, involving more than the application of previously designed best practice, but also the application of "best thinking" that enables police officers and their partners to exhaust the opportunities for what is thinkable and what is doable. Normatively, partnerships are surely about increasing deliberative processes among those who can make a difference and, most importantly, among those whose knowledge and capabilities have been previously unrecognized or untapped. The language of neighborhood policing, especially dominant in the UK and increasingly deployed in Australia, is normatively concerned with mobilizing *local* knowledge and capacity, not simply furthering a traditional, crime-fighting mission. In sum, if partnership policing in its most radical form is to be promoted, what other types of evaluative measures must be considered, and how can such measures be captured in everyday policing practice? This question is probably the biggest unfinished piece of business for Nexus and its sustainability plan.

In sum, we contend that partnerships matter for organizations like Victoria Police, and that they must be *made* to matter in sustained, organization-wide ways. If projects like Nexus—which seeks to push the conceptual and practical boundaries of partnerships—are to be sustained and organizationally embedded, the issues of capability formation, cultural change, and accountability structures must be aligned and interlocked to reinforce this agenda. Without a thorough and systematic commitment, Nexus, like many other partnership programs before it, is consigned only to having a ripple rather than a wave impact.

Conclusion

While the core roles of the public police may be unchanging, identifying and prioritizing these roles in concrete terms (within a complex and ever-changing environment) and mobilizing organizational capacity in order to achieve these goals constitute a continuous intellectual and moral challenge. Leaders can try to impose new visions upon their organizations by throwing their weight about and making lots of noise. But when the outcomes one wants to achieve are only deliverable through the practices and behaviors of one's people without the possibility to own, shape, and transmit such change, then invariably reform attempts can fail or only partially succeed. That is all too common in the history of police reform (Bradley, 2005). It has been insufficiently understood that all practitioners not only help develop solutions, but that they are essential to their delivery.

Partnerships matter. This is an uncontroversial point. How precisely partnerships should be conceptualized and institutionalized, however, is a considerably complex challenge. Our experience with Nexus is a story about pushing the boundaries of partnership thinking and practice, and it is a story that has raised some fundamental as well as more general issues that confront police reformers both nationally and internationally. Nexus has been devoted to fostering a new thinking process aimed at embedding the principles and practices of partnership building across different operational and geographical units of Victoria Police. In this paper we discussed the challenges we have encountered in implementing and promoting Nexus, and commented on the conditions required to support the Nexus enterprise in the future.

Partnership thinking must be supported by different and complementary levels of capability formation, beginning with police recruits and involving all ranks within the organization and at every point in their respective careers. Central to this capability formation is the creation of various reflective spaces that allow and encourage members to continually test, validate, or challenge the wisdom of previous generations. Furthermore, each police member must be regarded as an agent of cultural change who has the potential to spread new ways of thinking and doing to other parts of the organization. Together, such processes of capability formation and cultural diffusion must be supported by accountability structures that both require and nourish them. Throughout Nexus we have gained insight into how these three key dimensions of change can be pursued. Never before has Victoria Police opened itself up to so much external collaboration and the intellectual critique that comes with it. In this way, it has made more than a symbolic gesture about the necessity of partnerships as a new way of being.

References

Blair, I. (2005). *Dimbleby lecture*. Retrieved December 3, 2007, from http://news.bbc. co.uk/1/hi/uk/4443386.stm

Bradley, D. (1992). Escaping Plato's cave: The possible future of police education. In P. Moir & H. Eijkman (Eds.), *Policing Australia: Old issues, new perspectives* (pp. 132–159). Melbourne: Macmillan.

Bradley, D. (2005). Crime reduction and problem-oriented policing. *Police Practice and Research, 6*, 391–394.

Bradley, D., Nixon, C., & Marks, M. (2006). What works, what doesn't work and what looks promising in police research networks. In J. Fleming & J. Wood (Eds.), *Fighting crime together: The challenges of policing and security networks* (pp. 170–194). Sydney: University of New South Wales Press.

Braithwaite, J. (2006). Peacemaking networks and restorative justice. In J. Fleming & J. Wood (Eds.), *Fighting crime together: The challenges of policing and security networks* (pp. 195–217). Sydney: University of New South Wales Press.

Bratton, W. (2007). The unintended consequences of September 11th. *Policing: A Journal of Policy and Practice, 1*, 21–24.

Cohen, L. E., & Felson, M. (1979). Social change and crime rate trends: A routine activity approach. *American Sociological Review, 44*, 588–608.

Loader, I. (2000). Plural policing and democratic governance. *Social and Legal Studies, 9*, 323–345.

Mazerolle, J., & Ransley, J. (2005). *Third party policing.* Cambridge: Cambridge University Press.

Nygren, A. (1999). Local knowledge in the environment-development discourse: From dichotomies to situated knowledges. *Critique of Anthropology, 19,* 267–288.

Ratcliffe, J. (2008). *Intelligence-led policing.* Cullompton, UK: Willan.

Victoria Police. (2003). *The way ahead: Strategic plan 2003–2008.* Melbourne: Author.

Victoria Police. (2006). *Fit for purpose service delivery model for Victoria Police.* Melbourne: Author.

Wood, J., Fleming, J., & Marks, M. (2008). Building the capacity of police change agents: The Nexus Policing Project. *Policing and Society, 18,* 78–94.

Wood, J., & Marks, M. (2007). Cultural change through Nexus policing. In M. O'Neill, M. Marks, & A.-M. Singh (Eds.), *Police occupational culture: New debates and directions* (pp. 275–292). Amsterdam: Elsevier.

Serious Gun Violence in San Francisco

Developing a Partnership-Based Violence Prevention Strategy

ANTHONY A. BRAGA
DAVID ONEK
TRACEY MEARES

Contents

Beginning in the late 1980s and continuing through the early 1990s, the United States experienced a dramatic increase in firearms violence (Blumstein, 1995). The gun violence epidemic was highly concentrated among young minority males, who were often gang involved and well known to the criminal justice system, residing in disadvantaged inner-city neighborhoods (Braga, 2003; Cook & Laub, 2002). The peak year for gun homicide was 1993, with 17,075 homicides committed with firearms (U.S. Bureau of Justice Statistics, 2007). The increase was followed by a puzzling decrease. By 2000, gun homicide had decreased by almost 41% to 10,113 homicides with firearms and has remained relatively low, with 10,654 gun homicides in 2004 (U.S. Bureau of Justice Statistics, 2007). Criminologists and public policy analysts examined a wide range of factors—innovative policing strategies, a strong economy, higher imprisonment rates, stronger gun control, and stabilizing street-level drug markets—that may have been associated with the drop (Blumstein & Wallman, 2000; Zimring, 2006).

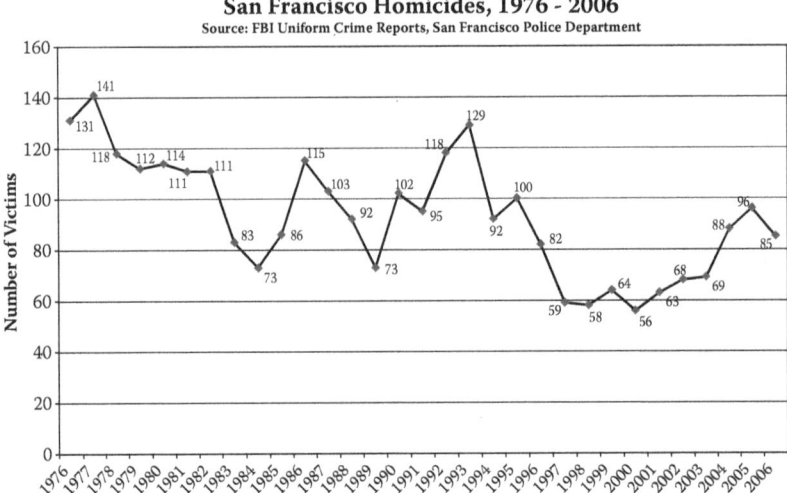

Figure 9.1 San Francisco homicides, 1976–2006. (From FBI Uniform Crime Reports, San Francisco Police Department.)

In 2005, for the first time in five years, the Federal Bureau of Investigation (FBI) reported an increase in the number of gun homicides. Nationwide, gun homicides had increased by 6.5% to 11,346 victims (U.S. Bureau of Justice Statistics, 2007). In media accounts, academics and practitioners have suggested that these recent increases in homicide were linked to a resurgence of urban gang violence and the availability of firearms (Johnson, 2006; Mansnerus, 2006).

Like many cities in the United States, homicide trends in San Francisco can best be characterized by peaks and valleys (Figure 9.1). Between 1977 and 1984, San Francisco homicide decreased from 141 to 73 victims. The next nine years included a peak of 115 victims in 1986 followed by a valley of 73 victims in 1989 and another peak of 129 victims in 1993. Over the course of the 1990s, homicide decreased and the new millennium started with a low of 56 victims in 2000. Unfortunately, since this low point, San Francisco homicide has increased, with 88 victims in 2004, 96 victims in 2005, and 85 victims in 2006. As Figure 9.2 reveals, much of the volatility in San Francisco homicide has been driven by gun deaths. Over the course of the time period 1976–2006, there has been a general, but entirely linear, decrease in the number of nongun homicides per year. The recent homicide increase has been entirely driven by offenders using guns.

A number of jurisdictions have been experimenting with new problem-oriented frameworks to prevent gang and group-involved violence, generally known as the "pulling levers" deterrence-based strategies (Kennedy, 1997, 2006). These new strategic approaches have shown promising results in the

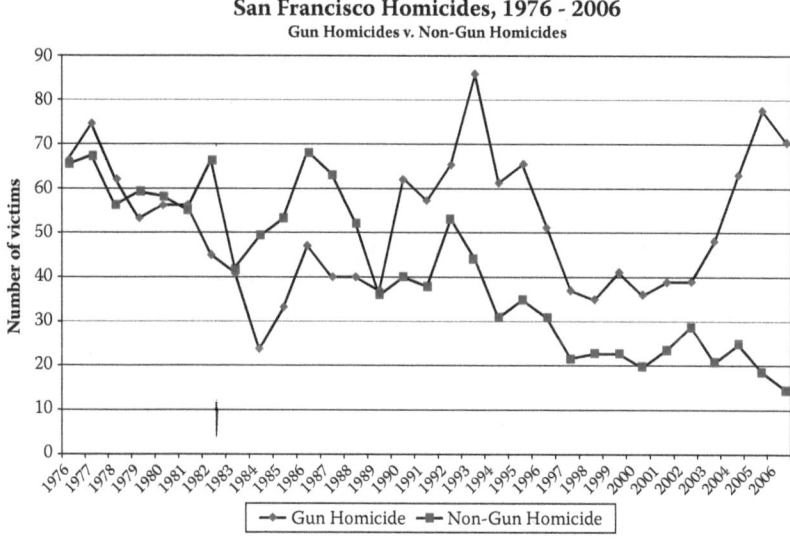

Figure 9.2 San Francisco homicides, 1976–2006. Gun homicides versus non-gun homicides.

reduction of violence (Braga, Kennedy, & Tita, 2002). Pioneered in Boston to reduce serious gang violence, the pulling levers framework has been applied in many American cities through federally sponsored violence prevention programs such as the Strategic Alternatives to Community Safety Initiative and Project Safe Neighborhoods (Dalton, 2002). In order to develop and implement this strategic approach to violence prevention, it is essential to establish a "network of capacity" consisting of dense and productive relationships from which a wide range of partners can be drawn (Braga & Winship, 2006; Moore, 2002). It is also important to customize the approach to local conditions through strategic problem analysis (Braga, 2008a).

In its simplest form, the pulling levers strategy consists of selecting a particular crime problem, such as gun homicide; convening an interagency working group of law enforcement, social service, community-based, and academic partners; conducting research to identify key offenders, groups, and behavior patterns; framing a response to offenders and groups of offenders that uses a varied menu of sanctions (pulling levers) to stop them from continuing their violent behavior; focusing social services and community resources on targeted offenders and groups to match law enforcement prevention efforts; and directly and repeatedly communicating with offenders to make them understand why they are receiving this special attention (Kennedy, 1997, 2006). One jurisdiction, Chicago, added a significant new component to the pulling levers strategy focused on changing offender norms about violence (Papachristos, Meares, & Fagan, 2007).

In this chapter, we closely examine the nature of homicide and nonfatal gun violence in San Francisco during the 2004–2006 time period and describe a pilot violence prevention strategy based on both a deterrence and norm-changing framework. We first describe the results of an analysis of homicides in San Francisco by a team of researchers from the Berkeley Center for Criminal Justice at the University of California, Berkeley. This problem analysis research was designed to unravel the nature of serious gun violence in San Francisco and support the development of a strategic violence prevention initiative by an interagency working group. Our research finds that a majority of San Francisco homicide is driven by ongoing violence committed by a small number of criminally active individuals in a small number of places in the city.

We then consider the available scientific evidence on pulling levers deterrence-based and norm-changing strategies to prevent serious gun violence. Next, we describe the development of a pilot project in San Francisco that seeks to reduce violence committed by a small number of serious offenders in one highly violent area of the city. Our chapter concludes by discussing the importance of interagency collaboration in providing a platform for strategic violence prevention interventions and problem analysis in framing appropriate responses to local violent crime problems.

The Nature of Homicide and Nonfatal Gun Violence in San Francisco, 2004–2006

It is well known that homicide offenders and their victims share essentially the same demographic characteristics (Cook & Laub, 2002; Lauritsen, Sampson, & Laub, 1991; Wolfgang, 1958). This was certainly the case in San Francisco between 2004 and 2006. Homicide victims were mostly male (90.0%, 241 of 268 victims) and largely from minority groups. The racial and ethnic breakdown of homicide victims was 60.8% Black, 15.7% Latino, 13.4% White, 7.1% Asian, and 2.7% other ethnic groups. Arrested homicide offenders were also mostly male (93.9%, 92 of 98 offenders) and largely from minority groups. The racial and ethnic breakdown of homicide offenders was 64.3% Black, 17.3% Latino, 10.2% White, 5.3% Asian, and 2.9% other ethnic groups. Homicide offenders tended to be younger than their victims. The mean age of a homicide offender was 27.6 years, and the mean age of a homicide victim was 31.4 years. A majority of both homicide offenders (69.4%) and homicide victims (60.9%) were ages 30 and under.

San Francisco homicide victims and homicide offenders were also both very well known to the criminal justice system before the homicide event. A large body of research documents the extensive prior criminal justice system involvement of an overwhelming majority of homicide offenders (Kennedy,

Piehl, & Braga, 1996; Kleck & Bordua, 1983; Swersey & Enloe, 1975; Wolfgang, 1958). Before the homicide occurred, 70.7% of homicide victims and 82.9% of homicide offenders had at least one adult arrest on their California Law Enforcement Telecommunications System (CLETS) record. For those individuals who were previously known to the adult criminal justice system, homicide victims had, on average, 11.1 prior arrests and homicide offenders had, on average, 11.0 prior arrests. The prior criminal histories of both homicide victims and homicide offenders were characterized by a wide range of offense types, including armed and unarmed violent offenses, illegal gun possession offenses, property offenses, drug offenses, and disorder offenses. In the gang literature, this wide range of offending is described as "cafeteria-style" offending (Klein, 1995).

Many homicide victims and homicide offenders had also been under some form of criminal justice system control before the homicide occurred. For homicide victims previously known to the justice system, 61.4% had been sentenced to serve time in an adult correctional facility, 57.9% had previously been on probation before they were killed, and 30.7% were under active probation supervision at the time they were killed. For homicide offenders previously known to the justice system, 51.7% had been sentenced to serve time in an adult correctional facility, 48.3% had previously been on probation before they killed, and 29.3% were under active probation supervision at the time they killed. Many homicide victims and homicide offenders were also previously convicted felons; 46.4% of homicide victims and 31.0% of homicide offenders had a prior felony conviction before the homicide event.

Urban homicide problems are often linked to ongoing gang violence. For instance, city-level studies have found gang-related motives in more than one-third of homicides in Chicago (Block & Block, 1993), 50% of the homicides in Los Angeles' Boyle Heights area (Tita, Riley, & Greenwood, 2003), and 70% of homicides in Lowell, Massachusetts (Braga, McDevitt, & Pierce, 2006). To collect data on gang violence, we used the crime incident review method (Braga, 2005; Klofas & Hipple, 2006) and definitions of *gangs* and *gang-related* violence developed in the Boston Operation Ceasefire research (see Kennedy et al., 1996). The research team interviewed San Francisco Police Department (SFPD) homicide inspectors on the circumstances of all homicides between 2004 and 2006—a total of 269 homicides. The review revealed that a large proportion of homicides during this time period was generated by gang-related violence. Almost 49% of homicides (131 of 268) involved gang-related circumstances. The remaining homicides were generated by personal disputes (16.8%), drug-related disputes (9.0%), robberies (7.1%), domestic violence (6.0%), and other circumstances (3.0%). The SFPD inspectors were not able to provide circumstance information on 22 homicide incidents (8.2%).

While a very small proportion of San Francisco youth participate in gangs, they generate a disproportionate share of homicide and gun violence.

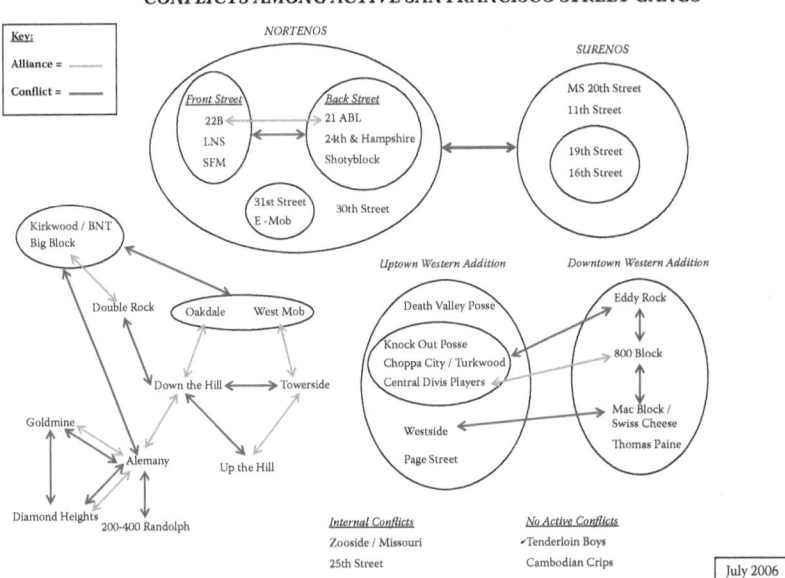

Figure 9.3 Conflict among active San Francisco street gangs.

In 2006, San Francisco had 41 active street gangs with an estimated total membership of between 1,241 and 1,660 youth. According to the 2005 U.S. Census estimate, this represented only 2.6% of 64,680 youth ages 15 to 24 in San Francisco. If the age range for gang members is expanded to include residents ages 15 to 34, only 1% of 198,011 residents of this age group participated in street gangs. In contrast to large and semiorganized gangs in Chicago and Los Angeles, San Francisco gangs were mostly small, informal, and loosely organized groups of youth. San Francisco gangs have, on average, 40 members and range in size from only 5 to nearly 150 members, and 46% have a total membership of 30 or fewer members. Gang membership was usually associated with a specific street, neighborhood, or housing development.

As Figure 9.3 shows, San Francisco gangs have a complex set of antagonisms and alliances. Chronic disputes, or "beefs," among gangs were the primary drivers of gang violence in San Francisco. A majority of San Francisco homicides identified as gang related were not about drugs, money, turf, or other issues in which the violence could be reasonably construed to be instrumental. They were usually personal and vendetta-like. Ongoing feuds often had a long social history and, depending on triggering events such as disrespectful treatment, were highly volatile and cyclical over time. Certain gangs were also much more central to violence than others. For example, two sets of Latino gangs, the Nortenos and Surenos, generated 22 homicides between 2004 and 2006.

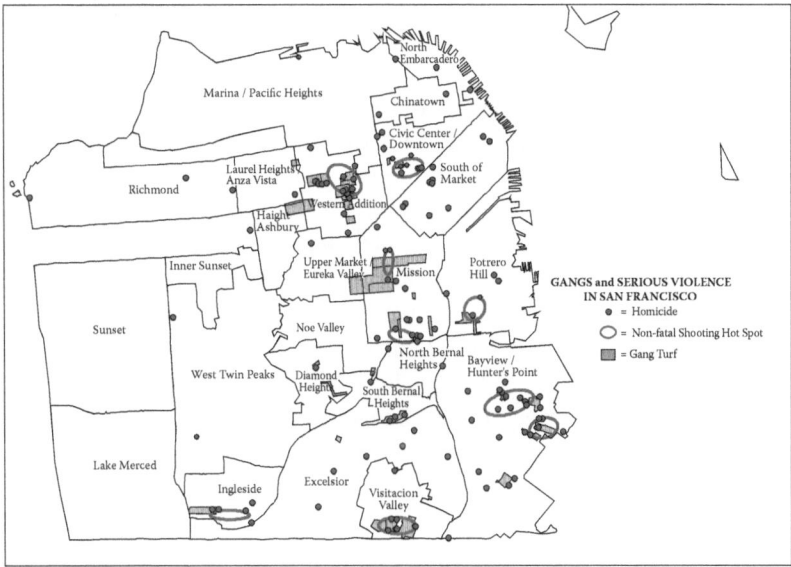

Figure 9.4 Gangs and serious violence in San Francisco.

Firearms are often the weapon of choice for violent gang members (Klein, 1995). Not surprisingly, a majority of homicide victims were killed by gunshot wounds (78.4%) between 2004 and 2006. As Figure 9.4 reveals, most of the homicides and shootings were concentrated in a small number of gun violence hot spots in San Francisco's disadvantaged, predominantly minority neighborhoods in the Mission, Western Addition, Bayview/Hunter's Point, and Visitacion Valley.* Research has consistently demonstrated that a very small number of hot spot locations generate a bulk of urban crime problems (Braga, 2001; Weisburd, 1997; Weisburd, Maher, & Sherman, 1992). In Minneapolis, for instance, 5% of the addresses generated more than 50% of citizen emergency calls for service to the police (Sherman, Gartin, & Buerger, 1989). These gun violence hot spots covered only 1.8% of San Francisco's 47 square miles, but generated nearly 58% of the homicides and nonfatal shootings in 2006. As Figure 9.4 reveals, San Francisco gun violence was generally concentrated in and around gang turf areas.

Evidence on the Violence Prevention Value of Pulling Levers Deterrence and Norm-Changing Strategies

There is a growing body of scientific research evidence that pulling levers deterrence strategies reduce violent crime. A rigorous U.S. Department of

---

* San Francisco gun violence hot spot locations were identified using Spatial and Temporal Analysis of Crime (STAC) tools available in the U.S. Department of Justice's Crimestat III software (http://www.ojp.usdoj.gov/nij/maps/crimestat.htm).

Justice (DOJ)-sponsored evaluation of Boston's Operation Ceasefire strategy used a quasi-experimental design to analyze trends in serious violence between 1991 and 1998. The evaluation reported that the intervention was associated with a 63% decrease in monthly number of Boston youth homicides, a 32% decrease in monthly number of shots-fired calls, a 25% decrease in monthly number of gun assaults, and in one high-risk police district given special attention in the evaluation, a 44% decrease in monthly number of youth gun assault incidents (Braga, Kennedy, Waring, & Piehl, 2001). The timing of the "optimal break" in the time series was in the summer months after Ceasefire was implemented (Piehl, Cooper, Braga, & Kennedy, 2003). The evaluation also suggested that Boston's significant youth homicide reduction associated with Operation Ceasefire was distinct when compared to youth homicide trends in most major U.S. and New England cities (Braga et al., 2001).

Other researchers, however, have observed that some of the decrease in homicide may have occurred without the Ceasefire intervention in place, as violence was decreasing in most major U.S. cities. Fagan's (2002) cursory review of gun homicide in Boston and in other Massachusetts cities suggests a general downward trend in gun violence that existed before Operation Ceasefire was implemented. Levitt (2004) analyzed homicide trends over the course of the 1990s and concluded that the impact of innovative policing strategies on homicide was limited. Using growth-curve analysis to examine predicted homicide trend data for the 95 largest U.S. cities during the 1990s, Rosenfeld, Fornango, and Baumer (2005) found some evidence of a sharper youth homicide drop in Boston than elsewhere, but suggested that the small number of youth homicide incidents precludes strong conclusions about program effectiveness based on their statistical models. In his examination of youth homicide trends in Boston, Ludwig (2005) suggested that Ceasefire was associated with a large drop in youth homicide, but given the complexities of analyzing city-level homicide trend data, there remained some uncertainty about the extent of Ceasefire's effect on youth homicide in Boston.

The National Academies' Committee to Improve Research Information and Data on Firearms concluded that the Ceasefire evaluation was compelling in associating the intervention with the subsequent decline in youth homicide (Wellford, Pepper, & Petrie, 2005). The panel also suggested, however, that many complex factors affect youth homicide trends, and it was difficult to specify the exact relationship between the Ceasefire intervention and subsequent changes in youth offending behaviors. While the DOJ-sponsored evaluation controlled for existing violence trends and certain rival causal factors, such as changes in the youth population, drug markets, and employment in Boston, there could be complex interaction effects among these factors not measured by the evaluation that could account for some meaningful portion of the decrease. The evaluation was not a randomized, controlled experiment. The nonrandomized control group research design cannot rule out these internal threats to the conclusion that Ceasefire was the key factor in the youth homicide decline.

The National Academies' panel also found that the evidence on the effectiveness of the pulling levers-focused deterrence strategy in other settings was quite limited (Wellford et al., 2005). The available evidence on the effects of pulling levers programs in other jurisdictions was scientifically weak. Sudden large decreases in homicide and serious gun violence followed the implementation of pulling levers in Baltimore, Minneapolis, and High Point, North Carolina (Braga et al., 2002; Coleman, Holton, Olson, Robinson, & Stewart, 1999; Kennedy & Braga, 1998). Unfortunately, these assessments did not use control groups and relied upon simple pre-post measurements of trends in homicide and nonfatal serious gun violence. In East Los Angeles, a DOJ-sponsored replication of Operation Ceasefire experienced noteworthy difficulty keeping the social service and community-based partners involved in the interagency collaboration (Tita, Riley, Ridgeway, et al., 2003). The law enforcement components of the intervention were fully implemented and focused on two gangs engaged in ongoing violent conflict. The quasi-experimental evaluation revealed that the focused enforcement resulted in significant short-term reductions in violent crime and gang crime in targeted areas relative to matched comparison areas.

Since the publication of the panel's report, four rigorous evaluations of the effects of pulling levers on gang violence in other jurisdictions have been completed. A quasi-experimental evaluation of the Indianapolis Violence Reduction Partnership found that the pulling levers strategy was associated with a 34% reduction in homicide in Indianapolis (McGarrell, Chermak, Wilson, & Corsaro, 2006). When compared to homicide trends in the nearby cities of Cleveland, Cincinnati, Kansas City, Louisville, and Pittsburgh, the evaluation found that Indianapolis was the only city experiencing a statistically significant decrease in homicide during the study time period. Similar quasi-experimental evaluations of pulling levers interventions targeted on gang violence found a 42% reduction in the monthly number of gun homicides in Stockton, California (Braga, 2008b), and a 43% reduction in assaultive gun violence in Lowell, Massachusetts (Braga, Pierce, McDevitt, Bond, & Cronin, 2008).

In Chicago, a quasi-experimental evaluation of a Project Safe Neighborhoods (PSN) gun violence reduction strategy found significant reductions in homicides in treatment neighborhoods relative to control neighborhoods (Papachristos et al., 2007). Four interventions were analyzed: (1) increased federal prosecutions for convicted felons carrying or using guns, (2) the length of sentences associated with federal prosecutions, (3) supply-side firearm policing activities, and (4) social marketing of deterrence

and social norms messages through justice-style offender notification meetings. The findings suggest that several PSN interventions are associated with
greater declines of homicide in the treatment neighborhoods compared to
the control neighborhoods. The largest effect, however, was associated with
the offender notification meetings that stress individual deterrence, normative change in offender behavior, and increasing views on legitimacy and
procedural justice.

Given its relevance to the San Francisco program, a more in-depth discussion of one aspect of the Chicago strategy is pertinent. Offender notification forums are Chicago PSN's unique intervention, and the one that is most
directly consistent with its goals of changing the normative perceptions of
gun crime by the offending population (Papachristos et al., 2007). The forums
began in January 2003 and are presently held twice a month. Offenders with a
history of gun violence and gang participation who were recently assigned to
parole or probation are requested to attend a forum hosted by the PSN taskforce. The forums are designed to stress to offenders the consequences should
they choose to pick up a gun and the choices they have to make to ensure that
they do not reoffend. These one-hour forums have three segments.

The first segment of the forum contains a strict law enforcement message
(Papachristos et al., 2007). For the first 15 to 20 minutes, representatives from
local, state, and federal law enforcement agencies discuss the PSN enforcement efforts in the target areas. Law enforcement personnel emphasize that
the levels of violence in the target communities warrant a collaborative
enforcement effort by local and federal agencies. In addition to highlighting
gun laws specific to ex-offenders, including minimum sentences, conviction
rates, and so forth, presenters speak candidly of the directed law enforcement
efforts in the area and the likelihood of ex-offenders being either a victim or
perpetrator in other acts of violence. Law enforcement officials also promote
high-profile cases featuring offenders from the neighborhood who many
in the audience may well know and who have been convicted through PSN
enforcement methods.

The second segment of the forum entails a 15-minute discussion with
an ex-offender from the community who works with local intervention programs (Papachristos et al., 2007). The speaker uses personal experience to
describe how he managed to stay out of jail and away from guns. The ex-
offender is usually an older, former gang leader who has turned away from
crime and who now works as a street intervention worker. His message
stresses the seriousness of the current levels of violence in the community,
the problem of intraracial violence, the troubles offenders face when looking
for work, and the seriousness of the PSN enforcement efforts.

The final segment of the forum stresses the choices that offenders can
make in order to avoid reoffending (Papachristos et al., 2007). For the final 30
to 40 minutes, a series of speakers from various agencies in the community

discuss their programs and what offenders need to do to enroll or participate. Programs include substance abuse assistance, temporary shelter, job training, mentorship and union training, education and GED courses, and behavior counseling. Often, several local employers attend and tell offenders the necessary steps to gain employment with their respective firms. Various literature, flyers, and business cards are given to the attendees in order to contact—free of charge—any of the services that were discussed. At the forum's conclusion, all the presenters talk and interact with the attendees, often staying late into the night in discussion or counseling.

This discussion of Chicago's strategy also implicates how to think about the mechanisms at work behind these strategies. While Boston's Ceasefire and similar strategies emphasized the deterrence aspect of these types of interventions, another theoretical construct is relevant here. Deterrence theories assume that individuals comply with the law because they fear the consequences of failing to do so. By contrast, norm-based theories grounded in social psychology of compliance connect voluntary compliance with the law to the fact that individuals believe the law is just or because they believe that the authority enforcing the law has the right to do so (Tyler, 1990). Their belief in the fairness of legal norms and procedures—and the underlying moral bases of law—creates a sense of obligation to cooperate with legal actors and comply with legal norms. These factors are considered normative because individuals respond to them differently from the way they respond to rewards and punishments. In contrast to the individual who complies with the law because he or she is responding to externally imposed punishments, the individual who complies for normative reasons does so because he or she feels an internal obligation. It is "the suggest[ion] that citizens will voluntarily act against their self-interest [that] is the key to the social value of normative influences" (Tyler, 1990, p. 24).

The architecture of the offender notification meetings makes these theories relevant. Although deterrence theory emphasizes the fact that the law enforcement message is conveyed to recently paroled gun offenders, norm-based theories of compliance emphasize both the content of the message conveyed to attendees in its entirety (the law enforcement message, the ex-offender transition, and the community organization message) and the context in which the message is conveyed.

In terms of context, the forums are held in a neutral and pleasant location, typically a public building in a local park. In fact, PSN taskforce members specifically rejected law enforcement facilities as a setting for the forums. Additionally, the room in which the forum takes place is set up in an egalitarian roundtable style. Chairs are set up in a square, and there is no podium for speakers, so that all participants are set on a level plane. In terms of the content of the message, all three components matter to the procedural justice account. If only deterrence were important, then the subsequent messages would be irrelevant. Yet, the Chicago PSN taskforce members believed—a belief consistent with theory— that each message component is necessary to emphasize the agency of the individuals in question who are capable of choosing appropriate paths in life.

These features of the forums find resonance in psychologist Tom Tyler's work, which develops a process-based model of regulation (Tyler, 2003). The process-based model of regulation argues that whether people comply with the law as a general matter or in specific instances—say, in particular encounters with law enforcement officials—is powerfully determined by people's subjective judgments about the fairness of the procedures through which the police and the courts exercise their authority. This model of compliance is explicitly psychological. That is, while it is true that people can be compelled to obey laws and rules through the use of threats by government authorities, it is also true that government authorities can gain the cooperation of the people with whom they deal through buy-in (Tyler, 2003, p. 286). Importantly, threats do not usually lead to buy-in. What does? Treating people with respect and dignity.

Developing and Piloting a Partnership-Based Violence Prevention Strategy in San Francisco

San Francisco officials built on the lessons of these previous efforts in crafting a new violence prevention strategy for the city. The norm-based messaging approach used in the Chicago offender forums was particularly influential in San Francisco's planning efforts. The development of the strategic violence prevention pilot project was framed as a "learning while doing" exercise (Kennedy & Moore, 1995) to determine whether a pulling levers/norm-based messaging approach was feasible in San Francisco.

San Francisco officials began their planning by reviewing the homicide and nonfatal gun violence analysis, which showed that homicides and nonfatal gun violence in San Francisco are highly clustered in a small number of places and among a small number of criminally active individuals. Based on this analysis, San Francisco leaders developed an approach to target this small number of high-risk individuals in specific high-risk neighborhoods. San Francisco chose to focus first on the Western Addition neighborhood, which the data showed was one of the major hot spots for street violence in the city.

Under the leadership of the Mayor's Office of Criminal Justice, with the strong support of the Berkeley Center for Criminal Justice, San Francisco developed a partnership among city and community agencies to implement this new approach in the Western Addition. Agencies that were involved in the initial partnership included the San Francisco Police

Department, San Francisco District Attorney's Office, San Francisco Probation Department, San Francisco Department of Children, Youth and Their Families, San Francisco Department of Public Health, California Department of Corrections and Rehabilitation–Parole, Western Addition Community Response Network, Westside Community Services, and St. Andrew Missionary Baptist Church.

The Mayor's Office of Criminal Justice and the Berkeley Center for Criminal Justice began meeting in January 2007 to lay the groundwork for a working group that included all of these partners. The working group was formed in March 2007 and began meeting weekly. The initial meetings were sometimes contentious, as agencies unaccustomed to partnering together worked through past issues and began to build trust. The agencies were able to do this by focusing on their common goal: stopping street violence.

A central component of the San Francisco strategy was a call-in session of probationers residing in the Western Addition who were deemed to be at risk of being the victims or perpetrators of violence. The call-in concept was greatly informed by the Chicago offender forums. On June 12, 2007, two call-in sessions were held with a total of 40 participants. The sessions were held in city hall, in the mayor's conference room. Chairs were arranged in a circle in the middle of the room, and both participants and presenters sat in the same circle. Food and refreshments were provided.

The call-in began with opening remarks by a mayor's office representative, followed by brief presentations from law enforcement representatives, then longer presentations from community representatives. The law enforcement presentations were about 2 minutes each; the community presentations ranged from 5 to 20 minutes each. Thus, the vast majority of the call-in involved community members speaking to the participants. The law enforcement agencies' presentations were made by the police department, district attorney's office, and adult probation department; the community presentations were made by a leading Western Addition service provider, a Western Addition faith-based leader, a former gang member, and a Western Addition community leader.

The essential message of the call-in, as written in the call-in script, was as follows:

> Each agency should start its presentation with a variation of the following: "We're here today because we care about you, we care about this community, and we are concerned about the safety of you and your loved ones. All of the agencies here are on the same page: The violence must stop. We know we may not have reached out to you in the past the way we should have, but we're reaching out now, all together, to do everything we can to help you and to help stop the violence."

The introductory remarks by the mayor's office were scripted as follows:

> All the community and law enforcement representatives here today are on the same page: We do not want you to get hurt or to hurt others. The violence must stop. We sincerely hope all of you will refrain from violence and take advantage of the services you will be offered today. Law enforcement is in full support of the community partners providing you with these services. But if you choose to continue the violence, the community is in full support of having law enforcement take you off the streets for your own safety and the safety of others.

The script called for similar messages from the law enforcement and community partners who presented.

Several key service providers were also present, sitting in chairs along the wall outside of the inner circle of chairs. These included employment services, child support services, substance abuse services, and mental health services. The service providers were introduced during the call-in session, and participants had the opportunity to connect directly with the service providers after the session ended; many participants took advantage of this opportunity rather than leaving directly after the call-in.

In Chicago, while forum attendees are offered services and can connect with service providers at the forum, there is no formal follow-up of any kind. The Chicago offender forum in and of itself was found to positively impact the reduction of gun violence. San Francisco, by contrast, organically devised a unique service follow-up component to the Western Addition call-ins. The call-in participants were all placed on the same caseload of one geographically-focused probation officer. In the days following the call-in, each of the participants had an appointment to meet with the Western Addition probation officer to follow up on the offers for services at the call-in. The Western Addition probation officer then worked collaboratively with the Western Addition Community Response Network, a community-based organization providing street outreach and case management services, to provide co-case management of participants.

The Western Addition experience served as an important proof of concept exercise that generated considerable interest among a wide range of social service, community-based, and law enforcement agencies that a pulling levers/norm-changing violence prevention strategy may be a viable approach in San Francisco. Using strategic analyses of data and the experiences from other jurisdictions, the City of San Francisco successfully assembled an interagency working group to deliver a strategic intervention to a small group of persistent offenders in one neighborhood suffering from high levels of gun violence. The lessons learned from the Western Addition pilot project will be used to refine the approach in the hope of developing a robust and testable intervention. The Berkeley Center for Criminal Justice is currently collaborating with the interagency working group to explore the possibility of implementing an adjusted version of the strategy with a rigorous evaluation in another San Francisco neighborhood.

Discussion

The research presented suggests there is much potential value in adopting the general strategic violence prevention framework and process developed in Boston and adapted in Chicago and other U.S. cities. It is important to note that these jurisdictions engaged the process of developing an appropriate response to their own gun violence problem rather than simply importing broad-based programs or tactics that may or may not fit their local conditions. The experience of San Francisco and the efforts in other cities reviewed in this chapter offer at least two key operational insights for other jurisdictions interested in developing pulling levers deterrence and norm-changing responses to highly complex gun violence problems: the importance of problem analysis research in crafting appropriate violence prevention responses and the need to create an effective network of capacity to prevent violence.

Many academics and practitioners have described the considerable value added to the development of crime prevention strategies by in-depth problem analysis (Clarke & Eck, 2005; Eck & Spelman, 1987; Goldstein, 1990). For complex problems such as gang violence, a deep understanding of the nature of the problem is crucial in framing appropriate responses (Braga et al., 2006; Decker, 2002). The San Francisco problem analysis research revealed that homicide and gun violence in the city were highly concentrated in a small number of places and among a small number of criminally active individuals. Considering this detailed description of local gun violence dynamics, an interagency working group decided that the Chicago PSN strategy broadly fit the nature of serious gun violence in the Western Addition, and then appropriately tailored the approach to the operational capacities of law enforcement organizations, social service agencies, and community-based groups in San Francisco.

Clearly, practitioner-academic partnerships add much value to the understanding of crime problems and the development of appropriate responses. While such partnerships are becoming more commonplace (see, e.g., McEwen, 2003), the challenge remains to encourage these collaborations through the education of practitioners and researchers in the principles and methods of problem analysis and the benefits of working together.

The development of the Western Addition pilot project was an exercise in building much needed violence prevention capacity in one city. In order for the City of San Francisco to develop an innovative gun violence prevention strategy involving a variety of partners, it was essential to begin to establish a network of capacity consisting of productive relationships from which partners could be drawn (Braga & Winship, 2006; Moore, 2002). Through the process of crafting a multidimensional response to gun violence in the Western Addition, the participating agencies greatly increased the network of capacity. The resulting network was well positioned to launch an innovative response to gun violence because criminal justice agencies, community groups, and social service agencies could coordinate and combine their efforts in ways that could magnify their separate effects.

Effective collaborations and the trust and accountability that they entail are essential in launching a meaningful response to complex gun violence problems (Braga & Winship, 2006). Without the establishment of an effective network, the Western Addition pilot project would not have been launched. However, the fact that such collaborations are needed does not guarantee that they inevitably rise or, once developed, are sustained. There are many significant obstacles to their development and maintenance, such as giving up control over scarce resources that could compromise agencies' traditional missions, aligning agencies' individual work efforts into a functional enterprise, and developing a collective leadership among a group of individuals aligned with the needs of their individual organizations (Bardach, 1998). A considerable amount of effort by the Mayor's Office of Criminal Justice, Berkeley Center for Criminal Justice, and partnering agencies was necessary to create and sustain the collaborative network. Important activities included identifying key players from relevant organizations, educating participants on the process and best practices from other jurisdictions, and facilitating ongoing meetings to seek input on strategy development and share information on implementation progress. While developing and sustaining a collaborative network of capacity can be very difficult work, it is certainly a worthwhile venture.

Acknowledgments

This research was supported by funds from the Evelyn and Walter Haas, Jr. Fund. The authors thank Jessica Hazard al-Tawqi, Sgt. Mikail Ali, Lenore Anderson, Sandra Bolden, Abner Boles, Rev. Ishmael Burch, Capt. Kevin Cashman, Rachel Diggs, Capt. Kevin Dillon, Capt. John Ehrlich, Art Faro, Steve Fitzpatrick, Chief Heather Fong, Russ Giuntini, Peter Grabosky, Kevin Grant, Marc Guillory, Tinisch Hollins, Ronda Jackson, Sarah Lawrence, Troy Lopez, Joe Marshall, Charlie Morimoto, Lt. John Murphy, Allen Nance, Mayor Gavin Newsom, Kyle Pedersen, Will Robinson, Ranon Ross, Maria Su, John Torres, Stewart Wakeling, Jessie Warner, Jeanne Woodford,

Chuck Weisselberg, and participants in the "Community Policing in Three Dimensions" conference at the Australian National University in December 2007. Points of view in this document are those of the authors and do not necessarily represent the official position of the Haas, Jr. Fund, City of San Francisco, San Francisco Police Department, or any of the collaborative partners.

References

Bardach, E. (1998). *Getting agencies to work together.* Washington, DC: Brookings Institution Press.

Block, C., & Block, R. (1993). *Street gang crime in Chicago* (Research in brief). Washington, DC: National Institute of Justice, U.S. Department of Justice.

Blumstein, A. (1995). Youth violence, guns, and the illicit drug industry. *Journal of Criminal Law and Criminology, 86,* 10–36.

Blumstein, A., & Wallman, J. (Eds.) (2000). *The crime drop in America.* New York: Cambridge University Press.

Braga, A. (2001). The effects of hot spots policing on crime. *Annals of the American Academy of Political and Social Science, 578,* 104–125.

Braga, A. (2003). Serious youth gun offenders and the epidemic of youth violence in Boston. *Journal of Quantitative Criminology, 19,* 33–54.

Braga, A. (2005). Analyzing homicide problems: Practical approaches to developing a policy-relevant description of serious urban violence. *Security Journal, 18,* 17–32.

Braga, A. (2008a). *Problem-oriented policing and crime prevention* (2nd ed.). Monsey, NY: Criminal Justice Press.

Braga, A. (2008b). Pulling levers focused deterrence strategies and the prevention of gun homicide. *Journal of Criminal Justice, 36,* 332–343.

Braga, A., Kennedy, D., & Tita, G. (2002). New approaches to the strategic prevention of gang and group-involved violence. In C. R. Huff (Ed.), *Gangs in America* (3rd ed., pp. 271–286). Thousand Oaks, CA: Sage.

Braga, A., Kennedy, D., Waring, E., & Piehl, A. (2001). Problem-oriented policing, deterrence, and youth violence: An evaluation of Boston's Operation Ceasefire. *Journal of Research in Crime and Delinquency, 38,* 195–225.

Braga, A., McDevitt, J., & Pierce, G. (2006). Understanding and preventing gang violence: Problem analysis and response development in Lowell, Massachusetts. *Police Quarterly, 9,* 20–46.

Braga, A., Pierce, G., McDevitt, J., Bond, B., & Cronin, S. (2008). The strategic prevention of gun violence among gang-involved offenders. *Justice Quarterly, 25,* 132–162.

Braga, A., & Winship, C. (2006). Partnership, accountability, and innovation: Clarifying Boston's experience with pulling levers. In D. Weisburd & A. Braga (Eds.), *Police innovation: Contrasting perspectives* (pp. 171–190). New York: Cambridge University Press.

Clarke, R., & Eck, J. (2005). *Crime analysis for problem solvers in 60 small steps.* Washington, DC: Office of Community Oriented Policing Services, U.S. Department of Justice.

Coleman, V., Holton, W., Olson, K., Robinson, S., & Stewart, J. (1999, October). Using knowledge and teamwork to reduce crime. *National Institute of Justice Journal,* 16–23.

Cook, P., & Laub, J. (2002). After the epidemic: Recent trends in youth violence in the United States. In M. Tonry (Ed.), *Crime and justice: A review of research* (Vol. 29, pp. 1–37). Chicago: University of Chicago Press.

Dalton, E. (2002). Targeted crime reduction efforts in ten communities: Lessons for the Project Safe Neighborhoods initiative. *U.S. Attorney's Bulletin, 50,* 16–25.

Decker, S. (2002). A decade of gang research: Findings of the National Institute of Justice gang portfolio. In W. Reed & S. Decker (Ed.), *Responding to gangs: Research and evaluation* (pp. 3–24). Washington, DC: National Institute of Justice, U.S. Department of Justice.

Eck, J., & Spelman, W. (1987). *Problem-solving: Problem-oriented policing in Newport News.* Washington, DC: National Institute of Justice, U.S. Department of Justice.

Fagan, J. (2002). Policing guns and youth violence. *The Future of Children, 12,* 133–151.

Goldstein, H. (1990). *Problem-oriented policing.* Philadelphia: Temple University Press.

Johnson, K. (2006, June 13). FBI reports increase in violent crimes in 2005. *USA Today,* p. 4A.

Kennedy, D. (1997). Pulling levers: Chronic offenders, high-crime settings, and a theory of prevention. *Valparaiso University Law Review, 31,* 449–484.

Kennedy, D. (2006). Old wine in new bottles: Policing and the lessons of pulling levers. In D. Weisburd & A. Braga (Eds.), *Police innovation: Contrasting perspectives* (pp. 155–170). New York: Cambridge University Press.

Kennedy, D., & Braga, A. (1998). Homicide in Minneapolis: Research for problem solving. *Homicide Studies, 2,* 263–290.

Kennedy, D., & Moore, M. (1995). Underwriting the risky investment in community policing: What social science should be doing to evaluate community policing. *Justice System Journal, 17,* 271–290.

Kennedy, D., Piehl, A., & Braga, A. (1996). Youth violence in Boston: Gun markets, serious youth offenders, and a use-reduction strategy. *Law and Contemporary Problems, 59,* 147–196.

Kleck, G., & Bordua, D. (1983). The factual foundation for certain key assumptions of gun control. *Law & Policy Quarterly, 5,* 271–298.

Klein, M. (1995). *The American street gang.* New York: Oxford University Press.

Klofas, J., & Hipple, N. (2006). *Crime incident reviews* (Project Safe Neighborhoods strategic interventions case study 3). Washington, DC: U.S. Department of Justice.

Lauritsen, J., Sampson, R., & Laub, J. (1991). The link between offending and victimization among adolescents. *Criminology, 29,* 265–291.

Levitt, S. (2004). Understanding why crime fell in the 1990s: Four factors that explain the decline and six that do not. *Journal of Economic Perspectives, 18,* 163–190.

Ludwig, J. (2005). Better gun enforcement, less crime. *Criminology and Public Policy, 4,* 677–716.

Mansnerus, L. (2006, June 15). Small cities in region grow more violent, data show. *New York Times,* p. 1.

McEwen, T. (2003). *Evaluation of locally initiated research partnership program* (NCJ 204022). Washington, DC: U.S. Department of Justice, National Institute of Justice.

McGarrell, E. F., Chermak, S., Wilson, J., & Corsaro, N. (2006). Reducing homicide through a "lever-pulling" strategy. *Justice Quarterly, 23*, 214–229.

Moore, M. (2002). Creating networks of capacity: The challenge of managing society's response to youth violence. In G. Katzmann (Ed.), *Securing our children's future: New approaches to juvenile justice and youth violence* (pp. 338–385). Washington, DC: Brookings Institution Press.

Papachristos, A., Meares, T., & Fagan, J. (2007). Attention felons: Evaluating Project Safe Neighborhoods in Chicago. *Journal of Empirical Legal Studies, 4*, 223–272.

Piehl, A., Cooper, S., Braga, A., & Kennedy, D. (2003). Testing for structural breaks in the evaluation of programs. *Review of Economics and Statistics, 85*, 550–558.

Rosenfeld, R., Fornango, R., & Baumer, E. (2005). Did Ceasefire, Compstat, and Exile reduce homicide? *Criminology and Public Policy, 4*, 419–450.

Sherman, L., Gartin, P., & Buerger, M. (1989). Hot spots of predatory crime: Routine activities and the criminology of place. *Criminology, 27*, 27-56.

Swersey, A., & Enloe, E. (1975). *Homicide in Harlem.* New York: Rand.

Tita, G., Riley, K. J., & Greenwood, P. (2003). From Boston to Boyle Heights: The process and prospects of a "pulling levers" strategy in a Los Angeles barrio. In S. Decker (Ed.), *Policing gangs and youth violence* (pp. 102–130). Belmont, CA: Wadsworth.

Tita, G., Riley, K. J., Ridgeway, G., Grammich, C., Abrahamse, A., & Greenwood, P. (2003). *Reducing gun violence: Results from an intervention in East Los Angeles.* Santa Monica, CA: RAND Corporation.

Tyler, T. (1990). *Why people obey the law: Procedural justice, legitimacy, and compliance.* New Haven, CT: Yale University Press.

Tyler, T. (2003). Procedural justice, legitimacy, and the effective rule of law. In M. Tonry (Ed.), *Crime and justice: A review of research* (Vol. 30, pp. 283–358). Chicago: University of Chicago Press.

U.S. Bureau of Justice Statistics. (2007). *Homicide trends in the United States.* Retrieved October 21, 2007, from http://www.ojp.usdoj.gov/bjs/homicide/tables/weapon-stab.htm

Weisburd, D. (1997). *Reorienting crime prevention research and policy: From the causes of criminality to the context of crime* (NCJ 165041). Washington, DC: U.S. Department of Justice, National Institute of Justice.

Weisburd, D., Maher, L., & Sherman, L. (1992). Contrasting crime general and crime specific theory: The case of hot spots of crime. In *Advances in criminological theory* (Vol. 4, pp. 45–70). New Brunswick, NJ: Transaction Press.

Wellford, C., Pepper, J., & Petrie, C. (Eds.). (2005). *Firearms and violence: A critical review.* Committee to Improve Research Information and Data on Firearms. Committee on Law and Justice, Division of Behavioral and Social Sciences and Education. Washington, DC: National Academies Press.

Wolfgang, M. (1958). *Patterns in criminal homicide.* Philadelphia: University of Pennsylvania Press.

Zimring, F. (2006). *The great American crime decline.* New York: Oxford University Press.

A Thin or Thick Blue Line? Exploring Alternative Models for Community Policing and the Police Role in South Africa[1]

10

MONIQUE MARKS
CLIFFORD SHEARING
JENNIFER WOOD

Contents

In his most recent book, Jonny Steinberg (2008) makes the point that communities in South Africa still shy away from being policed by the public police. This, he believes, is due to the fact that the police continue to lack legitimacy and demonstrate a poor record in crime combat and order maintenance. Through a detailed ethnography, he documents the daily interactions that the police have with local community members. What he demonstrates is that police are "always bluffing," (2008, p. 35) that they are effective in creating order, enforcing law, and solving crime. But communities, he says, "refrain from calling the bluff" (p. 36).

What is played out in the interface between police and communities is referred to by Steinberg as a script. This script, he says, is written by the audience (communities) rather than the playwrights (the police). When the police don't play the right lines, they are thrown off the stage and the audience (community members) become the actors. As Steinberg and others have shown, across South Africa, communities (both rich and poor) have come together to protect themselves from threats to their security. Their defense is neighborly cohesion, sometimes expressed as ethnic solidarity and sometimes based on ties that are political or traditional. What we see in Steinberg's book

Based on Marks, M., Shearing, C., and Wood, J. (2008). Who should the police be? Finding a new narrative for community policing in South Africa. *Police Practice and Research*, http://dx.doi.org/10.1080/15614260802264560

is that community initiatives have led to real reductions in the levels of crime in areas where there is social efficacy (Adams & Serpe, 2000). In the face of this, the police do not retreat from the center stage or try to find new roles for themselves. Instead, unsurprisingly, they continue to try to assert their authoritative position. They don't want to be made fools of, nor do they want to be seen as having failed as building the community policing project.

In Steinberg's view, the police have a poor act to follow (doomed by their own history and unabated rising crime levels). However, both they and those they serve know the officers in blue uniforms are important players in the safety game. But what roles should the police, communities, and other security actors play in the theatre of policing? Why do the police hold on to being the lead actors in every scene when there are clearly other actors who are willing and able to enter the stage and, indeed, have been welcomed there by the rhetoric of community policing? These questions are very real for South Africa, and indeed are fundamental to policing configurations the world over.

Since at least the inception of the community policing movement, public police organizations around the world have been on a quest to rethink their roles and, in particular, their relationships with non-state groupings. Reimagining policing, however, has been a very difficult task given that the public police cling tenaciously to identities and roles that often operate in tension. On the one hand, they desire to maintain what they view as their established monopoly of the policing enterprise, while at the same time, often in very instrumental ways, they use the language of partnerships and problem solving to devolve responsibility for sticky and thorny security problems to civic and private groupings.

The tensions and ambiguities that the public police feel about their current place in the world of policing are evident in a broad narrative they express through their policy statements, media presentations, and public commitments. We examine this narrative in this chapter, focusing particularly on the South African case where the discourse of community policing has been strongly articulated in recent years. We hope to situate this narrative, including its changed meanings and enactments, within what we see as the real world of policing. We then try to locate a place for the police that has instrumental appeal in terms of current policing configurations and that resonates with police as key actors in creating safety and preserving order. While we place the public police at the center of our analysis, we relate our discussion to the South African context, where the state itself is best described as emergent, fragile, and developmental.

In this chapter, we explore the contradiction between a police dream of realizing a monopoly over policing and the erosion of this monopoly through the (re)emergence or perhaps (re)assertion of other entities engaged in policing. We suggest that the dream of a monopoly of policing by police is no longer a viable one, and that police and public authorities should begin to look for another source of inspiration. We hope to provide a new imagining of community policing, one that moves beyond a conception of the police as all things to all people, an agency that will do almost anything to (re)gain legitimacy and to be at the center of all governance problems (see, for example, Skogan, 2007). In a sense, what we are doing is joining forces with the police in their questioning of their own role and the place of other security actors in a world of polycentric, nodal security governance.

In developing this argument, we advance a rather minimalist conception of the police, one that centers on both clarifying and bolstering their unique authority and capacities. We contend that within a nodal policing framework, this minimalist conception opens up a vista of opportunities for recognizing, linking with, and harnessing the unique forms of knowledge and capabilities that other nodes can bring to bear in the governance of security.

The Established Police Narrative in Post-Apartheid South Africa

In both established and transitional societies, the organizational field of policing is now characterized by a range of nodes or institutional actors with variable structures, legal status, resources, mentalities, and technologies (Dupont, 2006, p. 86). It is now broadly accepted by government actors (including the police) that the demand for security exceeds the capacity of the government to provide it (Wood, 2006a). This acceptance may be reluctant, but there is a basic appreciation that a more nodal or networked approach to governing security provides potential for greater effectiveness and a broader reach in service delivery (Rhodes, 2006).

South Africa is often cited as an ideal type of pluralization. It has one of the fastest growing—in size and influence—private security industries in the world (Berg, 2007). Further, there has been for some time now a wide range of non-state policing initiatives, particularly at the local level. These include street committees organized by politicized youth, traditional courts usually run by community elders, and neighborhood patrols and watches (see, for example, Brogden & Shearing, 1993; Dixon, 2000; Roche, 2002).

Historically, a fair amount of social ordering in South Africa has occurred in spite of the state (see Schärf & Nina, 2001). And today this tradition continues. Steinberg provides a number of examples of these. We will just refer to two. Street patrols in disadvantaged townships like Alexandra, north of Johannesburg, gather in the evening on weekends. They are made up of middle-aged or elderly men who divide into groups, and at least one person in the group has a licensed firearm and a cell phone. The patrol has been in existence for eight years, in which time three members have been killed and one paralyzed. As a group, they have confiscated over 600 illegal firearms from people on the streets of Alexandra. They act in ways that are not strictly legal, yet they are neither curtailed by the police nor hindered in their activities by the community they police (Steinberg, 2008).

On the other end of the social spectrum, in a wealthy Jewish (relatively homogenous) suburb called Glenhazel, residents have recognized the limits of fortifications, private security, and the public police in securing themselves. Glenhazel residents have thick bonds and have come together in an initiative called the Community Active Protection (CAP). CAP has created its own command and control center and hired people to monitor and respond to calls. Glenhazel residents call the command center to report suspicious activities or characters in the area. Police have refused to stop and search people identified as suspicious, and so it seems that the CAP uses intimidatory tactics to make suspects feel uncomfortable and leave. Police are well aware that groups like this displace crime, and harass people without good cause and in discriminatory ways. Yet they are also aware that in Glenhazel crimes such as armed robbery have decreased by 66% since the launch of this localized initiative (Steinberg, 2008). The police acknowledge the effectiveness of these community groupings, and they are well aware of the role played by the private security industry in preventing and responding to crime.

Notwithstanding these historical realities and new developments, the public police have not wished to recede into the background (see Dupont, 2006, p. 88). This impulse is not peculiar to South Africa. Police throughout the world do speak of, and generally advocate partnerships, but such talk is not the result of a coherent state governance project. Nor is it indicative of a state in retreat. Rather, as Garland has observed elsewhere, governments and state agencies "[tend] to combine responsibilisation moves with measures intended to consolidate central power, directing the actions of others, more or less coercively, to bring them into line with centrally defined goals" (Garland, 1996, p. 464). In South Africa, we find a fluid, fragmented, and ambiguous state policing framework that, if anything, is geared toward increasing the reach of the public police.

Policing policy in South Africa does emphasize partnerships. The term *community policing* was first formally used in 1997 when the Department of Safety and Security published its formal policy document entitled "Community Policing Policy Framework and Guidelines" (Pelser, 1999). In this text, community policing is presented as a collaborative partnership-based approach to (local-level) problem solving. Its logic is based on an acknowledgment that the objectives of the police can only be achieved through a collaborative effort of the police with other government organizations, structures of civil society, and the private sector (see Pelser, Schnetler, & Louw, 2002). An added, and perhaps unique, impetus in the South African case for embracing community policing was a commitment on the part of the new "democratic" government to bottom-up governance and civic participation. These practices have a strong legacy in South African society, particularly within the anti-apartheid/liberation movement.

A community policing narrative remains central to South African Police Service (SAPS) policy documents and is an integral part of their basic training programs. But just as is the case in other parts of the world, it has become focused almost entirely on ways of mobilizing non-state actors to legitimize and increase the effectiveness of the police. Contrary to early conceptualizations of community policing in post-apartheid South Africa, there is presently no real support for "counter-hegemonic policing initiatives" (Dixon, 2000, p. 17) or for lateral partnerships. Talk about partnerships is limited to conventional notions of the community assisting the police through providing information and supporting public policing initiatives (see, for example, Cachalia, 2007).

Over the past 10 years, new police narratives have emerged that now overshadow talk of community-oriented, collaborative problem-solving policing. As crime and fear of crime reached crisis levels in the 1990s, "the language and strategies of police ministers and commissioners became more aggressive ... the new thinking emphasised cordon-and-search operations in which whole city blocks were closed down, doors were kicked in and anyone suspicious was taken in for questioning" (Altbecker, 2007, p. 31). What we have witnessed is a remilitarization of police discourse (see Cachalia, 2007; Dixon, 2000). This trend is reflected in the continual increase of public police budgets, ongoing commitments to increases in police numbers, and an almost exclusive focus on traditional indirect indicators of police performance (Bayley, 1994), such as numbers of arrests and weapons seized (Rauch, 2002; Newham, 2005).

The dominant police narrative in South Africa now resounds with statements about police needing to assert their authority and their dominant role within policing networks. Instead of the public police speaking about the decentralization of policing resources (a central component of community policing), police leaders now want to centralize them. The national commissioner of the SAPS recently announced that he has plans to incorporate city and municipal police into a single South African Police Service. In his view, centralizing resources will increase the effectiveness and efficiency of the police through a shared system of line functions and accountability.

The police and their political authorities acknowledge that the public police are unable to meet even the most basic policing needs. Yet, there are no clear mechanisms or structures for mobilizing policing resources outside of the state. Where the idea of partnerships is actually used, it mostly refers to joint working arrangements with private security companies, not with civil society groupings. Arguably, this is partly due to the fact that police see private security companies as their natural allies and partners.

The relationship between the public police and private security officers is not always harmonious. There are disagreements about turf, strategy, knowledge flow, and lines of accountability. Yet, there is, in some ways, a shared cultural affinity between private and public police officers (Singh & Kempa, 2007). In a public statement, the minister of safety and security declared that "government is considering a ground-breaking plan to rope in the country's 300 000-strong army of private security guards to help the police fight crime." His proposed plan is to establish an "upgraded partnership" with security companies that "satisfy legal requirements" so they can be called upon in "emergency situations" (see Sekoana, 2007). Exactly how this upgraded partnership will work remains to be seen.

While private security partnerships appear to be the focal point of public police narratives, police leaders have made recent statements about the need to mobilize community members in the fight against crime. South African police policy frameworks have shifted fairly significantly since the transition to democracy in 1994. Initial policy frameworks such as the 1994 Interim Constitution were framed by broader post-apartheid governmental commitments to citizen participation (see Gordon, 2006). Newly elected government actors and policy makers were keen to incorporate communitarian ideals into new policies. The idea in these early days of democracy was for the new democratic state to loosen its monopolistic hold of law and order and to put in place mechanisms for the co-production of security. The Interim Constitution (unlike anywhere else in the world) provided for the establishment of community policing forums as a way of enabling consultation and fostering the legitimacy of the police at the local level, and as a way of getting local communities more engaged in local security governance solutions. The 1996 National Crime Prevention Strategy (NCPS) also spoke to the importance of community policing partnerships and multiagency approaches to the problems of crime and insecurity (Singh, 1997; Rauch & van der Spuy, 2007).

Yet, even in these early years of democratic government, there were signs that commitments to public empowerment were shaky. As Gordon puts it: "The pool of shared idealism that conceived of justice as co-produced by state and citizen was shallow, and officials of the formal system were ... reluctant to concede control over resources or authority to non-professionals who had recently been their antagonists" (2006, p. 216). It is not surprising, then, that we have witnessed a significant shift in national police policy, most evidenced in the 1998 White Paper on Safety and Security. This policy document focuses on ways of making the police more effective law enforcers (Rauch, 2002; Newham, 2005) and is no doubt partly a response to public outcries about high levels of crime and pressure for the state to deal more decisively with this problem.

Paul Graham, director of the largest nongovernment organization in South Africa, the Institute of Democracy in South Africa (IDASA), suggests that the shift away from community engagement on the part of both state and non-state actors is understandable. In his view, "after the intensity of engagement through the transition, the police revert to uniform type and civil society actors move on to the job of life.... Citizens increasingly see themselves as clients or customers" (Graham, 2007).

Also, Buur, Jensen, and Stepputat (2007) suggest that the hold that the state tries to retain over the authorization and provision of policing services has occurred in parts of Southern Africa that have emerged from protracted liberation struggles. Non-state, more informal groupings, they suggest, are perceived as threatening to security, rather than as contributors to it. But the desire from the center to hold on to security governance also results from an awareness (and anxiety) on the part of policy makers and state agency leaders that if the new democratic government is unable to deliver on the provision of basic services, it is likely to face a crisis of authority and legitimacy. A loss of confidence in the government's capacity to respond to people's need for security may have a dramatic impact on democratic values and engagement (Smit & Botha, 1990; Marks & Goldsmith, 2006).

This desire by the public police to reimagine policing as "their exclusive domain" (Wood, 2006a, p. 260) has been recognized as an international phenomenon (see Gordon, 2006). Studies of policing in places like Australia and the United Kingdom show that the public police are still trying to find ways of asserting their primacy (Fleming, Marks, & Wood, 2006; Johnston, 2007). But regardless of these attempts to monopolize, policing governance remains pluralized with the various players viewing themselves and others as (in varying degrees) significant or irrelevant players. The sticking point is that the ways in which these various players view themselves and each other may not align. There is, in short, a lack of clarity about the identities and roles of nodal players.

This role confusion, combined with strong directives and close monitoring from the center, has had very worrying consequences. It has resulted in limited possibilities (and support) for local innovation and responsiveness. It has created the space for private companies with a very narrow set of interests to take over a range of traditionally public police roles. But more positively, it also generates gaps or spaces for thinking more carefully about what the police should be doing, who they are, and what the community policing project now means.

Situating the Police as the Thin Blue Line

Interpretations and implementation practices of community policing are fluid. Partnership arrangements are *ad hoc* and instrumental, which has meant that all policing actors remain somewhat unclear about their roles, and even the public police remain weak actors struggling to find smarter ways of aligning themselves with other groupings keen to make South Africa a more safe and secure place for all. The time is ripe for experimentation, for discovering ways of making all actors as strong and effective as possible, and for enhancing state delivery capacity. Finding answers to the questions of who the police are and who they should be is, as Dupont, Grabosky, and Shearing (2003) argue, particularly urgent in countries that are characterized by conflict and instability, and where states are not able to effectively provide for the basic needs of their populations.

These questions are especially germane to South Africa, a country that stands out as having the highest levels of violent crime in the world. In a recently published book, Altbecker (2007) argues that instead of seeing South Africa as a "society in transition," we should view it as a "half-made" society. What he pessimistically argues (by his own admission) is that the lack of a clear strategy for making South Africa safer has meant that we cannot assume that South Africa is a society in transition. This phrase, he says, suggests that there is some well-thought-through plan of action geared toward a better end state. This is seriously lacking in South Africa, where policing policy is contextually inappropriate, police officers lack direction, and walls between people (literally and figuratively) are getting higher.

What is urgently required in South Africa, Altbecker argues, is "a state that can protect its citizens from the more dangerous of their compatriots" (2007, p. 180). This demands a corps of police who, first and foremost, can prove themselves able to "find, prosecute and incarcerate criminals" (2007, p. 137). What we require is "institutions that draw firm lines in the sand and then come down heavily on people who cross those lines" (Altbecker, 2007, p. 146). In Altbecker's view, we must shift away from what he considers "the absurd idea" that police officers are the "fulcrum around which the reengineering of society would turn" (2007, p. 140).

While Altbecker's view may be controversial, it is certainly not new. Indeed, the left realist school of criminology in Britain has argued for some time that a minimalist policing approach is the most appropriate way forward. By this they mean that for the police to be effective and accountable to the law, "police intervention should be confined to cases where there is clear evidence of law-breaking, and then should take the form of the invocation of legal powers and criminal process" (Reiner, 1992, p. 145). In other words, instead of widening the reach of the police, we need to confine them to what they are trained and resourced to do and restrict their interventions to what they are inclined toward.

We (the police, policing scholars, and the public) need to be clear about what the core competencies and functions of the public police are. Simultaneously, we need to have a firm understanding about which security governance functions should be outsourced to non-state agencies that hold resources or legitimacy that the police do not have in providing a range of security services (see Wood, 2006a). In countries like South Africa, and more especially in those where states are very weak or governance happens in spite of government, the need for this kind of delineation is even more pressing.

Good security governance requires strong and distinguishable policing nodes. For this to occur, all parties in networked arrangements need to be clear about what it is they can individually contribute and what they can realistically expect from the public police. Only once this is achieved will the public police move away from *ad hoc* and instrumental (sometimes exploitative) approaches to partnerships. And it is only then possible for non-state actors to be clear about what to expect from the public police and where their own interventions begin and end. It will, in short, allow for a formally agreed upon "negotiated division of labour" (Menkhaus, 2007, p. 106) between policing nodes.

A more minimalist view of the state police role and function, as suggested by Menkhaus (2007), would allow the police to get on with what they know best and to prove their effectiveness as a key agency within emergent or transitional states. This would provide a basis for certainty about who precisely does what, how, and at what cost. The result, hopefully, would be a state building exercise that harmonizes state authority with local systems. Such an approach, Menkhaus argues, is the "best hope for achieving something remotely approaching effective governance in communities desperate for a more predictable and secure environment" (2007, p. 108). What we don't want is arrangements that perpetuate half-made societies.

In thinking about core functions of the public police, we need to first consider what is unique about the *role* of the public police. We would like to make some suggestions about how we should think about this unique role. First, while the police no longer hold the monopoly over the legitimate use of force, they remain unique in their specialized training to use ubiquitous coercion in a graduated and discretionary way. Second, the police remain a fundamental representative of the legal system (Reiss & Bordua, 1967, p. 27) and through their presence demonstrate that a "regime of law exists" (Bayley, 1994, p. 34). Because of this, and because of their capacity to curtail individual freedoms in the most dramatic ways, the police are able to intervene authoritatively to restore order (Bayley, 1994), resolve conflict, control crowds, and curtail (rather than prevent) crime. The police, in this model, would distinctly outline actual functions that they feel they are uniquely placed to do because of this established role.

If the functions of the police were more clearly delineated, this would make institutions and mechanisms of accountability far simpler to design. In addition, the surest way to build legitimacy on the part of the police is for them to demonstrate that they are both democratic and effective in the means and ends associated with their core functions. Once the public police are clear about their own role, and feel less pressured to respond to an ever-widening demand for their interventions, a space will be created for them to actively encourage and even to learn from alternative (non-state) ways of social ordering. This is important because these local, non-state forms of ordering usually enjoy a high degree of legitimacy and local ownership, and their solutions to everyday security problems are often more effective than "inorganic, top-down" state interventions (Menkhaus, 2007).

One advantage of this perspective is that it fits well with what the police want to be. They want to be real police who can intervene effectively to combat crime, to restore public disorder, and to hold (at least symbolically) the "big gun" (Bjork, 2006). They don't want to be stretched beyond their capacities in terms of their resources, training, mandate, or skills base. In developing countries like South Africa, they simply cannot be the hub of all community/societal problem solving that is linked to broad notions of security.

A Community Policing Model for Emergent and Postconflict States

It may seem that what we are suggesting represents a retreat from community policing, a step backward toward professional, disassociated policing. To the contrary, we are trying to explore ways of making community policing work better and to avoid a situation where people in places like South Africa throw up their hands and say that it is simply a failed colonial import. We also want to move beyond a community policing narrative that the police own and control, toward a model that accounts for police limitations and the range of alternative policing sources that are already out there. The voices denouncing community policing have already become very loud in South Africa. For instance, some skeptics see it as a model that is too all-embracing and nefarious for countries struggling with basic governance issues (see Altbecker, 2007; Burger, 2007).

For us, community policing should be centered on the creation of horizontal and vertical matrixes between the police and other groupings involved in governing security. It should be about mobilizing as many resources and capacities as possible in making communities safer. It should be about joining forces to create a political environment in which citizens feel safe to demonstrate dissent and to engage in peaceful social conflict. For these principles to be actualized, the police have to be clear about their core role. They need to be confident in the knowledge that they have a unique right and requisite skills to use legal bureaucratic violence with discretion to resolve conflicts and create social order (Bjork, 2006).

Having carved out a specific role and function for themselves, the police should be much better placed to identify roles that need to be filled by other groupings to make societies safer. The process of acknowledging their own limited ambit would encourage them to work collaboratively with other actors (both state and non-state) to fill security gaps. In such a system, each node—each strong and distinguishable from the other—would need to develop the capacity to broker to other nodes, or put another way, to enlist the unique capacities and resources of other nodes around a problem or need that requires those special resources. In this process we need to allow for a certain degree of messiness and diversity. What is required is experimentation based on what resources are available locally and nationally, variable political and social historical trajectories, and perhaps most importantly, the reality of what it is that states are able to offer in an effective and accountable manner.

The coordinators of these systems, we suggest, should be local government who, together with the communities they govern, would identify which security problems exist, which resources (state and non-state) are available to fill these gaps, and what systems of accountability would need to be put in place so that all sectors of diverse communities are equally guaranteed of security outcomes. They would need to think of creative ways to encourage participation and volunteerism. This would have to involve incentive planning both for those privately funded non-police security activities and for those who get their own hands dirty in creating safer living, working, and leisure spaces.

Local governments could develop models for building neighborhood associations whose key function is to help create a secure environment. Such a model could outline how patrols are done, how security-related problems are identified and who they are reported to, at what point the police must be called in, and what to expect and demand of the police. This they could do by looking at the positive programs and outcomes of groupings such as those in Alexandra and Glenhazel. It is to local government authorities that problems with these groupings are reported, and it is to this body that a lack of responsiveness from the police would be relayed. They would become, in a sense, the hub of accountability and knowledge sharing. Given the current lack of legitimacy of the public police in places like South Africa, we suggest that this hub would work better than relying on the police as a state agency that exclusively determines which security-related knowledge is acknowledged and gathered.

The police should be central to these locally coordinated government systems. In particular, they should have the unique responsibility of nurturing otherwise weak nodes (i.e., lacking in political, economic, or other forms of capital), even if that simply means (1) acknowledging the unique abilities and resources of less resourced nodes, (2) allowing themselves to be enlisted by such nodes according to mutually agreed upon conditions/rules, (3) brokering traditionally weak nodes to other nodes so that the former can leverage up their capacities and resources and become stronger by drawing on the strengths of others, and (4) being more responsive (Ayres & Braithwaite,

1992) to the contributions that other nodes play, so that the specific interventions or roles of the public police are properly calibrated and complementary to the work that other nodes do.

The role of the police as government actors would be to ensure that publicly agreed upon norms for policing are adhered to, that due process is upheld, and that justice is enacted when arrests are made. The public police would also have to ensure that particular groupings (such as foreigners) are not targeted as suspects and are not excluded from public spaces through intimidatory tactics. They would have to configure ways to ensure that crime is not displaced from one locality to another, but instead that security problems are resolved in consultation with other actors. And perhaps most importantly, the public police would have to build their legitimacy with communities through being effective in resolving conflict, investigating crime, and being responsive to crimes or problems of disorder that communities identify as significant (Innes, 2004).

In this model, the public police would not monopolize policing, but they would be key government actors that ensure and facilitate public safety and security. We concur with Zedner, who argues that the public police should play the central role of delineating and upholding "the normative structures essential both to protect the public interest in policing and maintain the ligatures of civil society" (2006, p. 93). The onus on public police organizations (with the guidance and assistance of local government agencies if necessary) would thus be to resource, skill-up, and train their officers to be knowledge brokers (Ericson, 1994), facilitators, and experts in the discretionary enforcement of law and in the production of social order. Their role would be to ensure that force and the curtailment of freedoms is used effectively, and that democratic rights are protected for all citizens and residents.

Our approach to understanding who the police should be is consistent with the vision that Loader and Walker have recently advocated in their book, *Civilizing Security* (2007), where they argue for a role for the state as a guarantor of the public interest within a plural policing system. Together with local government, police should promote and support strategic and joined-up problem solving, particularly in preventing crime, so that a reversion to authoritarian or command and control approaches to problem solving are avoided, and so that prisons do not prosper as homes of excluded populations (i.e., those that engage in petty crime or disorderly behavior or conduct unbecoming). What we want in places like South Africa is certainty that serious crime will be dealt with effectively by the police. What we don't want is a society that is, to use Jonathan Simon's phrase (2007), exclusively "governed through crime," where criminals and the crime-prone are segregated into prisons and urban ghettos while law-abiding citizens are sheltered in gated communities, patrolled shopping malls, and secure workplaces (Davis, 1990).

Concluding Comments

In post-conflict, newly emerging democratic countries, states, and their police are looking for secured roles for themselves as well as ways of reaching out to other actors in a manner that enhances security while concurrently building state legitimacy and effectiveness. Developing and weak states are in no position to have police officers that are expected to be community activists and generalist problem solvers. Rather, what is required is police who have clearly defined and limited functions. They also need to be given the support and space to do their job in the best way possible. This places a responsibility on national governments to both develop clearer frameworks of core police functions and roles, and to enable local government actors (like municipalities) to act as facilitators and coordinators.

The transitional nature of South African state and society means that configurations of policing may be somewhat different from those in more established liberal democracies. In transitional societies there is less regulatory capacity, a greater correspondence of actual crime with fear of crime, less certainty about the role of the state, and a weary (yet historically mobilized) civil society. But the debate about who should be doing what in policing and how this should be done is equally relevant to post-conflict, transitional, and established democratic societies (Johnston, 2000, Wood, 2006b). This point is important because while police in established democratic countries may have greater legitimacy than those in places like South Africa, they are equally beset with questions about how they fit into new policing landscapes, and they too confront publics who question their effectiveness and commitment to providing an equitable and accountable service.

References

Adams, R., & Serpe, R. (2000). Social integration, fear of crime, and life stratification. *Sociological Perspectives, 43*, 605–629.

Altbecker, A. (2007). *A country at war with itself.* Johannesburg: Jonathan Ball Publishers.

Ayres, I., & Braithwaite, J. (1992). *Responsive regulation: Transcending the deregulation debate.* New York: Oxford University Press.

Bayley, D. H. (1994). *Police for the future.* New York: Oxford University Press.

Berg, J. (2007). *The accountability of South Africa's private security industry: Mechanisms of control and challenges to effective oversight.* Cape Town: Criminal Justice Initiative of the Open Society Foundation for South Africa, Colinton House.

Bjork, M. (2006). Policing agonistic pluralism: Classical and contemporary thoughts on the viability of the polity. *Distinktion, 12*, 75–91.

Brogden, M., & Shearing, C. (1993). *Policing for a new South Africa.* London: Routledge.

Burger, J. (2007). *Strategic perspectives on crime and policing in South Africa.* Pretoria: Van Schaik Publishers.

Buur, L., Jensen, S., & Stepputat, F. (2007). The security development nexus. In L. Buur, S. Jensen, & F. Stepputat (Eds.), *The security development nexus: Expressions of sovereignty and securitization in Southern Africa* (9–36). Cape Town: Human Science Research Council Press.

Cachalia, F. (2007). Operation iron fist after six months: Provincial police strategy under review. *Crime and Quarterly, 19,* 1–10.

Davis, M. (1990). *City of quartz: Excavating the future of Los Angeles.* New York: Vintage Books.

Dixon, B. (2000). *The globalisation of democratic policing: Sector policing and zero tolerance in the new South Africa.* Occasional paper series, Institute of Criminology, University of Cape Town. Retrieved March 23, 2008 from http://web.uct.ac.za/depts/sjrp/publicat/global1.htm.

Dupont, B. (2006). Power struggles in the field of security: Implications for democratic transformation. In J. Wood & B. Dupont (Eds.), *Democracy, society and the governance of security* (pp. 86–110). Cambridge: Cambridge University Press.

Dupont, B., Grabosky, P., & Shearing, C. (2003). The governance of security in weak and failing states. *Criminal Justice, 3,* 331–349.

Ericson, R. (1994). The division of expert knowledge in policing and security. *British Journal of Sociology, 45,* 149–175.

Fleming, J., Marks, M., & Wood, J. (2006). Standing on the inside looking out: The significance of unions in networks of police governance. *Australian and New Zealand Journal of Criminology, 39,* 71–89.

Garland, D. (1996). The limits of the sovereign state—Strategies of crime control in contemporary society. *British Journal of Criminology, 36,* 445–471.

Gordon, D. (2006). *Transformation and trouble: Crime, justice and participation in a democratic South Africa.* Ann Arbor: University of Michigan Press.

Graham, P. (2007, March 6). *Creating a civil society—The role of civil society organisations in security sector reform during political transitions.* Paper presented to Interpol Heads of Training Symposium, Emperor's Palace, Johannesburg.

Innes, M. (2004). Reinventing tradition? Reassurance, neighbourhood security and policing. *Criminal Justice, 4,* 151–171.

Johnston, L. (2000). *Policing Britain: Risk, security and governance.* Essex: Pearson Education Limited.

Johnston, L. (2007). "Keeping the family together": Police community support officers and the "police extended family" in London. *Policing and Society, 17,* 119–140.

Loader, I., & Walker, N. (2007). *Civilizing security.* Cambridge: Cambridge University Press.

Marks, M., & Goldsmith, A. (2006). The state, the people and democratic policing: The case of South Africa. In J. Wood & B. Dupont (Eds.), *Democracy, society and the governance of security* (pp. 139–164). Cambridge: Cambridge University Press.

Menkhaus, K. (2007). Governance without government in Somalia: Spoilers, state building and the politics of coping. *International Security, 31,* 74–106.

Newham, G. (2005). *A decade of crime prevention in South Africa: From a national strategy to a local challenge.* Research report written for the Centre for the Study of Violence and Reconciliation, Johannesburg. Retrieved May 20, 2007 from http://www.csvr.org.za/papers/papnwh17.htm

Pelser, E. (1999). *The challenges of community policing in South Africa*. Occasional Paper 42, Institute of Security Studies, Pretoria.

Pelser, E., Schnetler, J., & Louw, A. (2002). *Not everybody's business: Community policing in SAPS priority areas*. Monograph 72, Institute for Security Studies, Pretoria.

Rauch, J. (2002). Changing step: Crime prevention policy in South Africa. In E. Pelser (Ed.), *Crime prevention partnerships: Lessons from practice* (pp. 9–26). Pretoria: Institute for Security Studies.

Rauch, J., & van der Spuy, E. (2006). *Police reform in post-conflict Africa*. Pretoria: Safety and Security Programme of the Institute for Democracy in South Africa. Retrieved December 21, 2006 from www.idasa.org.za

Reiner, R. (1992). *The politics of the police* (2nd ed.). New York: Harvester Wheatsheaf.

Reiss, A. J., Jr., & Bordua, D. J. (1967). Environment and organization: A perspective on the police. In D. J. Bordua (Ed.), *The police: Six sociological essays* (pp. 25–55). New York: Wiley.

Rhodes, R. (2006). The sour laws of network governance. In J. Fleming & J. Wood (Eds.), *Fighting crime together: The challenges of policing and security networks* (pp. 15–34). Sydney: University of New South Wales Press.

Roche, D. (2002). Restorative justice and the regulatory state in South African townships. *British Journal of Criminology, 42*, 514–533.

Schärf, W., & Nina, D. (Eds.). (2001). *The other law: Non-state ordering in South Africa*. Johannesburg: Juta.

Sekoana, T. (2007). Police, security firms align forces. Bua News. Retrieved October 19, 2007 from http://www.southafrica.info/what_happening/news/security-110507.htm

Simon, J. (2007). *Governing through crime: How the war on crime transformed American democracy and created a culture of fear*. Oxford: Oxford University Press.

Singh, A. (1997, July 15–19). *Changing the soul of the nation? South Africa's National Crime Prevention Strategy*. Paper presented at the British Criminology Conference, Queens University, Belfast.

Singh, A., & Kempa, M. (2007). Reflections on the study of private policing cultures: Early leads and key themes. In M. O'Neill, M. Marks, & A. Singh (Eds.), *Police occupational culture: New debates and directions* (pp. 297–330). London: Elsevier.

Skogan, W. (2007, September 11). *Leadership from bottom to top: Chicago's model for community policing*. Paper presented at Apex Scotland Annual Lecture, Signet Library, Glasgow.

Smit, B., & Botha, C. (1990). Democracy and policing: An introduction to paradox. *Acta Criminologica, 3*, 36–45.

Steinberg, J. (2008). *Thin blue: The unwritten rules of policing in South Africa*. Cape Town: Jonathan Ball Publishers.

Wood, J. (2006a). Dark networks, bright networks and the place of the police. In J. Fleming & J. Wood (Eds.), *Fighting crime together: The challenge of policing and security networks*. Sydney: University of New South Wales Press.

Wood, J. (2006b). Research and innovation in the field of security: A nodal governance view. In J. Wood & B. Dupont (Eds.), *Democracy, society and the governance of security* (pp. 217–241). Cambridge: Cambridge University Press.

Zedner, L. (2006). Policing before and after the police: The historical antecedents of contemporary crime control. *British Journal of Criminology, 46*, 78–97.

Endnotes

1. This title is inspired by the name of Jonny Steinberg's most recent book, titled *Thin Blue: The Unwritten Rules of Policing South Africa* (Cape Town: Jonathan Ball Publishers, 2008).

Community Policing in China
A New Era of Mass Line Policing

11

LENA Y. ZHONG

Contents

Since 1949, policing in China has been guided by the mass line, whereby the work of the police is to work for the masses. Substantial emphasis was put on the mobilization of the masses at the grassroots level. Policing in China is essentially community policing, although the concept per se was not deployed until very recently, as observed by overseas community policing pioneers such as John Anderson in the UK and F. L. Masala in the United States (see Lu, 2001). However, with the implementation of the reform and open-door policy since 1978, the level of crime has escalated and the escalation trend shows no signs of abating despite successive waves of strike-hard campaigns. In the 1990s some cities started introducing community policing to fight crime and improve police-public relations. As an imported concept, community policing was widely embraced by some, namely, practitioners and academics. Others questioned its validity and challenged that it was similar to the guideline of combining the special work of the police with the mass line, long used by the Chinese police (Zhou, 2003); thus, it was mere repetitions of long-term practices and contained nothing new (Leng, 2003). So if the policing model prior to the economic reform is by nature community

Adapted from Zhong, L. (2008). Community policing in China: Old wine in new bottles. *Police Practice and Research,* http://dx.doi.org/10.1080/15614260802264594

policing, then is the current policing model labeled as "community policing" nothing more than simply old wine in new bottles? *

China has a rather low police-public ratio, compared with other juris-dictions. Currently the police-public ratio is estimated at 1.38/1,000.† How has community policing successfully operated in an overpopulated country with an insufficient police force? As Skogan (1990) has noted, certain features of American society severely limit the potential effectiveness of community crime prevention efforts, such as cultural diversity, high mobility, and strong orientation toward individual rights rather than collective responsibilities, which make it difficult for neighborhood residents to reach a consensus about the need to take specific action, mobilize, and work together. Drawing on Putnam (2000), Klinenberg (2001) questions whether we can achieve "bowl-ing alone and policing together." Although China was traditionally regarded as a communitarian society, the recent decades of economic reform have fundamentally transformed the whole society. So how has community polic-ing developed in current Chinese society, when compared with China before its economic reform took place?

This chapter will first delineate the history of policing in China since 1949, which is divided into three periods: mass line policing (1949–1980), strike-hard policing (1981–2001), and community policing (since 2002). The first period saw the implementation of the typical mass line policing. The second period witnessed the launch of strike-hard policing, which was a distortion of the general crime control policy of comprehensive man-agement of social order (CMSO) by overemphasizing its punitive prong at the expense of the preventive prong. The third period saw the full-scale launch of community policing at the national level and, most importantly, the explicit use of the label "community policing." The chapter will illus-trate what community policing is, and how it has been implemented since 2002, by drawing upon Building Little Safe and Civilized Communities (BLSCC), a community policing model in Shenzhen (a city at the vanguard of economic reform in China). Although policing in China demonstrates different characteristics in the three periods, the underlying rationale is community policing, as manifest by the mass line. In other words, com-munity policing per se in China since 2002 is nothing more than old wine in new bottles.

---

* There is a similar saying in Chinese to denote "old wine in new bottles" by drawing on cooking herbs in Chinese medicine: Change the soup but not the herbs (*huan tang bu huan yao*).

† The *China Law Yearbook* (1994) reported that in 1993 the national police force was 1.477 million, a ratio of 1.25/1,000. Afterwards the China Law Yearbook stopped reporting such data. I learned from a police friend that the current police force is around 1.8 mil-lion, a ratio of around 1.38/1,000 (the total population of 1.3 billion).

Mass Line Policing: 1949–1980

Policing during 1949–1980 was guided by the mass line. The mass line refers to "for the masses, relying on the masses, from the masses and to the masses" (Yu, Zheng, & Su, 1997, p. 152). It embodies two layers of meaning. First, policing is based on the interests of both the state and the masses, with a focus on "for the masses." Second, policing relies on the masses and the mobilization of the masses and on police function to win the understanding and support of the masses (Yu et al., 1997). The police-public relationship can be characterized metaphorically: The police are fish and the masses are water.* The mass line was operationalized as "mass prevention and mass management," whereby the public, social forces, and government agencies were mobilized to combat crime and maintain social order. The most notable mechanisms of mass prevention and mass management are neighborhood committees, work units, and social order joint protection teams.

The establishment of neighborhood committees as mass organizations of self-management at the grassroots level in urban areas is prescribed by Article 111 of the Constitution, which provides that the neighborhood committees

> establish sub-committees for people's mediation, public security, public health and other matters in order to manage public affairs and social services in their areas, mediate civil disputes, help maintain public order and convey residents' opinions and demands and make suggestions to the people's government. (*Constitution of the People's Republic of China*, 1982/2004, p. 72)

Members of the neighborhood committees are elected by residents. The subcommittees of people's mediation and public security are especially important for managing social order at the grassroots level. The former is responsible for resolving conflicts and disputes between individuals, groups, and organizations in the neighborhood and preventing them from escalating into criminal cases. In some places intentional homicides triggered by civil disputes account for 80% of homicide cases (Chen, 2002), and mediation, an alternative to dispute resolution, is believed to play an important part in reducing such crimes. The subcommittee of public security is aimed to educate residents on safety and legal matters, to report to the police criminals and suspicious individuals in the neighborhood, to provide assistance to the police for local crime control and population registration, to reeducate juveniles with mild offenses, and to report major discontent among residents to appropriate local authorities, *inter alia* (Wong, 1999; Yu et al., 1997).

---

* The metaphor goes like this: Fish cannot survive without water; the police cannot succeed without public involvement and support.

The work units, that is, where people are employed, also shoulder responsibilities for social control and sanctions of deviance. The police are directly involved in corporate security management—a corporate policing model as termed by Jiao (1997). In each medium-sized or large work unit, a public security division is set up—staffed with trained para-police personnel, equipped with law enforcement facilities, and in direct contact with the state police force (Shaw, 1996). The work units exert upon individuals social control through civil rewards or penalties, administrative disciplining, quasi-justice, and para-security (Shaw, 1996).

The social order joint protection teams are established through collaboration among several districts, work units, or organizations to jointly prevent crime and deviance and safeguard social order. A social order joint protection team differs from a subcommittee of public security under the neighborhood committee in three ways. First, members of a social order joint protection team are sent by their original work units to engage in full-time joint protection work, while members of a subcommittee of public security are elected by local residents as voluntary workers. Second, the former are paid by their original work units and enjoy the full benefits as employees, while the latter are not paid a salary, although certain allowances are provided. Third, in terms of duties, the former undertake crime prevention and control activities across neighborhoods under the guidance of the police, while the latter assist the police in maintaining law and order in a particular neighborhood (Yu et al., 1997). Nevertheless, the two form a huge self-help force at the grassroots level. Yu et al. (1997, p. 578) noted that by 1997, there were over 9 million subcommittees of public security members and over 2 million social order joint protection team members.

The above mechanisms of mass prevention and mass management operate under the general framework of the household registration system (*hukou*), which differentiates rural and urban registration status and attaches the status with both material and symbolic meanings. Under the household registration system, the Chinese citizens are classified into those with agricultural status and nonagricultural status. The former, mostly in the countryside, receive no state benefits except the right to farm. The latter are entitled to various privileges and benefits. Apart from the associated welfare and benefits, the household registration system also plays the role of identifying people, controlling the size of urban population, and providing demographic information. Most importantly, it serves to protect social stability. The system by and large dictates immobility; thus, it locks people, especially rural residents, into their native places. This immobility enhances mutual surveillance and conformity.

Household registration is under the jurisdiction of the local police station and charged by the registration officer. A registration form covers information such as the household head or relation to household head, name, sex, place of birth, date of birth, place of origin, nationality, education level, marital status, occupation, work unit, moving records, and re-registration records (Dutton, 1992). Based on the registered information, the registration officer identifies those adults with criminal records or those who pose a potential threat to social order. He also educates juveniles to obey social rules, and actively provides help and education (*bangjiao*)* services to ex-offenders to prevent reoffending. He is involved with local residents and spends much time on local affairs, such as inspections, street sanitation, local welfare, and family visiting. To a large extent, the household registration system and the information gathered through it serve as the basis for mass prevention and mass management.

It is notable that the police provide direct professional guidance to the mechanisms of mass prevention and mass management. For example, the neighborhood committees, especially the subcommittees of people's mediation and public security, work closely with the police. The latter subcommittee is considered to constitute a link between the police and the masses, and plays a key role in uniting and mobilizing the masses in crime prevention (Yu et al., 1997, p. 567). The police are directly involved in crime control and maintaining order in the work units through the latter's public security departments. The social order joint protection teams are under the direct charge and professional guidance of the police. The mass line policing model therefore demonstrates two interesting characteristics: On the one hand, the masses are mobilized to prevent crime and maintain social order, while on the other hand, the police play a tripartite role—crime control, order maintenance, and service provision. The following example vividly illustrates the mode of this service provision. During a visit to China in the 1980s, the American delegation explained their version of community policing: In a U.S. inner-city area, garbage collections were being made irregularly. The local police officer helped residents to identify the agency in charge of garbage collection, accompanied them to lodge a complaint, and was able to gain access to a ranking official in the sanitation department—successfully persuading the official to remedy the situation. In response, the Chinese police suggested that a Chinese police officer would have removed the garbage himself (Bracey, 1989, p. 138). During this period policing was guided by the mass line and manifested the mass line. The mass line policing reflects Sir Robert Peel's ideal of "the police are the public and the public are the police" (1829, cited in Shearing & Stenning, 1981, p. 215).

---

* In China *bangjiao* is a sort of aftercare services provided to ex-offenders by people at the local community. For both the receiver and provider of such services, it is mostly voluntary, not statutory. See S. Wong (2004) and L. Zhang et al. (1996) for details.

Strike-Hard Policing: 1981–2001

With the implementation of economic reform, China witnessed a surge in crime rates, especially crime committed by people under the age of 25 (see Bakken, 2000; Zhong, 2008). A sweeping crack-down campaign (referred to as strike-hard) was formally initiated in 1983.* Altogether, three national strike-hard campaigns were launched: the first from early August 1983 to late 1986/early 1987, the second from April 1996 to February 1997, and the third from 2001 to 2002. Under strike-hard, policing was characterized by catching criminals, cracking cases, and severe punishments. The ultimate goal was to reduce or at least control the rising crime rates. This period also saw the launch of the general crime control policy of comprehensive management of social order (CMSO), the initiation of police patrols and the 110 crime reporting hotline, and the emergence of the private security industry.

The general crime control policy of CMSO was initiated in the early 1980s and formally launched in 1991. Afterwards CMSO committees at various levels of the government were established to lead the work of CMSO. The guiding principle of CMSO lies in its "combining punishment and prevention, with the focus placed on prevention" (see Zhong & Broadhurst, 2007, p. 55). The strike-hard represents the punishment prong of CMSO. It seems that CMSO manifested into the mass line during a period of soaring crime by emphasizing prevention in the duality of punishment and prevention. Zhu and Wang (1995) argue that in principle, community policing and CMSO are two concepts with substantial convergence. However, in reality, a greater emphasis was put on the prong of punishment, as noted by both practitioners and academics in China (see, e.g., Wang, Qin, & Nie, 1998; Zhang, 2002).

Crime did not recede despite the successive waves of strike-hard campaigns, resulting in a formal national launch of police patrols in 1994 by the Ministry of Public Security to "put the majority of police force on the streets" (Fu, 2007, p. 40). The Ministry of Public Security promulgated the "Regulations on Urban People's Police Patrolling Work" and instructed local police departments to establish patrolling police teams based on the local situation (Ministry of Public Security, 1994). Article 3 of the Regulations stipulates that the police should use foot patrol as the main approach, supplemented with bicycle patrol and motor patrol. By the end of 2002, the patrolling police force had increased to 110,000 (Wei, 2006). In 2005, for example, Beijing had a patrolling force of more than 35,000 members: 3,300 patrolling police officers at the city level, 4,100 patrolling officers from the

---

* As noted by Tanner (1999), the initiation of the two campaigns—severe and rapid punishment in 1981 and strike severe blows against serious economic crime in 1982—set the stage for the launch of the first strike-hard. Hence, the year of 1981 is taken as the starting point for this period.

local police stations, 1,600 people's armed police officers, 1,900 traffic police officers, 9,400 social order joint protection team members, 12,000 security guards, and 2,900 auxiliary police officers. The three patrolling modes were used in combination: In the city center the ratio of foot to bicycle to motor was 4:3:3, in the suburbs 2:2:6, and in the remote suburbs 1:3:6 (Li, 2005). Given that the police-public ratio is rather low in China, the police force at the local level was further attenuated with the introduction of the patrolling police. Although in the West the effectiveness of police patrolling is an issue of debate (see, e.g., Clarke & Hough, 1980; Sherman, 1992), few rigorous research studies have been conducted in China to evaluate its effectiveness and impact.

The 110 crime reporting hotline was formally established on a national scale in China in 1996. By January 10, 2006, it had been available to 95% of police departments at the county level and 100% of police departments at the prefecture level. In 2005, the number of 110 reports reached 120 million nationwide, and served three purposes: seeking help, reporting crime, and receiving complaints on police officers in law enforcement (Sun, 2006). Rapid response to calls is required of the police, and police are expected to arrive within 5 minutes for urban areas, 10 minutes for suburban areas, and as soon as possible for rural areas (Mao & Zou, 2005). The guiding principle for the 110 hotline is four *have*'s and four *should*'s,* which basically means that the police should cater for all needs of any individual who dials the 110 hotline for anything. However, this principle imposes great pressure on police because the calls range from inquiries on buying flowers, breakfast delivery, and calling for a taxi to even harassment and nuisance. For example, in a city in Zhejiang province, the proportion of calls related to crime was only 15% (Zhejiang News Online, 2005). Indeed, there was a widely reported case in Wuhan, Hubei province, in which a man dialed 110 in the morning and asked the police to buy him breakfast, and the police officer did buy him breakfast! This illustrates how police often (mis)handle this particular service provision. Consequently, one police department in Zhejiang province has removed the four *have*'s and four *should*'s sign from its entrance (Zhejiang News Online, 2005). In 2003 the Ministry of Public Security published the guidelines of using the 110 hotline, which did not stipulate the four *have*'s and four *should*'s principle (Ministry of Public Security, 2003).

The emergence of private security is a result of the tension between the local policing model and the security needs of the foreign-owned enterprises and joint ventures in China, especially in the east coast areas. Those

---

* The slogan could be literally translated as "The police *should* handle any crime you *have*, *should* help with any difficulties you *have*, *should* save you from any dangers you *have*, and *should* meet any needs you *have*."

companies could not accept the police's direct involvement in their internal security, while the police were hard-pressed to meet their huge security needs. A compromise between the two parties led to the establishment of the first security service company in 1985 in Shenzhen. It is client oriented and based on fee-for-service. At the outset the security service companies raised eyebrows, but the market demands in the transitional economy attested to its importance for maintaining public order and reducing crime. It was gradually expanded to other cities in China. The security service companies are under the direct control of the police. Local companies, organizations, and communities started to employ a large number of security guards. The private security force constitutes an important part of mass prevention and mass management in the new era. For example, by December 2005, the number of security guards had reached 4 million nationwide, and in Beijing, security guards outnumbered police (China News Net, 2005). However, there is concern that the industry is not adequately regulated, and the professional training of guards is insufficient. The media periodically reported criminal cases committed by security guards, ranging from petty theft, burglary, and robbery to rape and even homicides. There was even a saying to depict the scenario: If security guards did not commit crime, the total crime rate would reduce to half (Southern Daily, 2004).

Apart from the above measures, this period also saw the passing of the Police Law 1995 (Ma, 1997). From the late 1980s to the early 1990s, policing in China underwent a period of radical reform (Wong, 2002). During the period of strike-hard policing, the mass line was still upheld as the guideline for police. But it seemed increasingly difficult to implement it in reality. Police-public relations deteriorated substantially, as noted by Du (1997). It was dubbed as oil and water (Ma, 1998), in stark contrast to the metaphor of fish and water for the period of mass line policing. To address the soaring trend of crime and to improve police-public relations, the police imported the model of community policing from the West to China. Thus *shequ jinwu*—the Chinese translation for "community policing"—was coined.

Community Policing: Since 2002

Community policing emerged in a number of cities in China in the late 1990s, mainly taking the form of Building Little Safe and Civilized Communities (BLSCC). In March 2002, the Ministry of Public Security launched community policing by calling for the full-scale implementation of community policing in major and medium-sized cities nationwide by the end of 2004 (Zhu, 2004). On August 15, 2002, the Ministry of Public Security and Ministry of Civil Affairs jointly promulgated the *Notice of the Ministry of Public Security and Ministry of Civil Affairs on Strengthening the Construction of Community*

Policing (Ministry of Public Security, 2002), which signaled the full-scale launch of community policing in China on a national level. The notice also stipulated that each local police station nominate an officer to participate in neighborhood committees, in order to better coordinate local affairs at the community level.

As noted earlier, during the mass line policing period, social order joint protection teams served as a self-help force at the grassroots level. Gradually, the joint protection teams became *de facto* police or auxiliary police, especially for local police departments short of police officers and under financial strain. In the process of carrying out their duties, some joint protection team members generated substantial grievances from the public (e.g., Gou, 2004). As a result, the Ministry of Public Security promulgated a notice to clean the police force by gradually abolishing the joint protection teams by January 1, 2008 (Ministry of Public Security, 2004). By cleaning the "bad apples" from the police, the abolishment was an important step toward police professionalism, and was highly acclaimed by the public. However, doubts were raised toward the wholesale abolition of joint protection teams, as they had made significant contributions to crime control and order maintenance during a period of soaring crime. Thus, there were additional concerns that the police force would be under even greater pressure to maintain social order, given the low police-public ratio.

Among the fundamental changes penetrating every nook and cranny of Chinese society in the reform era, the most notable is the tension exerted on the household registration system and the increased mobility of the population—hence the emergence of the so-called floating population (see Zhong, 2008). For example, in 2005 the migrant population was estimated to be 150 million, accounting for about 12% of the total population in the country (National Statistical Bureau, 2006). The policing model in a static society could not be applied to the current dynamic society. Nevertheless, can community policing provide a solution to crime and disorder and meet the security needs of the public? The following section will draw upon the experiences of implementing BLSCC in Shenzhen, a window of reform, and opening up in China, which has been characterized by rapid economic development, huge population growth, and increasing crime rates.

Community Policing in Shenzhen: BLSCC

BLSCC is intended to demonstrate the prevention prong of CMSO. It took shape in Shenzhen in the late 1990s. The important measures in implementing BLSCC can be grouped into four aspects: organizational features, safety measures, civilization measures, and the BLSCC rating system (see Zhong & Broadhurst, 2007, for more details).

Organization

BLSCC emerged from the two broader perspectives of "construction of spiritual civilization"* and the general crime policy CMSO. In fact, it gained legitimacy and momentum by anchoring onto these two essential doctrines of the socialist system. BLSCC bears distinctive marks of popular ideology (from which its slogans and methods are directly transplanted), including the leadership responsibility system, "learning from models," the setting of BLSCC yearly quotas, the strategy of mass prevention and mass management, as well as fund-raising.

The leadership responsibility system basically means that leaders at all levels of government, agencies, companies, and organizations should be held accountable for implementing BLSCC and maintaining social order. If a leader fails in BLSCC, he fails completely. It is the principle of whoever takes charge is held responsible, and is directly associated with a leader's year-end assessment, eligibility for model titles, and promotion (*Shenzhen Political and Legal Yearbook* [SZPLY], 1999, p. 135). In the official reports on BLSCC, the leadership responsibility system was always listed first for the successful implementation of BLSCC.

Mass prevention and mass management (as a manifestation of mass line policing in the first period of mass line policing) has two dimensions under BLSCC. It emphasizes the mobilization of all forces to fight crime and social disorder in concerted ways, and also aims to encourage individuals and work units to deploy crime prevention measures inside households or work units, as represented by the slogan "Manage well your own matters and watch out your own doors." In other words, it is both social crime prevention and situational crime prevention. Meanwhile, the mass media (including newspapers, television, and radio stations) publicized the launch and progress of BLSCC by reporting model individuals or work units, and even covering certain problems. But as the market economy has grown, it has become increasingly difficult to mobilize the masses. The ideological basis of mass prevention, which is reliant on voluntarism, now seems fragile.

Multiagency cooperation, an essential part of the mass prevention approach, is also problematic. This is acknowledged widely in crime prevention programs in the West. For example, Sampson, Stubbs, and Smith (1988) note that the multiagency approach should not be uncritically considered as a panacea for crime. Instead of an overblown, all-encompassing, multiagency approach, they advocate a "narrowly focused approach, with specific forms of inter-agency relationships, on specific themes and problems" (p. 491).

* Having achieved successful economic growth, the government emphasized the need to simultaneously pursue both material and spiritual civilization. Accordingly, the phrases "construction of material civilization" and "construction of spiritual civilization" are used.

Crawford (1998) also identifies important tensions between managerialist preoccupations of policy and the rhetoric of multiagency partnerships.

Since 1997, funding for BLSCC in Shenzhen has derived from four sources: the city government, work units, residents and households, and charges on convenience services. In the four communities where fieldwork was conducted, the situation varied between the communities. One community attracted a lot of external resources because it was designated as a national model in implementing BLSCC, while the other communities fared much worse. Put simply, funding solutions for BLSCC were dependent on both internal and external community resources.

Measures for Safety

Since its inception, the Shenzhen police have actively taken the lead in the BLSCC program. They have been involved in installing target-hardening crime prevention measures and played an important role in managing the migrant population via the *hukou* system. They also managed special professions, such as entertainment venues (i.e., dancing halls, sauna and massage parlors), hotels, secondhand dealers, and the publishing industry. The police have also linked BLSCC with wiping out pornography, gambling, and drugs, which go hand-in-hand with one of the more important criteria for BLSCC officers: "no drug addicts, no drug abuse dens and no drug abuse networks" (SZPLY, 1999, p. 140).

To better adapt to the tasks of BLSCC and CMSO, police actively adopted a series of tactics. For example, officers at local police stations engaged in "four *a*'s" activity* and "four *have*'s" activity,† in order to increase police-public contact and pledge good police service to the public. Consequently, local police officers have become one of the important assessment targets of BLSCC. The police have also become directly involved in maintaining private security, as referred to earlier. In BLSCC, security guards contribute to safety and civilization in the communities. All of the communities employed security guards—mostly decommissioned soldiers.

Similar to the West, situational measures were adopted to minimize the opportunities for crime. In BLSCC measures such as defensible space and crime prevention through environmental design were carried out. Fences

---

* The four *a*'s activity is literally translated as "to have *a* walk household by household, to have *a* meeting with the male, the female, the old, and the young, to say *a* hello when everything is under control, and to have *a* thorough handling when problems are detected" (SZPLY, 1998, p. 12).

† The four *have*'s activity is literally translated as "to *have* a thorough understanding of the beat situation, to *have* a good relationship with the beat public, to *have* a stable team for the management of beat public security, and to *have* a fundamental improvement of beat public security" (SZPLY, 1998, p. 136).

were built, community entries and exits were redesigned and electronically controlled, and antiburglary doors, infrared detectors, and CCTV cameras were installed in some communities. To "design out" crime, illegal structures* were demolished, an important means for managing migrants and a useful way to make the community look more civilized. Substantial emphasis was put on promoting residents' prevention awareness. Retired residents were organized as superintendents of individual staircases, buildings, and blocks. Regular patrolling by both subcommittees of public security members and security guards was arranged. Like the West, this kind of prevention proved costly: Communication and interaction between neighbors became much less frequent. Some old people complained about the iron doors, as it imposed a distance between neighbors, and people seemed more selfish.

Shenzhen has attracted a huge number of migrants from the inland areas. The proportion of the migrant population increased from 0.48% in 1979 to 77% in 2006. The Shenzhen government has treated the management of migrants as a top priority. Managing the migrants was crucial to the success of BLSCC because they reportedly committed a disproportionately high amount of crime in their cities and constituted a significant threat to social order (SZPLY, 1999, p. 224). The need to manage migrants required an adjustment to the *hukou* system, as it allowed for the issuance of temporary *hukou* or "residence permits" by police.

Measures for Civilization

The promotion of civilization is as important as that of safety in BLSCC. An inverse relationship was reportedly assumed between the construction of spiritual civilization and the level of crime (Gui, 1998). In BLSCC, the following measures are implemented to promote civilization levels at the community: (1) moral education, (2) promoting harmonious relationships, (3) building a community culture, and (4) purification of the environment.

Moral education is focused on enhancing individual awareness and compliance to socialist moral rules and party/government policies. This kind of moral education is achieved through the launch of seasonal campaigns, with the driving force being to evaluate and select models or civilize individuals or units. BLSCC also promotes good relationships and mutual help between neighbors. Residents are encouraged to actively fight crime and other social evils. Building a community culture seems to be an all-encompassing

---

* The illegal structures are residing places built without approval from the authorities. They are mostly in the suburban areas where migrants tend to stay when they first enter cities. The villagers-turned-landlords build temporary shacks to accommodate the migrants at a rate both sides accept. Also, some migrants build shacks or similar accommodation structures in the unoccupied wild hills or wild fields, thus becoming true squatters.

concept of civilization. Roughly put, its aims are to enrich community social life and enhance the residents' knowledge by organizing various recreational and educational activities. In the fieldwork, the four communities had all conducted such activities for its residents. The civilization of the community is also embodied in its physical environment. In BLSCC, measures were adopted to clean, improve, and "purify" the environment. For example, one of the achievements in BLSCC was environmental improvement, which was achieved by the establishment of greenbelts, paved roads, and the removal of rubbish. The stress on the improvement of the physical environment is based on the strong belief that the physical environment has a great impact on morality and mental health, a concept in line with the broken windows thesis in the West (see Kelling & Coles, 1996).

Rating System and Outcomes

A complicated rating system of the BLSCC was introduced in 1995 and revised in 1996. The BLSCC reports in Shenzhen are full of yearly achievements and statistics, for example, how communities are rated (either *pass* or *model*), how much money was invested, how much hardware was installed, and how many people were organized, *inter alia*. These achievements are based on the information submitted by local communities. Given the leadership responsibility system, local leaders have a strong desire to portray a positive picture. There were two surveys conducted in 1995 and 1998 by the government, but details of the methodology are not available. The 1998 survey showed that crime decreased in most communities under BLSCC, and some communities recorded no criminal cases (SZPLY, 1999, p. 225). No other rigorous empirical evaluations have been done on the effectiveness of BLSCC. In the whole city, the total number of recorded criminal cases in 1998 had slightly decreased, compared to 1997.

Discussion and Conclusion

To a very large extent, mass line policing (as witnessed in the first period) demonstrated all of the features of community policing, although the label was not used. The mass line of "for the masses, relying on the masses, from the masses, and to the masses" dovetails with the observations made by Nelken (1985) on the role of communities in community crime prevention: by the community, in the community, and for the community. Mass line policing should be understood in a historical context. During that particular period, the ideology of socialism and a planned economical model prevailed. As such, population mobility was very low, and it was not difficult to mobilize the masses for the common goal of crime prevention.

Strike-hard policing in the second period moved away from the tradition due to fundamental changes in Chinese society, although in theory the mass line was still upheld as the guiding line. With the implementation of reform and an open-door policy, crime increased in parallel with economic development. It became very difficult to mobilize the public. Successive waves of strike-hard campaigns did not arrest the trend of crime growth. This period also witnessed the professionalization and formalization of the police force. The police endeavored to cater to the public under a changing social environment by adopting a series of measures, among which are the designation of CMSO as the general crime control policy, the patrolling police force, the 110 hotline, and the emergence of the private security industry.

Community policing in the third period operated in a totally different social environment from the first period. During this period, the label of "community policing" was explicitly used. As an imported concept, community policing was aimed to provide solutions to crime and social disorder in the country. As BLSCC in Shenzhen demonstrated, the implementation of community policing was nothing more than old wine in new bottles. Some measures of BLSCC conform to situational crime prevention in the West. However, most of its measures are reminiscent of the mass line approach, such as its ideological underpinnings, mass prevention and mass management traditions, responsibility system, various kinds of contracts and pacts, heavy government investment (both administrative and financial), and the rating system. The new package of community policing did not change the nature of policing much. The same language was used and similar approaches were adopted. The difference lies in the fact that the police operated in a totally different social environment, which was less conducive to community policing. Community policing has encountered problems in China similar to those in the West. For example, the complaint of physical and social distance imposed by crime prevention hardware is in line with the lament of "fortress city" (Blakely & Snyder, 1997) and "barrack society" (Brown & Polk, 1996) in the West. Skogan's admonishment (1990) on the cultural bearings of the American society on the potential effectiveness of community policing seems to apply to current Chinese society. The mass line, as a locally initiated policing guideline, should be upheld now as in the past, but the problem is how to adjust it to meet the needs of a changing social environment.

References

Bakken, B. (2000). *The exemplary society: Human improvement, social control, and the dangers of modernity in China.* Oxford: Oxford University Press.

Blakely, E. J., & Snyder, M. G. (1997). *Fortress America: Gated communities in the United States.* Washington, DC: Brookings Institution and Lincoln Institute of Land Policy.

Bracey, D. H. (1989). Policing the People's Republic. In R. J. Troyer, J. P. Clark, & D. G. Rojek (Eds.), *Social control in the People's Republic of China* (pp. 130–140). New York: Praeger.

Brown, M., & Polk, K. (1996). Taking fear of crime seriously: The Tasmanian approach to community crime prevention. *Crime and Delinquency, 42,* 398–420.

Chen, X. (2002). Community and policing strategies: A Chinese approach to crime control. *Policing and Society, 12,* 1–13.

China law yearbook. (1994). Beijing: China Law Yearbook Press.

China News Net. (2005, December 6). *The number of security guards reached four million and in Beijing the police was outnumbered by security guards.* Retrieved November 2, 2007, from http://news.sina.com.cn/c/2005-12-06/10577635232s.shtml

Clarke, R. V. G., & Hough, J. M. (Eds.). (1980). *The effectiveness of policing.* Aldershot, Hampshire: Gower.

Constitution of the People's Republic of China. (2004). Beijing: Publishing House of Law. (Original work published 1982)

Crawford, A. (1998). *Crime prevention and community safety: Politics, policies and practices.* London: Longman.

Du, J. (1997). Police–public relations: A Chinese view. *Australian and New Zealand Journal of Criminology, 30,* 87–94.

Dutton, M. (1992). *Policing and punishment in China: From patriarchy to 'the people.'* Cambridge: Cambridge University Press.

Fu, D. (2007). On current situation of patrol police forces and its countermeasures in China. *Journal of Fujian Public Security College, 3,* 39–42.

Gou, Y. (2004, November 19). Abolishing joint protection teams is a consensus. *Gansu Daily.* Retrieved November 11, 2007, from http://www.gsjb.com/Get/jjlt/055171151323156.html

Gui, W. (1998). Reflection on the construction of spiritual civilization and crime prevention. *Juvenile Prevention Research, 1,* 35–40.

Jiao, A. Y. (1997). Crime control through saturated community policing: A corporate policing model. *International Journal of Comparative and Applied Criminal Justice, 21,* 79–89.

Kelling, G. L., & Coles, C. M. (1996). *Fixing broken windows: Restoring order and reducing crime in our communities.* New York: Touchstone.

Klinenberg, E. (2001). Bowling alone, policing together. *Social Justice, 28,* 75–80.

Leng, Y. (2003). Community policing in the process of urbanizations of the countryside. *Public Security Research, 1,* 50–54.

Li, L. (2005). Thoughts on improving the construction of patrolling control network in the capital. *Journal of Beijing People's Police College, 5,* 14–17.

Lu, Q. (2001). Community reform and community policing strategy. *Journal of Chinese People's Security University, 3,* 55–58.

Ma, J. (1998). On the police's mass work during the new era. *Journal of Beijing People's Police College, 2,* 10–15.

Ma, Y. (1997). The Police Law 1995: Organization, functions, powers and accountability of the Chinese police. *Policing: An International Journal of Police Strategy and Management, 20,* 113–135.

Mao, R., & Zou, R. (2005). The function of 110 and the service function of the police. *Economic and Social Development, 3,* 32–35.

Ministry of Public Security. (1994). *The regulation on urban people's police patrolling work.* Retrieved October 21, 2007, from http://vote.mps.gov.cn:9080/gab/flfg/info_detail.jsp?infoId=225

Ministry of Public Security. (2002). *Notice of the Ministry of Public Security and Ministry of Civil Affairs on strengthening the construction of community policing* (Ref. no.: Ministry of Public Security [2002, No. 42]). Retrieved December 1, 2008, from http://www.mca.gov.cn/article//zwgk/zcwj/200711/20071100002866.shtml

Ministry of Public Security. (2003, April 30). *Guidelines of using the 110 hotline.* Retrieved October 22, 2007, from http://vote.mps.gov.cn:9080/gab/flfg/info_detail.jsp?infoId=307

Ministry of Public Security. (2004, August 14). *Notice of the Ministry of Public Security on cleaning up the social order joint protection teams.* Beijing: Author.

National Statistical Bureau. (2006, March 16). *Press release of the main statistics from the 1% census.* Retrieved September 1, 2007, from http://www.stats.gov.cn/tjgb/rkpcgb/qgrkpcgb/t20060316_402310923.htm

Nelken, D. (1985). Community involvement in crime control. *Current Legal Problems, 38,* 259–267.

Putnam, R. (2000). *Bowling alone.* New York: Simon & Schuster.

Sampson, A., Stubbs, P., & Smith, D. (1988). Crime, localities and the multi-agency approach. *British Journal of Criminology, 28,* 478–493.

Shaw, V. N. (1996). *Social control in China: A study of Chinese work units.* London: Praeger.

Shearing, C. D., & Stenning, P. C. (1981). Modern private security: Its growth and implications. *Crime and Justice, 3,* 193–245.

Shenzhen political and legal yearbook. (1996–1999). Shenzhen, China: Haitian Press.

Sherman, L. W. (1992). Attacking crime: Police and crime control. In M. Tonry & N. Morris (Eds.), *Modern policing* (pp. 159–230). Chicago: University of Chicago Press.

Skogan, W. G. (1990). *Disorder and decline: Crime and the spiral of decay in American neighborhoods.* Berkeley: University of California Press.

Southern Daily. (2004, September 15). *One hundred and forty security guards became professionalized.* Retrieved October 22, 2007, from http://big5.southcn.com/gate/big5/www.southcn.com/news/dishi/shenzhen/szgc/200409150614.htm

Sun, Z. (2006, January 10). *The national 110 reports reached 120 million in 2005.* Retrieved October 29, 2007, from http://www.people.com.cn/GB/32306/32313/32330/4015070.html

Tanner, H. M. (1999). *Strike hard! Anti-crime campaigns and Chinese criminal justice 1979-1985.* Ithaca, NY: East Asia Program, Cornell University.

Wang, G., Qin, L., & Nie, G. (1998). Reflection on scientific yanda strategy. *Journal of Chinese People's Public Security University, 4,* 12–19.

Wei, G. (2006). On the relationship between patrol policing and policing power. *Journal of Shan Xi Police Academy, 14,* 13–17.

Wong, K. C. (2002). Policing in the People's Republic of China: The road to reform in the 1990s. *British Journal of Criminology, 42,* 281–316.

Wong, S. W. (1999). Delinquency control and juvenile justice in China. *Australia and New Zealand Journal of Criminology, 32,* 27–41.

Wong, S. W. (2004). Juvenile protection and delinquency prevention policies in China. *Australian and New Zealand Journal of Criminology, 37* (Suppl.), 52–66.

Yu, D., Zheng, X., & Su, T. (1997). *The encyclopedia for chiefs of local police stations.* Beijing: Red Flag Press.

Zhang, D. (2002). Quagmire and breakthrough: Thoughts on the strategy of community policing. *Journal of Fujian Public Security College, 16,* 44–47.

Zhang, L., Zhou, D., Messner, S., Liska, A., Krohn, M., Liu, J., et al. (1996). Crime prevention in a communitarian society: *Bang-jiao* and *tiao-jie* in the People's Republic of China. *Justice Quarterly, 13,* 199–222.

Zhejiang News Online. (2005, January 11). *Jiaxing 110 police do not meet all your needs.* Retrieved October 12, 2007, from http://www.zjol.com.cn/gb/node2/node138665/node138751/node138769/userobject15ai3757538.html

Zhong, L. Y. (2008). *Communities, crime and social capital in contemporary china.* Devon, UK: Willan.

Zhong, L. Y., & Broadhurst, R. G. (2007). Building little safe and civilized communities: Community crime prevention with Chinese characteristics? *International Journal of Offender Therapy and Comparative Criminology, 51,* 52–67.

Zhou, G. (2003). Correctly understand the further improvement of community policing with Chinese characteristics. *Public Security Research, 10,* 50–54.

Zhu, J. (2004). Thoughts on the function of community sub-stations. *Journal of Chinese People's Public Security University, 5,* 32–34.

Zhu, Q., & Wang, D. (1995). A comparison between community policing in the West and comprehensive management of public security in China. *Journal of Chinese People's Public Security University, 57,* 10–14.

The Effect of Community Policing on Chinese Organized Crime
The Hong Kong Case

12

LEE KING WA

Contents

David Bayley (1986) observed four basic elements in *Community Policing*: community-based crime prevention, patrol deployment for nonemergency interaction with the public, active solicitation of requests for service not involving criminal matters, and creation of mechanisms for grass-roots feedback from the community (p. 3). The main objective of this paper is to discuss how these four recurrent elements in community policing may help tackle organized crime in Hong Kong.

This chapter will proceed in three parts. First, it presents a case study of community policing in the Kwai Tsing District of Hong Kong. This case study illustrates the way in which Hong Kong Police promote community-based crime prevention and create a mechanism for feedback from the front-line public housing security guards. The distribution of anticrime propaganda in the neighborhood also allows police officers an opportunity to interact with the public in nonemergency situations. Second, it reveals the recent level of public confidence toward the Hong Kong Police, based on findings from the United Nations Hong Kong International Crime Victims Survey

(UNHKICVS). It explores the correlation of this confidence with public satisfaction with police services. This analysis indicates that the perception of good police services is significantly correlated to the perception of effective policing. Third, the chapter suggests that Chinese organized crime groups (such as the triad societies in Hong Kong) are rooted within the community. That is, triad groups frequently recruit youth from disadvantaged neighborhoods and also prey on street-level businesses for protection fees. To this end, community policing may help suppress organized crime activities at the community level, by encouraging community members to report incidents of extortion and blackmail, and by counterbalancing the influence of triad societies on neighborhood youth by creating a positive image of the police. The chapter concludes by suggesting that community policing can be used to control and suppress gang activity in neighborhoods, perhaps preventing the proliferation of organized crime in a community.

Community Policing in Hong Kong: A Case Study

The Policing Environment of the Hong Kong Special Administrative Region*

The Hong Kong Police Force is responsible for maintaining law and order in a total area of 1,104 km², populated by approximately 6.9 million (as of 2007). Recruited from the local population, nearly all members of the Hong Kong Police speak Cantonese (essential, as nearly 90% of Hong Kong residents speak Cantonese).† Made up of over 27,000 officers (14% of whom are women), the Hong Kong Police also maintain a backup staff of over 4,600 civilians. In addition to this force is the over 3,800 strong Hong Kong Auxiliary Police Force, a reserve force that consists of volunteers who assist in times of natural disasters or civil emergencies. The Hong Kong Police operate within the traditional constabulary concept of preserving life and property, preventing and detecting crime, and keeping the peace, with a strong emphasis on enlisting community support. In times of emergencies, it also has paramilitary capabilities.

---

* Hong Kong is a Special Administrative Region (HKSAR) of the People's Republic of China. China assumed sovereignty under the "one country, two systems" principle following British rule from 1842 to 1997. The current political situation will remain in effect for 50 years, ensured by the HKSAR's constitutional document, the basic law. The economy of Hong Kong is characterized by free trade, low taxation, and minimum government intervention. In 2007 the GDP per capita of Hong Kong was HK$232,836. Retrieved September 18, 2008, from http://www.gov.hk/en/about/abouthk/index.htm

† In June 2007, 88.7% of Hong Kong population were Cantonese speakers, 1.1% were Putonghua speakers, 5.8% were other Chinese dialect speakers, 3.1% were English speakers, and 1.3% were other language speakers.

The Hong Kong Police work closely with the Special Administrative Region (HKSAR) Home Affairs Bureau, District Fight Crime Committees, and other agencies at both regional and district levels to prevent crime and establish youth initiatives. The ideology of community policing is widespread within police ranks. Their primary strategy for maintaining law and order is projecting a highly visible and mobile police presence vis-à-vis uniformed officers,* and promoting a customer-focused culture of quality service. Their concept of community includes the public, community leaders, community organizers and activists, government officials, the business community, media, and all other public and private agencies (Siu, 2007). The following case illustrates the implementation of community policing at a district level in Hong Kong.

Implementation of Community Policing in Kwai Tsing District, Hong Kong

Kwai Tsing District (KWTDIST) is one of 18 districts of Hong Kong and part of the New Territories; it consists of Kwai Chung and Tsing Yi Island. It is one of the earliest towns of Hong Kong, housing the influx of Chinese who migrated to the region in 1949, and later, the baby boom experienced in Hong Kong. The KWTDIST has over 523,000 residents and, consequently, an extremely high population density (22,421/km²). Blocks of government-built public housing estates are common, and both light and heavy industries play an integral part in its development, and share substantial land use. The majority of local residents (approximately 75%) live in public housing and have below-average income, and the district itself is ranked the third least educated in Hong Kong.

The KWTDIST Police implemented a tailor-made scheme of community policing at the end of 2007. The scheme fosters close cooperation between the police (and in particular, the front-line officers) and the community, helping to establish and sustain mutual trust and enhancing social cohesion. As many contemporary police investigations are now intelligence-led, the community policing scheme desires an outcome in which the community plays a more forthcoming approach and willingness to come forward with information to assist police (Siu, 2007).

As Hong Kong Police do not patrol high-rise buildings, a main task of the community policing program is to foster the police's partnership with various private security companies within the area, which in turn become the front line of crime prevention. To this end, the KWTDIST Police have worked toward ensuring a greater presence in these areas. First, a security

---

* The Hong Kong Police Force: Controlling Officer's Report 2007. Programme (1): Maintenance of Law and Order in the Community.

communication network has been set up to enhance communication by e-mail between local police, security companies, and front-line security staff in public housing estates and commercial and industrial buildings. Second, taskforce hotline stickers have been placed at security company posts to ensure visibility at all times. The hotline itself serves as an additional channel for security personnel to make reports of any suspicious characters or circumstances, instead of going through supervisors or dealing with suspects directly. And finally, a police notice board has been set up at lobbies of public housing estates for the police to bring information on crime prevention to residents and front-line security personnel. These proactive measures promote communication between the KWTDIST Police, residents, and the personnel responsible for maintaining community security. Moreover, these initiatives have facilitated greater interaction between the public and the police force. Ultimately these plans have been incorporated with the hopes of greater citizen engagement and fostering greater creativity among the police force (Siu, 2007).

District-level community policing in Hong Kong is based on community-based crime prevention and feedback from the community (Bayley, 1986). The following section will elaborate on community-based youth initiatives and will discuss how community policing can help suppress organized crime. We turn now to public perceptions of the Hong Kong Police, and go on to explore the possible link between public perception and actual public satisfaction of the quality of nonemergency police services.

Hong Kong Public Confidence in Policing: Data from the UNHKICVS

Background of UNHKICVS

The UNHKICVS was carried out in mid-2005 by the Centre for Criminology and the Social Sciences Research Centre of the University of Hong Kong. It surveyed 2,283 Hong Kong residents concerning their crime victimization experience. The UNHKICVS followed the UNICVS sampling criteria and drew a sample of households through random telephone interviews. The eligible respondents were aged 16 or above and were Cantonese, Putonghua, or English speakers. Nonrelevant contacts, such as companies and private businesses, were ignored. The "next birthday" rule was applied; that is, within a household, another randomly selected household member (over the age of 16) whose birthday followed that of the interviewee was chosen, greatly reducing the overrepresentation of the elderly and housewives in the sample. The household member was not replaced if he or she refused to participate. The process continued until the designated number of completed interviews was

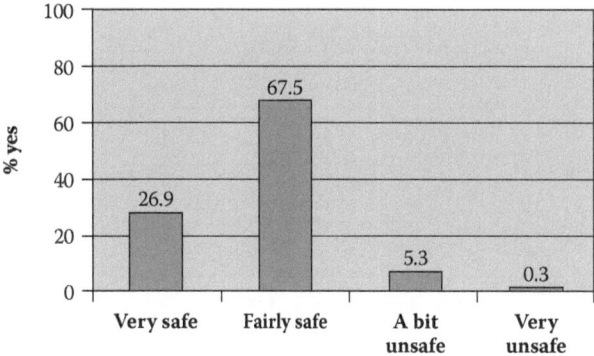

Figure 12.1 Note: Excluding 34 don't know/refusal cases and 8 cannot walk (on the street) cases.

reached. The corresponding maximum sampling error is ±2.1% at 95% level of confidence. The response rate is 49.0%.* We applied weighting to compensate for the over- and undersampling of particular groups, and to make the results more representative of the Hong Kong population (over the age of 16). The weights are the ratio of the age group by sex by region distribution of the population to that of the sample.† All missing cases were assigned a value of 1, and all findings reported here are based on weighted data.

During the interview, respondents were specifically asked about their fear of crime and attitudes toward the Hong Kong Police, apart from their household and personal victimization experiences. Below are the five questions that were posed, and their responses:

1. *How safe do you feel walking alone in your area after dark (after 6:00 p.m.)* (Figure 12.1)?

   A large majority (94%) of the respondents considered it very safe or fairly safe walking alone in their area after dark (6:00 p.m. or after), compared to only 6% of respondents who considered it a bit unsafe or very unsafe. Specifically, more than one-fourth (26.9%) of respondents felt very safe when walking alone in their area after dark, whereas more than two-thirds (67.5%) of respondents felt fairly safe. On the other hand, most respondents who considered it unsafe to walk alone in their area after dark tended to feel a bit unsafe (5.3%) rather than very unsafe (0.3%).

---

* 2,283 success/387 partial + 40 refusal during interview + 1,953 refusal to participate + 2,283 success = 49.0%.
† Weight = proportion of population/proportion of sample.

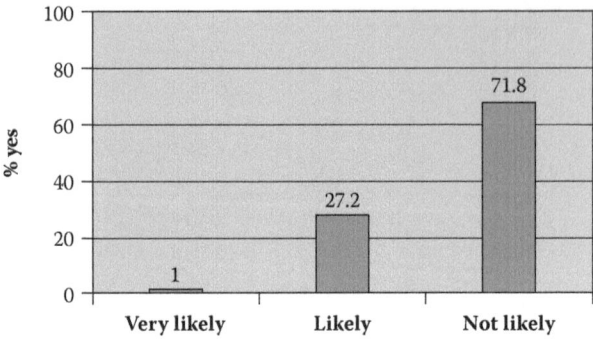

Figure 12.2 Note: Excluding 154 don't know/refusal cases.

2. *What would you say are the chances that over the next 12 months someone will try to break into your home (Figure 12.2)?*

Around 1% of respondents considered it very likely that over the next 12 months someone would try to break into their home. More than one-fourth of respondents considered it likely (27.2%). The majority of respondents, however, considered it not likely (71.8%) that someone would try to break into their home over the next 12 months.

3. *Over the last 12 months, how often were you personally in contact with drug-related problems in the area where you live (Figure 12.3)?*

Most respondents reported they had never been in contact with drug-related problems in the area where they lived in the last 12 months (80.2%). Some 12.4% said they were rarely in contact with drug-related problems in their living area. Around 6.1% were often in contact with drug-related problems, but even less (1.4%) indicated they were from time to time.

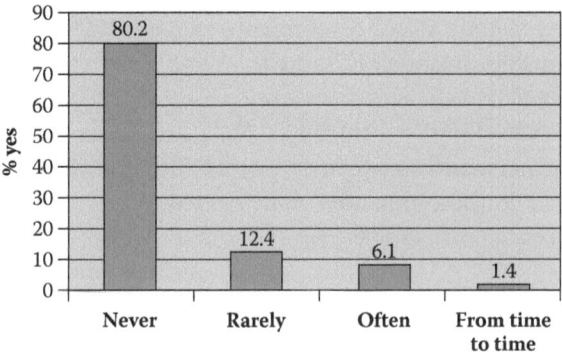

Figure 12.3 Note: Excluding 10 don't know/refusal cases.

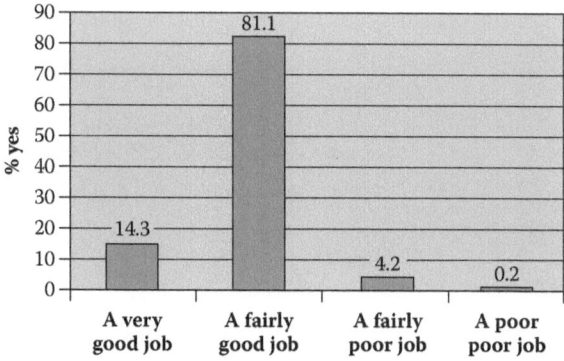

Figure 12.4 Note: Excluding 41 don't know/refusal cases.

4. *How good do you think the police in your area are at controlling crime* (Figure 12.4)?

   A large majority of the respondents (95.6%) felt the police in their area had done a very good job (14.5%) or a fairly good job (81.1%) at controlling crime. Only 4.2% of the respondents felt the police did a fairly poor job at controlling crime, whereas 0.2% thought the police did a very poor job.

5. *How much do you agree that the police do everything they can to help people and be of service* (Figure 12.5)?

   Most respondents (93.6%) either fully agree (12.2%) or tend to agree (81.4%) that police do everything they can to help people and be of service. Around 6% of respondents tend to disagree, and less than 1% of respondents (0.4%) totally disagree that police do everything they can to help people and be of service.

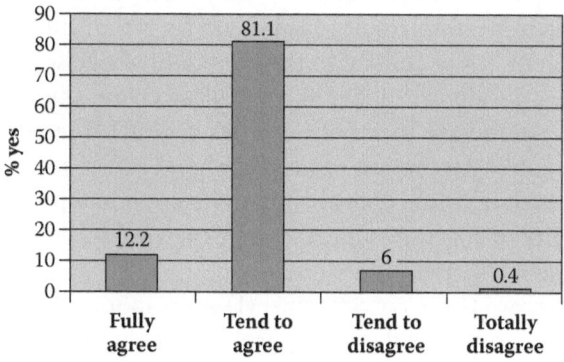

Figure 12.5 Note: Excluding 54 don't know/refusal cases.

Table 12.1   Correlation of the Five Questions in UNHKICVS Relevant to Community Policing

Question (score)	Walk in Dark	Break-in Likelihood	Drug Problem	Police Control Crime	Police Be of Service
Walk in dark	1.00	−0.19**	−0.14**	0.24**	0.18**
(1 very safe–4 very unsafe)					
Break-in likelihood	−0.19**	1.00	0.15**	−0.09**	−0.06**
(1 likely–3 unlikely)					
Drug problem	−0.14**	0.15**	1.00	−0.15**	−0.12**
(1 from time to time–4 never)					
Police control crime	0.24**	−0.09**	−0.15**	1.00	0.49**
(1 very good–4 very poor)					
Police be of service	0.18**	−0.06**	−0.12**	0.49**	1.00
(1 fully agree–4 totally disagree)					

**, $p < .01$ (two-tailed).

Correlation Test

A majority of respondents have a positive perception of the police's quality of service (93.6%) and their ability to control crime (95.6%). Respondents also tend to feel safe walking in their area after dark (94.0%), report never having been personally in contact with drug-related problems in the area where they lived in the last 12 months (80.2%), and consider it unlikely over the next 12 months that someone will try to break into their home (71.8%). The relationships between these questions (variables) are further explored by way of a correlation test. The attributes of each variable are scored so that a correlation index may be calculated. The scoring system and the result are shown in Table 12.1.

Analysis of these results indicates that all of the questions are significantly correlated with one other ($p < .01$). The Pearson correlation coefficients for each pair of tested variables vary from weak to moderate (see Table 12.1). One important result of this analysis is that the public seems to equate the result of crime control to the quality of police service. The better the respondents consider the police at controlling crime, the more they think police help people and are of service ($r = .49$, $p < .01$). The analysis has also found that the public perception of neighborhood safety seems to be associated with the result of crime control. The more confident respondents are in the police's ability to control crime, the safer they feel walking alone in their area after dark ($r = .24$, $p < .01$).

Table 12.1 shows three correlations: (1) As respondents feel safer walking alone in their area after dark, they feel less likely that they will become a victim of home burglary ($r = -.19$, $p < .01$). (2) The less likely they were personally in contact with drug-related problems in the area where they live ($r = -.14$, $p < .01$), the more agreeable they were to the idea that the police would help people and be of service ($r = .18$, $p < .01$). (3) The more likely respondents think someone will try to break into their home over the next 12 months, the more likely they were personally in contact with drug-related problems in the area where they lived ($r = .15$, $p < .01$). However, the break-in likelihood seems to be very weakly correlated to how effective the respondents consider police to be at controlling crime ($r = -.09$, $p < .01$) or how agreeable they consider police in helping people and being of service ($r = -.06$, $p < .01$). Finally, the survey found that as respondents came into contact with drug-related problems in the area where they lived, the less confident they were in the abilities of police in controlling crime ($r = -.15$, $p < .01$) and helping people ($r = -.12$, $p < .01$).

In summary, a positive evaluation of police performance at controlling crime is associated with a positive evaluation of the quality of police service and with a greater perception of neighborhood safety. These results suggest a possible link between trust in police, expectation of police services, and fear of crime. In the following section, the chapter discusses ways in which community policing in Hong Kong may enhance public trust in police, and how this increase in trust may help suppress organized crime groups, in particular the triad societies.

Community Policing and Organized Crime

The Hong Kong public shows a high level of trust toward their police. A major share of this confidence is a direct reflection of the excellent performance of the Hong Kong Police at controlling crime. The data further suggest that this high level of trust may be a result of community policing in Hong Kong. We suggest the emergence of community policing might also link to the special sociopolitical condition of Hong Kong (see Lau, 1982; Lui, 1989; Wong and Lui, 1992). For a different view, Lau (2004) questioned the effectiveness of the Hong Kong comuunity policing model. Police gain public support by actively engaging the community, using mass media channels to enhance public knowledge and confidence in police services, including providing timely responses to media inquiries and radio phone-in programs, holding regular press briefings to keep the press and the public updated on crime and police matters of public interest, and producing weekly TV programs, "Police Magazine" and "Police Bulletin" in Chinese and "Police Report" in English (Hong Kong Police Force, 2007). In a direct contact approach, the Hong Kong Police conduct biannual good citizen award presentation ceremonies to give recognition to members of the public who have rendered positive assistance to the police in fighting crime, and to promote community and voluntary services to Junior Police Call

(JPC) members with a view to fortifying their civic-mindedness and projecting a positive image of JPC members (Hong Kong Police Force, 2007). What effect do these measures have on suppressing organized crime?

Triad societies are the typical organized crime groups in Hong Kong. Relying on reputational and subcultural violence (Lee, Broadhurst, & Beh, 2006), Hong Kong triad members commit crimes such as extortion, blackmail, protection rackets, drug trafficking, syndicated vice, illegal gambling and bookmaking, smuggling, loan sharking, contracted violence, and money laundering. The ratio of triad involvement in overall crimes has remained stable at about 3.0% over the past 10 years (Security Bureau, 2008). Organized crime in Hong Kong can be described as a network composed of multicrime syndicates, enterprise crime, criminal gangs, youth gangs, and street gangs, all under the influence of triad subculture. The more sophisticated criminal groups obtain assistance from corrupt or delinquent professionals and politicians, whereas the lower-rank gangs absorb delinquent youth, school dropouts, unemployed and marginal persons, and drug addicts. The fact that triads are frequently recruited from disadvantaged communities implies that competent community policing can contribute to the suppression of organized crime. There is both theoretical and practical support for this argument.

From a theoretical point of view, Jansen and Bruinsma (2005) assert that organized crime members are not isolated from the community despite the fact that they act outside the law. They further point out that organized crime members operate within the community, recruit members from the surrounding neighborhood, live in the area where they commit their crime, and occasionally gain (often political) support from certain parts or strata of a community where the state has failed or is unwilling to exercise formal social control (Jansen & Bruinsma, 2005). We have found that triad societies, the traditional Chinese organized crime groups, operate similarly to those described by Jansen and Bruinsma. Triads may operate transnationally, but their power bases lie in the local Hong Kong community. Triad societies act as a role model for some youth in marginal economic and social situations, such as those living in public housing estates in Hong Kong. It is also difficult to eradicate triad influence from certain districts or neighborhoods in Hong Kong. Fortunately, like the Netherlands, there is no systematic infiltration or racketeering of triads in legal sectors, nor is there any systematic corruption of police, public prosecutors, judges, and civil servants in Hong Kong. This is empirically supported by the extremely low degree of street-level corruption in Hong Kong (0%) and Amsterdam (0.2%), as reported in the latest UNICVS (see Figure 12.6). In this regard, organized crime groups in both Hong Kong and the Netherlands are operating under a highly noncorrupt but extremely hostile environment. In Hong Kong, such a clean environment

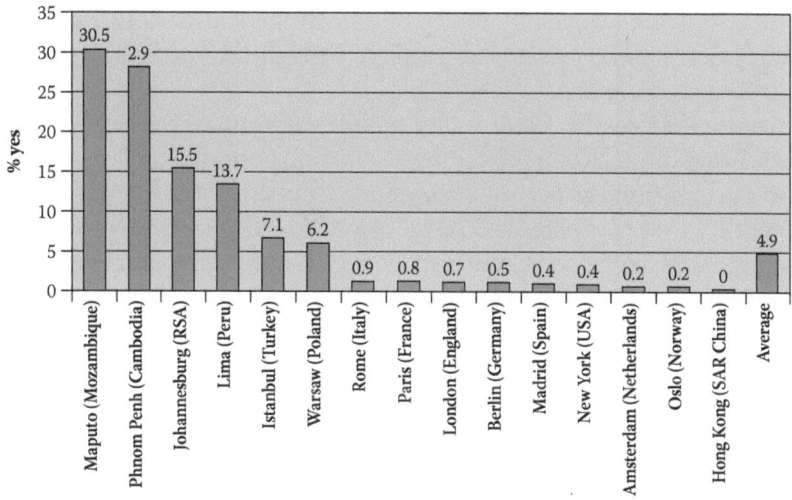

Figure 12.6 Percentage of UNICVS respondents who experienced street-level corruption in the latest sweep. Selected cities comparison. (From Dijk, Kesteren, & Smit, 2007. With permission.)

is ensured by the effective functioning of the Independent Commission Against Corruption (ICAC).*

The Hong Kong Police set up dedicated units—the Organized Crime and Triad Bureau (OCTB) and the Criminal Intelligence Bureau (CIB)—to take action against triads. These units are supported by the Regional Anti-Triad Units (RATUs) and District Anti-Triad Sections (DATSs) that are responsible for anti-triad enforcement at both regional and district levels. The Crime Prevention Bureau actively liaises with shops and businesses to encourage the reporting of triad activities. Such reporting is further encouraged by the Police Central Witness Protection Unit.† Community policing programs, like those implemented in the Kwai Tsing District, may work to enhance public confidence in the Hong Kong Police and encourage residents, private security services, and businesses generally to report elements of triads within their neighborhood.

To impede triad societies and organized crime groups from recruiting juveniles, there is a comprehensive publicity package that demystifies and disparages triad life. One of the well-established community-based programs is the Junior Police Call (JPC), a network consisting of over 140,000 members, aiming to disseminate anti-triad messages to youth. The JPC program

---

* For further detail of the role and function of ICAC refer to the following official website: <http://www.icac.org.hk/en/home/index.html
† The Witness Protection Ordinance 2000, which puts the witness protection program on firm legal footing, was enacted in June 2000 and commenced operation on November 9, 2000.

also develops the leadership ability of its members and motivates them to fight against juvenile crime and combat crime jointly with the community and other organizations.

Another successful community-based program is the School Liaison Officer Programme, Kong Police.* It was first introduced in 1974 as the School Liaison Programme as part of a community policing strategy to support at-risk youth. Currently there are 33 sergeants assigned to secondary schools and 25 sergeants assigned to primary schools.† The program effectively reduces young people's inclination to seek recognition and support from gangs. It also identifies potential at-risk youth for the purpose of early intervention.

Conclusion

As demonstrated in this chapter, the public perception of police crime control in Hong Kong is moderately correlated to their satisfaction of police service and helpfulness. Such an expectation, we argue, probably derives from various community policing programs that pair up issues of police services with issues of crime control. With such expectations, public confidence toward police is consolidated, regardless of whether police provide nonemergency services to a citizen or successfully control crime. Public confidence is critical to the intelligence-led investigation of organized crime groups, whose power bases frequently reside within the community. We therefore suggest that the influence of organized crime groups such as triad societies in Hong Kong is counterbalanced by the effective implementation of community policing by the Hong Kong Police.

---

* Other non-community-based policing of organized crime in Hong Kong includes legislation of constant review to ensure there is adequate legal power for the police to deal with the triads. Fully implemented in 1995, the Organised and Serious Crimes Ordinance (Chapter 455) has enhanced the police's ability to investigate organized and serious crimes, including triad-related offenses. It also empowers the police to apply to the court for heavier sentences and confiscation of proceeds arising from certain crimes, including money laundering. Close cooperation exists between the Hong Kong Police Force and overseas police, particularly those with a fairly large Chinese community, to tackle triad activities. Police continue to remain vigilant in the fight against all forms of triad activities by strengthening intelligence gathering and combating their financial sources.

† This strengthens police commitment in juvenile crime prevention work by focusing on secondary school children from form one level (approximately 12 years) under the multiagency approach. With the policy of nine years of free and universal primary and junior secondary education, it is believed that schools are the best contact point to reach students and parents.

Acknowledgment

This paper was an invited paper for the following workshops on policing: Community Policing in Three Dimensions (Generic Community Policing, Peacekeeping and Policing in the Post 9/11 Environment), organized by Security 21; and the International Centre for Security and Justice at the Australian National University (ANU) in collaborating with the Berkeley Center for Criminal Justice. The authors thank both organizers for their invitation and sponsorship. The author also thanks the School of Justice, Queensland University of Technology, for providing a research base during his visit to Australia.

References

Bayley, D. H. (1986). *Community policing in Australia—An appraisal: Working paper* (National Police Research Unit Report Series 35). Retrieved November 11, 2008, from Australasian Centre for Policing Research website: http://www.acpr.gov.au/pdf/ACPR35.pdf

Dijk, J. van, Kesteren, J. van, & Smit, P. (2007). *Criminal victimisation in international perspective. Key findings from the 2004–2005 ICVS and EU ICS*. WODC, Tilburg University, UNICRI, United Nations Office on Drugs and Crime. The Hague: Boom Juridische uitgevers. Retrieved November 11, 2008, from Wetenschappelijk Onderzoek-en Documentatiecentrum (WODC) website: http://english.wodc.nl/onderzoeksdatabase/icvs-2005-survey.aspx?cp=45&cs=6796

Facts about Hong Kong Police Force. Retrieved September 18, 2008, from Hong Kong Police Force website: http://www.police.gov.hk

Facts about Hong Kong Special Administrative Region. Retrieved September 18, 2008, from Hong Kong Government website: http://www.gov.hk/en/about/abouthk/index.htm

Facts about Independent Commission Against Corruption (ICAC). Retrieved September 30, 2008, from Hong Kong ICAC website: http://www.icac.org.hk/en/home/index.html

The Hong Kong Police Force: Controlling officer's report 2007. Retrieved November 11, 2008, from http://www.budget.gov.hk/2007/eng/pdf/head122.pdf

Jansen, F. E., & Bruinsma, G. J. N. (2005). Policing organized crime: A new direction. *European Journal on Criminal Policy and Research, 5*, 85–98.

Lau, R. W. K. (2004). Community policing in Hong Kong: Transplanting a questionable model. *Criminal Justice, 4*, 61–80.

Lau, S. K. (1982). *Society and politics in Hong Kong*. Hong Kong: Chinese University Press.

Lee, K. W., Broadhurst, R. G., & Beh, S. L. (2006). Triad-related homicides in Hong Kong. *Forensic Science International, 162*, 183–190.

Lui, T. L. (1989). The political role of Hong Kong's new middle class (in Chinese). In A. B. L. Cheung, T. L. Lui, & T. W. P. Wong (Eds.), *Class analysis and Hong Kong* (pp. 77–90). Hong Kong: Chingman Books.

Security Bureau. Facts about triad societies. Retrieved September 30, 2008, from Hong Kong Security Bureau website: http://www.sb.gov.hk/eng/special/bound/triads.htm

Siu, R. C. Y. (2007). Community policing in full steam in Kwai Tsing District (KWTDIST). *Offbeat*, Issue 860, November 21–December 4, 2007. Retrieved September 18, 2008, from http://www.police.gov.hk/offbeat/860/eng/

Wong, T. W. P., & Lui. T. L. (1992). *From one brand of politics to one brand of political culture* (Occasional Paper 10). Hong Kong: Hong Kong Institute of Asia-Pacific Studies, Chinese University of Hong Kong.

Police Development

13

Confounding Challenges for the International Community[1]

TONY MURNEY
JOHN MCFARLANE

Contents

Economically dominant nations have historically been responsible for the concurrent exploitation and development of emerging nations, frequently with catastrophic results. At the broadest international level, this form of engagement is inherently contradictory and self-defeating from a nation-building perspective as gains from international development, humanitarian assistance, and peacekeeping interventions appear, with few exceptions, to be ephemeral and elusive. The longer-term nation-building prognosis is particularly disturbing when the impacts of aid and development are considered empirically, as many analysts contend there is little evidence of lasting results (Hayward-Jones, 2008; Bayley, 2006; Fukuyama, 2004; Hughes, 2003; Hughes & Sodhi, 2006; Porter,

2003) and that benefits are at best "windfall gains" for recipient nations, with little if any link to the broader economic development of the target country.

We should not assume that field practitioners and associated agencies are naïve or otherwise unaware of the entrenched inhibitors that detract from aid and development effectiveness. Such inhibitors are not discussed in this chapter as they are well documented elsewhere, in relation to both aid and development more generally and, in some cases, traditional police development assistance (Fry & Kabutaulaka, 2008; McCawley, 2008; Ellison, 2007; Land, 2007; Morgan, 2007; Murphy, 2007; Marenin, 2005; Slatter, 2003). Pragmatic donor responses to these inhibitors have evolved as part of a disparate and ongoing regime of change in the international development field that, as a global methodology, appears little more sophisticated than trial and error due to its breadth, diversity, and broadly unstructured foundations.[2] It is important to stress that there is nothing inherently wrong with this from a field perspective, as it is commonly the only practical option for confronting debilitating aid and development issues.

The international search for solutions to the aid and development effectiveness problem has in recent years focused on the deployment of civil police into postconflict and other development scenarios as a method of establishing or reinforcing the fundamentals of social, economic, and political governance through strengthened public order and rule of law.[3] As a proposition, this shift has not been markedly controversial and, apart from minority debate about the role and cost of police in development (O'Connor, Chan, & Goodman, 2006; O'Connor, 2004), the move has generally been welcomed (McLeod & Dinnen, 2007; Goldsmith & Dinnen, 2007; McFarlane, 2005; Fullilove, 2006). Regrettably, however, this acceptance seems to be based more on a sense of fatalism driven by the seemingly intractable nature of the development effectiveness dilemma (stay and accept uncertain or negligible gains—leave and risk catastrophe) and an international history where frustration, failure, and waste stand alongside the highest of human ideals.

This acceptance creates a worrying philosophical position for policing (and one that is potentially difficult for practitioners in the field), as there is a lack of clarity in the international community as to how police will contribute to effective nation-building strategies. This aside, there seems to be some form of pervasive assumption that police from developed nations will engage with counterparts from emergent nations and that, by a physical presence in the field, along with some form of training, role modeling, mentoring, and coaching, an *osmotic* transformation will occur among indigenous police. It is further assumed that local police will increasingly come to resemble Western counterparts in conduct, behavior, and skill, with police organizations developing capabilities to provide indigenized security and rule of law, leading to a better future for the people of recipient nations. While these propositions may seem like artificially simplistic "stalking horses," they are a lamentably accurate reflection of international police development programs that reflexively focus on the institution of policing but ignore critical external factors (especially sociopolitical context and function).

The following analysis is designed to stimulate critical thinking on the roles of police in development and to assist in establishing realistic parameters for the successful application of policing strategies to some of the world's most serious nation-building challenges. This analysis will consist of four sections. The first section seeks to highlight the actual, as opposed to stated, role of policing in differing national circumstances and the confounding effect this can have on approaches to development. The second section extends this analysis by outlining two diagnostic structures that summarize the international rule of law challenges confronting police and the policy options for dealing with them. The third integrates these two structures in a way that provides insights into "more right" as opposed to "more wrong" combinations of problem and solution from an international policing perspective. Finally, the fourth section examines five issues identified from practical experience that have caused difficulty in a variety of mission settings, which will be used to ground theoretical conclusions in a much harder reality.

Policing Typologies

At a superficial level, policing across the world appears similar. Police are seen as being responsible for the preservation of internal order and security of the state through enforcement of the rule of law and using, if necessary, state-sanctioned powers of coercion and force. Differences between police organizations are perceived as being more of degree than type; that is, *police are still police.*[4] This perception is reinforced, especially in nonpolicing circles, by factors such as near-universal application of the term *police*, use of common symbols and uniforms, the application of related titles and structures, use of identical accoutrements, and inscriptions on vehicles and buildings, overlaps in vocational training, and at least partial parallels in function defined by idealized relationships to the community and judiciary. Based on these similarities, assumptions can arise about the role of police and how they might behave individually and collectively. Differences can be easily discounted by emphasizing similarities and making apologies for divergent demeanor, standards of conduct, and actual relationships to the community.

Assumptions of this type are entirely understandable and certainly true in some cases. The difficulty arises from nation-building and international development perspectives when apparent similarities between police are outweighed by unobserved or unrecognized differences, which may be of such magnitude that they substantially change the assumed role of the police. This is especially serious where they have transformed into criminal organizations of sometimes lethal proportions, representing a threat to both the populations of affected nations and those charged with providing external assistance to them.

This problem can be explored by considering the differing types of socio-political roles or functions performed by police in different contexts. Sung, drawing on the views of others, summarized:

> Good policing means different things to different social groups. To upper- and middle-class constituents, good policing leads to the maintenance of the status quo and the suppression of criminal activities; whereas to ethnic minorities and underclass citizens, good policing is characterized by the restraint and rectitude of individual officers (Sung 2002). Those more powerful segments of the population expect the police to bring order and those more powerless look forward to seeing their rights and freedoms respected. (Sung, 2006, pp. 348–349)

Sung's proposition identifies differentiated policing constituencies separated by major power imbalances and contravening public expectations. Acceptance of this view requires release of any belief that international policing delivers safety and security to communities as a whole, or that they are there to protect and serve[5] all members of the community equally. While these types of statements are true of some police organizations, they are definitely not of others, regardless of public claims, as there is far greater concern for, or even preoccupation with, the requirements of some elements in the community at the cost of others.

It is realistic in this context to portray police organizations on a spectrum (Figure 13.1) as being agents of *repression* (Murphy, 2008, p. 160) at one extreme (reflecting highly specific sectional interests) and agents of *expression* at the other (reflecting the needs of community members equally). Repressive policing is generally characterized by the arbitrary and unaccountable application of force on and coercion of significant elements of the population (Human Rights Watch, 2005, 2006), as opposed to expressive policing, which operates in support of the systematic application of laws that are compliant with international standards and conventions (for example, human rights) to reinforce the tenets and principles of representative government.

It is possible to populate this spectrum, for illustrative purposes alone, with distinct types of policing segregated by sociopolitical function in different contexts. At the expressive extreme, the generally accepted model from a Western viewpoint is *liberal democratic* policing (Bayley, 2001, 2006; Jackson & Lyon, 2002; Marenin, 1998). This model is variously defined by features relating to democratic processes and representative government, and is characterized by values including fairness, transparency, impartiality, accountability, and independence, with a service-oriented culture derived from adherence to the law and respect for individual rights. It is important to

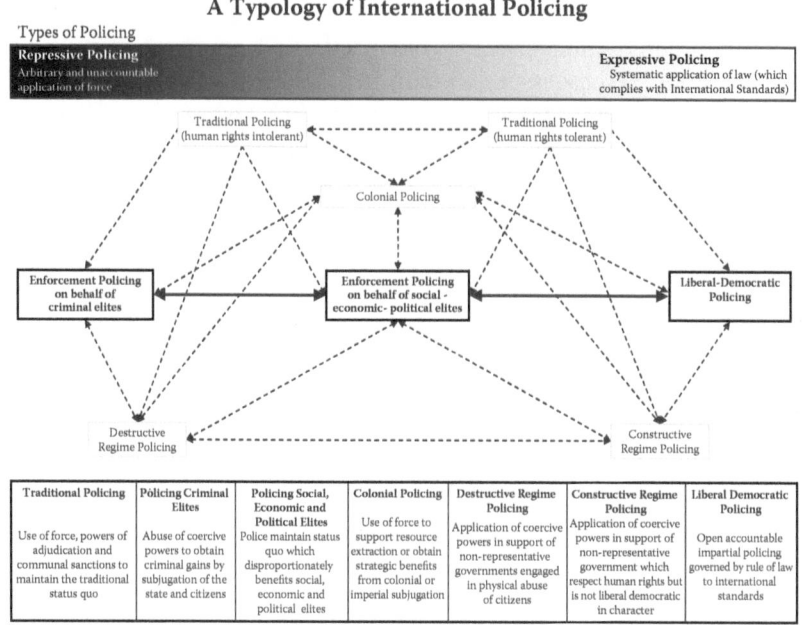

Figure 13.1 A typology of international policing.[6]

recognize that liberal democratic policing is more of an ideal than an actuality, and that while some nations tend toward this position, it would be difficult to convincingly argue that many, if any, actually achieve it in any purist form.

The idealized liberal democratic model contrasts with Sung's proposition that provides for scenarios where police can increasingly serve more discrete sectional interests at the cost of the general community. It is reasonable to presume that, as this occurs, representative legitimacy diminishes and the scope for arbitrary abuse rises. This proposition is represented in Figure 13.1 as a major divergence from the liberal democratic ideal in the form of *enforcement policing*. This is one of the most common forms of policing in the world today, with Freedom House reporting in 2007 that over 50% of the world's nation-states do not satisfy the fundamental criteria to be defined as free. The default function of police in these circumstances is to selectively control populations in the interest of elites that derive social, economic, and political benefits from the status quo.

At its least controversial level, this results in enforcement policing for the benefit of disassociated elites, which at best display benign neglect toward the population at large. At worst, however, policing becomes an active agent of criminally malignant elites that subvert the instruments of state for the purpose of propagating their illicit activities. These have been observed to vary from mass murder and extortion to corruption, torture, intimidation, and extraordinary exploitation of human, natural, and capital resources, with the ability to ultimately transform the state itself into a criminal entity. The evidence in relation to these issues is voluminous (Human Rights Watch, 2008).[7]

This description is, however, overly simplistic when the full spectrum of world police functions is considered. Other options, on different planes, include policing in *traditional* societies,[8] where conventional policing is not obvious, but the function, along with other justice practices (Dinnen, 2008; Peake & Brown, 2005; Goddard, 1992), continues to implicitly exist in the form of individuals (or groups) who possess powers of adjudication and sanction enforced by the social group or specific members of it. The characteristics of policing in these traditional groups can vary, depending on social behaviors, from tyrannically repressive to expressively utopian. Many traditional groups have been subjugated by foreign elites seeking advantage from resources or strategic position, and these have spawned forms of colonial policing (Cole, 1999)[9] that acted, with more or less force, to maintain order for the benefit of colonial or imperial powers.

The 20th century has also witnessed the emergence of regime states founded on philosophies (other than representative government) that stress the ascendancy of state power relative to the individual. They have taken the nuanced form of juntas, dictatorships, people's republics, and radical social experiments. These regimes have varied from being highly destructive,[10] resulting in mass extermination of citizens, to highly constructive, minimizing scope for violent internal conflict, achieving unheard of economic growth, and dramatically improving living standards for their citizens. Police in these states (including military and others performing internal security roles) have varied from murderously repressive to benevolently supportive of the community, but with major formal allegiances to the state and fundamental inabilities to develop liberal democratic philosophies of operation.

This typology now defines a structure that can be used to categorize different types of police organization and to speculate on what other forms of policing might exist, or are yet to evolve in a rapidly globalizing, technocratic world. In doing so, it should also be recognized that police organizations are not static in character (Johnston, 1999)—they can shift position, becoming stronger agents of expression or repression and adopting different combinations of characteristics and behaviors.

The elementary question from this discussion is, at what point do police actually cease to be police? Is this determined by extent of criminality among police, as the antithesis to the rule of law? Does the answer rely instead on legitimacy of the state and breaches of obligations by the state to its citizens in the form of abuses that are contrary to the role of a legitimate state (Chomsky, 2006, p. 40; International Commission on Intervention and State Sovereignty, 2001)? These questions are especially poignant in relation to colonial policing, so-called outlaw states and failed states.

The importance of this typology, however, is not that it describes specific forms of policing (this could be done using a host of different criteria), but in the recognition that, globally, policing is so dissonant that superficially similar organizations may in effect be completely different types of entities. This dissonance includes repressive and expressive organizations comprised of enforcement and regime police along with traditional, colonial, and liberal democratic police. They represent a range of behaviors, which may be highly criminalized, contain destructive or constructive state-centric views of the world, reflect the less well-recognized values of traditional societies, or possibly entail strong tendencies toward liberal democratic government. In the final analysis, police organizations differ not only in how they perform their core functions, but also in the nature of and reason for those core functions.

A failure to appreciate the strength of this dissonance is likely to lead to misspecification of police development programs, which all too commonly assume that "bad" policing in emerging nations is simply an underperforming variant of liberal democratic policing when, in reality, it is a distinct form of sociopolitical control serving specific sectional interests, based on vastly different objectives (regardless of public claims) and using different methods of operation that may include ingrained corruption, brutality, and abuse. Police development programs designed to deal with one type of policing (for example, an underperforming liberal democratic organization) will almost certainly fail if applied to another (such as those engaged in criminalized enforcement policing or destructive regime policing). Worse still, the wrong types of development support may strengthen such police organizations with adverse long-term consequences for the people of recipient nations.

Development Policing—Rule of Law Challenges and Policy Options

The most significant risk facing international police development programs is the restricted range of experiences (available to practitioners) that do not extend far beyond the peacekeeping paradigm. This paradigm, with few exceptions, is most relevant to immediate postconflict situations with a military emphasis on stabilization leading to a negotiated or enforced termination of armed conflict. There has been an increasing use of police in peacekeeping missions over the past 20 years (Greener-Barcham, 2007; Greener, 2007), including an increased concentration on capacity building (seen as training, equipment, and infrastructure). Peacekeeping initiatives have unfortunately tended to be short-term, with a reliance on other institutions (including other arms of the United Nations, nongovernmental organizations (NGOs), and bodies such as the World Bank and International Monetary Fund (IMF)) to support peace consolidation (United Nations, 2008, p. 23). Linden, Last, and Murphy (2007, p. 166) report frequent requirements for reengagement of peacekeeping missions due to relapses into violent internal conflict.

There is little scope in this paradigm to operate in preconflict environments, engage in the broader development agenda to strengthen the rule of law, or establish goals that reach past the immediacy of conflict and postconflict environments.[11] As a result, there is little guidance as to the full spectrum of challenges faced by police in this field and the policy options available to governments, multilateral organizations, and others when considering the international applications of development policing.

The Rule of Law Spectrum

Any review of failed and fragile states across the globe produces an almost indecipherably complex picture of political intrigue, warfare, irreconcilable ethnic differences, corruption, hardship, hunger, disadvantage, waste, and criminality (Fund for Peace—Country Profiles, 2008; Kaplan, 1994).[12] There is a strong need for a high-level conceptual examination of the rule of law challenges generated in these situations, as aggregate views can easily be obfuscated by interminable detail, situational dynamics, and the personal particularities of protagonists.

The fundamental starting point for police programs is that they should be inextricably linked to improvements in the rule of law as the formal governance mechanism for nation-states (Annan, 2006).[13] It is appropriate that the range of international police development challenges be cast in rule of law terms, as the policing function does not exist as an end in itself, but rather as an integrated part of law and justice processes that give effect to rules-based social, economic, and political development toward statehood. The link between social, economic, and political development is twofold: First, the formal and accountable rule of law underwrites production-based economies that are heavily reliant on the security of property rights to protect the benefits flowing from an accumulation of economic surpluses; and second, contemporary institutional rule of law is more likely to comply with the wide range of international standards and conventions designed to secure human rights and fundamental freedoms.[14]

Figure 13.2 describes a rule of law spectrum that ranges from no law at one extreme to refined rule of law at the other, and delineating four major situations likely to be encountered in development policing:

- *Internal conflict* (civil war and widespread internecine killing)—
  There is either no sustained rule of law internal to the nation-state, or it is highly tentative and under threat from the widespread use of armed force by military or related entities causing violent death, injury, and destruction, with affected populations living in battlefield or militarily contested circumstances where the rule of law has been

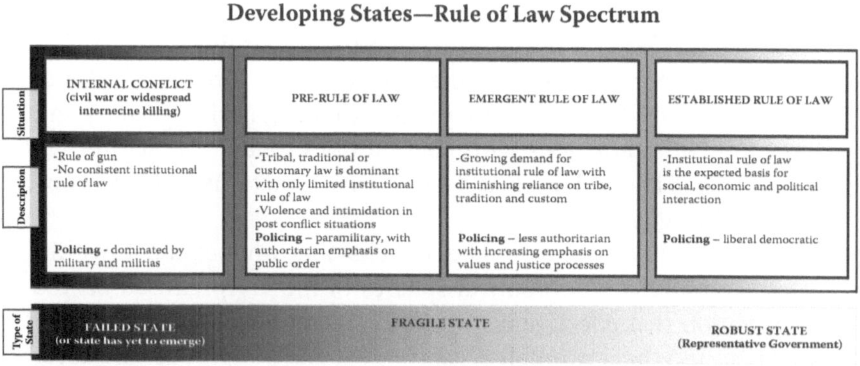

Developing States—Rule of Law Spectrum

	INTERNAL CONFLICT (civil war or widespread internecine killing)	PRE-RULE OF LAW	EMERGENT RULE OF LAW	ESTABLISHED RULE OF LAW
Situation				
Description	-Rule of gun -No consistent institutional rule of law **Policing** - dominated by military and militias	-Tribal, traditional or customary law is dominant with only limited institutional rule of law -Violence and intimidation in post conflict situations **Policing** – paramilitary, with authoritarian emphasis on public order	-Growing demand for institutional rule of law with diminishing reliance on tribe, tradition and custom **Policing** – less authoritarian with increasing emphasis on values and justice processes	-Institutional rule of law is the expected basis for social, economic and political interaction **Policing** – liberal democratic
Type of State	FAILED STATE (or state has yet to emerge)	FRAGILE STATE		ROBUST STATE (Representative Government)

Figure 13.2 Developing states—rule of law spectrum.

replaced by the *rule of the gun*. Østerud (2008) stresses that not only can the intensity of internal conflict change over time and between places, but also, and most critically, it can change in ways that escape definition (by, for example, becoming more criminal than civil in demeanor). Police functions, regardless of labeling, will generally be undertaken by formal militaries or militias that may be described and uniformed as police, but which continue to perform roles associated with the suppression of violence or movements that internally threaten the state. Police actions will have little to do with the courts or other legal institutions, while officers will tend to be poorly educated or illiterate and have little knowledge of institutional law. They will be armed with military weapons and work within military organizational structures.

- *Pre-rule of law*—Formal institutional rule of law has only limited direct implications for the majority of people in this scenario: The main form of law is derived from segregated traditional, tribal, and customary influences overlain by arbitrary violence and intimidation in some pre- and postconflict settings. The role of central government in the daily lives of affected people is minimal, ineffective, and disruptive of some customary authorities and behaviors. Central governments are often weak and fractured, with the population displaying little sense of nationhood (Fukuyama, 2008). Police functions tend to be paramilitary and authoritarian, with a significant emphasis on public order and the protection of elites.

- *Emergent rule of law*—Popular demand for institutional rule of law is emerging and increasingly being enforced in relation to key social, economic, and political behaviors that support transition to activities requiring interaction with groups beyond the bounds of traditional, tribal, or customary relationship systems, but which may continue to include illegitimate use of force and coercion in pre- and postconflict

settings. If effective, institutional rule of law progressively replaces
or formalizes aspects of these influences and marginalizes pre- and
postconflict emphases on the illegitimate use of force. Police functions will be undertaken, with an increased emphasis on values and
nonpunitive interactions with communities guided by the institutional rule of law and marked by stronger interactions with other law
and justice agencies.

- *Established rule of law*—General behaviors and conduct within
  social, economic, and political spheres of life are premised on the
  expectation that effective institutional rule of law is a normal daily
  practice, and that criminality, corruption, and malpractice are aber-
  rant and generally unacceptable to individual citizens, communities,
  and governments. Police will be agents of expression, values driven,
  and tend toward liberal democratic behaviors that emphasize the
  primacy of the institutional rule of law.

These four situations have also been illustratively aligned in Figure 13.2,
with three levels of state effectiveness—ranging from state failure through
state fragility to robust representative government.[15] This is done to indicate
the extent of state disability, which can be expected with each rule of law condition, and to describe the general circumstances in which policing development programs would need to be delivered. The most important of these
alignments are those between conflict, complete debilitation of the rule of
law, and state failure; pre-rule of law, emergent rule of law, and state fragility;
and the link between established rule of law and robust representative government. This pattern is borne out by empirical analysis of the association
between the World Bank Rule of Law Index and the Foundation for Peace
Failed States Index, which is in the order of 80–90%.

Three major factors are important when considering the rule of law spectrum. First, positions on the spectrum have been ordered sequentially from a
development point of view (increasing institutional rule of law), but nation-
states do not have to pass through all situations in a linear way. For example,
a state may fall from an emergent rule of law situation to one dominated
by internal conflict without passing through a pre-rule of law environment,
and vice versa, depending on the postconflict dynamics. Second, situations
on the spectrum can and do vary in intensity, so that alignment with other
categorizations, such as state failure, is a matter of degree rather than an
absolute condition. Third, the state fragility scale used in Figure 13.2 seems
almost benign in the context of the earlier discussion about the desperate
plight of state-abused citizens. This is particularly significant from a rule of
law perspective, as state failure implies victimization as the result of an omis-
sion by the state to fulfill the obligations of a state to its citizens, rather than
an active state malevolence that deliberately targets individual citizens or

groups citizens. The concept of a *malevolent state* needs to be considered with great care as an *off-spectrum* challenge in the planning and management of policing initiatives that differs from others not by degree but by quantum, with a destructive potential that creates uncontrollable threats.

The critical observation from the rule of law spectrum is that four broad challenges pervade most of the world's developing nation-states. Confusion between these situations can arise from a failure to appreciate that rule of law differences exist between nation-states, and that many of these differences are suitable for their time, place, and culture, with the consequence that short-term police development needs will be prescribed by them. Distorted perceptions about rule of law and policing needs in developing nation-states can result in an inability to comprehend what is necessary to transform one situation to another, or properly recognize features such as the malevolent state. The most common manifestation of this problem is the inappropriate transposition of theoretical or conceptual constructs onto actual situations, resulting in misguided efforts to solve the wrong problems. This condition is aptly described in colloquial terms as *seeing what you want to see, not what is there.*

The Policy Option Spectrum

As with the rule of law spectrum, the panoply of overlapping international development programs designed to alleviate the worst excesses of failed or fragile states, combined with the sheer volume of uncoordinated humanitarian assistance initiatives being delivered by innumerable contributors, debilitates meaningful appraisal of the strategic policy options for development policing. The underlying philosophies, motivations, and objectives of programs are extraordinarily difficult to discern from an intoxicating and disruptive milieu of competing national, organizational, and individual interests, spiked by altruism, greed, corruption, wealth, criminality, and helplessness. This is hardly the setting for cool and deliberate policy formation where rationality rules and best solutions are inevitable. This, however, does not mean that strategic policy options are inherently complex, especially when considered from an aggregate level.

Figure 13.3 describes a policy option spectrum for development policing, consisting of four limiting cases that transition from the most extreme alternative to the least:

- *Military intervention*—The deployment of military formations to suppress or deter warlike activity, with the objective of restoring or maintaining peace and security among affected populations. This type of activity is premised on dominance of the military and, by default, the imposition of martial law due to an inability of civil authorities to function across the state, or in significant parts of

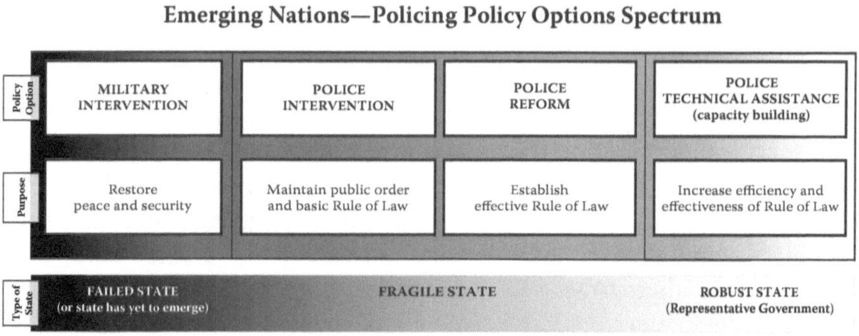

Emerging Nations—Policing Policy Options Spectrum

Policy Option	MILITARY INTERVENTION	POLICE INTERVENTION	POLICE REFORM	POLICE TECHNICAL ASSISTANCE (capacity building)
Purpose	Restore peace and security	Maintain public order and basic Rule of Law	Establish effective Rule of Law	Increase efficiency and effectiveness of Rule of Law
Type of State	FAILED STATE (or state has yet to emerge)	FRAGILE STATE		ROBUST STATE (Representative Government)

Figure 13.3 Emerging nations—policing policy options spectrum.

it, due to armed opposition. This is seen as a temporary condition pending a return to civil authority even though there is an attendant risk of rampant militarization in fragile states. Civil police are not trained, equipped, or organized as battlefield soldiers and have little place in war fighting with the notable exception of assignments involving advice to the military on criminal matters, planning for the transition to civil authority, and the investigation of war crimes and human rights abuses.

- *Police intervention*—The deployment of international police to perform in-line policing duties with executive powers and authorities bestowed by the state, with the objective of restoring or maintaining public order and the basic rule of institutional law. This type of activity is premised on a continuance of civil authority or rapid return to it, with arrangements for progressive return of policing functions to local agencies as they are reconstituted and re-formed with robust operational capabilities and behaviors suitable for the prevalent rule of law situation. This type of police work requires additional operational capabilities to support officers working in high-risk environments. These capabilities need to be managed very carefully to ensure that populations are not abused and that bad civil policing standards are not set for local police, with an unnecessary reliance on the use of force replacing respect and strong community relations.

- *Police reform*—The deployment of international police to in-line policing duties or as advisors to assist civil authorities to establish or reestablish basic policing principles to support the institutional rule of law. This may involve overcoming the usual technical assistance (capacity-building) problems, such as low levels of vocational skill, equipment shortages, and defective infrastructure. However, as modern or liberal democratic policing has evolved into a values-based pursuit, as discussed earlier, technical assistance alone will not have the desired result. Issues—both internal and external to police organizations—will need to be resolved. These will include entrenched criminality, corruption, patronage, politicization, absence of basic requirements for organizational effectiveness, and disempowered populations, along with even more rudimentary factors, such as poverty, illiteracy, lack of general education, and health among police and their extended families.[16] Reform requires not only professional development of police, but also high-risk political engagement designed to change the attitudes and behaviors of power elites and to mobilize popular demand for high-quality police services. This long-term endeavor requires strong local support in addition to vigorous links with other areas of the justice sector and donors working in those areas.

- *Police technical assistance* (capacity building)—The deployment of advisors to assist in identifying and eliminating barriers to the effective and efficient delivery of police services. This approach assumes basic police functions are performed to a workable standard that is free from major defects, but which could be improved by increases in effectiveness and efficiency.[17] Programs of this type should desirably be fully integrated with activities in other parts of the justice sector so as to maximize the balance with courts, corrections, and prosecutions, along with defense and advocacy services.

As with the rule of law, the policy option spectrum has been aligned with state functionality. Military and police interventions are associated with the more serious forms of state failure and fragility, whereas police reform and technical assistance are associated with emergent and established rule of law. While this seems self-evident in a conceptual model, such distinctions are more difficult to recognize in the field because they overlap and are confounded by the occurrences of daily life in development policing. How, for example, can low-level civil war be distinguished with any degree of certainty from high-level violent public disorder when, on the face of it, both are characterized by similar features in the form of social division, violent death, injury, and destruction of property?

Individual police development programs need to be created around the environment in which they will be delivered, with a deep cognizance of the type of police organizations that occupy the environment. The full spectrum of policy options is extremely wide and incorporates some of the most powerful policy tools available to contemporary nation-states. Military interventions and technical assistance have been used frequently by governments in the past (Organization for Economic Co-operation and Development, 2007) and are familiar to policy analysts. The policy spectrum, however, includes two new options unfamiliar to policy analysts: police interventions and police reform. These options are softer in posture than the application of military force (invited or not), but more vigorous than pure aid or development responses. They also have a major advantage over other forms of engagement, as they assimilate to varying degrees with the main organs of internal security in recipient nation-states while preserving civil authority that can otherwise be seriously impaired by state crises. This is a highly valuable capability, as it may decelerate any tendencies toward militarism or other forms of domination rule that are prone to arise in fragile states.

Linking Policing Programs to the Rule of Law and Policy Options

The main question at this stage is whether the propositions represented by the rule of law and policy options spectra can be meaningfully integrated to provide guidance on better or the best application of development policing resources. As discussed at the outset, the aim of this analysis is not to produce correct or incorrect solutions due to the inherent dynamism and complexity of the issues being examined, but rather to identify "more right" as opposed to "more wrong" combinations of problem and solution.

This integration can be achieved at a conceptual level by construing the rule of law and policy options spectra as the axis of a two-dimensional *guidance model*, with the limiting cases on each spectrum combining to represent changes in state against the types of challenge to be resolved and the policy options for achieving the required ends. The results of this integration are shown in Figure 13.4, with 16 combinations linking rule of law situations to policy options. Individual combinations are ordered horizontally according to the rule of law situation, and as can be seen from Figure 13.4, each of these is associated with four policy options. These combinations have been numerically graded (1 to 4) according to the coherence of problem and solution, with the severity of the problem equating to the extremity of the solution and vice versa. The grading system used is "more right" (1) or "more wrong" (4), with in-between grades of "less right" (2) and "less wrong" (3), noting that some combinations require more than one grading to accurately reflect the fit of problem and solution.

The overall picture from this attribution places some combinations in stark relief to others. "More wrong" combinations range across the guidance model and are predictably inclined to preclude police programs from internal conflict or civil war situations (A_1, A_2, and A_3) as these are, with minor exceptions, military environments. "More wrong" combinations also tend to disqualify military interventions in emergent rule of law situations (C_4), since these represent intensifying civil environments, and to prohibit both military and police interventions in established rule of law situations (D_3 and D_4), as these would unnecessarily disrupt functioning civil systems of government. "More right" combinations, by contrast, dictate that

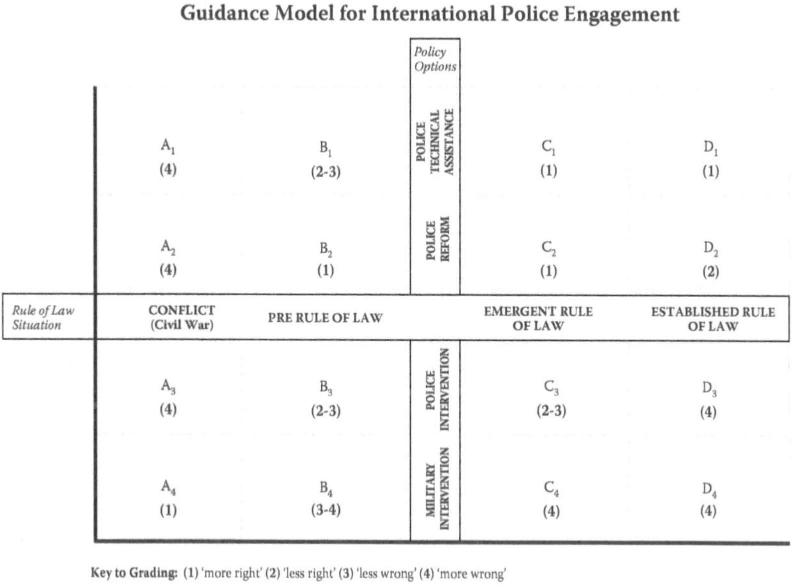

Guidance Model for International Police Engagement

Rule of Law Situation	CONFLICT (Civil War)	PRE RULE OF LAW	Policy Options	EMERGENT RULE OF LAW	ESTABLISHED RULE OF LAW
	A_1 (4)	B_1 (2-3)	POLICE TECHNICAL ASSISTANCE	C_1 (1)	D_1 (1)
	A_2 (4)	B_2 (1)	POLICE REFORM	C_2 (1)	D_2 (2)
	A_3 (4)	B_3 (2-3)	POLICE INTERVENTION	C_3 (2-3)	D_3 (4)
	A_4 (1)	B_4 (3-4)	MILITARY INTERVENTION	C_4 (4)	D_4 (4)

Key to Grading: (1) 'more right' (2) 'less right' (3) 'less wrong' (4) 'more wrong'

Figure 13.4 Guidance model for international police engagement.

military interventions are most appropriate in conflict zones (A_4) and that police reform is likely to best fit in pre-rule of law and emergent rule of law situations (B_2 and C_2), where local police organizations are in their early formative states. Police technical assistance or capacity building is also seen as "more right" in emergent rule of law and established rule of law situations (C_1 and D_1), as aspects of vocational training along with the provision of equipment and infrastructure may be necessary to solidify change management processes.

The "more right" and "more wrong" combinations are, superficially at least, relatively straightforward and uncontroversial until compared with the actual disposition of, for example, international peacekeeping activities. This type of comparison generates important questions relating to the fit between problem and solution, including the balance between civil and military elements in peacekeeping missions, and the processes needed to assist nation-states in progressing from a military orientation for survival to a civil one without the need for repetitive reengagement of peacekeepers at high human and financial cost to international donors (Collier, Chauvet, & Hegre, 2008; Linden, Last, & Murphy, 2007). These questions not only raise issues of the magnitude of challenges faced in peacekeeping, but also are the partial nature of most peacekeeping operations by comparison to the full spectrum of possible policy options, which may need to be implemented over long time periods.[18] Does this mean that the role of peacekeeping needs to be redefined in "fire brigade" terms, where interventions simply seek to restore peace and stop killing before moving on to the next crisis, and if so, where to from there?

Those combinations in Figure 13.4 with less definite fits are perhaps the most interesting because they commence a line of thought that deals with "less right" and "less wrong" types of fit. For example, military intervention in pre-rule of law situations (B_4) is not ruled out of contention because (despite not being a standard conflict situation) police may require military support to underwrite the security of programs where militias have been a feature of public order problems (Glenn, 2007). Similarly, police reform should be unnecessary in established rule of law situations (D_2) (as police organizations should have already passed this stage of development), but police reform may be necessary due to factors such as ingrained resistance to change, residual criminality, and resurgent corruption.

These observations require further development as they lead to questions of transition from one combination of problem and solution to another. The transition process means that, at some point, static problem and solution mixes shift from being "more right" (assuming they ever were) to "less right" and, subsequently, if suitable action is not taken, to being "less wrong" and possibly "more wrong." For example, unnecessary persistence with military suppression of violence may contribute to the repression of emerging civil society. It should also be acknowledged that several combinations of problem and solution might exist within one nation-state at the same time, depending on such factors as history, social organization, urbanization, and disparities in economic advantage. For example, conflict in one region may coexist with pre-rule of law in another, while major cities might display characteristics of emergent or established rule of law. The predisposition for interaction between areas and groups will also mean that problem and solution combinations may be less than optimal, with elements of one situation spilling over into others, contaminating the definition of problems and solutions, and reducing overall situational fit.

It is also important to stress at this juncture that movements on the failed state spectrum will not necessarily be positive over time (Collier et al., 2008; International Crisis Group, 2007; Hood, 2006). In fact, empirical observations in this area indicate exactly the opposite; that is, nation-states that have failed or not matured from a formative or fragile condition will be prone to experience repeated difficulties at great cost to all parties as policy solutions cycle backward and forward to adjust for development setbacks.[19] Cost becomes critical at this point from two perspectives. First, can donors afford the cost of "more right" solutions? If not, how effective are "less right," "less wrong," and "more wrong" solutions likely to be in achieving final goals? Second, can donors afford the cost of long-term transitions from one problem-solution combination to another, and if not, should engagement be avoided on the grounds of low effectiveness or the risks of being *sucked into a quagmire* where no workable solution has been defined?

The guidance model for development policing shows a wide range of problem-solution combinations that can be considered as part of the nation-building agenda. Many of these combinations are undesirable, while others are clearly compatible and likely to be "more right" than "more wrong." The guidance model described here highlights the need for policymakers and others to plan for transitions from one problem-solution mix to another, and to be agile in recognizing when actual policy changes need to occur. They also highlight the prerequisites for cooperation with, and interoperability between, key organizations, as no one participant will have the capability or mandate to manage the full spectrum of situations, from internal conflict and military intervention (A_4) to technical assistance and established rule of law (D_1).

Lessons Learned: The Reality Check

The guidance model in Figure 13.4 presents one possible rational framework for the systematic diagnosis of police development challenges and the policy options for resolving them. These types of framework are useful only to the extent that they are based on an accurate and complete diagnosis of the real problems. This, however, is frequently not the case in development policing, and there are often gaps between problem diagnosis and policy solutions. This analysis reflects the lessons learned from hard-won practical experience, which has assisted in the distillation of questions essential to successful police development in failed or fragile states. An awareness of these types of questions is an absolute requirement for policymakers in this field.

Unacknowledged and Hidden Problems

There are two dilemmas that are brought into sharp focus by police development programs because of the powerful association between expatriate police and accountability. The first of these is *the problem of the unacknowledged problem*. This arises from the temperament of relationships between donors and recipients (whether government agencies, multilateral bodies, or nongovernment organizations), where sensitivities limit or prevent meaningful discussion of profound problems on the grounds that they may jeopardize or impair relationships. As a result, police development programs can be crafted within safe parameters where these problems (especially those most responsible for defects in policing and the rule of law) cannot be properly acknowledged or discussed. The success or otherwise of subsequent police development programs may be directly related to this syndrome, as problems may be wrongly defined, focus on symptoms rather than causes, or become distracted by factors that are change irrelevant or change insensitive.

Unacknowledged problems are thematic phenomena that subvert entire governance structures in the form of human rights abuse, corruption, and patronage, which are deleterious to the interests of large groups within the population. While these problems may be too obvious to ignore in the design of development policing initiatives, discussion can be minimized, questions discounted as attacks on national sovereignty, positions defended by false or misleading claims that these matters are being addressed internally, and persistent abuse explained as cultural practice (Roth, 2008). These defenses are generally invalid to even casual observers due to the magnitude of such problems and their impacts on national development. Significant aspects of policing are prominent in the unacknowledged problem category.

The second dilemma is *the problem of the hidden problem*. This type of problem, by contrast to the unacknowledged problem, is highly specific from a rule of law perspective, as it involves the illegitimate actions of individuals that are deliberately hidden due to their inherent criminality. In descending order of significance, these actions include, for example, mass, multiple, or singular episodes of murder, torture, other forms of abuse, rape, theft, fraud, and major conflicts of interest. This raises questions about the depth and strength of agreed development programs in key agencies, but especially policing, as those who form part of the hidden problem may be integral to design processes and seek to neutralize resultant programs in order to protect themselves and other accessories, or to perpetuate a status quo that provides substantial personal benefits.

In arriving at this point, it is important to put these problems in context by acknowledging that, in even the most dysfunctional nation-states, there are individuals of outstanding character who perform their duties at very high personal risk to their careers and personal safety. It is also important to recognize that donors are not free of unacknowledged or hidden problems that include matters of extreme national self-interest and unconscionable individual behaviors involving abuse of power imbalances and other relationship issues when dealing with local people in recipient nations. This aside, the connotation of these two dilemmas is that care must be taken to separate what needs to be achieved from what can be achieved, whether resources are being committed in the interests of the relationship or in the interests of reform, and whether reform is possible with the resources available or other objectives are more realistic.

Each Mission Anew

Each mission has its own unique characteristics, and although certain common factors may exist, each mission has to be planned and organized. Each mission also has a unique context with its own background, special complexities and challenges, and opportunities and learning experiences. One lesson is that there are certainly no "one size fits all" solutions. As such, it is essential (drawing on the principles outlined earlier in this chapter) that there be an appreciation of what both sides aim to achieve, and whether, in all the circumstances, such aims are realistic (McFarlane, 2005).

Having established agreement on the outcome, how will both sides achieve this end? Is the basic concept viable in terms of outcomes and timings? Is the local criminal justice system, including the police service, capable of meeting these goals? Is there local government and community support for what is being undertaken, and how can government and community support be measured on an ongoing basis? Is it practicable to adjust the approach in the light of lessons learned or criticisms made? What languages will be used for documents? Is there the capacity to do this? What skill sets do the mentors need to contribute effectively under this program? Is the approach to training, capacity building, and institutional strengthening adjusted to meet local needs, or is the donor—perhaps inadvertently—trying to export its own model?

None of this effort will be sustained unless there are shared goals, mutual respect, cultural sensitivity, and above all, trust. What are the donor's underlying motives? Many in the recipient state will be suspicious of the donor's perceived motives, so it is essential to be honest and acknowledge that the donor state is serving its own national interests as well as endeavoring to assist a neighbor. The donor's motives could so easily be misunderstood or misinterpreted. The donor should not be afraid to acknowledge this and, in doing so, may well achieve a greater level of understanding and support. However, where misunderstanding or mistrust exists, the donor needs to carefully consider how it can honestly and transparently address this problem.

Finally, there is the question of the political involvement of other foreign states in the state where the advisers are deployed. The most likely involvement in the Australian region would be the competition for political influence and allegiance between China and Taiwan, and the host state. This could involve generous untied aid or even covert bribery of host state officials, including senior police officers, which complicates the operational environment of the advisers.[20]

Situational Awareness

Of all the issues of vulnerability in achieving joint objectives, none is more important or sensitive than cultural awareness. It needs to be acknowledged *and understood* that the donor is operating in another country, conditioned by the culture, history, social mores, networks of relationships, value systems, and religious or spiritual space of and between that country's inhabitants.

What are the cultural mores and protocols in, for example, Timor-Leste, the Solomon Islands, Papua New Guinea, or Afghanistan? Each country is different and unique. What is the village culture? How important is the *wantok* culture in the community?[21] How does land ownership work? Is it patriarchal or matriarchal? What are the *key* elements of local custom that differentiate one community from another? It cannot be expected that the community of the recipient state will change its basic values to accommodate the donor, although it might reasonably be expected that the donor's mentoring and professionalism might help to moderate bad behavior, such as violence, extortion, and corruption, where such behavior is clearly inimical to good governance, community relations, and sustainable policing. How can one engender changes in attitudes when such changes are necessary to achieve the agreed joint objectives?

As guests in the recipient state, the donor's predeployment training and preparations are of critical importance. Has the donor really tried to learn something about the country to which personnel are being deployed—its history (especially the recent circumstances that have resulted in crisis), its culture, its community complexities, its gender issues, its tribal animosities, its political and social dynamics, its attitude toward violence, its languages, and its long-term relationship with the donor state? What are the key issues that impact—either positively or negatively—on the policing role? What are the change agents in the community—the government and political processes, the young people and the educational processes, the security forces and the security processes, the churches or mosques and the religious processes, the NGOs and the social processes, the media and the exposure processes, the civil discourse and the community processes? How can these processes be harnessed for good without being perceived as infringing sovereignty or imposing cultural imperialism?

From a legal perspective, how well is the local legal system understood?[22] Is it the inquisitorial (civil law) system, or the accusatorial (common law) system?[23] To what extent does traditional (customary) law apply in the recipient state? What role do the police play in the local legal system? Are the training and experience provided appropriate to this role? If not, how should these approaches be modified?

An additional issue requiring consideration in this context is that of imprisonment for local offenders. Subject to the normal application of criminal law, this is not a critical issue in industrialized nations like Australia— "You do the crime, you do the time!" However, in many developing countries there is no social security blanket to protect the families of prisoners. If the primary breadwinner goes to prison, the family may well be left destitute. How does the family survive? Should this problem be taken into account by the courts, at least for minor offenses? Should the police exercise greater discretion in relation to prosecuting such cases, or are there other ways of dealing with the matter, involving, say, traditional law or compensation arrangements? The police are not social workers, but should they take into account the broader social issues impacted by law enforcement in developing countries? How would such an approach affect the mentoring of local police undertaken by advisers?

This is a long list, but unless these issues are given serious consideration, the mission is doomed to failure.

Local Politics

The political elites in a recipient country will have their own political and cultural agendas. These may be positive, negative, or neutral in nature when applied to the goals of the intervention. Causes for opposition to the intervention might include concern about issues of national sovereignty and security, or resentment over what might be viewed as foreign interference. Opposition could also be due to political ambitions, criminality, or corruption. Where does the power lie in the recipient state—with the politicians, with the street/youth gangs, or with the local security forces? What influence do the gangs have within the police and the military? Obviously, these are very sensitive issues, but they must be understood and addressed (Pearlman, 2008).

In order to understand the operational environment, it is necessary to make an assessment of the general level of social stability and crime within the country, and the community attitude toward these problems. Are there transnational crime influences that have an impact on the local social or political environment? How significant is the level of domestic violence? Can donors influence the local discourse on domestic violence? In a state where the most basic physiological and safety needs of Maslow's hierarchy of needs[24] are barely met, is it surprising that the law and order, and societal expectations of the donor are not necessarily the same as the priorities of a disrupted state with weak national institutions? Is it surprising that, in such circumstances, priority may be given to issues of compensation and revenge (payback)?[25]

How does traditional justice handle violent situations? When should the police intervene to apply formal justice? How does the community accept formal justice solutions instead of the traditional justice approach? For example, in Pakistan and Jordan, honor killings[26] are linked to the traditional justice approach. In Saudi Arabia, a young woman who had been raped was severely punished for being alone with a man who was not a relative, whereas the men who raped her were not punished at all. Are these examples of traditional justice? How should the donor respond in such circumstances? Do they respect the local customs, or do they try to change the culture? Is this a role for expatriate police? Clearly, police interventions in weak or failing states can lead to highly unexpected outcomes. This level of involvement with the local community raises issues unlikely to be faced by a military peacekeeping operation.

Mutual Obligations

For any police intervention to succeed, it is essential that both the local government and the community support the objectives of the intervention. However, it must go further; there must be local ownership of the process. The recipient state has a clear obligation to do all within its power to become actively involved, to publicly support the objectives of the project; to ensure that the local police and bureaucracy are in no doubt as to the expectations of the government; and to ensure that local officers are strongly encouraged to work closely with their foreign counterparts. The clients for the project are the local government and community: Both will be there long after the deployed police have returned to their own country.

Donor Perception and Perceptions of Donors

Donor governments put a great deal of effort and investment into supporting disrupted states and regions across the world. However, for a number of reasons, this contribution has not always been understood by recipient states. There is criticism over what some see as donor domination of the aid agenda and the perception that much of that aid comes back to donors in the form of payments to consultants, peacekeepers, aid workers, and for offshore overheads.

Donors do not always have a good reputation overseas. They are sometimes seen as arrogant, shallow, loud-mouthed, culturally insensitive, impatient, and overzealous. They need to give careful thought to national reputation and those values that underpin professional policing of the highest order.[27] Lack of local language skills may also be viewed as a disadvantage. Are police donors aware that wraparound sunglasses inhibit eye contact with locals, thereby acting as a communication barrier? Have they considered the importance of getting out of their vehicles to "walk and talk" as a major contribution to encourage communication and trust? In the capacity-building role, would it be better to deploy a small number of advisers, each targeted to a specific counterpart officer or role, or can bigger impacts be achieved through greater numbers?

Police capacity building is made even more difficult if it is isolated from other elements of the criminal justice system, such as the courts, the judiciary, public prosecutors, the prison service, the probation service, and the agency responsible for collating crime statistics. Sometimes the Australian Federal Police has become involved in the capacity building of other elements of the criminal justice system, such as the staff of the prosecutor general, and the results have been highly commendable. On other occasions, capacity building in the other agencies of the criminal justices sector is provided by the Australian Agency for International Development (AusAID), or other providers, and again the results have been very positive. Yet, a successful outcome requires the close coordination of all the donors.

Furthermore, consideration needs to be given as to whether the capacity building provided will be limited to the police headquarters and capital city personnel, or whether the outlying districts should also be targeted. Is there a capacity available to do this? What would be the consequences if this were not done? Is there a risk of establishing a headquarters elite, and does this magnify any existing divisions between the headquarters and the field? Obviously, none of these questions can be resolved without the agreement of the recipient state.

Conclusion

Development policing has the potential to provide substantial support to worldwide nation-building efforts. The first major lesson, however, is that great care must be taken in identifying the functions performed by police, the *modus operandi* of police in performing these functions, the sensitivity of police and policing organizations to change, and most importantly, the recipients of those policing functions. It is contended here that policing is individual to each context. Assumptions of similarity are invalid, with formidable scope for misapplied development policing to damage the nation-building agenda.

Subsequent examination of development policing has been constrained in this analysis to the most aggregate level so as to limit the effects of monumental detail that obfuscates underlying structures. In this context, development policing is interpreted as being elemental to the rule of law rather than as an end in itself. This proposition assisted recognition of limiting cases for the rule of law challenges facing developing nation-states, and the conclusion that improper transposition of inappropriate theoretical constructs onto actual development situations will result in predestined efforts to solve the wrong problems. Discussion of the policy spectrum created to deal with these situations revealed two new options arising as a direct consequence of development policing. These are police intervention as opposed to purely military intervention, and police reform as opposed to traditional technical assistance. These options offer new advantages to policymakers in terms of in-between postures and the preservation of civil structures, the demise of which might accelerate shifts toward militarism or domination rule.

The two spectra used to demonstrate these issues were then integrated into a guidance model that identified a range of "more right" from "more wrong" combinations of problem and solution. More importantly, this guidance model brought together a range of situations that raised questions of transition from one state to another, and the simultaneous coexistence of differing problem-solution combinations. This highlighted the need for policy agility in dealing with dynamic problems that interact in ways prone to confound purist solutions. Rationalism is useful in representing the calculus of development policing. However, rationalism can be destabilized by factors such as *the problem of the unacknowledged problem*, a failure to treat each mission separately, an inability to understand culture, ignorance of local politics, and most importantly, misplaced perceptions of self and others. These factors can undermine all but the most sincere union of donor and recipient. Where this does not exist, development success will necessitate artful disentanglement of intentions and behaviors to ensure police programs are not wasteful or, even worse, counterproductive.

The overpowering advantages of development policing have yet to be realized, and these will rely on police preserving an awareness of their special identity in the aid and development field. To achieve this, police must not be confused with diplomats or other aid practitioners despite requiring the skills and guidance evident in both. Those disciplines have different roles and responsibilities in the nation-building arena. The role of police would be undermined if they used only the skills and guidance required in diplomatic and aid-related roles.

References

Annan, K. (2006). *Uniting our strengths: Enhancing United Nations support for the rule of law*. Report of the Secretary General of the United Nations to the General Assembly, Sixty-first Session, Item 80.

Bayley, D. H. (1999). Policing: The world stage. In R. I. Mawby (Ed.), *Policing across the world: Issues for the twenty-first century*. London: Routledge, 3–12.

Bayley, D. H. (2001). *Democratising the police abroad: What to do and how to do it*. Washington, DC: U.S. Department of Justice, National Institute of Justice.

Bayley, D. H. (2006). *Changing the guard—Developing democratic police abroad*. Oxford: Oxford University Press.

Brahimi, L. (2000). *Report of the panel on United Nations peacekeeping*. Report to the General Assembly, Fifty-fifth Session, Item 87 (provisional agenda). New York: United Nations.

Chomsky, N. (2006). *Failed states: The abuse of power and the assault on democracy*. Crows Nest, NSW: Allen and Unwin.

Cole, B. A. (1999). Post-colonial systems. In R. I. Mawby (Ed.), *Policing across the world: Issues for the twenty-first century*. London: Routledge, 88–108.

Collier, P., L. Chauvet, & H. Hegre. (2008). *Conflicts—The security challenge in conflict prone countries*. Copenhagen: Copenhagen Consensus Center.

Dinnen, S. (2001). *Law and order in a weak state: Crime and politics in Papua New Guinea*. Adelaide: Crawford House Publishing.

Dinnen, S. (2008). Beyond state-centrism: External solutions and the governance of security in Melanesia. In G. Fry & T. T. Kabutaulaka (Eds.), *Intervention and state-building in the Pacific: The legitimacy of cooperative intervention*. Manchester: Manchester University Press, 102–18.

Dobell, G. (2007). *China and Taiwan in the South Pacific: Diplomatic chess versus political rugby*. Lowy Institute Policy Brief. Sydney: Lowy Institute for International Policy.

Ellison, G. (2007). Fostering a dependency culture: The commodification of community policing in a global market place. In A. Goldsmith & J. Sheptycki (Eds.), *Crafting transnational policing: Police capacity-building and global police reform.* Portland, OR: Hart Publishing, 203–42.

Freedom House. (2007). *The worst of the worst—The world's most repressive societies.* Washington, DC: Freedom House.

Fry, G., & T. T. Kabutaulaka. (2008). *Intervention and state-building in the Pacific: The legitimacy of cooperative intervention.* Manchester: Manchester University Press.

Fukuyama, F. (2004). *State building: Governance and world order in the twenty-first century.* London: Profile Books.

Fukuyama, F. (2008). *State building in the Solomon Islands.* Memo reporting to the World Bank. Washington, DC: Johns Hopkins University.

Fullilove, M. (2006). *The testament of Solomons: RAMSI and international state building.* Lowy Institute Policy Brief. Sydney: Lowy Institute for International Policy.

Glenn, R. W. (2007). *Counterinsurgency in a test tube—Analysing the success of the regional assistance mission to the Solomon Islands.* Santa Monica, CA: Rand Corporation.

Goddard, M. (1992). Big-man thief: The social organisation of gangs in Port Moresby. *Canberra Anthropology, 15,* 20–34.

Goldsmith, A., & S. Dinnen. (2007). Transnational police building: Critical lessons from Timor-Leste and the Solomon Islands. *Third World Quarterly, 28,* 1091–1099.

Greener, B. (2007). *UNPOL: UN police as peacekeepers.* Unpublished.

Greener-Barcham, B. (2007). Crossing the green or blue line? Exploring the military-police divide. *Small Wars and Insurgencies, 18,* 90–112.

Hayward-Jones, J. (2008). *Beyond good governance: Shifting the paradigm for Australian aid to the Pacific Islands region.* Lowy Institute Policy Brief. Sydney: Lowy Institute for International Policy.

Hood, L. (2006). Missed opportunities: The United Nations, police service and defence force development in Timor Leste, 1999–2004. *Civil Wars, 8,* 143–162.

Hughes, H. (2003). *Aid has failed the Pacific.* Issue Analysis 33. Sydney: Centre for Independent Studies.

Hughes, H., & G. Sodhi. (2006). *Annals of aid: Vanuatu and the United States Millennium Challenge Corporation.* Issue Analysis 69. Sydney: Centre for Independent Studies.

Human Rights Watch. (2005). *"Making their own rules": Police beatings, rape, and torture of children in PNG.* Washington, DC: Author.

Human Rights Watch. (2006). *Tortured beginnings: Police violence and the beginnings of impunity in East Timor.* Washington, DC: Author.

Human Rights Watch. (2008). *World report 2008.* Washington, DC: Author.

International Commission on Intervention and State Sovereignty. (2001). *The responsibility to protect.* Ottawa: International Development Research Centre. Retrieved October, 15, 2008, from http://www.idrc.ca/en/ev-9436-201-1-DO_TOPIC.html

International Crisis Group. (2007). *Reforming Afghanistan's police.* Asia Report 138. Washington, DC: Author. Retrieved October 15, 2008, from http://www.realinstitutoelcano.org/especiales/especialFuerzasArmadas/ICGreformingpolice2007.pdf

Jackson, A., & A. Lyon. (2002). Policing after ethnic conflict: Culture, democratic policing, politics and the public. *Policing: An International Journal of Police Strategies and Management, 25,* 221–41.

Johnston, L. (1999). Private policing: Uniformity and diversity. In R. I. Mawby (Ed.), *Policing across the world: Issues for the twenty-first century.* London: Routledge, 226–38.

Kapalan, R. D. (1994). The coming anarchy. *Atlantic Monthly*, February 1994. Retrieved October 15, 2008, from http://www.theatlantic.com/doc/199402/anarchy

Kaufmann, D., A. Kray, & M. Mastruzzi. (2008). *Governance matters VII: Aggregate and individual governance indicators 1996-2007.* Washington, DC: World Bank.

Land, T. (2007). *Joint evaluation study of provision of technical-assistance personnel: What can we learn from promising experiences?* Canberra: Australian Agency for International Development (AusAID).

Linden, R., D. Last, & C. Murphy. (2007). Obstacles on the road to peace and justice: The role of civilian police in peacekeeping. In A. Goldsmith & J. Sheptycki (Eds.), *Crafting transnational policing: Police capacity-building and global police reform.* Portland, OR: Hart Publishing, 149–76.

Marenin, O. (1998). The goal of democracy in international police assistance programs. *Policing: An International Journal of Police Strategies and Management, 21,* 159–177.

Marenin, O. (2005). *Restoring policing systems in conflict torn nations: Process, problems, prospects.* Geneva: Geneva Centre for Democratic Control of Armed Forces.

McCawley, D. (2008). *How should aid donors work in fragile states?* Seminar Series: State, Society and Governance in Melanesia. Canberra: Australian National University.

McFarlane, J. (2005). Regional and international cooperation in tackling transnational crime, terrorism and the problems of disrupted states. *Journal of Financial Crime, 12,* 301–309.

McFarlane, J. (2007). The thin blue line: The strategic role of the Australian federal police. *Security Challenges, 3,* 91–108.

McLeod, A. & S. Dinnen. (2007). Police building in the southwest pacific. New directions in Australian policing. In A. Goldsmith & J. Sheptycki (Eds.) *Crafting transnational policing: Police capacity-building and global police reform.* Portland, OR: Hart Publishing, 295–328.

Morgan, P. (2007). *Direct and indirect approaches to technical assistance: RAMSI interventions in the Solomon Islands.* Canberra: Australian Agency for International Development (AusAID).

Murphy, C. (2007). The cart before the horse: Community oriented versus professional models of international police reform. In A. Goldsmith & J. Sheptycki (Eds.), *Crafting transnational policing: Police capacity-building and global police reform.* Portland, OR: Hart Publishing, 243–61.

Nelson, H. (2007). *The Chinese in Papua New Guinea.* State Society and Governance in Melanesia, Discussion Paper 2007/3. Canberra: Australian National University.

O'Connor, T. (2004). Australian police are no solution to PNG's problems. *Green Left Weekly,* Issue 570, February 11, 2004.

O'Connor, T., S. Chan, & J. Goodman. (2006). *Australian aid: Promoting insecurity? The reality of aid.* Retrieved October 15, 2008, from http://www.realityofaid.org/roareport.php?table=roa2006&id=1

Organization for Economic Co-operation and Development, Development Assistance Committee. (2005). *Security system reform and governance.* Paris: OECD Publishing. Retrieved October 15, 2008, from http://www.oecd.org/dataoecd/8/39/31785288.pdf

Organization for Economic Co-operation and Development, Development Assistance Committee. (2007). *Handbook on security system reform: Supporting security and justice*. Paris: OECD Publishing. Retrieved October 15, 2008, from http://www.oecd.org/dataoecd/43/25/38406485.pdf

Østerud, Ø. (2008). Towards a more peaceful world? A critical view. *Conflict, Security and Development, 8*, 223–240.

Peake, G., & K. S. Brown. (2005). Police building: The International Deployment Group in the Solomon Islands. *International Peacekeeping, 12*, 520–532.

Pearlman, J. (2008). Officers back—but not on the beat. *Sydney Morning Herald*, October 4, 2008. Retrieved October 15, 2008, from http://www.smh.com.au/articles/2008/10/03/1223013791406.html

Porter, M. E. (2003). *Microeconomic foundations of competitiveness—A new agenda for international aid institutions*. Worksop with UNDP Leadership Team. New York: United Nations Development Program.

Roth, K. (2008). Despots masquerading as democrats. In *World report 2008*. Washington, DC: Human Rights Watch, 1–24.

Slatter, C. (2003). *A commentary on Helen Hughes' "Aid has failed the Pacific."* Suva: Department of History/Politics, University of the South Pacific. Retrieved October 15, 2008, from www.acfid.asn.au

Sung, H. (2002). *The fragmentation of policing in American cities: Towards a theory of police-citizen relations*. Westport, CT: Praeger.

Sung, H. (2006). Police effectiveness and democracy: Shape and direction of the relationship. *Policing: An International Journal of Police Strategies and Management, 29*, 347–367.

United Nations. (2007). *UN peacekeeping 2007: Excerpts from the report of the secretary general on the work of the organisation* (UN document A/62/1). New York: United Nations Department of Public Information (Peace and Security Section).

United Nations. (2008). *United Nations peacekeeping operations: Principles and guidelines*. New York: United Nations Department of Peacekeeping Operations.

Wainwright, E. (with contributions from J. McFarlane). (2004). *Police join the front line: Building Australia's international policing capability*. Canberra: Australian Strategic Policy Institute.

Endnotes

1. Much of this chapter is derived from practical experiences gained over the past four years during establishment of the International Deployment Group (IDG) of the Australian Federal Police. The IDG represents one of the few successful efforts to implement the recommendations of the Brahimi Report (2000) in relation to UN member nations creating standing bodies of internationally deployable policing personnel. Since its formation, the IDG has been heavily committed to international operations across 10 countries, including post-crisis interventions in the Solomon Islands, Timor-Leste, and Tonga. As of October 2008, the IDG had some 519 people deployed, including 50 officers in the Northern Territory Emergency Response, in aboriginal communities. See Wainwright (2004) for further discussion of the IDG concept.

2. Great care needs to be taken with the proliferation of cross-pollinating solutions generated by this process, as it represents a major source of confusion, especially to policymakers, and there is significant potential to compound congenital weaknesses incorporated within individual solutions by inadvertently transferring them into new contexts where other weaknesses may already exist.

3. This represents an extension of a much broader governance debate (Kaufmann, Kray, & Mastruzzi, 2008) in the international development field and may also have foundations in the maturing heritage of police peacekeeping with its increased focus on police capacity building.

4. Bayley (1999, 2001), Marenin (2005), and Dinnen (2008) note tendencies by Western police delivering international development programs to replicate the practices and processes from their personal experience. This reflects three things: (1) a view that they have been selected to perform such roles because their personal experience is relevant, (2) a judgment that practices and processes from one set of circumstances can and should be transferred to another (regardless of major contextual differences), and (3) a lack of wider experience that would provide further options. All three factors point to an assumption that underlying policing solutions will be similar across the world, when this may not be the case. It should also be understood that when missions are deployed in response to a serious apprehension of violence or state failure, the skills being sought are those already provided, and that the local systems have often already collapsed or been implicated in violent behavior.

5. These types of statements can be found by reviewing police department websites and output-based budget statements (available on a profusion of Internet websites).

6. The authors acknowledge the support of Brenna Lindsay in preparing the final versions of all the figures used in this chapter.

7. Human Rights Watch publishes prolifically on these subjects at http://hrw.org

8. The term *traditional policing* is used here in the sense of original peoples and not in the way Western policing was conducted, for example, some 30 years ago.

9. The positioning of colonial policing in Figure 13.1 is possibly contentious, as it could be argued that, as with other types of policing, it should be represented according to degrees of repressiveness or contemporary views of outlaw behavior. This has not been presented as such only because the basic function was arguably specific to colonial or imperial objectives, which were essentially exploitative on behalf of foreign elites. There are, however, several different ways this could be represented in Figure 13.1, including extreme repression.

10. See P. Scaruffi for an indicative history of genocide in the 20th century, at http://www.scaruffi.com/politics/dictat.html (retrieved October 15, 2008).

11. A continuing high demand for peacekeepers has stretched UN resources (United Nations, 2007, paragraph 61) and restricted opportunities for missions to remain *in situ* for any longer than necessary to achieve stabilization objectives.

12. See the Fund for Peace at http://www.fundforpeace.org/ (retrieved October 15, 2008).

13. Solutions need to integrate formal and traditional governance as required, for example, in the constitutional arrangements for the Solomon Islands and Samoa.

14. This is not to argue an inherent superiority in contemporary over traditional systems, as the latter is often founded in spirituality and beliefs that are a living part of tribal or customary societies. There are also questions concerning the affordability of contemporary institutional rule of law in these contexts, and the need for such systems at certain stages of development where people have yet to make choices about their futures. This position is idealistic in many cases, as either traditional people are not given any choices to consider or other circumstances dictate courses of action that must be taken in the interests of survival.

15. These terms are now well understood and empirically documented (see earlier references). Accordingly, they do not require definitional treatment in this chapter. It should be emphasized at this point that the parameters for state failure used here are restricted to rule of law for the purposes of this analysis only, and it is acknowledged that state fragility or failure can and does arise from a number of other sources.

16. The issues raised here are often discounted in police development programs for practical reasons or seen as the responsibility of other programs. As a result, they remain untreated, and police development programs risk entering a cycle of failure as the fundamentals for good policing are not established.

17. Initiatives of this type are also often seen as establishing entry points for reform (Organization for Economic Co-operation and Development, 2007). It has yet to be established if this is successful or whether it is simply another way for aid-savvy elites to generate windfall cashflows, with no intention of embracing reform in all but the most superficial way. While this approach to engagement is suboptimal, it does reflect the reality of police and other reform efforts in many emerging nations—a reality that is in bleak comparison to the ideal.

18. In making these observations, it should be recognized that the simple advent of peacekeeping has arguably contributed to reductions in the loss of life through warfare in the second half of the 20th century (*Human Security Report 2005* (New York: Oxford University Press, 2005); see http://www.humansecurityreport.info/index.php?option=content&task=view&id=28) (retrieved October 10, 2008)). The question is: How can this result be improved in the 21st century?

19. Policy responses being applied to worst-case situations (e.g., internal conflict) will need to incorporate elements of later policy options (even if it is only planning) if they are not to become *stuck* at one point in the development process and disrupt further progress because of their own inflexibilities.

20. See, for example, Dobell (2007) and Nelson (2007).

21. The term *wantok* in Melanesian Pidgin means one who speaks the same language (literally, "one talk"), but is popularly used to describe relations of obligation binding relatives, members of the same clan or tribal group, and much looser forms of association. In the context of modern institutions, *wantokism* is generally used in a negative sense to describe the practice of nepotism (Dinnen, 2001, p. 203).

22. The system of law in countries whose legal systems originate in Roman or civil law, under which the judge initiates all necessary investigations and summons and examines witnesses, and in which a trial is an inquiry by the court. See Roger Bird, *Osborn's Concise Law Dictionary*, 7th ed. (London: Sweet and Maxwell, 1983), 181.

23. It is a common law principle that the responsibility for collecting and presenting evidence lies with the party who seeks to introduce the evidence. See Bird,
Osborn's Concise Law Dictionary, 9.
24. U.S. psychologist Abraham Maslow argued that each person has a hierarchy of
needs that must be satisfied. These are physiological needs; safety needs; needs
of love, affection, and belongingness; needs for esteem; and needs for self-actu-
alization. See *honolulu.hawaii.edu/intranet/committees/FacDevCom/guidebk/
teachtip/maslow.htm (retrieved October 10, 2008)*.
25. Sinclair Dinnen (2001, p. 15).
26. See Amnesty International, *Honour Killings of Women and Girls*, September
1, 1999, http://www.amnesty.org/en/library/info/ASA33/018/1999 (retrieved
October 12, 2008).
27. Claire Bukis, "Arrogant Australians! We Have a Bad Reputation Overseas,"
Age, December 10, 2007, http://www.theage.com.au/articles/2007/12/09/
1197135284098.html (retrieved December 11, 2007).

Policing Peace
Evolving Police Roles in UN Peace Operations

14

B. K. GREENER

Contents

The United Nations (UN) has provided civilian police to help support its peace operations for decades. Yet those police, known initially as CIVPOL and more recently as UNPOL, are increasingly being called upon to undertake peace-building as well as peacekeeping tasks. This chapter outlines the move from nonexecutive SMART (support, monitoring, advising, reporting, and training) models of policing in traditional peacekeeping operations to more assertive peace operations that have required executive policing roles, and thence to a new focus on institutional reform and rebuilding efforts. In charting these changes, the chapter then outlines how the UN Police Division at UN Headquarters in New York has changed in recent years in light of the challenges posed by these shifts, before closing with a discussion of future issues that will impact upon ongoing reform efforts.

Beyond Peacekeeping

Article 24 of the charter states that the UN has "primary responsibility for the maintenance of international peace and security," while additional articles within Chapters VI and Chapter VII of the charter provide more detail as to how the UN was originally intended to operate as a collective security organization. One of the most significant of these is Article 43, which

Adapted from Greener, B. K. UNPOL: UN Police as peacekeepers. *Policing and Society*, forthcoming.

asks member states to make some of their armed forces and facilities available to the UNSC "on its call and in accordance with a special agreement or agreements," though, as John Hillen has pointed out, none of the special agreements have ever been concluded, and if they had been, the UN would have much stronger authority to mobilize, direct, and use military forces in operations (Hillen, 2000, p. 11). Instead of operationalizing Article 43 in any meaningful way, the UN has instead come to look to the concept of peacekeeping as an important instrument in helping to manage international security issues. Yet there has of late been much confusion as to what peacekeeping is, and what we are to call those missions that go beyond conceptualizations of peacekeeping as traditionally understood.

The concept of peacekeeping does not formally appear within the UN Charter, and there has been much interpretation as to how best to deploy UN personnel to uphold its responsibility to maintain international peace and security. Given the Cold War constraints of the political and strategic context of the time, the initial genesis of peacekeeping saw the introduction of a fairly limited role for UN personnel whose main role was to "maintain quiet" to try to allow political solutions to develop as well as they might (UN Department of Public Information, 1990). Key peacekeeping principles were thus ones that insisted that UN peacekeeping operations be: UN missions (formed by the UN with a UN-appointed general in the field under the authority of the UN secretary general), deployed with the consent of all parties after political settlement was reached, and strictly impartial. Furthermore, personnel were to be provided on a voluntary basis, and military and other units were to operate under strict rules of engagement that emphasized a minimum use of force (Goulding, 1993).

However, the events of the early and mid-1990s drew the UN into the possibility of peace enforcement, with Secretary General Boutros Boutros-Ghali's *Agenda for Peace* foreseeing a potential shift away from consent-based operations. With the resultant problems in Somalia, however, the future of peace enforcement as a UN pursuit was stymied. Instead, there arose what was then termed second-generation peacekeeping. Second-generation peacekeeping shifted the UN and other actors into aspects of nation building and necessitated the development of increasingly multipurpose military forces as well as the deeper engagement of civilian and nongovernmental organization (NGO) actors (Williams, 1998). Second-generation peacekeeping was said to go much further than pure military action in presenting challenges to the traditional peacekeeping norms of consent of the parties (a more "heart and minds" approach with civil information campaigns), impartiality (the assertive nature of the new peacekeeping requiring a greater awareness in dealing with the parties involved), and the use of force (Findlay, 1996). However the term *second-generation peacekeeping* has fallen out of favor, and other terminology has been created to avoid definitional confusion.

Instead of talking about the blurring of impartial, neutral peacekeeping into broader and deeper peace roles, there is now much discussion of the rise of the peace-building agenda as a closely related but qualitatively different kind of function. UN personnel have increasingly been involved in

creating viable political and social institutions, rebuilding basic social and economic infrastructures, strengthening the rule of law and protecting human rights, and demobilising former combatants and reintegrating them into society … [with] the new efforts aimed to reconstitute viable states. (Weiss, 2001, p. 3)

This type of activity has come to be known as peace building. The new peace-building consensus has seen a greater role ascribed to actors that can engage in both security and developmental roles, as the objectives of peace missions have moved from the simpler act of the separation and monitoring of warring parties, to the much more complex and difficult aim of establishing a self-sustaining positive peace (Richmond, 2004). Such state and peace-building activities have not been neutral in that peace building has been associated with both democratization and marketization, and thus is a "specific *kind* of social engineering, based on a particular set of assumptions about how best to establish durable domestic peace" (Paris, 2004).

It is this overarching context of a broadening and deepening of UN missions as a whole, one that has most obviously seen UN personnel given potentially increased mandates to engage much more actively in countries where they operate in peace keeping and postconflict peace-building efforts, that has demanded a complementary broadening and deepening of engagement with regards to the more specific aspect of the *policing* part of such operations.

The Practice of Policing in Peace Operations

In assessing police involvement in recent peace operations we can begin by noting that police simply have an increased presence in peace operations. Policing numbers grew from 35 in 1988 to 1,500 during Namibia, and by February 2000 the UN had deployed 9,000 CIVPOL around the world (Bayley, 2001, p. 4). In even more recent times, numbers of UN Police officers deployed on operations increased from 7,300 in August 2006 to 8,800 in January 2007 to 9,600 in August 2007 and in September 2008 reached nearly 13,000 (UNDPKO, 2008).

Moreover, the tasks of these police professionals have widened and deepened in scope in line with the overarching changes in peace missions outlined above. Here, for many years, UN Police functioned under the SMART model of civilian policing abroad: SMART meaning support, monitoring, administering, reporting, and training (Hartz, 2000). Such tasks fit with the narrow emphasis on peacekeeping as defined during Cold War times. However, throughout the later 1990s UNCIVPOL personnel were increasingly tasked with greater responsibilities as needs and expectations changed in line with broader changes to peace operations. Both executive policing and peace-building roles were increasingly pressed upon policing personnel.

Executive policing roles had been allocated on an *ad hoc* basis to police in Cambodia and Haiti, but in Kosovo and East Timor these roles were brought in from the beginning of the mission. Executive mandates essentially allowed for such police officers to have powers of arrest, search, and detention in those states. In addition to this significant development, innocuous-sounding tasks like monitoring similarly evolved as previously fairly haphazard observation was replaced with reviews that monitor compliance with internationally accepted standards of human rights and the UN Criminal Justice Standards (UNCJS) (Hansen, 2002). And, in developing the notion of police reform in other countries, the content of such reform programs has also changed. There has been a move away from police reform, which focuses only on technical and structural issues (size, organizational structure, equipment, etc.) to that which focuses on building the public's confidence in the police as a force for public safety and security that is independent of political agendas (Hansen, 2002, p. 13). In reflecting on such changes, the Brahimi Report of 2000 specifically called for a "doctrinal shift" in the use of CIVPOL and other personnel involved in rule of law institutions to reflect an increasing focus on strengthening human rights and the rule of law in postconflict situations, and asserted that CIVPOL actively retrain and restructure local police, not just "observe and scold" (UN Secretariat, 2000).

By 2004, UN Police personnel deployed to missions around the world were typically tasked with the following roles:

- Advisory
- Mentoring
- Law enforcement
- Selection, recruitment, training, establishment of a credible local police force
- Human rights
- Humanitarian
- Elections
- Internally displaced persons (IDPs) and returnees

The emphasis is now often on capacity building, on the support and restructuring of institutional systems in fragile or transitional states as well as in postconflict situations, and this requires a great depth and breadth of skills. Operations may require interim law enforcement and operational support. Or they may involve reform efforts based on democratic policing principles, on restructuring police forces to depoliticize them, or on rebuilding indigenous forces to ensure they are capable of carrying out their policing roles (Smith, Holt, & Durch, 2007). As Ban Ki-Moon (2007, p. 1) recently stated:

> In our effort to help countries ravaged by conflict, the work of UN Police is indispensable to establishing law and order—not temporarily, but for the long haul. That is why, in police reform, we no longer focus only on mentoring and monitoring national force, but even more on building capacity through training, advising and leading by example.

Key tasks for personnel therefore increasingly involve the three R's—*reform, restructuring*, and *rebuilding*. Police may be deployed as *peacekeepers* but there is also a growing demand for UNPOL to act as *peace builders*.

In particular, in line with the ideological drivers behind the peace-building agenda, police personnel are undertaking roles that mean that these three R's are being carried out so as to replicate *liberal democratic* policing principles. Recent efforts in Kosovo, Bosnia, and later deployments to Timor-Leste under the UN Integrated Mission in Timor-Leste (UNMIT), in particular, indicate efforts to ensconce and reinforce democratic policing. The last day of 2002 saw the conclusion of the UN Mission in Bosnia and Herzegovina (UNMIBH), which had been the largest police reform and restructuring operation in UN history, beginning in 1995 following the adoption of UNSC Resolution 1035 (Thomas, 2004). This deployment essentially aimed to transform the broader organizational culture of policing in Bosnia—as evidenced by the requirement that all 10 federation cantonal police and the Republika Srpska police sign a commitment to democratic policing before they received assistance. Similarly, the UN Mission in Kosovo (UNMIK) was tasked with assisting with policing and police administration, while (from September 1999) the Organization for Security and Cooperation in Europe (OSCE, 2005) was to train police officers according to international human rights and community-based policing standards. The two institutions together aimed to produce a new police service that was "organized and functioning according to internationally recognized standard of democratic policing," and both UNMIK police and the OSCE Department of Police Education and Development were heavily involved in processing potential police recruits who were, moreover, to

> work with all ethnic groups; follow the rule of law and protect human rights of all people, regardless of ethnicity, and to be intolerant of ethnic violence; and to have sufficient intellect, stability and strength of character to learn, apply and reinforce law enforcement techniques and concepts in the context of principles of democratic and community-oriented policing and internationally recognized human rights standards. (Kosovo Police Service School, date unknown)

In early missions to East Timor, on the other hand, the UN failed to strongly pursue such democratic policing models. Therefore, under the UNTAET and then UNMISET mandates, the UN created a police force that was criticized for having a lack of democratic civilian oversight and control (Hood, 2006). Here it was felt in the lead up to major political and security troubles in 2006 that such institutional deficits allowed for the politicization of the police. Indeed, the United Nations Commission of Independent Inquiry (2006) believed that the situation

> can be explained largely by the frailty of the state institutions and the weakness of the rule of law. Governance structures and existing chains of command broke down or were bypassed; roles and responsibilities became blurred; solutions were sought outside the existing legal framework.

Following the problems of 2006, the UN has since attempted to implement a Policia Nacional de Timor-Leste (PNTL) Organizational Strategic Plan for Reform, Restructuring, and Rebuilding (RRR) that focuses on operational and administrative capacities, oversight mechanisms, and coordination with other agencies involved in the security sector (though so far the effectiveness of this effort has not been proven).

Given the pursuit of these new broader peace-building and democratic policing agendas in UN missions, there has been an urgent need for a concomitant growth and utilization of certain skills in this new environment—skills in business administration, human resources, and management, among other things. What this has meant is that the UN Police Division within the UN Department of Peacekeeping Operations in New York has had to begin to look to source senior management and strategic advisors as well as good street cops. This has necessitated the development of a new approach to recruitment and has highlighted the need to match staff to tasks. Such changes in institutional culture and capacity (changes both within the division and in terms of the missions the division is becoming involved in) may well bring about an increased civilianization of some roles. Though this is a sensitive issue in terms of trying to establish when there is a need for uniformed personnel as opposed to when a well-informed civilian with specialist skills may be the right choice, it is nonetheless crucial to match needs with appropriate skill sets to enhance chances of success in the rather daunting tasks the UN takes on. Andrew Carpenter, head of Strategic Planning and Development, has strongly asserted that international policing is increasingly "different from the day job," not only in terms of the kinds of cultural, political, social, and economic environments within which police may have to work, but also in terms of the work at hand—in terms of the particular tasks that are undertaken. Personnel must be matched to these tasks at hand, and this could see an increasing presence of nonuniformed personnel in certain jobs or in certain phases of a mission. This revision of just who can undertake policing tasks and why is an ongoing one, though it is clear that one civilian position is always of vital importance to all of those involved in the policing part of UN peace missions.

Two positions are particularly key for how UNPOL operates on the ground in all of its peace missions: the civilian role of the special representative of the secretary general and the top policing position on the ground, that of the police commissioner. The SRSG is the head of mission, and the police commissioner (who exercises control over UNPOL personnel and coordinates activities with other actors on the ground) reports directly to him or her, not back to the Police Division in New York. Once the mission is in place, the police commissioner can operate quite autonomously from the division. In the past this has sometimes meant that the division has acted more as mailman than adviser to those in the field, though this is starting to change. The SRSG is a political appointment who can override advice from the division, while the police commissioner is selected by a panel that includes police, military, political, and other input.

Lastly, in terms of the nuts and bolts of policing in UN missions, there have been some changes forthcoming in terms of the increased use of Formed Police Units (FPUs) and minor changes with regards to logistical support. FPUs or Stability Police Units (SPUs) now constitute a significant part of UN Police numbers. These units are valuable in providing an interim force between military and community police responses in peace support operations because, as Michael Dziedzic and Christine Stark (2006) note, they are

> robust, armed police units that are capable of performing specialized law enforcement and public order functions that require disciplined group action. They are trained in and have the flexibility to use either less-than-lethal or lethal force, as circumstances dictate.

These forces specialize in the harder edge of policing: riot control; protection roles; organized crime, counterterrorism, and counterinsurgency; border patrol; and intelligence collection. The UN has increasingly looked to utilize these forces as they present a flexible option in responding to this hard edge of policing; they help to fill what was a previous gap in capabilities when it came to dealing with civil unrest and the like. These FPUs are therefore increasingly used as a presence in missions, patrolling the streets—albeit with the need to clearly display police insignia and the requirement to report to the police commissioner rather than any military figure. And lastly, with regards to the second issue of logistics, the UN system, despite the establishment of the base at Brindisi, has been criticized for being too slow and cumbersome. (Indeed at times Brindisi has added to the problem. This is because if equipment is needed for a mission and is available locally for quick delivery, it cannot be brought in if the same equipment is held in Brindisi, acting to slow UN missions even further.) The UNSC has to approve a mission before the UNDPKO can start procurement, and there has not been luck thus far with stockpiling mission kits (Perito, 2004, p. 96). And all of these operational shifts require the parallel development of broader strategic and conceptual frameworks to accommodate and support such changes.

Guiding Principles and Strategic Development

In terms of the development of guiding principles, long-term strategic planning, and doctrinal development, the UN has long had a general code of conduct for law enforcement officials. Significant parts of this code include:

> [Article One] Law enforcement officials shall at all times fulfil the duty imposed upon them by law, by serving the community and by protecting all persons against illegal acts, consistent with the high degree of responsibility required by their profession.
>
> [Article Two] In the performance of their duty, law enforcement officials shall respect and protect human dignity and maintain and uphold the human rights of all persons.
>
> [Article Three] Law enforcement officials may use force only when strictly necessary and to the extent required for the purpose of their duty. (Kroeker, 2007)

Similarly, a number of other documentation in the form of practitioners' handbooks and guidelines have been forthcoming from the UN. For example, the *United Nations Criminal Justice Standards for Peace-keeping Police* handbook was released by the UN Crime Prevention and Criminal Justice Branch in 1994 with the help of CIVPOL members who had served in UNPROFOR and UNTAC, in the hope that it would prove useful in future UN operations "acting as a catalyst for change in law enforcement and police behaviour, as well as a guide for effective and fair criminal justice administration" (1994, p. 3). The handbook covers the role of police as it relates to fulfilling duties imposed by law, serving the community, protecting persons against illegal acts, and respecting and protecting human rights. It also outlines the procedures for lawful arrest, the use of force and firearms, trials, the handling of victims, refugees, detainees, and prisoners, and the need for law enforcement officers to resist corruption, the use of torture, illegal executions, and genocide.

However, there have continued to be a number of gaps in terms of the development of an overarching comprehensive doctrine and a more robust standardization of policing efforts (Mobekk, 2005; Lewis, Marks, and Perito, 2002). In an effort to fill such gaps, the UN Police Division has therefore recently brought about Doctrine Development Groups. These groups have been developed to undertake work on the development of doctrine and policy in areas such as policy relating to FPUs and predeployment training. These doctrines are still being finalized but present the first real chance for all of those personnel involved in policing roles to be on the same page in terms of a much more comprehensive and systematic set of common rules and guidelines.

Here, for example, with regards to predeployment training, it is clear that a lack of common standards has significantly hampered UN efforts (Morrison, 1996). In the later 1990s and into the new century the UNDPKO brought into being the *Selection Standards and Training Guidelines for United Nations Civilian Police* (1997) and the *United Nations Police Officers Course* (2000), which looked to outline more stringently the requirements for personnel operating in UN policing missions. Basic UN standards that have been in place for a number of decades and that are considered to be the bare minimum for consideration for deployment include professional status as members of the police force, good mental and physical health, minimum five years' policing experience, mission language proficiency, valid driving license from member state, and personal and professional integrity. Yet this issue of recruitment standards has received unprecedented interest within the Police Division in very recent times. Indeed, for the first time the division, in cooperation with the DPKO Integrated Training Service (ITS), is drafting tailored predeployment curricula as well as creating a standard predeployment curriculum that may become *de rigueur* for UNPOL personnel (Rolf Landgren, personal communication, 2007).

In addition to more systematic approaches to initial recruitment of personnel, the Police Division is also seeking to introduce a Performance Appraisal System that is linked to promotions and extensions and to launch an FPU evaluation and training system (Kroeker, 2007). (With regards to this latter ambition, there have been some advances already, as the UNDPKO teamed with CoESPU to conduct command development seminars for FPU commanders and their police commissioners, with the first seminar being held in mid-March 2006 (Dziedzic & Stark, 2006).) Though such measures are vital for ensuring the quality of UNPOL personnel in the field, they also, admittedly, narrow the potential candidates for selection—presenting the UN with something of a catch-22 situation as it aims to deploy good quality police in enough numbers to actually be able to make traction in peacekeeping missions.

All of these initiatives are part of a concerted effort to overcome past operational problems. Many of these problems have occurred because of the wide variations in quality of police personnel that are offered up for service on UN missions; thus, additional efforts at increasing the size of the pool of potential police for deployment as well as other quality control efforts have been undertaken in tandem with these more general guiding statements of principle sketched above. After all, the UN Police Division is first and foremost tasked with the recruitment of police officers for deployment in UN missions, and the quality of those police needs to be such so as to enable the UN to achieve the objectives of the mission at hand.

In terms of finding enough qualified personnel, the Brahimi Report of 2000 explicitly called on UN member states to establish a pool of police officers ready for deployment to United Nations peace operations on short notice. This document was the result of a very comprehensive review of United Nations Peace Operations, which, among other things, sought to augment and invigorate member state commitment to international policing to address the key issue of recruiting and retaining good police personnel. By the time of the report the UN was finding it very difficult to sustain adequate numbers of qualified policing personnel in the field. For example, in February 2000 member states had provided only 5,122 police officers to fill the nearly 9,000 posts that had been authorized by the Security Council (Crossette, 2000). The increasing demand for such a policing capability helped bring about a realization that ensuring greater commitment to international policing by member states was a necessary part of successful peace operations. In October 2004, then, the UN Police Division established a Police Generation Service in the hope of bringing to life this recommendation. There was a call for member states to have rolling rosters of experts to share the recruiting burden and to pool police in support of this standby concept. However, this concept was hampered by a rather patchy response across police contributing countries (PCCs) and never really gained the momentum needed. More recently, this concept been replaced by other initiatives, such as Operation 100, which hopes to increase the number of police contributing countries, which stood at 88 in mid-2007 and 92 at the end of 2007. In terms of numbers of personnel provided, the top 10 PCCs in respective order were: Jordan, Pakistan, Bangladesh, Nepal, Senegal, Nigeria, India, Portugal, United States, and Turkey (Top contributing countries graph, *UN Police Magazine*, 2007, p. 11). And lastly, another sensitive topic that is also beginning to be tackled is the question of when a uniformed police officer is required versus when non-police officers may carry out certain jobs. The civilianization of certain parts of policing and military establishments has proceeded apace since the end of the Cold War and the reassessment of those institutions.

However, such increases in the qualitative and quantitative nature, length, and breadth of police involvement in UNPKO have happened with surprisingly little fanfare, as have changes at the UN Police Division that is tasked with overseeing the development of both operational and strategic planning needs.

The UN Police Division

In keeping with the changes outlined above, a number of complementary changes unfolded with regards to the place of police within the DPKO. In

May 1993 a separate Civilian Police Unit at the DPKO was established and was tasked with planning and coordination of all matters relating to policing activities in UN peacekeeping operations (Hansen, 2002, p. 21). In 1997 the president of the Security Council (1997) recognized the growing role of police in peace operations, as noted above, by stating that

> the civilian police perform indispensable functions in monitoring and training national police forces and can play a major role, through assistance to local police forces, in restoring civil order, supporting the rule of law and fostering civil reconciliation[; moreover the UNSC] sees an increasingly important role for civilian police.

The Civilian Police Unit was upgraded to a Civilian Police Division in October 2000, and the division's head was promoted to the same level as the military adviser to the under-secretary general for peacekeeping (Hansen, 2002, p. 22). More recently, the military advisor for DPKO has been promoted to the level of assistant secretary general, while the Office of the Rule of Law and Security Institutions was created in mid-2007 to enfold the Police Division alongside the Criminal Law and Judicial Advisory Section, DDR Section, and Mine Action Service, and entails the office as a whole to its own assistant secretary general. (This raises the profile of the office as a whole, improving its status relative to the other agencies within UNDPKO: the Office of Operations, Office of Military Affairs, and Policy, Evaluation and Training Division.)

The Police Division is currently comprised of around 33 staff at any one time. Five of these positions are professional five-year posts (P posts) that are "galaxy" positions (positions that are open to competition), while the other posts are either temporary contract staff or national secondments that are on one-year rolling contracts for up to three years. Though there is no strict geographical allocation for such positions, PCCs are naturally interested in having a presence within the division, though countries are usually represented by a maximum of two or three personnel. These staff are posted as part of either the Office of the Police Advisor, Strategic Policy and Development Section (SPDS), or the Mission Management and Support Section (MMSS). According to the Police Division website, key tasks for the division include:

- Support police components of UN peacekeeping missions
- Enhance planning capacity for police components of UN operations
- Assist as appropriate in strengthening the performance, effectiveness, and efficiency of local criminal justice systems, including police and corrections
- Enhance ability to deploy rapidly a functional police component
- Improve quality representation in the field (date unknown)

In order to help augment these staff permanently based at the UN, a new Standing Police Capacity (SPC) that consists of 27 personnel who are to always be ready to go has been created. It includes 25 personnel with backgrounds in areas such as police reform, transnational crime, and transitional justice, as well as two administrators. And in addition to such in-house reshuffling, the division has also created a Rule of Law Index (ROLIX) to assess a cross section of rule of law factors in a mission area. Similarly, the division is seeking to establish a database of prospective leaders, police commissioners, and senior police advisors (Kroeker, 2007). The Police Division has also enlisted the help of an International Policing Advisory Council (IPAC) to provide strategic advice and a "specialised and dedicated high-level forum for critical discussion and policy-level input on international policing matters" made up of prominent policy makers, experts, and specialists in the field (UNDPKO, 2006, p. 6). At the same time, a concerted effort has also been made to systematize the information side of the division's undertakings, with the production of a *Portfolio of Police and Law Enforcement Projects* being produced in 2007 to give details on existing projects, with a new oral history project, and with the publication of *UN Police Magazine* to provide a forum for stories about those projects.

In addition to these internal developments there has also been some effort at strengthening relationships within DPKO and the broader UN family as a whole. The emergence of the concept of Integrated Operations Teams (IOTs) is an important initiative in this way in that they bring together police, military, political, and logistical/support components in mission-based teams—hence the creation of Team Darfur—which are co-located and whose role is to provide advice, coordination of response, and essentially be a multitasking New York-based contact point for missions in the field. In addition to the IOT concept, there are ongoing efforts to strengthen relationships with other law and justice actors within the UN family, and with member states' permanent missions too. Most countries at the UN do not have a permanent police advisor, and as Smith et al. (2007, p. 6) have pointed out, the Police Division has therefore had to work with military advisors who may not understand requirements of policing.

All of the above demonstrate that major changes have occurred and are ongoing for both the Police Division at UNHQ in New York and UNPOL personnel deployed in mission. As noted in the first section with regards to the evolution of the concept of peacekeeping, such changes have not occurred in a vacuum. As such, any future changes will have to take into account two significant reviews currently under way at a more strategic level within the UN family.

The Future of Police in Peace Operations

Police have moved from more limited roles to deeper and broader involvement in UN missions, involvement that may bestow executive powers or that may require the complete rebuilding of a country's police service. Yet the Police Division and UNPOL personnel must work within the broader UN framework and will therefore again have to adapt to any changes that may be rung in under the new reviews into Security Sector Reform (SSR) and into the broader concept of peacekeeping and peacekeeping doctrine that are currently under way.

Prompted by the increased demands being placed upon the UN to support national authorities in SSR, a UN system-wide SSR Task Force was recently established by the secretary general, to lead in the development of a holistic, coherent, and coordinated UN approach to SSR. The task force is co-chaired by UNDP and DPKO. The most immediate priority of the SSR Task Force is the preparation of a comprehensive report on SSR, as requested by the General Assembly in May 2007. This report will propose a framework for future UN engagement in SSR, which is expected to assist UN actors in this important area. For example, UN training on SSR, to civilians as well as police and military personnel, may assist in ensuring better governance of security sector actors, while enabling UN staff to better support national counterparts in this important area. This process will therefore impact upon both the Police Division and UN policing more generally, though these effects are obviously yet to be played out.

An even broader review is under way to define the doctrinal foundation of UN peacekeeping writ large. This review process, called the Capstone Doctrine, is assessing the overarching status of UN peacekeeping—its purpose and key principles. This is a major task that has not been undertaken since the mid-1990s. Beginning at the end of 2005 the process was moved through a number of iterations. Retired Major General Robert Gordon was brought in to draft an initial document, the draft was reworked in light of initial feedback at the UN, then sent out for consideration within six regional workshops held in Stockholm, the United States, Singapore, Ottowa, Jordan, and at the Conference of American Armies from late 2006 to mid-2007. Think tanks, field workers, NGOs, bureaucrats, and practitioners have been brought in to comment on draft documents, and an initial summary of some of the key ideas was published by Ahmed, Keating, and Solinas (2007) in the *Cambridge Review of International Affairs* in 2007. The document is now under consideration by member states. Here the major concern is to clearly demarcate what the UN can do through peacekeeping and what it cannot. Though there is some concern to try to push the envelope with regards to issues such as whether or not defense of a mandate qualifies as self-defense, and with regards to the potential to shift from terminology that talks of the nonuse of force to that which opens the possibility for "restraint in the use of force," there is also concern to recognize the limits of peacekeeping. Thus, the notion of consent has been stressed, the idea of peace enforcement by and large ignored, and the idea of peace building entertained but again mainly sidelined while the core business of peacekeeping is first reinscribed ("UN Peacekeeping," 2007).

These broader developments will undoubtedly impact upon the work of police as peacekeepers *and* peacebuilders no matter what the eventual outcome, but their effects are as yet unknown.

Conclusion

UN peace operations have broadened out from limited peacekeeping to peace missions where the UN may take over "key administrative functions, from taxation to garbage collection," whereby deeper peacebuilding efforts are necessarily engaged in (Paris, 2004, p. 213). Within this broader rubric the practice of UN policing in these peace operations has also changed dramatically. Executive policing and the three R's are now potential tasks for UN Police personnel—personnel that number in the high thousands and that may range from civilian advisers to specialist FPUs. Clearer standards, guidelines, and strategic planning are now being pursued to try to keep pace with these operational challenges, though the Police Division is underresourced, with 33 staff to manage 13,000 or so personnel in the field in 2008.

Given that the underlying but often implicit political agenda of the peacebuilding consensus is one of a process of liberalization, UN Police efforts of all kinds present a chance to pursue a key part of this agenda. Democratic policing principles that emphasize the supremacy of the (democratic, accountable, and transparent) rule of law and that aim first and foremost to serve and protect the local community present a chance to ensconce such values at a fundamental level in societies that may have been driven by conflict. Much of the challenge lies in tailoring this process to the local context. And although international policing as undertaken by the UN is not a panacea for the world's ills, indeed there are ongoing concerns about the efficacy of efforts in Kosovo and Timor-Leste today; for example, international policing under UN auspices presents a resource with as yet untapped and unrealized potential.

Acknowledgments

Thanks to Andrew Carpenter, Gerard Beekman, Rolf Landgren, and Kevin Steeves of the Police Division as well as Ugo Solinas and Jared Rigg (and others from throughout the Department of Peacekeeping Operations who do not wish to be directly acknowledged) for their discussions with the author in New York in November 2007. Thanks too to the participants of IPAC III for a fascinating few days of discussion in August 2007, and to the Australian Federal Police for hosting that meeting; to RegNet at the ANU and their co-host, Berkeley University, for a community policing workshop in December 2007, where I presented a first draft of this paper; and lastly to those many unnamed but not forgotten others who have helped with this project in various ways. As always, however, this paper, its argument and content, and any mistakes within are the work of the author alone.

References

Ahmed, S., Keating, P., & Solinas, U. (2007). Shaping the future of UN peace operations: Is there a doctrine in the house? *Cambridge Review of International Affairs, 20,* 11–28.

Ban, K. M. (2007, June). Message from Ban Ki-Moon. *UN Police Magazine,* 2nd ed., p. 1.

Bayley, D. H. (2001). *Democratizing the police abroad: What to do and how to do it.* Washington, DC: U.S. Department of Justice.

Boutros-Ghali, B. (1992) *An Agenda for Peace: Preventive Diplomacy, Peacemaking, and Peacekeeping.* New York: UN.

Crossette, B. (2000, February 22). The UN's unhappy lot: Perilous police duties multiplying. *New York Times,* p. A3.

Dziedzic, M., & Stark, C. (2006, June). *Bridging the security gap; the role of the Center of Excellence for Stability Police Units (CoESPU) in contemporary peace operations.* USIPeace Briefing. Retrieved October 8, 2007, from http://www.usip.org/pubs/usipeace_briefings/2006/0616_coespu.html.

Findlay, T. (1996). The new peacekeeping and the new peacekeepers. In T. Findlay (Ed.), *Challenges for the new peacekeepers* (SIPRI Report 12). Oxford: Oxford University Press for SIPRI.

Goals of the division. Retrieved May 13, 2008, from http://www.un.org/Depts/dpko/dpko/civpol/4.htm

Goulding, M. (1993, June). The evolution of United Nations peacekeeping. *International Affairs,* p. 455.

Hansen, A. S. (2002). *From Congo to Kosovo: Civilian police in peace operations.* Oxford: IISS.

Hartz, H. (2000). CIVPOL: The UN instrument for police reform. In T. Holm & E. Eide (Eds.), *Peacebuilding and police reform* (pp. 27–42). London: Frank Cass.

Hillen, J. (2000). *Blue helmets: The strategy of UN military operations* (2nd ed.). Washington, DC: Brassey's.

Hood, L. (2006). Security sector reform in East Timor. *International Peacekeeping,* 13, 73.

Kosovo Police Service School. Retrieved December 21, 2005, from http://www.civpol.org/unmik/KPS.htm

Kroeker, M. (2007, August). UN Police presentation. Third meeting of the international policing advisory council. National Museum of Australia, Canberra.

Lewis, W., Marks, E., & Perito, R. (2002, April). *Enhancing international civilian police in peace operations.* USIP Special Report.

Mobekk, E. (2005). *Identifying lessons in United Nations international policing missions.* Geneva: Geneva Centre for the Democratic Control of the Armed Forces.

Morrison, A. (1996). Methodology, contents and structure of UN civilian police training programmes. In N. Azimi (Ed.), *The role and functions of civilian police in United Nations peacekeeping operations: Debriefing and lessons.* London: Kluwer Law International.

OSCE. *Police education: Establishing Kosovo police service.* Retrieved December 20, 2005, from http://www.osce.org/kosovo/13216.html

Paris, R. (2004). *At war's end: Building peace after civil conflict.* Cambridge: Cambridge University Press.

Perito, R. (2004). *Where is the Lone Ranger when we need him? America's search for a post-conflict stability force.* Washington, DC: USIP.

Richmond, O. P. (2004). UN peace operations and the dilemmas of the peacebuilding consensus. *International Peacekeeping, 11,* 83–101.

Smith, J. G., Holt, V. K., & Durch, W. J. (2007, August). *From Timor-Leste to Darfur: New initiatives for enhancing UN civilian policing capacity.* Henry L. Stimson Center Issue Brief.

Thomas, L. M. (2004). Peace operations and the need to prioritize the rule of law through legal system reform: Lessons from Somalia and Bosnia. *Small Wars and Insurgencies, 15,* 70–76.

Top contributing countries graph, May 2007. (2007, June). *UN Police Magazine,* 2nd ed., p. 11.

UNDPKO. (1997). *Selection standards and training guidelines for United Nations civilian police.* New York: UN.

UNDPKO. (2000). *United Nations police officers course.* New York: UN.

UNDPKO, Government of the United Kingdom, of Great Britain and Northern Ireland, and Government of Norway. (2006, August). *International policing advisory council (IPAC) summary meeting report.* Wilton Park, UK.

UNDPKO. (2008). UN police warn of organized crime threat to peacekeeping. Retrieved March 2, 2009 from http://www.UN.int/wcm/content/site/portal/cache/offonce/home/pid/6114

United Nations Crime Prevention and Criminal Justice Branch. (1994). *United Nations criminal justice standards for peace-keeping police.* Vienna: UN Office at Vienna.

United Nations Department of Public Information. (1990). *The blue helmets: A review of United Nations peacekeeping* (2nd ed.). New York: UN.

United Nations Police Division. (2007). *Portfolio of police and law enforcement projects 2007* (1st ed.). New York: UN Police Division.

United Nations Secretariat. (2000, August 21). *Report of the panel on United Nations peace operations* (Brahimi Report, UN Document A/ff/305, S/2000/809). Retrieved October 8, 2005, from http://www.un.org/peace/report/peace _operations

United Nations Special Commission of the Inquiry for Timor-Leste. (2006). *Report of the United Nations independent special commission of inquiry for Timor-Leste.* Geneva: Author.

UN peacekeeping: Capstone doctrine. Retrieved December 6, 2007, from http://pbpu. unlb.org/pbps/Pages/Public/viewprimarydoc.aspx?docid=481

Weiss, T. G., Forsythe, D. P., and Coate, R. A. (2001). *The United Nations and changing world politics* (3rd ed.). Boulder, CO: Westview Press.

Williams, M. C. (1998). *Civil-military relations and peacekeeping* (Adelphi Paper 321). London: International Institute for Strategic Studies.

"It Wasn't Like Normal Policing"
Voices of Australian Police Peacekeepers in Operation Serene, Timor-Leste, 2006

15

ANDREW GOLDSMITH

Contents

While Australia's history of police participation in peacekeeping goes back more than 40 years to the beginnings of the United Nations (UN) peacekeeping operation in Cyprus, involvement of significant numbers of Australian policing personnel in overseas operations including peacekeeping is relatively recent. Significant participation began with the Australian-led regional intervention in the Solomon Islands in 2003 (Regional Assistance Mission to the Solomon Islands (RAMSI)). Since 2003, more than 1,000 Australian federal, state, and territory police officers have served in a variety of missions in addition to the Solomon Islands. These have included Papua New Guinea (PNG), Tonga, Nauru, Vanuatu, Sudan, Afghanistan, and Timor-Leste (TL). These missions have had capacity-building as well as peacekeeping functions, and in some cases the two functions have coexisted formally in the same mission (e.g., RAMSI).

Adapted from Goldsmith, A. (2008). It wasn't like normal policing: Voices of Australian police peacekeepers in Operation Serene, Timor-Leste 2006. *Policing and Society*. http://dx.doi.org/10.1080/10439460802187548

In many of these settings, stabilization of preexisting conflicts and tensions remains incomplete or tenuous. International police are being asked to operate in more volatile and potentially dangerous environments and to draw at times upon a range of more robust operational techniques than they have been accustomed to (Centre on International Cooperation, 2008, p. 9; Durch, 2006; Oakley, Dziedzic, & Goldberg, 2002). In many instances, this has meant working alongside military peacekeepers, at least for some period of time during deployment. It has also led to placing greater reliance upon special operations and riot control police units (in the UN setting, known as Formed Police Units (FPUs)). Australia's participation in these dynamic environments and its significant role in providing police to these kinds of missions, especially in the Asia-Pacific region, have resulted in greater demands upon, and challenges for, police peacekeepers and capacity builders and their commanders.

This chapter presents some findings from a pioneering study of Australian police peacekeepers and capacity builders conducted over 2005–2007. The study comprised in large measure a series of face-to-face interviews with more than 120 police personnel who had served on overseas missions in Timor-Leste, Solomon Islands, and Papua New Guinea. The deployment of international police personnel in peacekeeping environments has been critically understudied. The major contribution to the literature in this field has been in the form of a few personal accounts published in recent years that deal with such involvements (e.g., Savage, 2002; Cole, 2007). Systematic research has been in short supply. David Bayley has noted this phenomenon by stating that: "At the moment ... the people who do [police] assistance work, both at home and abroad, know a great deal about what works and what doesn't, but this knowledge isn't being captured" (2001, p. 76).

In order to capture knowledge, the interview method was adopted. This qualitative method enables the researcher to focus upon the narratives of the police peacekeepers interviewed. The interview materials should be considered "narrative accounts rather than as true pictures of reality" (Denzin & Lincoln, 2005, p. 647). As Chase has pointed out (2005, p. 656), narratives of the kind discussed in this chapter "communicate ... the narrator's point of view, including why the narrative is worth telling in the first place," adding that in addition to describing what happened, narratives "also express emotions, thoughts and interpretations." The point in this chapter is not to establish to what extent these narratives fit or don't fit with reality or reflect official policy applying to Operation Serene, or indeed whether Operation Serene can be considered successful. It is rather to bring to light themes emerging from a close reading of the personal accounts rendered that might bear usefully upon future planning and conduct of police peace operations.

This chapter contains an analysis of a subset of 44 interviews, conducted with policing personnel who served in TL at some point between May 28 and December 1, 2006, as part of Operation Serene. Operation Serene was the

Australian police component of an intervention in TL following the breakdown of civil order and the virtual paralysis of the TL government in April–May 2006. The police interviewed represented a sample drawn from state and territory police (26 respondents) as well as members of the Australian Federal Police (18 respondents). Of this group, 36 were male and 8 female. Police from across all serving ranks were interviewed.

While Australian police service in Timor-Leste dates back to 1999, Operation Serene appeared to raise two particular challenges for the officers involved. The first was the difficulty presented by youth gangs and disorderly crowds on the streets of Dili. Groups of youth, sometimes numbering 100 or more, would frequently confront international police patrols in the narrow streets of Dili throughout the entire period of the intervention. These confrontations were often violent, involving the use of catapults, knives, machetes, dart guns, and mass stoning against police personnel and their vehicles. In many instances, police patrols of four or five officers, equipped only with radios, capsicum spray, and collapsible batons, were required to seek urgent backup from more heavily armed military and paramilitary units. The second challenge was the political situation in the country during this period. The Australian police component of the intervention had to negotiate the often opaque and contradictory ideas of local political and community expectations of its role, and accommodate the increasing involvement of UN police from different countries during the period September to December 2006. This chapter will focus specifically on aspects of these two challenges.

Operation Serene: Australian Police in Timor-Leste

In late May 2006, the Australian Federal Police participated in Operation Serene upon request from the TL government for assistance in dealing with civil disorder, which had been getting worse over the preceding two months. It reached crisis point on May 25, when several defense force (F-FDTL) members opened fire upon a group of unarmed Timorese police officers, resulting in 9 deaths and 25 seriously injured. The breakdown in order has been extensively reviewed and canvassed in a series of official reports and academic commentaries (UN, 2006a, 2006b; Goldsmith & Dinnen, 2007). Operation Serene was charged with assisting the Australian Defence Force (ADF) in restoring order, and with initiating investigations into a range of serious offenses committed during the April–May crisis, including the massacre of National Police (PNTL) personnel on May 25. What is important to note was that the disorder was largely confined to Dili and its immediate environs. Policing had become increasingly absent over the weeks leading up to May 25, with many police fearing for their own safety. The government, preoccupied with political in-fighting, lost effective control over its security forces. In the hours after the May 25 events, calls for assistance were made by the TL government. These extended not only to Australia, but also to Malaysia, New Zealand, and Portugal. Operation Serene was launched on May 29, less than four days after the start of the ADF-led military intervention, code named Operation Astute (Slater, 2006).

Deployment of the Australian police began on May 28 with a six-member assessment team, followed the next day by 45 more police. Deployment continued in a progressive manner over the next few weeks, with numbers of deployed personnel reaching as high as 200. Immediately prior to the intervention, six Australian police had been working in Dili in a small capacity-building program known as the Timor-Leste Police Development Program (TLPDP). This program effectively became suspended during the crisis, with just a skeleton staff remaining in the country, though some civilian members continued to work with the Ministry of the Interior. The Australian police presence continued until the United Nations Mission in Timor (UNMIT) began in late August 2006 (Security Council Resolution 1704), after which Australian police, while continuing to participate in urban patrols and other policing tasks under formal UN control, began preparations for their withdrawal on December 1, when the UN assumed full control of a broader multilateral police peacekeeping force. During the intervention, Australian police worked cooperatively with the ADF contingent of more than 1,000 soldiers, as well as with military personnel and police from Malaysia, New Zealand, and Portugal, who gradually joined the operation from June onward. In both police and military terms, Australia contributed the largest contingent to this intervention and had provided the first on-ground response (Slater, 2006).

In many ways, Operation Serene provides a telling example of a complex 21st-century peace operation. The Australian intervention was not peacekeeping in its traditional meaning. There was no negotiated peace to monitor or uphold. TL did not constitute a failed state in the sense that an executive administration was needed. It has to be remembered that, despite loss of control over the security forces and other symptoms of governmental dysfunction, there was nonetheless a government in office claiming sovereignty. Until this moment in the nation's short history, TL had been widely touted as a UN nation-building success story (Hood, 2006; Ashdown, 2007). Australia's 2006 response was a classic case of cooperative intervention, premised upon an invitation by the government to outside governments to assist. However, as might be predicted in such cases, such operations are often complex and poorly defined. Establishing clear lines of responsibility (and hence authority) in sensitive matters such as civil order and security sector operations has then and since proved difficult and often impossible (Wilson, 2008).

Dealing With the Gangs

Yeah, they're quite friendly really, when they weren't throwing rocks at you. [Respondent 35]

Dili is the capital of Asia's newest and poorest nation-state. After centuries of colonialism and foreign occupation, it has only existed as an independent nation since May 2002. The country itself has a population of around 1 million, with one of the world's highest birth rates—around eight live births per female. The capital has an official population of just under 200,000 persons, though this number is likely to be conservative given the trend of many youth moving there in search of excitement and economic opportunity. During the civil disorder of 2006, an estimated 150,000 persons were forced to flee or chose to move out of their homes in Dili into displaced persons camps and other forms of temporary accommodation, many of which were in the immediate surrounds of Dili. Needless to say, such an irregular, massive displaced population only added to the difficulties faced by the Timorese government and the challenges facing the peacekeeping forces.

A key element of the setting confronting Australian peacekeepers was the so-called east/west tensions, or tensions arising from regional differences between persons from the east of the country (*lorosae*) and those from the west (*loromonu*) (Devant, 2008; International Crisis Group, 2008). Dili is an inevitable meeting point between the two parts of the country for trade, employment, and governance purposes. In such a small country, these tensions became increasingly visible within national institutions (particularly the military and police forces) in the months preceding the crisis of 2006. They culminated in a series of clashes between elements of the two institutions and their civilian supporters. Much of the political tension during April and May can be linked to a significant group within F-FTDL (the petitioners, numbering nearly 600 out of the 1,400 defense force members), which accused the military leadership, widely viewed as having eastern (*lorosae*) allegiances, of discrimination against westerners within the F-FDTL. It is now widely accepted that the issue was mishandled politically, and as such, it led to a deepening of tensions and rising levels of disorder in the period leading up to May 25 (UN, 2006a).

Ironically, as tensions built during the first few months of 2006, the United Nations Mission in Support of East Timor (UNMISET) was winding down after three years of assisting the newly independent government. However, even if the UN mission saw the crisis coming, its small scale made it ill-equipped to act quickly or decisively. On May 25, the day of the massacre of the local PNTL officers, Australia was well placed to respond quickly to an invitation to intervene. It already had a naval vessel, *Adelaide*, nearby, anticipating the potential need to evacuate Australian citizens should things deteriorate further. The ADF was able to deploy troops within hours of the invitation from the government to intervene, which followed quickly after the massacre. When the first Australian military and then police personnel arrived, they encountered widespread public disorder, including looting, burning of houses, and gang fights between rival easterner and westerner gangs (Slater, 2006). As noted earlier, many persons affected, mainly easterners, were forced from their homes in Dili into temporary camps around Dili, many of which still remain (International Crisis Group, 2008).

The "Youth Bulge"

A significant contextual variable for peacekeepers seeking to restore order is the enormous youth bulge in the population—approximately 50% of the country's population is 15 or under, and many Timorese of this age bracket have been drawn to Dili to live (Scambary, 2006). Another factor is the lack of economic development and high levels of unemployment and underemployment in urban areas such as Dili. This is particularly evident in Dili, which resembles many other developing country capital cities undergoing urbanization, as people, again, mainly youth, flock to the city from the countryside to live typical, economically marginal lives.

Timorese youth have a significant history of involvement in martial arts groups, dating back at least to the period of the Indonesian occupation (1975–1999) (Scambary, 2006). While these groups seem to have begun as a way of channeling youthful energy into productive, disciplined forms, the picture has become more complex over time, reflecting changes in the local environment. The mayhem surrounding the holding of elections and the Indonesian withdrawal in June to September 1999 was largely attributable to Indonesian-trained and supported militias, directed against those favoring independence (Savage, 2002). Since that time, it is widely accepted that some persons involved in these groups have become involved in petty criminal activities such as extortion, as well as being drawn into conflicts within the local political elites and the intercommunal violence that continues to plague TL.

As political in-fighting within government and between political groupings escalated during the first half of 2006, levels of civil disorder rose in frequency and seriousness. These "gangs" played an observable and significant role in this disorder (Scambary, 2006). In short, prior to the crisis in 2006, Dili was increasingly the home for significant numbers of disaffected, martially trained, young men with few legitimate economic opportunities. As the crisis deepened over April and May, PNTL officers in Dili abandoned their posts. Many of these police, rather than withdrawing from the conflict, went to join various irregular groups, including militias and gangs, involved in burning of houses and intergroup fights. From the end of May onward, these groups confronted the new international police on the streets of Dili.

The quick deployment of Australian military peacekeepers, supplemented progressively by police personnel over the first few weeks, did little initially to quell the serious disorder. Many of the police, as well as the military personnel, were surprised by what they encountered:

When we dropped out of the sky, basically, the—a lot of gangs roving around, a lot of houses burning, still firearms present with the gangs and machetes and darts and such. [Respondent 96]

Early images in the Australian media appeared to show Australian military peacekeepers standing around helplessly as Timorese people on the streets engaged in looting, arson, and other forms of civil disorder. One of the difficulties was that there were many more such instances of disorder taking place than could be responded to by the peacekeepers available. Thousands of houses were destroyed during this period.

Another difficulty was that there was a lack of basic geographical knowledge. This lack of understanding was such that even when a unit was available to respond to a call, it would often not know how to find the location of the incident (Interviews, Australian military and police personnel, Dili, November 2006). This meant that for an extended period, until local intelligence could be obtained, the international peacekeeping presence could not prevent gangs and others from burning the homes of many ordinary Dili residents, turning them into displaced persons. Such early displays of impotence by peacekeepers augured badly for subsequent efforts at building local confidence.

Once Australian police arrived in significant numbers, in early June, the ADF and Australian police began joint patrols, consisting of 9 or 10 military and 2 police personnel. These patrols took place on foot as well as using armored personnel carriers (APCs), and were under the control of the ADF. During this period, police could only patrol according to military rules of engagement, including only operating during restricted hours. During July 2006, police started assuming greater responsibility for patrols, moving about in four-wheel-drive Toyotas, with the capacity to call for military or police operational support backup. By July, these patrols had become increasingly multinational in composition, consisting of a mixed team of four or five officers, of Australian, Malay, and in the last few months of 2006, returning PNTL officers. During this period, it should be noted that the Portuguese National Gendarmerie (GNR) remained operationally separate.

On many occasions, police patrols could only react to house burnings and gang fights. They then became vulnerable to ambush by large groups of stone-throwing, dart-firing, and at times, machete-wielding youths. As one Australian officer recounted, the situations they faced were sometimes highly precarious:

In the beginning they [youth gangs] never threw a rock at us; now, one night it just turned. They got two [police] vehicles, ambushed them, set up barricades. They were testing the waters, how we would react. They set up a roadblock, they sucked a car in with a false allegation, roadblock behind it, and then they came out and ran at the car and the car had to [go] over and through the barricade to get out of there. And then they sucked two coppers in, and one of the copper's lives was saved because another ex-Timorese police officer, who somehow was with the gang, grabbed him and said. "You run or they will kill you." One made it over the wall running and the other one didn't. Got grabbed by the crowd about to get beaten up and killed, and the ex-Timorese copper grabbed him, saved him, threw him over the wall. [Respondent 84]

The sense of being inadequately prepared, in terms of training, direction, and equipment, for the circumstances they faced is reflected in the comments of many peacekeepers interviewed. Attempts to apply everyday, familiar Australian policing methods, such as arresting suspected offenders, often appeared pointless or even counterproductive in such volatile circumstances. Police patrols faced "hit and run" type encounters with the gangs, in which the gang members would escape, barefooted if necessary. As one respondent experienced:

You just ended up with a street full of empty thongs [rubber casual beach footwear] and you're standing there in your full kit. [Respondent 39]

This kind of exchange proved very frustrating for many police:

"This is the police, stop." Well, in Australia, 99.8% of people stop, whereas over there, 99.8% of people basically turn and hoofed it. So it was quite a—quite a shock and very frustrating, because as I said, you were so used to 10 years of people obeying your lawful commands, and then you'd go there and, you know, they just basically run down the street and turn around and pelt you with rocks. [Respondent 39]

During the entire period of Operation Serene, baiting police and avoiding detention was a common practice among local youth, which Australian police felt ill-equipped to counter. The equipment supplied and required to be worn by them (helmets, shields, and body armor) meant they were not well placed to chase the mainly young males who constituted these gangs over unfamiliar terrain. The sense that Australian police were fair game under these conditions seemed to exist in some quarters of the local community. During my visit to Dili in November/December 2006, I was told by several persons that some gang members believed the acronym for the Australian Federal Police (AFP) stood for "Awfully Fat Police," pointing to a local perceived difference between Australian police and members of the

Portuguese GNR (known to the youth as "Guns 'n Roses"), composed on average of younger, apparently fitter personnel equipped with a wider range of nonlethal weaponry, including gas and rubber bullets. This view held among Timorese youth may well have contributed to the relative attractiveness of Australian police as targets for ambush. Such an interpretation, if correct, would help to make sense of the level of frustration felt by many of our respondents.*

Australian police peacekeeping patrols initially, for the most part, lacked weaponry capable of projecting nonlethal force over more than a few meters. When this was required, they were obliged to call for military and operational response or FPU-type support (Respondent 86). Among the deployed personnel interviewed for this study, this was seen to put them at a disadvantage in terms of dealing with gangs and large groups of youths in street encounters. Australian police, while armed with side arms, could otherwise resort only to collapsible batons and capsicum spray. Equipped in this manner, calling for backup became commonplace when surrounded by stone-throwing mobs. This meant that until backup arrived, they often felt, and probably often were, at significant risk of personal injury or worse. In some incidents, side arms were drawn and warning shots were fired while biding time until backup assistance arrived (Interview, NZ police officer). Overall, it was remarkable that no serious injuries or deaths of international police personnel or Timorese occurred during any of these incidents.

As an interim response, in addition to the handful of operational response personnel within the Australian contingent, a further dozen Australian police were certified to carry shotguns that fired beanbag rounds on patrols. These were used mainly to target ringleaders in ambush-type situations, and were widely seen by Australian police interviewed as having improved their crowd control capacity considerably. Still, this change was not sufficient to supply the level of robust support needed by the Australian police patrols, meaning that military or FPU-type support was still required from time to time.

In dealing with the gangs, some Australian police began to experiment with different techniques. One officer observed:

> Sometimes we'd manage to talk them into going home. Other times we'd use tactics, you know, like at one stage we were driving our vehicle at the crowds to disburse them, to stop them from throwing rocks. That sort of thing and various techniques to try and prevent, you know, arresting a few of them, searching them, taking weapons off them, arresting them if it's a serious weapon,

* There is little doubt Australians were not the only group in TL during this period that were subject to negative perceptions among local people. While the GNR were admired by some, they were also feared and resented by other local people for what were seen as often excessively robust interventions and handling of detainees.

taking photographs of them. I found out they didn't like their photograph being taken, so if there's a gang there and they were looking like they were going to get—going to cause trouble, I'd walk around with my camera taking photos of them, and then the next thing, they're all gone home. If I'd walked there and asked them to go home or told them to go home, they wouldn't have. They'd walk five minutes and stand in the next spot, but taking a photo, off they go. So we've learned on the go. [Respondent 51]

Such experiments can lead, in effect, to examples of *reverse capacity building*, referring to the acquisition of new skills and capacities by the putative capacity builders (or, in this case, peacekeepers) for potential use in their home policing environments.*

Another lesson for many respondents from Operation Serene was the crucial importance of FPU-type rapid response groups. The demonstration effect provided by the sorts of confrontations described above, as well as similar experiences in the Solomon Islands in April 2006, led to the decision during the course of Operation Serene to train additional Australian police in the operation of beanbag-firing shotguns (Respondent 86). As one noted:

Our biggest problem was we were relying on the GNR and other police forces to be our heavy hammer, we didn't have the capabilities, and the AFP hasn't thought of what force. Like we have that beautiful circle and the commissioner's orders and you will consider this, but what is between spray and baton, which are only effective in two-meter ranges, and deadly force? Absolutely nothing. So when someone throws a rock at you or the darts and they are 20 meters away, what have you got to defend yourself? Nothing except deadly force. [Respondent 84]

A number of respondents indicated the futility of normal models of police patrol work in situations when violence suppression became a major objective. The sense of vulnerability felt in these volatile environments inevitably led them to innovate their own approaches as well as to think about the need in such operations for more robust forms of engagement.

Meeting Local Expectations

That was probably the biggest challenge, that if they couldn't see that we were being totally unbiased in about who we were policing and why we were doing it. [Respondent 34]

---

* The phenomenon of reverse capacity building is examined in Harris and Goldsmith (2009).

One of the very early challenges in interventions of this kind is to get the local community, whose expectations are often extremely high and indeed unrealistic, to support peacekeeping objectives. In a highly fractious and volatile environment in which the community has become fearful and factionalized, this critical first challenge is often quite difficult. The result is that peacekeepers, despite even their best efforts to provide assistance, will often end up bewildered, feeling the hostility of local residents:

> The actual police work was a lot tougher there, yeah. You felt like you weren't really making much of a difference. You felt like you were just chasing your tail every day. You'd sort out one skirmish where people were throwing rocks at each other, and you'd turn up and then they'd throw them at you, and then the next day you'd be talking to them and they'd think you're fantastic and not just one nationality or one state or anything like that, but everyone. Then later on that night, they'd be throwing rocks at your police barrier. I just couldn't understand it, and it just seemed like you weren't going to achieve anything. You know, it just seemed like a more hopeless sort of mission. [Respondent 14]

Rumor and Gossip

One of the challenges facing Australian police in TL was the impact of rumor and gossip. Local rumors can affect peacekeepers' reputation and standing within the community. Stories circulating among local populations in tense environments can easily spill over into local attitudes and acts of hostility, or at least indifference and noncooperation toward the peacekeepers. Often they are blamed without foundation for particular attacks or acts against one party to a conflict or dispute. One occurrence in late 2006 makes this point clearly:

> The Sacred Heart gang led by two PNTL officers with guns (who have been arrested for it) attacked en masse the Hotel Timor refugee camp. They shot … without killing anyone. Two Australian Defence Force personnel were driving by when the shooting started, went to ground, and called in assistance. A rumor quickly spread among the locals that the ADF had participated in the initial attack because they were seen calling in during shooting, and that the Australian police who arrived to protect community, had joined in. Then the Australian police came under attack. And they came under attack next day elsewhere after word spread by mobile phone that Australia launched this attack on IDP camp. They went back to camp next day to explain what had happened. They also explained to the camp residents that they were there to protect them and had arrested two leaders of the attack. [Respondent 121]

Even if these rumors were untrue, on occasions even countered by official statements from the TL government as to their falsity, such stories, as communal narratives, can leave a residue of resentment among local people, reinforcing and adding to existing narratives about the character and motives of international peacekeepers. Several Australian police personnel interviewed commented on the local perception that the Australians favored the westerners—in the case just given, the fact that "eastern" residents of the Hotel Timor displacement camp had not been protected from the "western" gang attack by Australian police or military peacekeepers served to corroborate the content of this communal narrative about the real motives of Australian peacekeepers. The perception that the Australian police were taking sides constituted a fundamental difficulty, not only challenging the image of peacekeeping as a neutral activity, but also undermining the peacekeepers' capacity to meet local expectations. In an environment where there is local will in certain quarters to politicize the activities of peacekeepers, there are no obvious or easy solutions.*

Building Confidence

The inherently political nature of peacekeeping and the strangeness of the local settings in which peacekeeping is being attempted, present a range of difficulties for peacekeepers. As noted earlier, the sheer infeasibility of making arrests on many occasions raises questions about the relative priorities for ordinary police peacekeepers in these environments, in which there are rule of law needs to suppress violence, maintain order, and investigate criminal offenses. This is not a mixture of objectives that many Australian police are accustomed to juggling in the course of a normal day's police work in their home police forces. Moreover, as we have also seen, there are often underlying currents of distrust and suspicion in the local population that make cooperation in achieving criminal investigative and intelligence objectives within peacekeeping operations highly problematic.

Among our respondents, these obstacles were sometimes attributed to cultural differences. As one officer noted:

> The cultural differences were to do with people not giving information ... sometimes the assurances you gave people were very uncomfortable assurances.... Like people would ask, "If we give you information, are you going to be able to protect us?" ... At the end of the day, I don't think we're in a position to give people the assurances that they were all looking for. [Respondent 52]

---

* See further below the discussion of Australian police dealings with the TL government. Australia's interest in Timor gas and oil has helped to muddy the waters for Australia in terms of how different Timorese groups view Australia's motives for humanitarian and security assistance. As became clear to me during my visit in November–December 2006, some Timorese views of Australian police activities in TL have been shaped by critical assessments of Australia's wider foreign policy agenda.

In a divided, conflict-prone society where the peacekeepers are a temporary and often tentative presence, the challenge of reassuring potential local witnesses in a future prosecution is much greater than it is in most Western societies. In part, the reason for this lies in the histories of places like TL, for whose residents the previous experience of policing under colonial and later Indonesian authorities had been repressive and brutal. Given these jaundiced histories, the proposition that peacekeepers could persuade Timorese to give up information so as to ensure greater security for all concerned is deeply unrealistic. The inability of the peacekeepers to stop widespread burning and looting of homes and businesses over many weeks, as noted earlier, was reminder enough to local people of the limited protection available from peacekeepers, putting aside the problem of feelings of fundamental distrust and perceived bias held by certain sections of the population living in Dili.

Dealing With the Timorese Government

Unlike the Australian-led intervention (INTERFET) in 1999 following the withdrawal by the Indonesians, the operation by Australia in 2006 occurred alongside, and indeed at the invitation of, a standing national government (Slater, 2006). In 1999, when the Indonesians left and the militias were exacting their revenge on the Timorese population, INTERFET in effect entered a failed state scenario. In May 2006, while Timorese *de facto* sovereignty and state capacity were clearly in question, there was nonetheless no doubt that formal sovereignty continued to reside in the Timor-Leste Fretilin-dominated government.* It was not a trusteeship-type situation, in which executive authority was vested in another agency (Chesterman, 2004).

The novelty and complexity of this set of circumstances require further specification and better understanding in terms of lessons for the future than is possible here. However, it needs to be borne in mind that in addition to having a government in power, the Australian-led peacekeeping force was supplemented relatively quickly in 2006 by police and military personnel from several other countries; two UN investigations of the problems surrounding the crisis and the massacre on May 25 were undertaken; several UN Security Council resolutions were passed; and by August 2006, it was clear that a new UN mission with peacekeeping and capacity-building mandates was to succeed the limited, multinational *bricolage* of Australian, New

---

* Fretilin is the political party that dominated government since 2002 until 2007, and that was in power at the time of the 2006 crisis. Historically, it has claimed to be the natural party of government, given its long-standing association with the resistance movement during the period of Indonesian occupation (1975–1999).

Zealand, Malaysian, and Portuguese peacekeepers that was in the process of winding down (Goldsmith & Dinnen, 2007). Such a complex picture inevitably makes international police peacekeeping operations on the ground complicated, often difficult, and frequently contested.

Given the complex political terrain upon which Operation Serene took place, it is hardly surprising in many ways that the setting was not well understood by Australian police peacekeepers at the time. Conventional understandings of peacekeeping or humanitarian assistance would not prove adequate in this setting, both for those leading the peacekeeping operations and for those police personnel involved in street patrols. Local, particularly elite, perceptions of Australian involvement and its strategic interests in TL policing were inevitably going to be shaped by its established capacity-building program that had been under way for two years at the time of the crisis (the Timor-Leste Police Development Program (TLPDP)), as well as by its peacekeeping role in Operation Serene. Moreover, during the period of the peacekeeping operation, it became clear to members of the TL government that Australia sought an expanded role in the future rebuilding of the PNTL. One might well have predicted that any proposed shift from a limited, bilateral capacity-building role to a peacekeeping and then to an expanded capacity-building role in the future might well encounter significant resistance given the local political complexities and the range of other international participants present during the peacekeeping phase.

The following comment by a senior Australian police peacekeeper is suggestive of the difficulties that may be encountered when trying to pursue simultaneously different policing agendas in such environments:

> We spent quite a deal of time and negotiated with all the key stakeholders in a reintegration plan, did a presentation to what would be the equivalent of our Cabinet. They all nodded their heads, yes, yes, yes, and the next day there's a totally different plan. [Respondent 33]

This comment is also a reminder of how often peacekeepers and capacity builders can, at their peril, presume their proposals and plans to be technical and professional (rather than political) in nature, especially when dealing with a government *in situ*. Though unlikely to have been intended in this case, an overly programmatic approach to deeply political issues can too easily appear like arrogance to locals who possess a different view of the environment and its needs, and result in obstruction and resistance at the local level (Interview, UN official, New York, February 2007).

In the case of TL in 2006, the UN's renewed interest in the country's troubles, following a request for its assistance in June, served to provide the TL government with a counterpoint to the clear ongoing interest shown by Australia in shaping the future of TL policing. In effect, it allowed the government respite, at least for a while. This became palpable among senior Australian police peacekeepers at the time. As one observed:

> [The government] was very keen on having the UN come in and take over, and I think we ended up with a stalemate ... where they were just going to hold off as long as they could until the UN got there.... Mr. Ramos Horta [prime minister] ... clearly made it known that no one was going to tell him how to run his police and how to run his army, and wanted to make sure that everyone clearly understood that, despite what had occurred. [Respondent 96]

The Transition to the United Nations Integrated Mission in Timor-Leste (UNMIT)

Operation Serene officially ceased on December 1, 2006, though transitional arrangements for handing over to UNPOL had been taking place since late August. As the prospect of the Australian withdrawal grew closer, and as more UN police contingents arrived in TL, the Australian role inevitably diminished in significance. Around 40 Australian police officers from Operation Serene stayed on as part of the UNPOL operation under UNMIT. For these officers, the transition presented certain difficulties:

> My conversations with people that were left behind ... is that they were pretty much targeted—or bullied if that's the word I would use—by the UN forces because they had lost that power base, and I think the appendum was, well you may have been in charge, but now we're in charge and we're the UN and we know better; and you're not in that lead role anymore, you're down the bottom here. [Respondent 21]

From an Australian police perspective, as many of our interviews revealed, the UN, and UNPOL itself, can sometimes appear weak and open to manipulation by politicians in a country such as TL. Many respondents expressed strong reservations about the level of operational proficiency shown by some police units from other countries involved during Operation Serene, as well as noting the difficulties of coordinating an efficient multinational policing operation in a peacekeeping situation. Many of these challenges are, of course, not unique to TL. However, it is a reminder that the perception among many Australian police respondents that peacekeeping missions are basically straightforward, technical, and professional, rather than political, complex exercises needs to be challenged and corrected quickly. Apart from avoiding unnecessary provocation of other interested parties, adopting a more realistic, and hence modest, view of the peacekeeping role will also help to avoid some of the feelings of resentment and disappointment evident among peacekeepers during Operation Serene and the handover to the UN mission.

Conclusion

> In the end, it really came down to us doing Australian policing and prob-
> ably not being overly successful in that environment and probably because
> we just didn't have enough numbers to accomplish it, because, you know, our
> response as Australian police is great. If somebody breaks the law there's—it's
> "We'll catch you and we're going to chuck you in the bin." And we didn't have
> enough numbers to do that to everybody, and consequently, there was a bit of
> a perceived [bias among the community]. [Respondent 34]

Two clear themes emerge from remarks such as this one and from those of
many other respondents interviewed and discussed here. The first is the sense
of surprise among police peacekeepers about the environment into which
they were placed, and the second concerns the limited skills they felt they
possessed to respond appropriately in that environment. Two-thirds of those
interviewed for this study had no prior in-country experience, though some
had served elsewhere on other overseas missions. Inevitably, many then had
only a superficial understanding of the culture, social composition, political
arrangements, and languages spoken. To the extent that these limitations were
also present among some of the mission command, this could be expected to
reduce their effectiveness in terms of their ability to negotiate the sensitive
political terrain on which they were operating. It also could be expected to
result in uncertainty and imprecision in directions to operational peacekeepers. The terrain was shaped largely by shifting involvements of other nations,
the UN, and last but not least, the local political complexities of a fragile, new
nation-state. There is some strong evidence that these limitations did impact
subsequently upon the TL government's response to Australia's agenda for
police capacity building. Why Australian police were also not better placed
at the start of Operation Serene on issues such as local intelligence, language,
and cultural knowledge, given previous involvements in various missions in
TL dating back to 1999 (e.g., Savage, 2002), is an important question for the
purposes of learning for future missions. There has been some response since
then by the International Deployment Group of the AFP, in the form of local
language training for police capacity builders working in TL. Further development in terms of interoperability between police and the ADF is also ongoing, which may point to more effective intelligence at the commencement of,
as well as during, future operations of this kind.

The point about relevant skills sets not only raises questions about proper
predeployment training. It also raises questions about clarity of mission objectives among police peacekeepers on the front line, and particularly what tasks
they can reasonably and competently be expected to be doing. Stabilization
and criminal investigation objectives, as noted, can work at cross-purposes and
induce uncertainty among front-line police working under novel and deeply

challenging circumstances. The quickly changing nature of these circumstances, and the limitations of capacity possessed by peacekeepers to respond, means that juggling different potential goals of policing activity becomes even more vexed and unclear on the ground than it can be in the course of Australian policing experiences. Our interviews suggest that further effort may be required in terms of preparing peacekeepers for responding operationally to these objectives. In part, this should cover anticipating the sense of impotence felt among a number of our respondents, and being clear about what counts as appropriate and sufficient responses in situations such as responding to larger-scale gang fights. For the future of police peace operations, new thinking about what it is to restore law and order is needed urgently. Upholding the rule of law in postconflict and fragile societies may mean a reassessment of Western policing priorities, and even looking beyond Western understandings of policing, to how calls for improved security as well as for justice can be balanced in societies deeply traumatized by violence. Changes of this kind will inevitably require significant adjustments from current practice in relation to selection, training, equipment, and command of police peacekeepers.

Acknowledgments

This chapter forms part of a body of work emerging from the Policing the Neighbourhood project [LP0560643], an Australian Research Council Linkage grant, supported by the Australian Federal Police. I thank Dr. Vandra Harris, research fellow on the project, for her assistance in locating data for this chapter; Russell Brewer, who conducted most of the interviews relating to this chapter; and Christine Nam for her editorial work. The chapter has also benefited from frank and detailed feedback provided by three senior members of the AFP International Deployment Group. Their assistance is gratefully acknowledged. However, the views presented here do not purport to reflect the official views of the AFP.

References

Ashdown, P. (2007). *Swords and plowshares: Bringing peace to the 21st century*. London: Weidenfeld and Nicolson.

Bayley, D. (2001). *Democratizing the police abroad: What to do and how to do it*. Washington, DC: U.S. Department of Justice.

Centre on International Cooperation. (2008). *Annual review of global peace operations: Briefing paper*. New York: Center on International Cooperation at New York University.

Chase, S. (2005). Narrative inquiry: Multiple lenses, approaches, voices. In N. Denzin & Y. Lincoln (Eds.), *The sage handbook of qualitative research* (pp. 105–117). London: Sage.

Chesterman, S. (2004). *You, the people: The United Nations, transitional administration and state-building*. New York: Oxford University Press.

Cole, R. (2007). *Under the gun in Iraq: My year training the Iraqi police*. Amherst, NY: Prometheus.

Denzin, N., & Lincoln, Y. (2005). *The sage handbook of qualitative research*. London: Sage.

Devant, S. (2008). *Displacement in the 2006 Dili crisis: Dynamics of ongoing conflict* (Working Paper 45). Oxford: Refugee Studies Centre.

Durch, W. (2006). *Twenty-first-century peace operations*. Washington, DC: U.S. Institute of Peace Press.

Goldsmith, A., & Dinnen, S. (2007). Transnational police building: Critical lessons from Timor-Leste and Solomon Islands. *Third World Quarterly, 28*, 1091–1109

Harris, V., & Goldsmith, A. (2009). International police missions as reverse capacity building: Experiences of Australian police personnel. *Policing: A Journal of Policy and Practice, 3*, 50–58.

Hood, L. (2006). Security sector reform in East Timor, 1999–2006. *International Peacekeeping, 13*, 60–77.

International Crisis Group. (2008). *Timor-Leste's displacement crisis* (Asia Report 148). Brussels: Author.

Oakley, R., Dziedzic, M., & Goldberg, E. (Eds.). (2002). *Policing the new world disorder: Peace operations and public security*. Honolulu: University Press of the Pacific.

Savage, D. (2002). *Dancing with the devil: A personal account of policing the East Timor vote for independence*. Melbourne: Monash Asia Institute.

Scambary, J. (2006). *A survey of gangs and youth groups in Dili, East Timor: A report commissioned by Australia's Agency for International Development, AusAid*. Canberra: AusAID.

Slater, M. (2006). An interview with Brigadier Mick Slater, Commander JTF 631. *Australian Army Journal, 3*, 9–14.

United Nations. (2006a). *Report of the secretary-general on Timor-Leste pursuant to Security Council Resolution 1690, S/2006/628*. New York: Author.

United Nations. (2006b, October). *Report of the United Nations Independent Special Commission of Inquiry for Timor-Leste*. Geneva: Author.

Wilson, B. (2008, February). *Smoke and mirrors: Institutionalizing fragility in the policia nacional Timor Leste*. Conference paper at Democratic Governance in Timor-Leste Conference, Darwin.

What Happens Before and After

16

The Organizational and Human Resources Challenges of Deploying Canadian Police Peacekeepers Abroad

BENOÎT DUPONT
SAMUEL TANNER

Contents

Unlike most contributions on civilian police peace operations (also known as CIVPOL), this chapter does not focus on the impact these missions have on the postconflict societies where they are conducted (Gregory, 1996; Sysmanidis, 1997; Oakley, Dziedzic, & Goldberg, 1998; Murray, 2003)—or their lack thereof. Nor will it conclude with a list of suggestions for improvements that could make police contingents more effective at peace building (Call & Barnett, 2000; Bayley, 2001; Latham, 2001; Perito, 2004). We will also leave alone the psychological

Adapted from Dupont, B. and Tanner, S. (2008). Not always a happy ending: The organisational challenges of deploying and reintegrating civilian police peacekeepers (a Canadian perspective). *Policing and Society*, http://dx.doi.org/10.1080/10439460802187555

impact on police peacekeepers of participating in missions whose outcomes are ambiguous to others (Drodge & Roy-Cyr, 2003). Instead, we have chosen to explore another facet of the CIVPOL story: the selection and preparation process of police officers that temporarily leave their jobs in stable societies to undertake often challenging tasks in postconflict environments (Chappell & Evans, 1998), and the subsequent overall failure of contributing organizations to fully take advantage of the skills and experience their returning officers have acquired in the process. From this perspective, we conceptualize civilian police peacekeeping missions through a much broader temporal and organizational window than the one defined by its purely operational component, which usually falls under the responsibility of the UN. Instead, we envisage CIVPOL operations as a continuum made up of three phases.

The first phase consists of the mobilization of public—and sometimes private—organizations in contributing countries to provide suitable police officers to the UN. The second phase involves the deployment and management by the UN of CIVPOL contingents in receiving countries. Finally, the last phase (which in our opinion has not attracted enough interest so far) relates to the reintegration of police peacekeepers by their main employer. The emphasis placed on the operational phase can certainly be explained by the numerous specific challenges associated with the promotion and maintenance of the rule of law in postconflict settings (Holm & Eide, 2000). However, from a sustainability point of view, we believe that the initial and final stages are crucial elements that need to be incorporated into the overall assessment of CIVPOL operations. The mobilization stage determines to a large extent the quality of police officers who are made available to CIVPOL missions, while the reintegration phase provides an opportunity for contributing organizations to benefit from the experience and skills gained by their officers. It is also closely monitored by returning officers' colleagues who are considering volunteering for future CIVPOL operations, in order to determine the level of support the organization is providing and the impact such deployments have on career paths. Agreeing to contribute police officers to CIVPOL operations represents a significant commitment for police organizations whose resources are usually already stretched thin. Therefore, beyond altruistic motives, one would expect that organizations that are unable to embed the mobilization and reintegration phases into their routine processes will be less likely in the long run to maintain their CIVPOL commitment, seeing it as a costly distraction (Donais, 2004).

What distinguishes the mobilization and the reintegration phases from on-the-ground efforts is the intense level of inter- and intraorganizational negotiations going on between police units that frequently contest one another's rationalities and motives, despite the collaborative ties that bind them. In order to assess the extent to which these contests and negotiations determine the outcome of the mobilization and reintegration phases, we focused on

Canada—a country that has made regular contributions to CIVPOL operations since its inception.

The involvement of police officers in peacekeeping operations is a fairly recent phenomenon. Apart from the deployment of two small civilian police contingents in the Congo and Cyprus—where the term *CIVPOL* originated (Schmidl, 1998; Hansen, 2002)—in the early 1960s, the first large-scale UN police mission occurred in 1989 in Namibia, when 1,500 officers were dispatched from 25 countries in order to monitor the independence from South African rule and the ensuing elections (Broer & Emery, 1998). Up until then, peace missions had almost exclusively involved cross-border ceasefire monitoring tasks, and were therefore staffed by military personnel. As the Cold War was drawing to an end, this traditional peacekeeping approach was expanded to include peace building activities, whose stated objectives are to restore the rule of law, promote democratic values, and facilitate the reconciliation process between intrastate enemies (Chappell & Evans, 1998; Brahimi, 2000, p. 3). In 2008, more than 10,700 police officers from more than 100 countries were deployed in 16 peacekeeping missions. With an average of 125 officers contributed between 1989 and 2005 (International Peacekeeping Branch, 2005), Canada hardly ranks among the countries providing the largest contingents, which include Jordan (909 officers in 2006–2007), Pakistan (813), Bangladesh (776), and even Nepal (514) (Department of Peace Keeping Operations, 2007, p. 19). However, the quality of its officers and the skills they bring to CIVPOL operations (such as some officers' capacity to work in both English and French) make Canada a valued contributor. Its distributed staffing model involves a mix of officers temporarily seconded from more than 30 federal, provincial, and municipal police services. By contrast, the U.S.-devolved model delegates the selection of recruits with prior police experience to a private contractor (Bronson, 2002; Perito, 2004), whereas the Australian integrated model relies on a standing unit of 500 officers (the International Deployment Group, or IDG) available at short notice (Peake & Studdard Brown, 2005).

Hence, this chapter will examine what happens in Canada before and after the CIVPOL deployment per se, and how the different organizations involved coordinate their efforts and resources (while at the same managing their constraints) in order to meet Canada's commitment. We will also question the gap between the resources invested in this process and the benefits contributing police organizations derive from their participation in UN peacekeeping efforts. Our chapter is based on empirical data consisting of semidirected interviews with 22 police officers from three different organizations. Our sample is composed of 4 higher-level managers and 18 mid-level managers and rank-and-file officers who had participated (or were about to) in one or more CIVPOL operations. The three organizations that accepted to participate in this project represent a diversity of perspectives that include the federal police (Royal Canadian Mounted Police) as well as one provincial and one municipal police service.* We also interviewed the head of CANPOL,† a nongovernmental organization that maintains a roster of more than 500 recently retired police and security sector volunteers who can be called upon by the Canadian government to supplement the pool of police expertise. These interviews were conducted from October 2004 to May 2006 and included questions that addressed the experience of the respondents before, during, and after their deployment.

This chapter is organized in three sections. The first section delineates the Canadian model of CIVPOL participation, outlining the various responsibilities that structure government and police organizations at the federal and local levels. The second section examines the interorganizational negotiations that are conducted between these actors and the specific rationalities that inform these negotiations. The final section analyzes the intraorganizational challenges that are faced by officers on their departure and return.

The Canadian Model: A Distributed Structure of Responsibilities

In order to understand the intense negotiations that characterize the deployment of Canadian police peacekeepers, the distribution of roles and responsibilities between a range of government and law enforcement agencies must be outlined. Three levels of responsibilities must be delineated with regards to the Canadian context: (1) the federal government, (2) the federal police (also known as the Royal Canadian Mounted Police, or RCMP), and (3) local police forces.

The Federal Government

The whole process of deploying Canadian police officers to postconflict peace operations begins with a request addressed by a multilateral organization, such as the United Nations or the European Community, to the Foreign Affairs and International Trade Ministry (FAC). FAC appoints a special committee called the Canadian Police Agreement (CPA). This permanent entity is composed of senior public servants from the Canadian International Development Agency (CIDA), Public Safety Canada (PSC), and the RCMP. CPA's mandate is threefold. First, it must assess the request made by the multilateral organization, and consider its feasibility. Second, it coordinates

---

* Respondents respectively identified as PP and MP officers.
† http://www.canpol.ca/

the different partners' involvement, and designs the policy framework and guidelines for a police contingent (selection and preparation). Finally, because the participating police officers' salaries are covered by the multilateral organization, the CPA manages the funds allocation among the federal government, CIDA, and the RCMP. As mentioned in the introduction, some peacekeepers may also be selected by FAC from a nongovernmental organization, CANPOL.

The Royal Canadian Mounted Police

As soon as the FAC has decided to participate in a CIVPOL mission, the whole organizational responsibility to form and train the police contingent rests on the RCMP's shoulders. To that end, structural changes were made to the RCMP organization in 1996, with the creation of the International Peacekeeping Branch (IPB). Its mandate is to organize the selection of Canadian police peacekeepers. It is responsible for the administration of predeployment medical and psychological tests, as well as predeployment training. The IPB is also responsible for emotional and logistical support to deployed officers. Due to its upstream consultation role and downstream executive responsibility, the RCMP is a strategic and central actor in this process.

The RCMP's selection criteria are prescribed by both the UN's CIVPOL branch (the Department of Peace Keeping Operations (DPKO)) and the FAC. These criteria, for example, require that candidates should be clear of any criminal record, pass medical and psychological tests successfully, and have at least seven years of experience as a police officer.* Candidates must show that they are above-average practitioners, and that they can adapt easily to new environments. Candidate training is mostly determined by the mission's mandate as established by the UN. The length of a CIVPOL mission is nine months. Yet in some cases the mission may be extended to 12 months. These responsibilities make the RCMP the most powerful actor in the entire deployment process. Huge amounts of time, equipment, and human resources are spent to form, train, and deploy Canadian police peacekeeping contingents.

---

* The candidates must meet the following criteria: (1) Police officers must have a minimum of five years of operational police service. (2) RCMP police officers must indicate their interest on their personnel file. (3) Canadian police officers from municipal, regional, and provincial police services must channel their request through their respective police service, which then liaises with IPB. (4) Canadian police officers chosen for peacekeeping duties must meet specific selection criteria set by the UN and other participating multilateral organizations, as well as the RCMP and municipal, regional, and provincial police departments. (5) Criteria include, but are not limited to, extensive operational experience; strong interpersonal, organizational leadership and coaching skills; flexibility and innovation; team-oriented skills; and oriented fitness. (6) The selection process also includes the RCMP's Physical Abilities Requirement Evaluation (PARE), a medical examination, a psychological test, and a suitability interview.

Local Police Forces

Although it is the largest Canadian police service with more than 26,000 employees, the RCMP is not capable of staffing every single Canadian police contingent deployed at any given time. Unlike the Australian Federal Police, the RCMP does not have a permanent unit dedicated to CIVPOL missions. Consequently, it must rely on key partners, namely, provincial, regional, and municipal police services, to provide additional officers. In this chapter, we will focus on two local police services that contribute to Canadian CIVPOL contingents. One is a provincial police department of 5,000 officers, and the other is a large municipal police department of 4,000.

The provincial police service's first participation in peace operations started in 1995. Two additional contingents were then provided in 1996 and 1997. It suspended its participation until 2004, mostly for financial reasons. By that time, and following the decision to resume its contribution to peace operations, the service established a unit dedicated to the management of its CIVPOL-related operations in 2003, which is mainly responsible for the selection of police officers to be recommended to the RCMP.

The municipal police department's involvement in peacekeeping operations also started in 1995. Since then, police officers have been participating in CIVPOL missions without interruption. The department has also undergone structural changes and created an external missions division within its administrative branch. Among other responsibilities, this division manages the selection of volunteers who will be recommended to the RCMP. The selection process is based on voluntary participation, and candidates apply individually to new missions. In both local police services, volunteers attend information meetings related to upcoming missions. They are mandatory for police officers working in the municipal police department, and are organized in partnership with the RCMP. Former peacekeepers from the organization also participate and provide relevant information to their colleagues about major issues they were confronted with once in the field (contacts with the local population, climate issues, and conditions of work abroad). Each organization is free to set its own selection criteria, as long as they fit the minimum federal requirements.

Interinstitutional Negotiations and the Collision of Contested Rationalities

In the previous section, we focused on the organizational and structural features linked to the deployment of Canadian police officers in peacekeeping operations. We considered each level of responsibility separately in order to illustrate the decision-making and implementation chronology for each new mission. However, the various organizations involved in this joint effort do not share the same incentives, nor do they unconditionally accept the current distribution of power. While some occupy a central and comfortable position, others are very limited in the control they have over their involvement. To borrow Wendy Espeland's (1998) terminology, each participating organization brings to this collective endeavor a "rationality" that is often "contested" by its partners. This section examines the rationalities of three contributing police organizations and focuses more specifically on the different incentives that justify their participation in CIVPOL operations. Since this type of international activity adds significant constraints—namely, the selection and training of personnel—on already severely understaffed police organizations, why is it that they choose to participate in these missions and send some of their best employees to remote areas for extended periods of time? In order to understand the rationality behind this apparent paradox, we will proceed sequentially and examine how each of the three police organizations perceived its involvement, and positioned itself with regard to the two others. Before we continue, we must address the issue of CANPOL, a hybrid actor that is actively contributing to a peace operation in Haiti as of December 2007. Despite the initial plan that led to the creation of this nongovernmental organization (NGO) of qualified volunteers who are either retired police officers or active officers on leave without pay, it seems that such participation is exceptional, in the words of its former manager:

> One of the difficulties is that there is a direct interference from the FAC, which always favors the RCMP. Even if CIDA is the principal sponsor, there won't be any external project without the agreement of the FAC. And as soon as the FAC sees somebody other than the RCMP, it can't stand it. In the field, you cannot talk about partners; instead, there are competitors. In Canada, it is the same: [CANPOL] and RCMP compete with each other. (CAN-01)

RCMP's First Choice

Based on the organizational and structural description above, it is obvious that the RCMP holds a strategic role in the whole process of deploying Canadian police officers abroad. The RCMP defines its own requirements, norms, and guidelines—as long as they comply with the UN criteria. Since local police services are participating under the RCMP umbrella, they have no other choice but to adopt the same set of norms. Several incentives can explain the RCMP's decision to participate in such missions. They mainly revolve around four crucial issues: helping other countries to rebuild their democratic institutions, promoting international responsibility and solidarity, countering insecurity surges, and promoting Canada abroad.

As representative of the Canadian government, we are here … to help people rebuild a democratic government with its democratic institutions. I think that as a developed country, we have a responsibility toward the international community to take part in such missions. As I mentioned, since 1989 the Canadian police is involved in such missions. Since that moment, we have earned a lot of credibility in the eyes of many people around the world. Then I know that Foreign Affairs and other departments want the Canadian flag to be put up. (RCMP-01)

If we consider Haiti, for example, it takes four hours by plane to get to [Canada], where an important Haitian community lives. We saw that when the UN withdrew (UNMIH: 1993–1996) from Haiti, the country fell into chaos. It became a place were crime was high as well as a drug trafficking hub, generating negative impacts on both the United States and Canada.… Thus, it is crucial to bring stability to that area to counter such negative impacts. Criminality is now a global phenomenon. (RCMP-02)

Here we have many people who now live in Canada but come from places where there is political instability. I think it is important that they see that Canada sends people over there to help. (RCMP-03)

Since peace operations are associated with high levels of symbolic capital (Dupont, 2006), sending police officers serves as a highly rewarding gesture that ultimately brings credibility to contributing organizations. As such, the more a police department provides police officers, the more prestige it will build up. Accordingly, strategies are being developed by each organization to maintain or improve their status. Still, the struggle is biased from the beginning due to the strategic position held by the RCMP.

… For missions such as Bosnia-Herzegovina, the RCMP won't even call us.… They know they will be able to fill in the ranks with their own staff. Even if they are short of staff, they will do that so as to keep the upper hand.… At the present moment, they represent 33% of the [Canadian] staff around the world. They want to take over, but to keep control, you need staff. (MP-01)

The [RCMP] pretends there is no competition, but if they could, they would fill 100% of the positions with their own staff. We would even not be here, that is for sure. Yet, they don't have our experience in urban environments.… There is a kind of friendly competition, everyone wants to be present as much as possible.… When you take part in a mission, it is a reward. For a policeman, to participate in a mission is an extraordinary experience.… (MP-01)

As a consequence, the RCMP plays a hegemonic role, which not only is the result of its coordinating responsibilities, but also manifests itself through staffing strategies that reserve the most desirable positions to its own personnel. Our interviews show that local police organizations—not to mention

CANPOL—are called upon only when the RCMP is unable to fulfill a CIVPOL commitment by itself, and some of the most prestigious missions are exclusively staffed by RCMP personnel, even if it strains the home organization.

The International Ambitions of a Provincial Police Service

Two different strategies were observed among the local police organizations we investigated. The first one is tied to the particular conditions of Canadian politics, where one province has developed over the past 50 years a discrete international relations policy based on privileged ties with French-speaking countries and international organizations. This policy has been updated in 2006 to include a security component, whose relevance became manifest in the aftermath of the 9/11 terrorist attacks. In this context, the provincial police service we studied is encouraged to develop a presence on the international policing scene, and contributing to police peacekeeping operations is definitely considered relevant experience by the department's managers. While referring to the strategy followed by the provincial police, a senior officer from the municipal police department states:

> [The provincial police] only decided to come back to the field of international peacekeeping missions in 2004. They have an international relation section; it is because of the former [separatist] government. [It] expected the provincial police to become a national police, so they wanted to get known and they created the international relation section. They are mostly involved in training French-speaking missions [for Haiti]. They then created a niche with all the French-speaking countries. (MP-01)

At the present time, the provincial police focus on a specific region, Haiti, as revealed by its members:

> If we extend our involvement to other missions, that means there will be fewer … police officers in Haiti, but the RCMP doesn't want a reduction [of our members] there. That is where we have acquired most of our experience so far. (PP-06)

> I have heard that [the provincial police managers] wanted to resume international missions and that they wanted to target Haiti first and see how we could handle it before expanding to the rest of the world. (PP-04)

But the decision to focus on Haiti was also triggered by local contingencies, and more specifically by the presence of a huge Haitian community in the province serviced by this organization.

The financial dimension should not be underestimated when it comes to understanding the incentives or disincentives of sending police officers abroad. If most of the individual participants are motivated by reasons other than money, very few officers would be allowed to participate if their salary had to be paid by their department alone. On that specific issue, a senior police officer acknowledged that before a financial agreement had been signed between the three institutional levels—the UN and the federal and provincial governments—the provincial police never provided more than two or three police officers for such missions. This agreement compensates contributing police departments so that they may hire temporary staff to fill in for deployed officers, and do not experience shortages as a result.

> When [the provincial government] agreed to have the funds [from the UN] transferred directly to the provincial Public Safety Ministry and the police department, we stopped losing money.... Otherwise, we would still only be capable of supplying one, two, or three officers per mission. We could not afford more. (PP-06)

The extension of this agreement to the provincial police slightly modified the balance of interinstitutional arrangements between the different police partners.

> Without insisting too much on the frictions it generated, one could notice that [the municipal police department] was taking a lot of room [in peace missions]. It was related to the fact that the money allocated by the United Nations for our salaries was not transferred to us. Therefore, we could not afford to send many people.... Now we send a group of 25–30 people and we have control, and we can exercise very, very direct power [on decisions related to the mission]. (PP-06)

Police organizations do not systematically compete with each other. Sometimes, alliances are forged when there is a perception that organizational values converge.

> Our [provincial police service] is more similar to the RCMP than to the [municipal police service] in the sense that we both work in rural and remote areas.... We work in the same environment; we are used to similar things. The RCMP has different ethical rules than any municipal police department.... The provincial police force and the RCMP have more in common. For example, the municipal police force wanted to take the lead of the mission [in Haiti], but still, the RCMP is in charge of Canadian police missions, ... and for that particular mission, out of the five highest ranking officers, three were from our organization. (PP-06)

Another provincial police manager (PP-07) also acknowledged the presence of competition between the different police departments, mostly due to the limited number of high-ranking positions left by the RCMP. Moreover, PP-07 points out that the competition becomes even more palpable in the context of French-speaking missions, when all possible partners come from the same province. Yet, the provincial police and municipal police forces routinely negotiate the distribution of positions, and as soon as the contingents are formed, a true solidarity emerges between the officers sent to Ottawa for training.

The Revenue-Generating Rationale of a Municipal Police Force

Although the deployment protocol exposed in the first section explicitly states that municipal police services cannot participate in a peace mission unless they do so at the request and under the authority of the RCMP, the respondents we interviewed in a large municipal police organization mentioned alternative strategies that were used to get around it. However, such strategies were not without risks, and interorganizational tensions could increase when discovered.

> 99.9% of the time, we are contacted by the RCMP.... However, once, through a contact here, and in spite of the current mission, the [country name] embassy came and asked us directly for help. They needed our expertise in crowd control and order maintenance. We decided to send several police officers but, in the end, the RCMP took over because they found out, they felt offended, and it violated the protocol. Even the federal government intervened.... Despite all of that, our officers remained in the mission. (MP-01)

He adds:

> For [country name], the [country name] government directly came to us. They were looking for bilingual officers who were experienced in homicides in a large city, so they came to us.... In other provinces, they do not have as many crimes as we have. Sometimes, I "sell" international training, it is part of my mandate.... China even asked us to provide them with a forensic identification expert once. (MP-01)

In spite of political, ethical, or symbolic reasons that may come into play upon deciding to participate in international peace operations, the same respondent acknowledges that money is definitely an important incentive:

> [The motivation] is also budgetary, we cannot hide it. When we send an experienced police officer, the RCMP reimburses his salary. In the meantime, we hire someone [less qualified] for the duration of his deployment. We make huge savings, even if we always replace our personnel. You send a $70,000 policeman and you hire a $30,000 substitute. You save a lot of money, it is worth it. (MP-01)

Pushing his rationale further, the manager explains that sending police officers abroad fits perfectly with his marketing objectives, which involve

finding governmental or corporate customers willing to purchase his organization's services. Like in other businesses, competition comes into play.

> I have a profitability threshold. I want at least 10 people away per year to be
> worth it.... I don't want any competition. The competition is not related to
> individual positions, but rather to the number of positions available. But the
> RCMP decides, and when there is an English-speaking mission starting, other
> police departments are also involved: the Ontario Provincial Police, Calgary,
> Halifax, Edmonton.... (MP-01)

Competition is definitely a recurring theme in the discourse of the provincial and municipal police departments. Due to their local police service
status, they compete to maintain a privileged relationship with the RCMP.

> The RCMP pretends there is no competition, but if they could, they would fill
> all the available positions with their own staff. We would not be here, that is
> for sure. Yet they don't have the same depth of experience in urban environ-
> ments.... There is a kind of friendly competition; everyone wants to be there
> as much as possible. (MP-01)

Despite very open references to financial incentives, the municipal police
organization also expected to derive a certain amount of prestige from its
involvement in peacekeeping operations. The department has also expressed
concern regarding the potential mismanagement of its police officers during
the deployment, and the possible skills decay that may result.

> Once in the designated country, there are some hitches. For example, I went to
> Kosovo, to Mitrovica, and I found the mandate strange. They had assigned one of
> my best police officers as a prison warden. He was the prison's chief. I guess it was
> interesting for him [laughs], but ... We send our best police officers so that they
> come back with a certain cultural experience. And they do.... But very often, the
> mandate branches off. I haven't sent him to work in a prison.... In Guatemala, we
> had five police officers who were very badly assigned. Two of them were secretar-
> ies and they had to answer the phone, and three were drivers. This is nonsense. I
> told them that I wasn't sending policemen that I have to pay CAD 100,000 a year
> to be drivers or receptionists. I want them to be police officers and to help local
> police, to help prevent crime.... I should not tell that, but our policemen will
> not complain about it because they are comfortable there while it is snowing in
> Canada. For the police organization, it is important because we want to develop
> experiences. When the mandate changes, we have a right to express our view,
> and when it goes bad, you have to officially complain. (MP-01)

As we can see, the incentives and benefits that each organization expects
to derive from its contribution to CIVPOL operations vary greatly, and they
directly influence the negotiations that regulate interactions between the

agencies involved. But rationalities are not only contested at the interorganizational level. Within each of the three police services we surveyed, there was a lack of consensus on the desirability of sending experienced and well-trained personnel abroad, even if the moral imperative to do so was hardly questioned. This internal clash of rationalities produced very concrete repercussions for police peacekeepers, at both the selection stage and upon their return.

Intrainstitutional Paradoxes: Competition and Indifference

Although local police organizations are financially compensated by the federal government to cover the costs associated with their contribution to CIVPOL missions, they still invest a lot of time and energy to make sure that only the most suitable candidates are selected. It is therefore surprising to witness the apparent lack of interest to which returning police peacekeepers are confronted at the organizational level, considering the care and efforts that characterize the predeployment phase.

Selecting Police Peacekeepers: The Poacher's Dilemma

If the attractiveness of CIVPOL operations among police officers means that there is rarely a lack of volunteers, contributing police organizations are faced with several challenges linked to the selection and replacement of departing officers. The first challenge concerns the competition that this process generates inside the organization to secure the best officers, especially in specialist areas. Usually, the units responsible for the management of CIVPOL commitments are staffed with a limited number of managerial and administrative positions. As a result, they can be perceived by other police units as "poachers" of strategic resources, especially when they recruit among specialists such as serious crime investigators or SWAT team members.

> When I need someone for Rwanda, a police officer with experience in investigations, homicides, or even war crimes, I go to the homicide section. And we all know how it works in homicide: The officers are involved in long-running projects, most of the time because they arrested somebody and they took charge of the case and they have to go to court.... All I want is to send the best policeman there is, but I poach on his boss's territory, who doesn't want his man to leave. This is where my role starts. I usually tell him: "Look, he is the best candidate in here. In the meantime, you can get a new guy assigned to your section. You will start to train new members, and when the investigator comes back, the other guy will reintegrate his former unit.... But it really turns out to be a problem when a unit loses its best officers, its specialized personnel. They usually have a false idea of these missions and think that their men are going to be on holidays, while they will have to work twice as much. (MP-04)

To be considered for the selection process, volunteers must first obtain their superior's permission. Some managers are very reluctant to free up some of their best officers, either because the organization lacks the resources to fill the temporarily vacant position, or due to the belief among older managers that CIVPOL operations are nothing more than subsidized holidays.

[When you return] they have to assign you to the position you had before you left. But the reality is that when you occupy certain positions, they just don't want you to go on a mission. In some units, if you go on a mission, you are not valued anymore when you come back. In some other units, they will tell you that if you want to go on a mission, you shouldn't even think about applying [for transfer], because they ... do not want to lose their personnel for a nine-month period. (MP-09)

Even today, often people will say: "Hey, here is [name of respondent, in charge of CIVPOL deployment], the department's traveling agent.... People think these missions are a good opportunity to have some rest and take a holiday.... There still remains a lot of work to educate our managers. (MP-05)

Some people wondered: "What is the purpose to send people abroad when the police lack personnel?" This is a recurring comment. (PP-01)

In some instances, the unions also represent a constraining factor, since they require that CIVPOL management units give priority to older staff, even though they usually fail the rigorous medical and physical tests. Once a police officer has been cleared by his manager, he must attend an information session on the application process and the specific CIVPOL mission for which he would like to be considered. The selection process varies from one organization to another, but it is not uncommon to see a police service supplement the UN and RCMP minimum requirements with its own criteria, in order to ensure the success of the secondment. Once police officers have demonstrated that they meet all the professional, medical, and discipline-related requirements, they undergo in-depth interviews in order to assess their motivation, coping skills when confronted with stressful and uncertain situations, general capacity to adapt to new settings and unfamiliar environments, and the suitability of their family arrangements for long-term deployments. Clearly, police officers who volunteer for CIVPOL deployments undergo stringent selection procedures that indicate how serious the two local police organizations we studied are about them, despite the intraorganizational frictions and service delivery perturbations caused by such contributions. In this context, one would expect contributing organizations to offset their temporary inconvenience by maximizing the delayed benefits that derive from welcoming back officers with increased skills and experience.

Reintegrating Police Peacekeepers: Missed Opportunities

Adjusting back to a normal personal and professional life is not always a smooth process: Some peacekeepers suffer from posttraumatic stress disorder, leave their spouse, or have to deal with problems of substance abuse. The police organizations we surveyed were very much aware of these potential difficulties. They offer the services of psychologists in order to facilitate the transition, and try to monitor the performance of returning officers in order to detect behavioral problems. Still, most of the returning officers we interviewed were convinced that their CIVPOL experiences had made them better police practitioners. Some of them developed strong management skills and learned how to work in uncertain and culturally diverse environments. Others felt they had become more autonomous and flexible, and believed they were able to better structure their workload as a result. Another benefit frequently mentioned by our respondents was the informal benchmarking and knowledge transfers occurring between police peacekeepers from different countries (mainly developed countries).

> I think that for a police officer who leaves for his first mission, the perspective to be exposed to the world is huge. From the moment he arrives, he will meet new colleagues. His eyes open through exchanges with German or Swedish colleagues. Everyone has his own experience and ways of doing things that are all effective in their own way. Being in contact with so many different people is like attending a big school. (MP-04)

> The experience is not limited to the fact that you go abroad. You also meet people in your contingent. Police officers from all over Canada, you listen to them, and you can assess how it works in their job, in their work environment, and compare with your own. You come out of this a winner because you improve your perception of many things you are doing routinely, without necessarily being aware of their implications. (MP-07)

CIVPOL missions also provided interesting opportunities for social networking with colleagues from other departments within Canada or abroad (who might facilitate access to criminal intelligence in future cases) or with community leaders whose own networks extend to immigrant communities in Canada.

> I made some contacts in Haiti and here, I have kept in touch with people from the Haitian diaspora. They are doctors, ministers, and famous people. If there are things we need to do more directly, or through the department, we have contacts now. (PP-06)

However, most of these increased skills and competencies were mentioned as personal gains that would remain virtually ignored by their organization.

They were pleased to find a generally supportive reception among their colleagues and managers, but they were confounded—and even frustrated—by how little was being done to take advantage of their experience at an organizational level.

A majority of respondents indicated that their organization seemed to limit its assessment of a mission's success to the maintenance of a good reputation on the international stage and the recovery of the costs involved. They regretted that no organizational attempt was made to systematically learn from returning peacekeepers how they could individually or collectively improve police work in Canada.

> You come back with more experience, and I don't think they [the police service] take advantage of it. There is no opportunity for us to provide feedback: "What did you learn over there and how could it help us?" (MP-02)

> I have not seen any initiative from my organization or from the RCMP ... to try to gather pieces of information related to our experience. What do we get from the experience our members have gained? They just don't care.... We don't really feel our organization is willing to take something out of it. (MP-03)

Another strong indicator of this indifference was the fact that promotion procedures sometimes failed to take stock of the CIVPOL experience.

> Some people conducted investigations during their deployment, and when they took their exams, the promotion panel did not recognize that experience. (MP-09)

During their deployment, police peacekeepers are assigned by the UN to positions that may or may not correspond to their rank and qualifications at home. In worst case scenarios, officers whose yearly salary approached CAD 100,000 ended up answering the phones and driving UN officials. In several instances, peacekeepers assumed much more responsibility during their deployment than they would have at home.

> I was in [country name] and I almost was the detachment's head. There were 25 people. When I came back, I returned to my patrol car, with my radio, working for someone who had 25 people under his command. I did not have the responsibility or the prestige attached to the position anymore. It sounds arrogant, but still, the chief of the country's battalion called me "mister," and I could sit at his table and his troops would cook something for us. And here, if you take 62 minutes for your lunch instead of 60, they will blame you. You come back in the system. From that perspective, it was irritating. (MP-05)

One year ago, I was in a deciding position, I was on top, I had people working for me. Here, there is still the same administration as when I left, I have the same position as when I left. It is like a doctor … that you send to work for Doctors Without Borders, and when he comes back, you ask him to remove stitches…. It is not the same…. I had big responsibilities but it was fun. And when I came back, it was like … pffffff … I am just a sergeant, I have my team. It took me a while before I realized that, OK, it was part of my past, it's in the memory box and now I have my role. (MP-07)

It is not uncommon for those who are unable to adjust to a slower pace, and who are not offered new challenges by their organization, to develop a general boredom that results either in their resignation or in withdrawal from their work.

When you come back, your job may seem boring, very, very ordinary and boring. What I consider the most difficult here is the fact that it is not very demanding compared to what we do on mission, where we can be confronted with extreme criminal behaviors that are rare here…. When you come back, you feel that you don't do that much here. There are two extremes: People apply for other positions or resign. (PP-06)

I would say that my biggest problem now … is that nothing really turns me on. I need to feel the adrenaline to be satisfied. I mentioned that my present job is a transition because I really want to go back. If they [the UN] offered me a job to go back to Africa, I would think about it twice, but it would be very difficult for me to stay here. (MP-04)

I understand that the context is not the same, but I tell you that the motivation at work at the beginning was limited. My mind was on something else, but it gets better and better. Still, there is always a part of me that will remain [on the mission]. (MP-03)

From these statements, it would seem that the reintegration is experienced by many police peacekeepers as an anticlimax. The emotional and professional investment they made into the mission is followed by a period of disenchantment that can be partly attributed to their organization's lack of follow-up. Considering the care taken to screen and train volunteers and the costs involved, the outcomes associated with the organization's incapacity to offer returning officers opportunities commensurate with their experience is disappointing. Instead of feeling welcome and valued, these high achievers become estranged from their workplace.

Conclusion

Although our focus in the last section was an analysis of the most problematic aspects of the reintegration phase, our intent is not to overdramatize the experience of police peacekeepers when they return home. Many end up much more disillusioned with the UN bureaucracy and its notorious mismanagement of peace operations than with their own organization. In fact, some of our respondents claimed that their deployment had made them more philosophic about their work environment in Canada. They felt lucky to be members of well-resourced organizations whose management was supportive, and were quick to admit that they were more reluctant to complain after having experienced extremely chaotic situations.

Nevertheless, we maintain our assessment of a fundamental discrepancy between the considerable upstream investments made at the mobilization stage and the limited downstream yields (or even losses) that are observed at the reintegration stage. Managers in each organization's unit responsible for CIVPOL operations were very much aware of this paradox and deplored it. However, there was little they believed that could be done to solve it. The number of officers involved in police peacekeeping deployments represents less than half a percent of the total workforce for a large metropolitan or provincial police service at any given time, and this is clearly insufficient to alter existing internal policies. Moreover, contributing police organizations are eager to promote their participation to CIVPOL missions externally, as a demonstration of their good global citizenship. But even if such activities are valued from a public relations perspective, the professional prestige that former police peacekeepers command cannot match the aura attached to serious crime investigators or tactical unit members in the police informal hierarchy.

Does it matter in the long run for CIVPOL operations? In our opinion, it does. Eventually, organizations whose internal support for returning peacekeepers is found lacking will have more difficulty attracting high-caliber recruits that have a chance of making a difference in post-conflict societies. Facilitating the "metabolism" of police peacekeepers' experiences would certainly increase their satisfaction and improve their retention rates, while making the organization more responsive to its environments and more creative in its responses. It would also enhance the support of colleagues, such as the police brotherhood, which definitely matters for police officers facing health or psychological issues related to their experience in peace operations. This could, for example, involve programs that provide better planning for the reintegration of returning officers, increased opportunities for officers to formally share their knowledge with colleagues, or assignment policies that take advantage of the skills and needs of former CIVPOL officers. These measures would solidify the organization's commitment to future CIVPOL operations and guarantee their sustainability by aligning the interests of the former with the goals of the latter.

Acknowledgments

We thank the police officers who accepted to share their CIVPOL experience, as well as their organizations and their superiors for facilitating their interviews.

References

Bayley, D. (2001). *Democratizing the police abroad: What to do and how to do it.* Washington, DC: National Institute of Justice.

Brahimi, L. (2000). *Report of the panel on United Nations peace operations A/55/305-S/2000/809.* New York: United Nations.

Broer, H., & Emery, M. (1998). Civilian police in U.N. peacekeeping operations. In R. Oakley, M. Dziedzic, & E. Goldberg (Eds.), *Policing the new world disorder: Peace operations and public security* (pp. 365–397). Washington, DC: National Defense University Press.

Bronson, R. (2002). When soldiers become cops. *Foreign Affairs, 81,* 122–132.

Call, C., & Barnett, M. (2000). Looking for a few good cops: Peacekeeping, peacebuilding and CIVPOL. In T. Holm & E. Eide (Eds.), *Peacebuilding and police reform* (pp. 43–67). London: Routledge.

Chappell, D., & Evans, J. (1998). The role, preparation and performance of civilian police in United Nations peacekeeping operations. *Commonwealth Law Bulletin, 24,* 1248–1316.

Department of Peacekeeping Operations. (2007). *UN police magazine.* New York: United Nations.

Donais, T. (2004). Peacekeeping's poor cousin: Canada and the challenge of post-conflict policing. *International Journal, 59,* 943–963.

Drodge, E., & Roy-Cyr, Y. (2003). Police peacekeeping: Health risks and challenges in a post-conflict environment. *International Journal of Police Science and Management, 5,* 229–244.

Dupont, B. (2006). Power struggles in the field of security: Implications for democratic transformations. In J. Wood & B. Dupont (Eds.), *Democracy, society and the governance of security* (pp. 86–110). Cambridge: Cambridge University Press.

Espeland, W. (1998). *The struggle for water: Politics, rationality and identity in the American Southwest.* Chicago: University of Chicago Press.

Gregory, F. (1996). The United Nations provision of policing services (CIVPOL) within the framework of 'peacekeeping' operations: An analysis of the issues. *Policing & Society, 6,* 145–161.

Hansen, A. (2002). *From Congo to Kosovo: Civilian police in peace operations.* Oxford: Oxford University Press.

Holm, T., & Eide, B. (2000). *Peacebuilding and police reform.* London: Frank Cass.

International Peacekeeping Branch. (2005). *2004-2005 review.* Ottawa: Royal Canadian Mounted Police.

Latham, E. (2001). Civpol certification: A model for recruitment and training of civilian police monitors. *World Affairs, 163,* 192–203.

Murray, J. (2003). Who will police the peace-builders? The failure to establish account-
    ability for the participation of United Nations civilian police in the trafficking of
    women in post-conflict Bosnia and Herzegovina. *Columbia Human Rights Law
    Review, 34*, 475–527.

Oakley, R., Dziedzic, M., & Goldberg, E. (1998). *Policing the new world disorder: Peace
    operations and public security.* Washington, DC: National Defense University Press.

Peake, G., & Studdard Brown, K. (2005). Police building: The international deploy-
    ment group in the Solomon Islands. *International Peacekeeping, 12*, 520–532.

Perito, R. (2004). *Where is the Lone Ranger when we need him?* Washington, DC: U.S.
    Institute of Peace Press.

Schmidl, E. (1998). Police functions in peace operations: An historical overview. In
    R. Oakley, M. Dziedzic. & E. Goldberg (Eds.), *Policing the new world disorder:
    Peace operations and public security* (pp. 19–39). Washington, DC: National
    Defense University Press.

Sysmanidis, R. (1997). *Police functions in peace operations.* Washington, DC: U.S.
    Institute of Peace.

Policing Business Confidence? Controlling Crime Victimization in Papua New Guinea

17

MARK FINDLAY

Contents

By any measure, Papua New Guinea (PNG) has a serious crime problem. Human Rights Watch (HRW) recently described PNG as "one of the more dangerous countries in the world not at war" (HRW, 2005). Up until the administration of several comprehensive community crime surveys, data on crime in PNG are highly unreliable (Findlay, Guthrie, Hukula, & Laki, 2004, 2005, 2006; Guthrie, Hukula, & Laki, 2006; Zveic & Alvassi del Frate, 1995; Sikani, 1999; Dinnen, 2002). What data exist indicate that violent crime is high and is proportionately greater than in many of Papua New Guinea's Pacific neighbors (Dinnen, 2001, pp. 61–62; 2002).

Despite the bleak picture for community safety in PNG, a 2004 household survey of crime in Port Moresby found that most residents believed that crime, while high, had stayed the same or decreased in the last year (Justice Advisory Group and National Research Institute, 2004). In addition, while vulnerable communities in the capital city expressed an alarming distrust in state police personnel and services, a large majority of those surveyed looked forward to more police protection if the quality and integrity of community policing could be raised.

Particularly in urban centers, the conditions that exacerbate crime as a consequence of socioeconomic development and modernization are prevalent in PNG (see Findlay, 1999). Papua New Guinea's population is young and growing rapidly: With almost 6 million people, the population has almost tripled since independence. Nearly half are children (UNICEF, 2003). As a consequence of a growing cash economy, limited rural employment opportunities, and the breakdown of customary community ties, which comes at a social cost of development, urban drift into transient and criminogenic town settlements has fueled gang crime (Dinnen, 2002).

The government is struggling to provide basic health and education services, especially in rural areas. The country's infant mortality rate and maternal mortality rate are among the highest in the world; life expectancy at birth was 58 in 2003 (UNICEF, 2003). Poverty and unemployment increased in the 1990s and 2000s; only 5% of those who left school found employment in the formal sector in 2002 (AusAID, 2002, p. 5). The country ranks the lowest in the Pacific on United Nations Development Program's (UNDP) Human Development Index, and in the lowest third of all nations (UNDP, 2004, p. 141).[1] Rural poverty is particularly acute, spurring migration to urban areas that lack the infrastructure to receive them, and employment opportunities to relieve the criminogenic consequences of socioeconomic disparity (Braithwaite, 1979).

The economic consequences of crime victimization have been a concern for both national economic development in PNG and principal aid donors. In a briefing paper as far back as 1979 the National Centre for Development Studies estimated significant direct financial losses from property crime and argued that crime control resourcing was crucial for the healthy growth of the small business sector (National Centre for Development Studies, 1997). A year later the Centre for Democratic Institutions hosted a conference in Canberra to discuss crime as the central consideration for the Australian-PNG bilateral relationship. The conference identified the negative impact crime has on business confidence as being a dangerous impediment to the mutual political and economic interests of the two states (Centre for Democratic Institutions, 1998).

Against this background, Australia's aid development agency (AusAID) in 2006 sponsored a business community crime survey in Port Moresby to empirically evaluate the influence of crime victimization on business crime confidence and investment (PNG Justice Advisory Group, 2006). A total of 172 business managers and spokespeople were surveyed as part of the questionnaire phase. They represented business enterprises widely spread throughout sites in Port Moresby. Their businesses were a mixture of single and multiple business locations. There was a fairly even mix of local, foreign, and shared ownership behind these businesses surveyed.

The survey obtained the views of businesses recently established in Port Moresby, those that had been in business over the medium term, and some that had a lengthy record of business activity within the nation's capital. In terms of turnover, the businesses surveyed ranged from single-person, low-budget operations through to extensive high-capital, high-turnover organizations. As for the nature of business enterprises represented, the survey covered retail, manufacturing, professional, wholesale, transport, hospitality, and other commercial operations. The businesses surveyed were in industrial, business, and commercial sites, professional offices, and local area situations such as shopping centers. They ranged from single-person operations to organizations of over 400 personnel.

The broad purpose of the survey was to provide a balance to reported crime data so that the law and justice sector in PNG, and the stakeholder business community, could ascertain trends in crime levels and construct appropriate strategies in response. Specifically, the survey was designed to:

- assess the extent and nature of crime victimization among the business community in PNG;
- identify the environmental indicators and concerns regarding business crime and victimization;
- evaluate opinions held within the business community regarding provision of state criminal justice services and policing in particular;
- examine the manner in which the business community is taking responsibility for crime prevention, and in particular through the use of private security agencies;
- evaluate the cost of crime victimization and prevention measures on business activity, and (where possible) confidence;
- provide information for policy development in the area of integrated business crime prevention; and thereby
- improve the law and order environment for business in PNG (and beyond), which may impact on business confidence and investment.

Perceptions of crime victimization and criminal justice service delivery within the business sector are vital for the health and activity of that community. The influence over business confidence in turn is a central concern for the economic development of countries such as PNG.

Crucial to the policing dimension of this chapter, the survey results gave an indication of whether attitudes to crime and justice services, and crime victimization, are impacting on a positive business climate, and the extent to which state policing in particular impacts on any such determination. *Can bad policing deter good business?*

The business crime victimization survey (PNG Justice Advisory Group/ NRI, 2006; hereafter referred to as "the survey") built on past experience of community crime surveys of PNG and similar developing countries. Specifically, the detailed work of the United Nations and the Australian Institute of Criminology (AIC)[2] in the small business crime field informed the design of the PNG business crime survey. The survey team also had the benefit of perusing internal business surveys identified through an eventual focus group process.[3]

One of the most compelling observations emerging from the survey data and expanded upon in later focus group discussions was the almost wholesale rejection by the business community of the relevance of state-sponsored policing to controlling crime victimization. Faced with this conclusion, the business community in Port Moresby either seems to take policing and community safety into its own hands, or has simply accepted crime as a business cost that can be negotiated in a commercial sense.

The ramifications of these governance and commercial responses to crime victimization, for the relationship between state-centered criminal justice and the conditions for effective modernization, are the concerns for this chapter, focusing particularly on policing styles and business enterprise. First, however, it is useful to sketch out the nature of the business community in a high-crime/low-development context.

Doing Business in PNG

In Port Moresby, the business community, while relatively small, is identifiable, established, and responsible.[4] As in many small developing state economies, the Port Moresby business community incorporates large, medium, and small business with local, foreign, and combined sources of ownership. Business activity ranges across the common forms of secondary and tertiary business and commercial enterprise. Business relies on a variety of support services. These include a developed financial sector, government supervision, insurance protection, transportation and communication networks, and in PNG in particular, private sector security facilities. International agencies, including donor groups, also influence commercial and investment climates that then affect business activity (World Bank, n.d.).

Doing business in PNG is commonly perceived as difficult and dangerous. Crime is thought to present a significant challenge to profitability and a safe and supportive enterprise environment. Therefore, business crime victimization needs to be reduced, and businesses should be guaranteed more secure operational settings if confidence in business is to grow and investment to follow.

The survey provides a stark picture of business crime victimization. Equally significant is the tendency for business to see crime as endemic, and its prevention or control as largely a business responsibility. The business community declared itself isolated in the face of crime and generally cynical about reducing crime and making the business environment more secure.

There is mutual benefit in business and local communities engaging, where appropriate, in a positive and constructive fashion, and crime prevention is one important level of such engagement (Findlay, 2004). As the survey revealed, distorted perceptions in the community about business can exacerbate crime victimization and make crime prevention more difficult. Further, misunderstandings about the needs of business and the potential of the police to meet these needs have fragmented the business crime control effort.

In order to introduce the relationship, or absence of it, between state police and business in Port Moresby, it is elucidating to focus on the survey responses to questions concerning police service delivery. In this context the survey looked at the location of business within the wider community, and then the connections between workplace crime victimization and the police.

Community/Policing/Business Engagement

Business in Port Moresby largely operates in isolation from the community in which it is located. Such isolation is reinforced by the impressions in the business community that:

- the public believe that business is an easy mark for crime, that businesses can afford crime, and that business crime is not a community responsibility;
- the local community is out to fleece business at every opportunity, is self-interested, and is largely incapable of promoting crime prevention;
- the police are disinterested in business crime victimization and are not a competent crime prevention alternative to private security;
- the private security sector is sometimes too close to crime, or is not efficient in providing crime prevention services, but still they are preferable to the police;
- that government is corrupt, bereft of leadership, and largely not worth engaging; and
- it is up to business to secure itself, and remain profitable in the face of high crime and prevention costs, despite the impact on the community and the economy.

Some of these views are obviously a consequence of crime victimization.

A disturbing feature of business attitude to policing was not so much a connection between poor experiences with the police and a reluctance to involve the police in business crime, but rather the prevailing view that the police were useless at best, or that their involvement compounded the problem of crime victimization. Over 70% of respondents expressed views that the police were disinterested, wouldn't do anything, or if they did, it would make no difference.[5] This obviously influences a willingness to engage with police beyond crime victimization and its consequences. Some of the extended answers provided by respondents when asked about providing police with information evidence a significant distrust in police professionalism:

- A lot of people fear the police: Grassroots community informants find difficulties going to the police and they do nothing about it.
- Fear of payback: Fear that they will be identified as informants, intimidation by criminal elements.
- Half the time the police do nothing, and secondly, they side with clan members and threaten informants.
- No confidence in police performance: They are not confidential. Informants are threatened later on.

Business in Port Moresby was not confident that the police had a positive impact on crime and crime prevention. Just over 10% of the sample believed that the police were doing a good job and that this was influential on crime, while 14% disagreed with this suggestion. The vast majority had no view on police involvement. The disinterest or uncertainty about the effectiveness of state criminal justice was more marked when the question turned to the courts and prisons.

Conclusions to draw from this disaffection with formal criminal justice service delivery are that business in Port Moresby, while suffering frightening rates of crime victimization:

- has little positive experience of state criminal justice agencies;
- does not want to be involved with these agencies due to the assumption that they are ineffectual;
- believes that other areas of intervention are more effective; or
- is not sufficiently well enough informed about the practice and potential of state criminal justice agencies to construct a critical opinion.

Interestingly, it should not be drawn from this that business accepts the state should have, or continue to have, a diminished role in crime prevention. Rather, it is a question of utility as well as responsibility. According to business community responses, the police (86%) have the most responsibility for crime prevention and community safety. Sixty-three percent of respondents also recognized that the community, including business, should have a role in crime prevention/community safety, and 45% of the sample stated that crime prevention and community safety are the responsibility of the individual.

In practice, it became clear from survey and focus group elaborations that business takes on almost the entire responsibility for business crime prevention, does not engage in community initiatives, and does not rely on the police.

When discussing the manner in which the police could be better assisted by business, a recurrent theme was mutual respect and the need for businesses to further recognize their role as good corporate citizens. Seventy percent[6] of the business sample believed that members of their workplace community could better assist the police by calling the police when they see criminal activity. Cast against a notable reluctance of business to report crime to the police (see the section to follow) or to recognize the police as doing a good job in crime control, this might be seen as wishful thinking. Fifty-nine percent of the sample believed that their workplace community might better assist the police by cooperating with the police, and a similar percentage also thought that the workplace community could better assist the police by providing them with more information. In each of these areas there was at least the will for greater engagement of staff with police, even if businesses themselves were reluctant to be involved with the police at an organizational level.

There remains much ambiguity on the side of business about their responsibility to cooperate with the police, and the utility of doing so. Forty-eight percent of respondents stated that generally people are willing to give information about crime to the police. Yet around half of those who responded (and a third of the sample) did not report to the police crimes for which their business was victimized. Interestingly, against this, 92% of businesses indicated that they would report to the police if their business were a victim of crime in the future. The decision to call in the police seems to be contextual to crime, situation, and loss. In addition, lower rates of insurance against property crime and low levels of confidence in property recovery by the police militate against reporting.

Reporting Crime to the Police

Table 17.1 lists reasons for business crime victims not reporting these events to the police.

The responses that indicated a dissatisfaction or disillusionment with policing services are consistent and high, and this translates into low reporting rates, and reduced opportunities for positive engagement. Given the high nonresponse to the question about reasons for reporting, it could be assumed that dissatisfaction with police is higher than the actual response percentages suggest.

Table 17.1   Reasons for Victims Not Reporting Crimes to the Police

Reason	% of Responses[7]
Not serious enough	29
Wouldn't have changed anything	30
Police are not interested	11
Police would not have done anything about it	27
Police take too long to respond	28
You were frightened	2
You knew the offender	4
Offender was a staff member	14
Got property back or compensation	13
Relied on security to deal with it	5
Would take too much time and paperwork	10
Insufficiently insured	1

Even for those who did report (around 100), the police response times nominated were over 2 hours on average, and this exacerbated the negative interpretation of police engagement and utility. Satisfaction with police service delivery was also very low on the scores of decision to investigate, conduct of the investigation, keeping the business informed, and returning property.

In detail, business crime victims observed other reasons for nonreporting to police:

- The police are not efficient or active in dealing with fraud.
- Company policy is not to report employee crime.
- Sometimes when businesses do report, the police give excuses about not having fuel in the vehicle to come to the crime scene.
- The business solved it themselves.
- Police reports always lie.
- The offense needed to be dealt with right away, otherwise it would recur.
- Nothing can be done about staff stealing.
- The police wanted payment for their services.
- Some crimes are handled by the local community.
- The business wanted to give the staff a chance.
- Sometimes crime was perpetrated by police.

It appeared that the predisposition to report to the police was offense specific. Obviously, where insurance rates were high, and the police report for the purposes of loss claims, as with motor vehicle theft, reporting rates were correspondingly high (35% of sample—100% of responses). Other high reporting situations were with burglary (27% of sample—94% of responses) and armed robbery (11% of sample—86% of responses).

Regarding theft from the premises, where property recovery was unlikely, reporting rates were consequentially low. Also relatively low were reporting practices on theft from motor vehicles at 13% of the sample (66% of responses), malicious damage at 7% (60% of responses), and nonemployee theft from premises at 7% (54% of responses). These would all be instances of where the individual financial loss was small or prospects of recovery were unlikely.

For offenses such as fraud, where the reputation and internal security protocols of the business might be challenged by the publicity of reporting and investigation, rates of police reporting were also down. In the focus groups the representatives of big business in particular indicated a reluctance to report employee or financial services theft or fraud if it reflected badly on the security and operations of the business concerned. Therefore, it is not difficult to explain that employee theft from premises at 9% (34% of responses) and fraud by employees at 11% (58% of responses) were low relative to the general reporting, where it occurred.

There were clear differences between the reporting rates for attempted and completed crimes. This might be explained by the belief either that an attempted crime was less serious or, on the other hand, that an attempt might be effectively addressed through police intervention, by deterring future victimization. For instance, reporting attempted vehicle theft was 20% less likely than if the offense was completed, whereas with check/credit card fraud the reporting rates were roughly the same for attempted and completed crimes. In the latter crime, particularly where employees were involved, the individual exposure and the collective sensitizing of other staff could be viewed as imbuing police involvement with deterrent potential.

Self-Help Policing

Private sector security fared little better than did the state police when it came to the confidence of business. This has led larger business entities to create their own security facilities in order that they might be more accountable in response to the businesses themselves. There was significant suggestion that private security services may in fact be involved in crimes against the businesses they are hired to protect, as a result of clan affiliations or other interests that would compromise their independence or contractual obligations.

Business disillusionment with state institutions and the private sector when it comes to crime prevention was not counterbalanced by a positive belief in effectiveness of community intervention more generally, as had been evidenced in the Port Moresby community crime survey. Only 6% of the business survey sample believed that good community practices were influencing crime in their area, and around the same figure saw poor community practices as negatively influential. The only strong indication of a correlation between community environments and current business crime victimization was the 18% of the sample that believed the threat from "rascals" (local crime gangs) was becoming worse, and thereby degenerating the safety of the local environment.

Businesses admitted to changing their behavior in response to crime victimization, in physical and commercial ways. Seventy-five percent of respondents identified the nature of the change as including:

- Being more alert
- Having more electronic protection
- Having better security and a more careful routine with security already installed
- Restricting the use of checks
- Moving premises
- Encouraging credit customers
- Having alarms and immobilizers in vehicles
- Paying payroll directly into bank
- Not going into "no go" zones
- Cautioning the community
- Changing transport routes
- Banking done irregularly by two or more staff
- Having more security, less insurance
- Addressing business procedures with security in mind
- Learning from mistakes

These self-help changes commonly indicated something internal to business that could be remedied in order to minimize risk. Almost 90% of respondents (44% of the sample) changed their crime prevention methods as a result of victimization. These changes involved:

- Upgrading security
- Having more camera surveillance
- Increasing vigilance
- Having more prevention technology
- Having more after-hours surveillance
- Restricting vehicles in settlement areas
- Employing auditors and systems managers
- Creating staff awareness
- Selecting staff with references
- Having security escorts

Regarding specific changes to business operations, 47% of respondents (23% of the sample) suggested changes such as:

- Consolidating in order to control better
- Having ongoing security upgrades
- Constantly revising attitudes to checks
- Controlling logistics and having no cash on premises
- Limiting activity in public areas
- Employing their own security personnel
- Overhauling the total conduct of their business

The business sector in Papua New Guinea is a relatively large consumer of private sector security. This takes the form of perimeter security as well as policing and patrols. Financial investment in private security and security facilities by the business sector is high both in real terms and as a proportion of turnover.

Generally, however, there does not appear to be a positive correlation between higher investments by business and private security, and lower rates of victimization. This should not simply be read as a criticism of the quality and effectiveness of security services. It may be that those business sites that are highly secured are also particularly attractive to crime opportunities.

The general disengagement of business from state-sponsored and private sector policing in PNG has significant consequences not only for crime victimization, but also for business economies and the "costing" of crime (Findlay, 2001, pp. 109–131). In addition, the possibility of a communitarian approach to policing is compromised when business accepts crime victimization as out of control of its own limited environmental adjustments.

Crime Victimization Beyond Control?

The stark realities of business crime victimization in Port Moresby are that:

1. Rates are high.
2. Costs are substantial.
3. Impacts are negative.
4. Business seems resigned to the crime problem, and isolated in crime prevention.

In detail:

- Crime victimization of businesses in Port Moresby is running above 75% for the surveyed financial year 2004–2005.

- Business crime victimization rates are generally higher than community crime victimization rates revealed in the general 2004 community crime surveys for Port Moresby and Bougainville.
- If victimized, businesses were more often than not subject to multiple incidents of the same crime.
- Actual crime victimization rates explain and could support the perceptions of business that crime in their location remains constant or is on the rise.
- All business crime types are significantly represented in business crime victimization, with the most prominent being theft, burglary, fraud, and armed robbery.
- Theft from businesses was three times more likely to be committed by staff than outsiders. Staff defrauded their business more than outsiders did.
- Low levels of financial loss for employee-related theft tend to suggest that individual incidents of employee crime, while common, were not significant. For employee-generated fraud, while average losses were low, the total financial cost of the offense was among the highest recorded.

This is a description of a business environment anything but compatible with investment and confidence. However, business is surviving and profiting in PNG, and some are very profitable despite crime. The state-sponsored police that generate low levels of community approval are still receiving substantial capital and resource benefits through aid and government subvention. So, could it be said with any certainty that high crime and poorly perceived state policing are bad for business?

What can be said is that businesses are surviving in unsafe environments. Over 70% of businesses surveyed felt unsafe and insecure in their locations as a consequence of crime, or only felt safe some of the time. Private security services may not have a significant influence on rates of actual crime victimization. They may, however, be deterring a greater increase in crime. The cost of crime and the provision of prevention and security services are high in terms of annual business turnover. With crime by staff featuring in business victimization, and businesses seeming alienated from the communities in which they operate, environments for the expansion and development of commerce and enterprise are far from supportive.

What are the consequences for the business community of a self-help approach to crime victimization, policing in particular? While businesses in PNG are making large investments in their own crime prevention, they do not see crime rates falling as a result, or that their locations are becoming safer. Business largely is not turning to the state or the community to assist in crime prevention or control. Of the 129 businesses surveyed that experienced crime and the 1,124 crime incidents reported by them in the survey, only 33 such incidents resulted in arrests and 11 went to court. Business was generally unsatisfied by this. The proportion of businesses not reporting crime to the police can reach up to 50%. Business practice modification is an important theme in crime prevention. Particularly in the areas of financial and stock management, staff auditing, and alternative transportation routing, businesses were varying their operations to account for potential victimization.

Is there a connection between crime victimization, the fear of crime, perceptions of security, business confidence, and business investment? Business in PNG strongly believes that crime and the fear of crime are negatively influencing business confidence and investment. The vast majority of businesses suspect public corruption in PNG is high, and therefore very negatively influential over business confidence. Corruption in government was increasing according to 54% of respondents in the survey. Further, 39% indicated that corruption in government remained the same for the last 12 months. Nineteen percent of respondents identified public corruption concerns as affecting business operations and future business decisions. Also, 47% of respondents wanted the government to fight corruption.

Seventy-seven percent of respondents identified the fear of crime, including government corruption, as impeding business confidence. In the view of business, crime and the fear of crime (including corruption) are the main reasons for poor business confidence and investment in PNG. Business is generally concerned about the negative impact that government rules, regulations, and policies, and the law and order situation are having on their operations and enterprise. Allied with public sector corruption, this tends to suggest that government intervention does not promote business confidence and investment. Business sees government as unable to provide stable economic and market conditions that would stimulate business activity.

Corruption, law and order issues, and the cost of crime prevention topped the list of concerns for business operations and future investment. More particularly, law and order issues, staff safety, and public corruption were most regularly nominated as the primary concern.

The Failure of a Police/Business/Community Compact in Crime Prevention

From the earlier community crime surveys administered recently in PNG, community crime prevention appears to be progressing well at a general community level. In fact, the community, even in the poorest settlements of Port Moresby and the most transitional parts of Bougainville, is filling the gaps left by ineffective state policing to ensure community safety. Then why when it comes to business crime victimization are business and the community not working together for crime prevention? Answers may lie in the following:

- The business community is a heavy investor in private security measures and at the same time does not anticipate a fall in rates of business crime victimization any time soon.
- Business is generally not engaging with the community in which it is located in order to promote local and cooperative crime prevention initiatives.
- Business does not see the state or the general community as doing a good job in crime prevention.
- Business directs responsibility for crime prevention first to the police, then the community (including business), and finally the individual. Even so, it does not tend to generally or uniformly resort to the police or the community to assist in business crime prevention.
- There was division within the business community about whether it should increase its support for and engagement with broad community crime control initiatives, as there was with assessing its value.

A Way Forward

Arising from the major concerns of business about crime prevention and control in Port Moresby, the challenge for policy development is to turn around crime-related negative influences over business confidence and investment. From the experience of the general community crime surveys, and recognizing the central themes of the PNG National Law and Justice Policy and Plan of Action (2000), which advocate communitarian and restorative justice, an important solution to crime victimization and the passed-on costs to the market in developing countries, an answer to business crime victimization, lies in an integrated approach to the problem. Unless this occurs, then the propensity for surviving businesses simply to divert the cost of crime victimization to the consumer will continue to the detriment of national economic viability.

Business is reluctant to engage with the state, its criminal justice agencies, and the community in any consensual or collaborative crime control effort. Community crime surveys in Port Moresby indict the police in particular for failing to provide leadership and impact over crime victimization. However, there is convincing evidence that community empowerment has led to improvements in public safety and advanced locality conflict resolution. A safe and secure business environment will have positive influence over business confidence. A reduction in business crime victimization to produce that safer environment, I would argue, is possible by top-down engagement, business to business, and business with the communities in which they reside. Along with this, a constructive reinterpretation of the business crime victimization within the wider community, and its negative consequences for standards of living, will provide an incentive for constructive engagement, community to business. Unfortunately, the formal state-sponsored criminal justice agencies may be sidelined from these developments, and as such, community policing in high-crime developing societies may take on a distinctly different authority and direction.

Community Engagement

It is important that business and the general community in Port Moresby work together at the very least to address certain fundamental misconceptions that tend to exacerbate business crime victimization and the fear of crime. Even among those businesses surveyed that anticipated little benefit in community engagement for crime prevention, there was a strong view that public opinion should be reeducated on the capacity of business to carry crime costs.

The public should be made better aware of how much the cost of crime is impacting on the cost of living. If community attitudes to business crime are made more realistic and supportive, then the business community can move from seeing the public as the problem, and reconsider their commercial preference for passing on the cost of crime to the consumer, as the expedient response to crime victimization. The consequences for the cost of living and enhanced consumer capacity in turn will be beneficial for business and the economy.

Local communities need to become more realistic in their expectations of business welfare. Business priorities are fundamentally profit driven, and as such, for communities to attract financial support from business, the business should be convinced of the manner in which such support will benefit business priorities as well as broad community interests.

Against this, business more uniformly needs to embrace corporate citizenship. Businesses exist in community locations and benefit from community stability and cohesion. In this respect, business has a responsibility to invest in that stability and cohesion in the same way it invests in the protection of its premises, property, and operations.

From no more than the perspective of good business practice, a safe, secure, and supportive community environment for business enterprise will promote business confidence and a stronger climate of competition and investment. This applies no matter what the business structure or enterprise, and no matter how diverse the general community may be. Those businesses surveyed that have a productive working relationship with their local communities reported benefits such as improved staff safety and diminished investment in private security services. Other businesses that were less disposed to community engagement blamed divided and inconsistent community interests.

Interaction between business and the general community, consistent with a cross-sectoral approach to crime prevention and control will depend on a repositioning of responsibilities and expectations. The success of any such interaction, even at basic levels, also will be dependent on more effective and confident associations with the formal justice agencies, the police in particular. As with the general community crime survey results, this survey reveals fundamental dissatisfaction from business in the delivery of state criminal justice services.

Engagement With Government

Business and government are far from equal partners in business crime victimization, control, or prevention in PNG. The almost universal concern from within the business community about endemic public sector corruption no doubt colors the necessary interactions between government and business. This shaky reputation for government and public sector administration in the eyes of business has further reduced the value of state criminal justice to the business community.

The marginalization of business from the state involves more than crime prevention and control concerns. Business views government regulation as another factor undermining business enterprise and even viability.[8]

The survey reveals that, from the perspective of business opinion, government and business have some fairly fundamental rebuilding to do if their essential interactions and mutual interests in a stable and progressive economy are to be enhanced. Government will not be in a legitimate position to stimulate or regulate business for the benefit of the community in PNG unless it can at least get more involved in business crime victimization prevention and control. More involvement will also depend on better involvement. The police, for instance, must provide a more efficient and effective service to business victims of crime.

Engagement With Formal Criminal Justice
Agencies, State Policing in Particular

It would be wrong to suggest that business is not engaging with the police. However, up to half the businesses surveyed preferred not to call on the police as a first response to crime victimization. Along with other explanations is a prevailing disaffection from within business toward state criminal justice. If state police are to retain any utility and legitimacy with the business community, and contribute thereby to a stronger growth environment, this trend needs to be countered. For cross-sectoral crime prevention and control to be achieved in the area of business crime victimization, business needs to work with formal criminal justice agencies, as well as community-based crime prevention. If this does not happen, then the significant investment of donor funding into the formal institutions of criminal justice is hard to justify in terms of economic as well as personal community security.

In order to promote a more productive engagement between business and government crime control institutions, improved service delivery is crucial. Business has indicated a greater willingness to call on a better-trained and more professional police organization.

Leadership and Anticrime Consciousness

The concept of good corporate citizenship is as important in helping change negative or unsupportive attitudes to business crime prevention as it might be in showing the way forward to better leadership in all levels of life in PNG. Business alone is not well placed to call for change in the attitudes of the public on business crime victimization and responsibility without in turn passing on any savings in crime prevention investment that may flow from more supportive community crime prevention.

Consistent with the business commitment to self-help in crime prevention is the opportunity for business to lead other interests, whether they are state or community centered, to address crime victimization. Working against this are the apparent tendency toward individualism in the business response to crime, a limited organizational presence from business in crime prevention, fragile networking across business activities where crime opportunity is high, and an isolationist attitude to business enterprise in general. Each of these issues needs to be addressed by business in any engagement strategy wherein business takes a leadership role.

Business is critical of political leadership and the will of government when responding to the business crime issue. While recognizing the importance of a more productive relationship between business and government in crime prevention, the challenge is for business leaders to demand and support best practice in government. This will stimulate rewarding interchange between business and government as government agencies recognize and respond to the legitimate expectations from business for support and protection.

Business Engagement With Business

The theme of isolation recurred in the survey even within the business community itself. Respondents gave examples of where crime victimization was exacerbated by the suspect commercial practices of other service organizations. For example, concern about fraud as a result of check and credit card irregularities suggested poor communication between some businesses and the financial services sector.

Business respondents were sometimes critical of the probity and effectiveness of some private security services. This led to an in-house preference for the provision of these services, particularly within vulnerable businesses.

The business community needs to work on effective lines of communication to minimize the opportunity for crime victimization as a consequence of careless business or incompatible business security practices. In addition, businesses should routinely communicate information and experience on what works and doesn't work in crime prevention practice.

Investment in a Safer Society

The general community crime surveys in Port Moresby and Bougainville indicated that energy and confidence are being broadly directed to crime prevention at a community-initiated level. Communities are not necessarily relying on the state or waiting for the police to deal with crime and make life safer. Community policing in this respect is more about communities policing than police working with and within communities. The business community also has revealed through the survey a strong self-help ethic. However, it is individualized and not well organized.

If business investment in crime prevention and security were to be coordinated where appropriate with effective state and community initiatives, it would produce better value for money. The climate, framework, capacity, and mechanics for such cooperation should be collectively explored and enhanced. The reservations of business against coordination or engagement should be listened to and addressed by state agencies in particular.

Finally, if the message is that crime victimization decreases business confidence and thereby negatively influences economic development, the PNG experience reveals that this will not be arrested simply by further resourcing failing state criminal justice agencies (Government of PNG, 2004), the police in particular. A better productive strategy seems to rest in promoting:

1. More constructive community crime prevention through engagement between business and the communities in which they operate
2. More realistic understandings of the cost of business crime victimization and its consequences for the economy, particularly for consumers
3. More genuine effort from all stakeholders in community crime prevention to reduce rather than pass off business crime victimization
4. More effective leadership from the state and from business in promoting an anticrime consciousness in which business no longer anticipates crime victimization as a significant and prevailing commercial cost

References

AusAID. (2002). Framework: Australia's aid program to Papua New Guinea. Retrieved April 30, 2000 from http://www.ausaid.gov.au/publications/pdf/png_framework.pdf

Australian Institute of Criminology. (2004). Crimes against business: A review of victimisation, predictors and prevention (Technical and Background Paper No 11).

Braithwaite, J. (1979). *Inequality, crime and public policy*. London: Routledge.

Centre for Democratic Institutions. (1998). *Australia/Papua New Guinea: Crime and the bilateral relationship*. Canberra: Australia Defence Study Centre.

Dinnen, S. (2001). *Law and Order in a Weak State*. Honolulu: University of Hawaii Press.

Dinnen, S. (2002). Building Bridges: Law and Justice Reform in Papua New Guinea, discussion in paper.

Findlay, M. (1999). *The Globalisation of Crime: Understanding Transitional Relationships in Context*. Cambridge: CUP.

Findlay, M. (2001). The cost of globalised crime: New levels of control. *International Journal of Comparative Criminology*. 1(2), 109–131.

Findlay, M. (2004). *Introducing Policing: Challenges for Police and Australian Communities*. Melbourne: OUP.

Findlay, M., Guthrie, G., Hukula, F., & Laki, J. (2005a). *Port Moresby community crime survey 2004* (Special Publication 36). Waigani: NRI.

Findlay, M., Guthrie, G., Hukula, F., & Laki, J. (2005b). *Bougainville community crime trends 2004* (Special Publication 37). Waigani: NRI.

Government of PNG. (2004). *Ministerial review of police services*. Waigani: Author.

Guthrie, G., Hukula F., and Laki, J. (2006a). *Bougainville community crime trends 2005*. Waigani: NRI.

Guthrie, G., Hukula F., and Laki, J. (2006b). *Lai community crime survey 2005*. Waigani: NRI.

Guthrie, G., Hukula F., and Laki, J. (2006c). *Mt. Hagen community crime survey 2005*. Waigani: NRI.

Guthrie, G., Hukula, F., and Laki, J. (2006d) *Port Moresby community crime survey 2006*. Waigani: NRI.

Human Rights Watch. (2005). PNG report. Retrieved April 30, 2008 from http://www.hrw.org/reports/2005/png0905/4.htm

Justice Advisory Group and National Research Institute. (2004). *Community crime survey data: Port Moresby and Bougainville*. Retrieved April 30, 2008 from http://www.lawandjustice.gov.pg/resources/documents/YLM_IMPACT_EVALUATION_REPORT_FINAL_2201071.pdf

Law and Justice Sector Working Group. (1999). *National law and justice policy and plan of action toward restorative justice*.

National Centre for Development Studies. (1997, July). *A big push to curb crime in Papua New Guinea*. NCDS Briefing Paper.

NRI. (2006). *Law and justice sector; Highland's highway crime study, 2005*, Port Moresby: NRI.

PNG Justice Advisory Group/NRI. (2006). *PNG Law and Justice Sector, Port Moresby business crime victimisation survey 2005*. Port Moresby: NRI.

Sikani, R. (1999). Criminal threat in Papua New Guinea, in *Australia—Papua New Guinea: Crime and the Bilateral Relationship*. B. Bohea, ed., Port Moresby: National Research Institute.

Stringer, W. (2000). Royal Papua New Guinea constabulary: Review of community policing approaches.

UNICEF. (2005). *At a glance: Papua New Guinea, statistics*. Retrieved May 4, 2005 from http://www.unicef.org/infobycountry/papuang_statistics.htmlhttp://www.unicef.org/infobycountry/papuang_statistics.html

United Nations Development Program. (2004). *Country fact sheets: Papua New Guinea*. Retrieved April 30, 2008 from http://hdr.undp.org/statistics/data/country_fact_sheets/cty_fs_PNG.html

World Bank. (n.d.). *Doing business, economic rankings*. Retrieved April 30, 2008 from http://www.doingbusiness.org/EconomyRankings/

Zveic, U. and Alvassi del Frate, A. (1995). *Criminal victimization in the developing world*. New York: U.N. Interregional Crime and Justice Research Institute.

Endnotes

1. Papua New Guinea ranked 133 out of 177 countries on UNDP's Human Development Index. UNDP's Human Poverty Index for Papua New Guinea is 37%, placing the country 62 out of 95 developing countries for which the index has been calculated. The Human Poverty Index (HPI) "focuses on the proportion of people below a threshold level in basic dimensions of human development—living a long healthy life, having access to education, and a decent standard of living, much as the poverty headcount measures the proportion of people below a certain income level" (United Nations Development Program, 2004). See also International Bank for Reconstruction and Development, International Development Association, "Interim Strategy Note for Papua New Guinea," No. 31790-PG, March 18, 2005, para. 1, 16.

2. See Australian Institute of Criminology, *Crimes Against Business: A Review of Victimisation, Predictors and Prevention* (Technical and Background Paper 11).

3. For instance, staff survey from Fin Corp/GC, in which business/staff work practices were related to a range of quality of life issues for business.

4. The focus group experience, an essential component of the wider survey exercise, indicated that the Port Moresby business community was a diverse collection of interests with a clear commitment to the economic development and business enterprise expansion in Papua New Guinea.

5. It is likely that this percentage as a total would be less due to multiple reporting.

6. It should be remembered that the nonresponse rate for these issues varied from around 30 to 70%.

7. Here there was a nonresponse rate of over 70.

8. The World Bank's costs of business (http://www.doingbusiness.org/) analysis of PNG, which shows that the PNG government's regulatory procedures do indeed hamper the efficiency of business relative to other countries in the region.

Police Capacity Development in the Pacific

18

The Challenge of the Local Context

ABBY MCLEOD

Contents

> In Papua New Guinea there are 800 cultural groups. When the Australian police came there were 801.
>
> **Senior member of the Royal Papua New Guinea Constabulary, 2006**

While capacity development has long been at the forefront of international development practice, police involvement in capacity development has increased significantly in the past decade. Such is its importance to the Australian Federal Police (AFP) that in 2004, Commissioner Keelty described regional capacity development as "core business" (Keelty, 2004). Despite its increasing popularity, police capacity development remains poorly documented and understood, as evidenced by the limited—albeit growing—body of literature dedicated to its analysis. This paper seeks to address this

Adapted from McLeod, A. Police capacity development in the Pacific: The challenge of the local context. *Policing and Society,* forthcoming.

lacuna by exploring challenges to Australia's involvement in police capacity development in the Pacific, specifically in Papua New Guinea (PNG).

In particular, it interrogates the oft-cited criticism that capacity development initiatives—not only of police, but of institutions generally—fail to take adequate account of local context (McLeod, 2007; McLeod & Dinnen, 2007; Hegarty et al., 2004). Reflecting upon the author's own transition from academia to the Australian public service, this chapter calls for greater policy-relevant discussion of the ways in which police (and other) capacity development initiatives can be tailored to local contexts. It will argue that even where local conditions are reasonably well understood and local people have been widely consulted, the process of negotiating donor and recipient values, needs, and policies frequently compromises the local relevance of foreign capacity development initiatives.

The chapter comprises four distinct sections. The first section outlines the nature of police capacity building, providing an overview of existing literature before familiarizing the reader with the PNG case study in the second section. Papua New Guinean perceptions of a specific foreign police support program—the Australian Enhanced Cooperation Program (ECP)—are presented in the third section, followed by an analysis of the ramifications of these perceptions for future support of the Royal Papua New Guinea Constabulary (RPNGC) in section four.

While the focus of the case study is the period of capacity development that occurred under the ECP, the purpose of the chapter is not to critique that intervention. Rather, it seeks to employ interview data and ethnographic material gathered at a particular point in time in order to illustrate key challenges to police capacity development in PNG more generally. To this end, the chapter draws upon interviews and focus groups conducted with approximately 100 Papua New Guineans who worked with Australian police deployed under the ECP, and interviews and discussions with 33 Australians who worked with the RPNGC. Data gathered during interviews, focus groups, and discussions are complemented by the author's participant observation in both the RPNGC (prior to, during, and after the ECP) and the Australian Federal Police (after the ECP).

Police Capacity Development: An Overview

Definitions of capacity development, and analogous terms such as *capacity building* and *institutional strengthening*, are plentiful. The subject of capacity development—namely, capacity—is defined by the United Nations Development Program (UNDP) as "the ability of individuals, organisations and societies to perform functions, solve problems, and set and achieve objectives in a sustainable manner" (2007, p. 24). By extension, capacity development is the process through which these abilities are obtained, strengthened, adapted, and maintained over time by internal and external stakeholders (UNDP, 2007). Capacity development must therefore be seen not only as an externally driven exercise, but also as an indigenous process of change and evolution (Morgan, 1998, p. 3).

Unlike the term *capacity building*, which implies that capacity is yet to be built, capacity development assumes existing capacity, with the focus being on improvement rather than establishment. To the external stakeholder, capacity development typically involves a suite of activities targeting both individual and organizational capacity, including, but not limited to, the provision of additional financial and physical resources, technical assistance, training, systems improvement (e.g., financial and personnel management), the provision of policy and strategic advice, constitutional and legislative reform (to create an enabling environment), organizational redesign, and the development of performance incentives (Morgan, 1998, pp. 7–12). Despite the terminological shift from capacity building to development, the prominence of technical assistance in external capacity development initiatives highlights the ongoing unspoken assumption that outsiders "know" how to do the things that "locals" ought to do in order to improve their capacity. That is, while recipients view the external skill set as one of many options, the very practice of technical assistance presumes the external skill set to be superior.

In the context of policing, externally driven capacity development initiatives range from attempts to reinstate failed or critically fractured policing institutions (such as in postconflict countries like Sierra Leone, Timor-Leste, and Solomon Islands) to less ambitious programs targeting specific skills, such as criminal investigations and training. The latter capacity development initiatives are often offered in explicit support of donor goals, such as strengthening the ability of recipient countries to detect and manage transnational crime, particularly within close vicinity of the donor country. For example, the AFP's Law Enforcement Cooperation Program (LECP) has assisted countries throughout Asia and the Pacific to establish transnational crime units (TCUs), with subsequent small-scale capacity development support being provided to countries in which TCUs have been established (AFP, 2008).

While some police capacity development programs morph out of peacekeeping operations (as in Timor-Leste), others form part of a broader nation or state building agenda, including agency-specific and sector-wide institutional strengthening activities that are collectively designed to strengthen the state. The antecedents of police capacity development in the name of nation building can be found in the immediate postindependence eras of many recently decolonized states (e.g., PNG) (Goldsmith & Dinnen, 2007, p. 1094), with the strengthening of state institutions having recently gained further impetus from the global good governance agenda (see, for example, Fukuyama, 2004).

Existing literature dealing with police capacity development focuses primarily upon the reestablishment of police organizations postconflict (Marenin, 2005), the democratization of foreign (usually developing country) police organizations (Bayley, 2001), broad guidance for improving policing in developing country contexts (Clegg, Hunt, & Whetton, 2000), and case studies of specific external attempts to strengthen policing in developing countries (see, for example, Goldsmith & Dinnen, 2007; Hood, 2006; Horn, Olonisakin, & Peake, 2006; McLeod, 2007; McLeod & Dinnen, 2007).

Much of this literature is characterized by universal prescriptions about best practice and lessons learned, although the need for local specificity is frequently highlighted. For example, in outlining lessons for police reform abroad, Bayley makes 18 points in regards to democratization, including the necessity of political will for reform, the need to adapt programs of foreign assistance to local settings, and the need to create effective disciplinary systems within host police organizations (2001, pp. 35–40). Similarly, in drawing upon police capacity development experiences in Africa, Asia, and Latin America, Clegg et al. (2000) suggest that police capacity development initiatives work best when long-term strategic assistance is grounded in stakeholder analysis and participatory planning, when support recognizes and encourages the roles that other formal and informal actors play in the maintenance of social order, and when local community infrastructure is developed.

Together, the various prescriptions for police capacity development outlined in the policing literature differ little from the recommendations made in the literature pertaining to capacity building/development and institutional strengthening more generally. While highlighting key issues to be mindful of when designing police capacity development programs, existing literature falls short of providing tangible guidance for those involved in the design and implementation of police capacity development endeavors. This is particularly so in the case of the widely touted "lesson learned" that foreign assistance to police must be adapted to local conditions, begging the questions: What must be adapted to local conditions, and how might this adaptation occur?

As highlighted by Clegg et al. (2000), stakeholder analysis and participatory planning are key to ensuring the appropriateness of foreign assistance programs to the country settings in which they are implemented. Capturing local voices is similarly important in the context of extracting lessons learned from previous attempts at supporting foreign police. In presenting Papua New Guinean perceptions of the ECP, however, this article highlights tensions between the objectives, needs, and values of Australian and Papua New Guinean police, leading to questions about the practicality of adapting foreign assistance to suit local conditions. For example, what does one do when foreign and local needs are at odds? More significantly, to what extent can foreign assistance to police be tailored to a local context in which certain practices, values, and beliefs are fundamentally incongruent with the very principles upon which Western policing institutions are based? The following section addresses these questions via an exploration of police capacity development in PNG.

Police Capacity Development in Papua New Guinea

Papua New Guinea lies immediately to Australia's northeast and is populated by approximately 6 million people, 85% of whom live rural subsistence lifestyles. The people of PNG face significant human development challenges, including low life expectancy (56.9%), low adult literacy (57.3%), and a low standard of living, in terms of purchasing power parity (UNDP, 2008). Ranked 145th out of 177 countries on the United Nations Human Development Index (HDI), PNG is a developing country that receives a significant amount of foreign aid, most notably from Australia. In 2005, foreign aid accounted for 22% of the national budget (PNG Government, 2005).

Australian aid to PNG is delivered under the auspices of the Australia Papua New Guinea Development Cooperation Treaty, amounting to AUD$300 million per annum. Much of this aid is targeted at strengthening state institutions, with 34% going toward core institutions responsible for governance (Heinecke, Dollery, & Fleming, 2008, p. 56), including law and justice sector agencies.

Since 1975, PNG, like many other fledgling states, has been beleaguered by problems of internal disorder. Despite the absence of reliable crime statistics, scholarly research suggests that raskolism (a Papua New Guinean Pidgin word for gang crime), white-collar crime, sexual violence, domestic violence, sorcery, and electoral violence feature frequently in contemporary Papua New Guinean life (Dinnen, 2001). Rather than playing a role in the detection and management of such crimes, the RPNGC is deeply implicated in internal disorder: Its members have a reputation for their brutal treatment of the public and for their heavy involvement in corrupt activities (Human Rights Watch, 2005).

Western-style policing in PNG began in 1890 with the Armed Native Constabulary in Papua. In 1965, the RPNGC was established, and today boasts a funded strength of just over 5,000 members. Government commitment to the RPNGC is minimal, with inadequate annual budgets severely curtailing its ability to fulfill its primary functions. The majority of police members occupy uninhabitable barracks, and basic operational costs such as uniforms, vehicles, fuel, stationery supplies, and communication infrastructure are not met by government funding. Public perception of the RPNGC is consequently poor, and the detection and processing of crime is of a low standard.

Against this backdrop, the RPNGC has received extensive Australian support, including 15 years of police capacity development support under the Australian Agency for International Development (AusAID) RPNGC Development Project (1989–2005) and the short deployment of just over 100 police to Port Moresby and Bougainville under the Enhanced Cooperation Program. While the ECP was too short-lived to provoke extensive comment, the RPNGC Development Project has been harshly criticized for failing to impact positively upon the RPNGC. Significantly, the issue of local appropriateness was not strategically addressed in either of these programs (McLeod, 2007).

Prior to the RPNGC Development Project, Australian police officers were involved in the *ad hoc* provision of specialist training for RPNGC officers, and many RPNGC officers undertook placements with Australian state police forces. Conducted in three distinct phases, the RPNGC Development Project delivered capacity development and institutional strengthening initiatives using advisers drawn primarily from Australian and New Zealand police forces, in addition to technical civilian specialists.

Despite the differing foci of each phase, a number of key areas received consistent attention over the years, including fraud and anticorruption, prosecutions, community policing (since 1993), corporate planning, information management, human resources, logistics and infrastructure, leadership and management, training, finance, discipline, general duties, and gender mainstreaming.

On June 30, 2004, Australia and PNG signed a treaty establishing the Enhanced Cooperation Program (ECP), committing an additional AUD$800 million to PNG over a five-year period for the police-led intervention. Under this program, it was anticipated that in-line personnel would be placed in central government agencies (including legal, economic, and financial specialists), and that approximately 230 Australian police officers would be seconded to the RPNGC, where they would hold line positions in Port Moresby, Lae, Mt. Hagen, the Highlands Highway, and Bougainville. The policing component of the intervention, however, was somewhat short-lived, with the withdrawal of the entire contingent on May 13, 2005, due to a high court decision that rendered the deployment of Australian police officers with full immunities unconstitutional (McLeod & Dinnen, 2007).

While short in duration, the policing component of the ECP saw Australian police deploy to both Port Moresby and Bougainville. Australian police deployed under the ECP were collectively known as the Australian Assisting Police (AAP), being sourced from both the AFP and various Australian state police forces. While it was originally envisaged that the Australian police would hold line positions, upon deployment they worked strictly as advisers, being instructed to assist, rather than do. Australian police and civilians worked in a variety of specialist policing, general policing, and support areas, including, but not limited to, human resources, finance, logistics, fraud, legal, communications, criminal investigators, prosecutions, and general duties in stations throughout Port Moresby, as well as in Buka and Arawa in Bougainville.

Australian police deployed under the ECP were by and large welcomed by the community. Their deployment occurred amidst community percep-tions that PNG police inadequately policed the community, resulting in increasing crime and decreasing public safety. While many people noted the gross wealth disparities between the Australian police and themselves— a disparity that exists between the majority of expatriates and Papua New Guineans—people welcomed their presence, reported increased feelings of safety, demonstrated greater willingness to report crime, and subsequently publicly mourned the departure of the AAP.

Since the withdrawal of the policing component of the ECP in 2005, the RPNGC has received minimal donor support, with the exception of technical assistance provided by a handful of advisers employed under the AusAID/ PNG Law and Justice Sector Program. However, in the context of a new Australian government committed to long-term engagement with the Pacific and dedicated to the establishment of Asia-Pacific partnerships for security and development (Rudd, 2007), future Australian support to the RPNGC is likely. It is therefore timely to consider the ways in which future support to the RPNGC might be better tailored to the local context than previous Australian police capacity development initiatives in PNG.

By presenting interview and focus group data obtained from Papua New Guineans who worked with the AAP, this chapter seeks to highlight the ways in which members of the RPNGC view foreign assistance to their organization. In highlighting these diverse views, it becomes apparent that while some issues raised by members of the RPNGC are easily addressed, such as enhancing Australian attention to language and cultural com-petency, other issues are less easily tackled, such as influencing RPNGC attitudes toward police brutality. This suggests that a more nuanced appre-ciation of the complex web of issues involved in adapting foreign assistance to suit local circumstances would assist in translating this lesson learned into practice.

Listening to Capacity Development Recipients

By the time the Australian Assisting Police deployed to PNG in 2004, mem-bers of the RPNGC were experienced consumers of development assistance, having had 15 years of Australian support under the RPNGC Development Project. RPNGC members therefore held preconceived ideas about external assistance, the role of advisers, and the relative gains and losses to be made within the context of Australian assistance to their organization.

Prior to deployment of the AAP, RPNGC members spent a significant amount of time discussing what the Australian police were coming to do and what they would bring with them. While one particular adviser from the RPNGC Development Project (which was soon to end, yet continued throughout the duration of the AAP deployment) provided an information session for police based at the station in which he worked, the vast majority of RPNGC members received no information about the deployment and were unclear about the form or purpose of the assistance they were to receive.

The reactions of RPNGC members to Australian assistance varied greatly, on the basis of not only individual difference, but also age, organizational seniority, and gender. While members raised a variety of issues in regard to the presence of the AAP, they overwhelmingly focused upon the reasons that they wanted assistance (primarily material gain), their perceptions of capacity development, and the ideal attributes of advisers, each of which is outlined below.

Motivations for Assistance

While the ECP sought to strengthen the RPNGC through the provision of technical support and infrastructure, when discussing support received under this program, RPNGC members focused overwhelmingly upon the resources and logistics provided to them by the AAP. Comments such as "We already have the knowledge and skills, we just need resources and logistics" and "They should just give us the cars and let us do our jobs" were common. When discussing material gains made under the program, RPNGC members referred to stationery, photocopiers, accoutrements, guns, computers, and even food and water.

The provision of resources and logistics no doubt addressed a real constabulary need. Officers are frequently unable to do their jobs due to a lack of basic resources, such as pens, paper, and fuel, and members of the public (and RPNGC members) often purchase such items themselves in order to get a complaint attended to. During deployment of the AAP, RPNGC members had increased access to resources, which they claim enhanced their ability to perform policing duties. However, the provision of materials was not entirely uncomplicated, with many people commenting that equipment (particularly cars) was monopolized by Australians and that resource promises remained unfulfilled.

RPNGC attention to the issue of resources must also be seen within the broader context of comparative resource poverty and attendant beliefs about Australian "cargo." Cargo cults featuring "white men" have long existed in various Papua New Guinean societies, and the association between white men and goods remains strong. Material gains made as a result of the Australian aid program have further strengthened this association for members of the

RPNGC, who have come to expect that cargo will be a significant element of any assistance offered.

Perceptions of Capacity Development

While all members interviewed alluded to resources when discussing the benefits of Australian assistance to the RPNGC, few referred to skills and knowledge obtained as a result of technical assistance. RPNGC attitudes to capacity development under the ECP appeared to be closely related to two primary factors: age and seniority. While few RPNGC officers based in Port Moresby expressed a specific desire to learn from the AAP, recently recruited members of the organization based in Bougainville indicated a keenness for mentoring and knowledge transfer.

When discussing capacity development, experienced officers (branch heads, superintendents, etc.) unanimously made three key points. Firstly, they noted that they possessed adequate policing skills and required assistance not in the basics, but in specialist areas to which they had limited exposure (e.g., the detection of white-collar crime) and areas of identified weakness, such as management, leadership, and discipline. These officers suggested that significant improvements to management and discipline occurred while the AAP were in country, yet these improvements were contingent upon AAP presence and could be largely attributed to absence of kin pressures upon AAP members. These benefits ceased upon removal of the AAP.

Second, experienced officers saw the AAP as "manpower," rather than advisers. According to this cadre of RPNGC members, the AAP assisted them to clear significant backlogs and their primary contribution to the organization was as "workers." This perception informed contrasts between previous assistance to the RPNGC (which was strictly advisory) and the ECP, as captured by a senior member who noted, "We want them back but we don't want advisers, supervisors, or spectators, we just want them to do police work. I don't need drivers, I need workers." Such comments demonstrated the different power relations at play, with many senior officers expressing a desire to command Australian human resources and use them to their advantage. In practice, this was not possible, due to the existence of parallel command structures—a major RPNGC criticism of the ECP intervention.

Third, senior officers unanimously unpacked the assumptions informing technical assistance and capacity development by questioning the direction of knowledge and skills transfer. Several officers interrogated the assumption of a universally applicable "right way of policing," over which Australian police have a monopoly. Indeed, this line of questioning extended to junior officers, who noted that Australian police had much to learn about PNG, including familiarity with local dispute resolution processes, ideas about right and wrong, and understanding how local policing operates.

It is perhaps this line of questioning that is the most interesting in the context of analyzing capacity development. All Papua New Guineans interviewed referred to the need for Australian police officers to understand PNG before they could be of "use to them." This, they believed, was possible only in the longer term and could not be achieved through short-term deployments. From a policing perspective, it was noted that while certain knowledge and skill sets deemed to be Western (the use of computers, for example) were considered useful, senior officers found the notion of capacity development by Australian police offensive.

Senior officers explicitly challenged the usefulness of Australian policing knowledge and techniques, arguing that PNG has its own way of policing, which is appropriate in the local context. Many officers commented that the soft Australian approach was inappropriate in PNG, and that they would simply revert to beating people when the AAP departed. Senior officers expressed particular disdain for Australian officers who lacked operational and general duties experience, given the importance of these skills in their environment. This disdain was exacerbated by the placement of a small number of Australian officers in roles for which they were ill-equipped (e.g., people with white-collar crime experience working in the sexual offenses squad). Given their perceptions about the usefulness of Australian policing knowledge and skills, senior RPNGC officers questioned the language of capacity development, with comments such as "We taught them [the Australians] a lot" and "They were just starting to understand" being commonplace.

Less experienced RPNGC officers also questioned the language of capacity development (on the basis that Australian police officers had learned from the experience), yet simultaneously referred to knowledge that they themselves gained in specific areas, such as communications, data management, customer service, use of force, discipline, and the handling of suspects.

Ideal Adviser Attributes

Despite significant social change and contemporary challenges to the authority of elders, age remains an important factor in PNG social relations. Within the policing realm, age does not necessarily intersect neatly with organizational seniority, although both the elderly and those of senior rank are afforded deference. Regardless of rank, elder members of the RPNGC are acutely aware that the policing environment in which they operate is challenging, and characterize themselves as "experienced police officers." To such officers, while the energy and dynamism of younger officers deployed under the ECP were appreciated, the implication that young Australian officers had something to offer was offensive. Consequently, regardless of their own age, the majority of RPNGC members consulted noted that Australian police would be best placed to offer assistance if they were of "mature age."

What constitutes mature age is arbitrary. In this context, RPNGC members are likely alluding as much to experience (in both life and policing) as they are to biological age. Factors that impact upon Papua New Guinean assessments of maturity include, but are not limited to, grey hair (a sign of wisdom), marital status (a sign of social completeness), parenthood, exposure to violent crime (professional experience), experience in a broad range of policing specialties (particularly general duties), and respect among peers. This preference for advisers of mature age is consistent with the findings of a recent AusAID (2004) evaluation of capacity building in public finance in the South Pacific, whereby ni-Vanuatu noted that culturally, it is unacceptable for young people to give advice and direction to older people.

While PNG is generally described as egalitarian, organizationally, the RPNGC is characterized by extreme rank consciousness. In light of limited opportunities for promotion, rank progression is highly valued, and those of senior rank zealously guard their seniority. As with age, partnering an Australian police officer with an RPNGC officer of higher rank is deemed highly problematic. While many members of the AAP were deployed at rank (and a limited few deployed below rank), there was constabulary-wide awareness that a number of Australians had deployed to PNG above rank. This was deemed insulting by those paired with an Australian junior and was seen as an indication of Australian paternalism and perceived seniority. Indeed, Australian comments such as "He might be an inspector, but in Australia he'd be a constable" demonstrated that RPNGC perceptions of this dynamic were in many cases substantiated. Ultimately, Papua New Guinean police officers expressed a desire for Australian advisers who treated them as equals, wanted to learn—not only advise, were culturally sensitive and willing to learn Pidgin, and were willing to try and see the world through a different lens.

The Challenge of Adapting Foreign Police Assistance to Local Circumstances

Being aware of local conditions and the needs and aspirations of recipient country police officers is an important first step in the development of police capacity development programs that aspire to be locally meaningful. This awareness requires significant consultation with the host police force and, preferably, immersion in the host community for some time prior to program design. Ideally, someone from the donor country with a solid understanding of host country dynamics—such as an anthropologist or experienced development practitioner—can play an important role in negotiating cultural differences and advocating for consistent attention to local voices. Moreover, involvement of local people is fundamental to the proper planning of capacity development initiatives.

The preceding summary of RPNGC perceptions of the ECP illustrates the complexity of incorporating local voices into police assistance programs. To demonstrate the difficulty of adapting foreign assistance to local conditions, the following section will explore the three key themes raised by members of the RPNGC—motivations for assistance, perceptions of capacity development, and ideal adviser attributes—and consider the ways in which these local ideas intersect with the practical realities of providing Australian policing assistance to PNG.

Motivations for Assistance

The tension between Australian and Papua New Guinean motivations for the provision of policing assistance is an important yet poorly understood issue. While policing organizations are frequently at pains to publicize their assistance as invited, little thought is given to the motivations behind such invitations. Given the basic development tenet that institutional reform is dependent upon local ownership and political will, the reasons that assistance is sought require scrutiny. Interviews with Australians who have served in capacity development missions in the Pacific demonstrate the pervasive belief that requests for assistance are expressions of a keenness to learn from "more experienced foreign police." Conversely, the significant majority of Papua New Guinean police openly express a desire for material gain, albeit in the professional context, as the primary motivation for receiving foreign assistance to their organization.

The focus on material gain of RPNGC police interviewed following the ECP does not negate the fact that many senior members of the executive (past and present) harbor genuine reform aspirations. It does, however, suggest that the day-to-day relationships between Australian police and PNG police are not premised upon a shared understanding of purpose. This poses challenges to the donor police organization that wishes to harness local energy for reform yet can only do so via the provision of material infrastructure. While it is acknowledged that capacity development requires a combination of "quick wins" and long-term development objectives, sustaining motivation for behavioral change following the provision of goods is extremely challenging. Many donor programs (not only police capacity development initiatives) have attempted to circumvent this challenge by tying the provision of material goods to performance incentives, although the ability of incentives to induce behavioral change is dependent upon a variety of factors (AusAID, 2003).

Engendering local energy for reform is among the key challenges of institutional strengthening, be it of police or other government agencies. Failing to consider the nuanced nature of local motivations for foreign assistance diminishes the ability of donor organizations to harness energy for change, and precludes opportunities for generating drivers of change within recipient institutions (albeit noting that the majority of change is internally driven). To this end, it is the *acknowledgment* of local contingencies, rather than adaptation to local circumstances, that is required.

Perceptions of Capacity Development

Reconciling donor and recipient perceptions of capacity development is the core challenge facing those intending to deliver capacity development assistance in a locally meaningful manner. The very language of capacity development, with which members of the RPNGC are intimately familiar, presupposes a capacity deficit on the part of the recipient organization. Although many members of the RPNGC acknowledge deficits in certain areas (for example, computer literacy, knowledge of forensic and financial investigation), members' self-perceptions center largely upon their experience (the RPNGC is an aging workforce) and their knowledge of how to police Papua New Guineans. To this end, while expert Australian knowledge is valued, members of the RPNGC, particularly senior members, contest Australian understanding of the PNG police context and, more specifically, Australian capacity to impart knowledge that is locally meaningful.

At the heart of this challenge is the acceptability of violence in Papua New Guinean society. While the acceptability of violence varies greatly throughout the country, violence is seen as a legitimate form of discipline and dispute resolution in many Papua New Guinean cultural settings (Weiner, McLeod, & Yala, 2002). Police play a significant role in the perpetuation of violence. Paradoxically, although police receive significant public criticism of their violent modus operandi, many communities simultaneously express a desire for strong law enforcement, without which respect for authority is absent (McLeod, 2004). This cycle of violence is further perpetuated by the poor conditions under which Papua New Guinean police operate, rendering violence among the few means available to police wishing to assert their position in society. To the Australian police officer, the acceptability of violence is incomprehensible and antithetical to principles underpinning modern policing, such as respect for human rights.

The notion of nonstate dispute resolution procedures poses a similar challenge to Australian police. Although Papua New Guinean wrongdoers may be prosecuted through the legal system, disputes and wrongdoings are rarely deemed resolved in the absence of nonstate dispute resolution processes. Indeed, nonstate dispute resolution is in most cases paramount, with state intervention in wrongdoings seen as an unnecessary adjunct. Even though legislation defines the parameters of wrongdoings to be dealt with by the state, in practice Papua New Guinean police officers exercise significant discretion when dealing with wrongdoings. In many cases "talk" is seen as the most important process in resolving a dispute or wrongdoing, and criminalization by the state is believed to further damage social relations. Australian police faced with this situation experience the challenge of encouraging their Papua New Guinean colleagues to uphold the law, or allowing them to resolve local problems in ways that are deemed appropriate to local people.

These brief examples demonstrate the practical difficulty of adapting foreign policing assistance to suit local circumstances. While universal declarations and recipient country commitments to international conventions are often mentioned in justification of the primacy of donor value systems, such references lack meaning and influence over recipient institutions. Despite the use of language such as "We're working to assist them to police their own people in a way that is sustainable," foreign police assistance is ultimately premised upon foreign values. For those offering assistance, values such as human rights, impartiality, and respect for the law are basic assumptions, yet to members of the recipient institutions, they are simply another way of looking at things, and one that doesn't necessarily make sense. This poses the most fundamental qualification to the dictum that foreign police assistance must be adapted to local circumstances, exposing the reality that foreign policing assistance *always* entails the imposition of foreign values, ultimately requiring adaptation on the part of the recipient institution, rather than on that of the donor.

Ideal Adviser Attributes

Incorporating Papua New Guinean ideas about ideal adviser attributes into planning for future assistance to the RPNGC is among the most tangible means of adapting foreign assistance to local circumstances. It is not, however, without its challenges. Members of the RPNGC expressed a preference for members of mature age, with cultural competence, linguistic abilities, significant operational policing experience, and respect for Papua New Guineans.

While institutions such as the AFP can develop rigorous assessment methodologies for the selection of members to serve overseas, personal characteristics such as beliefs about ethnic differences are notoriously difficult to assess, even through psychometric testing. Interviewed Australians who have served in the region frequently highlighted this point, acknowledging the difficulty of predicting responses to foreign circumstances prior to deployment. Consequently, while the ongoing refinement of selection processes may assist in the deployment of appropriate members to countries such as PNG, there will always be a number of people who prove ill-suited to the task. The onus, then, is on donor institutions to remove such people—with reasonable cause—when they are proven to be unsuitable.

The issue of age is a contentious one, as antidiscrimination legislation promotes workplace decision making on the basis of merit, and not personal bio data. While requirements for operational experience may preclude very young Australian police from serving overseas, they might not, for example, preclude a person in his or her early 30s with a decade of policing experience from such work. For the selection panel faced with a 30-year-old and a 50-year-old, the younger of whom has the specific skills required for the area in which he or she will operate, it is necessary to consider the sociocultural environment in which he or she will be required to work. In this instance, adapting foreign assistance to local circumstances requires a familiarity with local ideas about status, knowledge transmission, and respect, all of which should be considered when selecting members to serve offshore. AusAID experiences in the PNG law and justice sector demonstrate that Papua New Guinean participation in adviser selection increases local ownership of decisions made, promoting best practice in tailoring foreign assistance to local circumstances. This experience could be usefully replicated in the policing arena.

Conclusion

In considering the nature of police capacity development in PNG, and Papua New Guinean motivations for assistance, perceptions of capacity development, and views on ideal adviser attributes, this chapter has sought to demonstrate practical limitations to the widely touted lesson learned that foreign assistance to police must be adapted to local conditions. Frequently, criticisms of police assistance missions are premised upon the assumption that donor institutions lack an understanding of host country contexts, as demonstrated by their failure to provide assistance in a locally meaningful way. In examining Papua New Guinean perceptions of the ECP, it is hoped that this chapter has demonstrated that even where knowledge of local circumstances is apparent, the practical realities of harnessing that knowledge are at best challenging.

Ultimately, there are issues upon which no compromise can be made. For example, Australians working in PNG will not accept violence as a normal part of policing, but rather, they will continue to discourage its use. This example does not seek to misinterpret claims made about the need for locally meaningful capacity development initiatives, but rather, it seeks to identify the problems that they can entail. In the event that we fail to acknowledge the realities of aid, including unequal power relations and the imposition of foreign values, the notion of adapting foreign assistance to police will simply remain a moral dictum. Alternatively, deconstructing exactly what can and cannot be adapted to local conditions will provide tangible guidance to those seeking to influence policing organizations in a manner that is locally meaningful.

Acknowledgments

The author acknowledges support provided by the Australian Research Council (LP0560643) for fieldwork undertaken in Papua New Guinea.

References

AusAID. (2003). *Review of incentives and the Australian aid program*. Evaluation and Review Series 32. Retrieved February 20, 2008, from http://www.ausaid.gov.au/publications/pdf/qas32_incentives.pdf

AusAID. (2004). *Capacity building in public finance: An evaluation of activities in the South Pacific*. Evaluation and Review Series 36. Retrieved February 20, 2008, from http://www.ausaid.gov.au/publications/pdf/qas36_capacity_pacific.pdf

Australian Federal Police. (AFP). (2008). *Law enforcement cooperation program*. Retrieved March 2, 2008, from http://www.afp.gov.au/international/liaison/LECP.html

Bayley, D. (2001). *Democratizing the police abroad: What to do and how to do it*. Washington, DC: U.S. Department of Justice.

Clegg, I., Hunt, R., & Whetton, J. (2000). *Policy guidance on support to policing in developing countries*. Swansea, UK: Centre for Development Studies.

Dinnen, S. (2001). *Law and order in a weak state: Crime and politics in Papua New Guinea*. Honolulu: University of Hawaii Press.

Fukuyama, F. (2004). *State-building: Governance and world order in the 21st century*. New York: Cornell University Press.

Goldsmith, A., & Dinnen, S. (2007. Transnational police building: Critical lessons from Timor-Leste and Solomon Islands. *Third World Quarterly, 28*, 1091–1109.

Hegarty, D., May, R., Regan, A., Dinnen, S., Nelson, H., Duncan, R. et al. (2004). *Rebuilding state and nation in Solomon Islands: Policy options for the Regional Assistance Mission*. State, Society and Governance in Melanesia Project Discussion Paper 2004/2. Canberra: SSGM Project, Australian National University.

Heinecke, D., Dollery, B., & Fleming, E. (2008). The Samaritan's dilemma: The effectiveness of Australian foreign aid to Papua New Guinea. *Australian Journal of International Affairs, 62*, 53–71.

Hood, L. (2006). Missed opportunities: The United Nations, police service and defence force development in Timor-Leste, 1999–2004. *Civil Wars, 8*, 143–162.

Horn, A., Olonisakin, F., & Peake, G. (2006). United Kingdom-led security sector reform in Sierra Leone. *Civil Wars, 8*, 109–123.

Human Rights Watch. (2005). *Making their own rules: Police beatings, rape and torture of children in Papua New Guinea*. Retrieved January 29, 2008, from http://hrw.org/reports/2005/png0905/

Keelty, M. (2004, July 7). *The AFP—25 years and beyond*. Address to the National Press Club, Canberra.

Marenin, O. (2005). *Restoring policing systems in war torn nations: Process, problems, prospects.* Geneva: DCAF.

McLeod, A. (2004). *Royal Papua New Guinea constabulary community perceptions survey.* Report produced for the AusAID RPNGC Development Project.

McLeod, A. (2007). Police reform in Papua New Guinea. In A. Browne (Ed.), *Security and development in the Pacific Islands: Social resilience in emerging states* (pp. 73–88). Boulder, CO: Lynne Rienner Publishers.

McLeod, A., & Dinnen, S. (2007). Police building in the Southwest Pacific—New directions in Australian regional policing. In A. Goldsmith & J. Sheptycki (Eds.), *Crafting transnational policing: Police capacity-building and global policing reform* (pp. 295–328). Oxford: Hart Publishing.

Morgan, P. (1998). *Capacity and capacity development—Some strategies.* Note prepared for the Political and Social Policies Division, Canadian International Development Agency. Retrieved December 21, 2007, from http://www.impactalliance.org/file_download.php?location=S_U&filename=10343697570CIDA_Strategy_Paper.pdf

Neild, R. (2001). Democratic police reforms in war-torn societies. *Conflict, Security, and Development, 1,* 21–42.

PNG Government. (2005). *Medium term development strategy 2005–2010.* Waigani: Government Printing Office.

Rudd, K. (2007, July 5). *Fresh ideas for future challenges: A new approach to Australia's arc of instability.* Speech to the Lowy Institute. Sydney, Australia.

United Nations Development Program (UNDP). (2007). *Capacity development practice note.* Retrieved December 10, 2007, from http://www.capacity.undp.org/indexAction.cfm?module=Library&action=GetFile&DocumentAttachmentID=1507

United Nations Development Program (UNDP). (2008). *Human development reports.* Retrieved February 29, 2008, from http://hdr.undp.org/en/statistics/

Weiner, J., McLeod, A., & Yala, J. (2001). *Aspects of conflict in the contemporary Papua New Guinea highlands.* State Society and Governance in Melanesia Project Discussion Paper 2002/4. Canberra: SSGM Project, Australian National University.

Reinventing Policing Through the Prism of the Colonial *Kiap*

19

SINCLAIR DINNEN
JOHN BRAITHWAITE

Contents

Early Modern Police in the West

The early modern idea of police in the West differs from the contemporary notion of an organization devoted to fighting crime (Garland, 2001). Police from the 16th to the 19th centuries in continental Europe meant institutions for the creation of an orderly environment, especially for trade and commerce. The historical origins of the term through German back to French are derived from the Greek notion of "policy" or "politics" in Aristotle (Smith, 1762/1978, p. 486; Neocleous, 1998). It referred to all the institutions and processes of ordering that gave rise to prosperity, progress, and happiness, most notably the constitution of markets. Actually, it referred to that subset of governance that many contemporary scholars conceive as regulation.

Police certainly included the regulation of theft and violence, preventive security, and the regulation of labor, vagrancy, and the poor, but also the regulation of weights and measures and other forms of consumer protection: liquor licensing, health and safety, building, fire safety, road and traffic regulation, and early forms of environmental regulation. The institution was rather privatized, subject to considerable local control, relying mostly on volunteer constables and watches for implementation, heavily oriented to self-regulation and infrequent (even if sometimes extreme) in its recourse to punishment. The lieutenant de police (a post established in Paris in 1667)

Adapted from Dinnen, S. and Braithwaite, J. (2008). Reinventing policing through the prism of the colonial kiap. *Policing and Society,* http://dx.doi.org/10.1080/10439460802187571

came to have jurisdiction over the stock exchange, food supplies and standards, the regulation of prostitutes, and other markets in vice and virtue. Police and the "science of police" that in 18th-century German universities prefigured contemporary regulatory studies[1] sought to establish a new source of order to replace the foundation laid by the estates in the feudal order that had broken down.

English country parishes and small market towns, as on the continent, had constables and local watches under a Tudor system that for centuries beyond the Tudors regulated the postfeudal economic and social order. Yet there was an English aversion to conceptualizing this as police in the French, German, and Russian fashion. The office of the constable had initially been implanted into British common law and institutions by the Norman invasion of 1066. The office was in turn transplanted by the British to New England, with some New England communities even requiring Native American villages to appoint constables. Eighteenth-century English political instincts were to view Continental political theory of police as a threat to liberty and to seek a more confined role for the constable. Admittedly, Blackstone, in his fourth volume of *Commentaries on the Laws of England* (1769), adopts the Continental conception of police, and Adam Smith applauds it in his *Lectures on Jurisprudence* (1762–1764/1978).

Peel's creation of the Metropolitan Police in London in 1829 and the subsequent creation of an even more internationally influential colonial model in Dublin were watersheds. Uniformed paramilitary police, preoccupied with the punitive regulation of the poor to the almost total exclusion of any interest in the constitution of markets and the just regulation of commerce, became one of the most universal of globalized regulatory models. So what happened to the business regulation? While the Victorian ideal was laissez faire, from the mid-19th-century factories, inspectorates, mines inspectorates, liquor licensing boards, weights and measures inspectorates, health and sanitation, food inspectorates, and countless others were created to begin to fill the vacuum left by constables now concentrating only on crime. Business regulation became variegated into many different specialist regulatory branches.

The shift from generalist regulatory police to paramilitary crime control police has created an important public policy problem in countries like Australia, where rural people have become the new poor, yet miss out on all the protections of the regulatory state available in the city. In the move from the police economy (in which the local constable was responsible for all forms of commercial rip-offs in a country town) to the galaxy of specialized regulatory agencies that only find it economic to base inspectors in offices in major cities, rural citizens are the big losers. In the city, if the butcher's scales increase the weight of meat or if suburban petrol stations fix prices, something might be done about it. But there are no inspectors in the bush today to do anything about such rip-offs. Regulatory redesign is needed to reverse the sad effects of the abolition of the multidisciplinary constable for those who live in villages and farms. Peel's invention of paramilitary police preoccupied with the discipline of crime control was a disaster for the village dwellers of all the world's nations, especially their poorer ones. The remedy may be the reinvention of rural constables as multidisciplinary regulators of plural forms of domination.

Policing Villages in the Developing World

The British Empire's colonies were mostly founded long before the Peelian revolution specialized policing in 1829. Colonial policing was therefore shaped initially from the institutional clay of the 18th-century nonparamilitary regulatory model of police. There were constables who were post-Peelian in the capital, but rather more pre-Peelian in rural areas.

> 'The police department in India,' wrote Sir Edmund Cox shortly before the First World War, 'is the very essence of our administration. There is no other which so much concerns the life of the people. To the ordinary villager the ... constable ... is the visible representative of the Sirkar, or Government'. This view was echoed two decades later by J.C. Curry when he remarked that 'The Indian policeman is the ubiquitous embodiment of the government', and went on to claim that millions of villagers who had never seen a squad of soldiers or encountered a British administrator has nevertheless had frequent contact with the police. (Arnold, 1992, p. 43)

Arnold also quotes Jawaharlal Nehru as having a similar view of the centrality of Indian police to dispersed governance immediately after independence. Yet perhaps district officers, or *kiaps* in the New Guinea case, which we will consider in detail later, were even more important regulatory police (in the 18th-century sense) in 19th- and 20th-century colonies. These colonies also started as almost exclusively village societies, with few and small towns. When colonial administration and comprador capitalism created cities, it happened much later than in the West, so the rise of paramilitary police to control riots and urban crime was also later. And the paramilitary police remained until the end of British colonialism a less powerful institution than the diaspora of village-based district officers. Colonial policing had more than its share of corruption, incompetence, and excessive use of force. But for all that, the argument of this article is that colonial policing had a structurally healthier hybrid of rural regulatory policing and urban paramilitary crime control police than Western societies like Australia have today. While it would be folly for Sydney to do without crime control police with specialized capabilities from forensics to traffic to riot control, our hypothesis is that outback towns might do better with a *kiap*. Of course, such a contemporary Australian bush *kiap* would regulate different things from the New Guinea colonial *kiap*. She would not have to worry about regulating community disruption from threats of sorcery. But she might have to warn the two petrol stations in town that they are breaking the law when they agree to increase their prices in concert. She might have to warn a local foundry to put a fence around dangerous machinery, or head off serious conflict by warning a farmer to stop polluting a stream with agricultural chemicals. Before returning in our conclusion to the idea of a contemporary *kiap* of regulatory capitalism, first we consider the experience of the colonial *kiap* of Papua New Guinea.

Policing the Frontier: The Colonial *Kiap*

Papua New Guinea (PNG), comprising the eastern half of the island of New Guinea, gained independence in 1975 and inherited the familiar array of institutions that constitute modern statehood. These were assembled by the former Australian administration over a relatively short period of institutional modernization in the late colonial period. They included the standard components of a modern criminal justice system, notably a centralized police force, hierarchy of courts, and prisons. In the fourth decade after independence, this system continues to struggle to gain effective traction in PNG's famously diverse social settings, and does so against a background of burgeoning law and order problems. The police, in particular, have experienced major difficulties in fulfilling their constitutional role of preserving peace and good order, and maintaining and enforcing the law in an impartial and objective manner. An expanding litany of police failings includes incompetence, brutalization, nepotism, corruption, politicization of senior ranks, as well as poor responsiveness to community needs. Decades of Australian development assistance have had little impact on police performance, with a recent review concluding that the police force "was close to total collapse" (Royal Papua New Guinea Constabulary, 2004, p. 40).

Australian assistance has assumed the merits and feasibility of transplanting an urban-centered policing model, even though 85% of the population live in rural villages. Disappointing outcomes have been viewed as technical and administrative challenges to be overcome by improved modalities of delivery, such as the recent deployment of serving Australian police officers to work alongside their PNG counterparts (McLeod & Dinnen, 2007). The notion that the model being transplanted may itself be flawed, and that more innovative approaches to policing are required, is rarely raised. PNG's overwhelmingly rural character is but one indicator of the many ways in which its circumstances differ from those of the metropolitan donors seeking to shape its modernization and development. With over 800 languages spoken among a population of almost 6 million people, PNG is one of the most sociolinguistically diverse countries in the world. Government and commercial facilities are concentrated in urban centers, while most people live in rural villages, surviving through a combination of subsistence agriculture and cash cropping. Transport and communications infrastructure is still rudimentary. Bonds of kinship, shared language, and ties to ancestral land, along with *kastom*[2] and Christianity, provide the basis for individual identities and allegiances among most Papua New Guineans rather than abstractions of citizenship and nation. Most citizens live on the margins of the modern state, including its formal justice system. Accessing the nearest police post, magistrate, or government office often entails a long journey by foot, truck, or canoe. Everyday disputes are addressed informally in the community. In some areas, notably in the Highlands, significant disjunctions still separate local perceptions of right and wrong from those inscribed in state law. Violent forms of self-help, including payback and warfare, are considered legitimate responses to grievance in certain places.

As with other facets of the modern state, the history of institutionalized policing in PNG is a remarkably short one. In its current form, the Royal Papua New Guinea Constabulary (RPNGC) dates from the period of institutional modernization that began in the 1960s as part of the larger process of decolonization. Throughout most of the colonial period, policing was an integral part of an overall system of administration marked by a lack of institutional differentiation. This was, in part, a practical response to the enormous challenges of extending government control in such a large, fragmented, and topographically diverse territory.

The northern half of modern PNG was colonized originally by Germany in 1884, prompting Britain to declare a protectorate over the southern part of the island in the same year. British New Guinea was subsequently transferred to Australia and renamed Papua in 1906. Following World War I, German New Guinea became a mandated territory of the League of Nations and was administered by Australia. After World War II, the two territories of Papua and New Guinea were administered jointly, becoming self-governing in 1973 and finally independent in 1975. The key official in colonial policing was an administrative official, sometimes called a patrol officer or district officer, and more popularly known by the pidgin term *kiap*.[3] *Kiaps*, typically young Australian men, played a critical role in the extension of government control. Patrols led by the *kiap* accompanied by his armed native constabulary provided the most visible face of colonial government. The *kiap* has been described as a "multi-powered boss" (Rowley, 1972, p. 76) who was viewed by local people as "almost God's shadow on earth" (Nelson, 1982, p. 35).

The expansion of the administrative frontier was uneven and incremental. European exploration of the densely populated Highlands only commenced in the 1930s and was led by gold prospectors rather than by government agents. At independence, while some communities had experienced over a century of centralized administration, others had less than 20 years. Limited resources and the difficulties of local topography impeded a timelier and more uniform process of consolidation. In the early years there were relatively few *kiaps* scattered across vast tracts of land. At the height of Australia's prewar administration in 1938, a total field staff of 150 men existed to govern three-quarters of a million people, while a similar number of people lay beyond official government control (Nelson, 1982, p. 33). By 1940 approximately two-thirds of the inhabitants of the two territories were governed by patrol (Griffin, Nelson, & Firth, 1979, p. 61), including most of the previously neglected Highlands by the late 1940s. According to Downs, "For the greater part of this history the Territorial Government operated through fifteen district offices, fifty-eight sub-districts and a score of remote patrol posts serving a total of 11,920 villages" (1980, p. xv). As late as the 1960s, young patrol officers and a dozen police might have responsibility for the administration of a subdistrict comprising around 10,000 people (Nelson, 1982, p. 33).

Magistrates in British New Guinea provided the prototype for the *kiap* as developed by later administrations (Banks, 1993, p. 12). These officials had considerable powers and occupied multiple roles. As described by Wolfers:

> A 'magistrate' in Papua was more than a judicial officer. He was, and his successor the patrol officer still is, in many areas, the sole personification of the government: policeman, explorer, road-builder, health inspector, social worker and prison warder; even in court, where he deals with most of the 'lesser offences' against the law, and civil disputes between Papuans, he acts as prosecutor, defence counsel, judge and jury. (1975, p. 19)

The Germans and British developed a similar system of administration based on districts. Each district had a headquarters and three or four dispersed government stations. *Kiaps* and their police undertook regular patrols radiating outward from stations. A major part of their early work was the exploration of new territory and pacification of warring tribes (Sinclair, 1984, p. 7).

Prior to World War II, New Guinea *kiaps* were part of the auxiliary police establishment within the New Guinea Police Force. In Papua, members of the magisterial service, resident magistrates, and patrol officers were appointed as officers of the Royal Papuan Constabulary. They had no formal ranks or uniforms. The two police forces were brought together for administrative purposes after World War II. Patrol officers and district officers remained as commissioned officers in the Field Constabulary Branch up to and beyond independence. In the prewar years there were a small number of uniformed professional police with European officers in both territories. Their role was primarily confined to the small urban centers of Port Moresby and Rabaul, which were the main expatriate enclaves in both territories.

English common law and selected Australian legislation, including the Criminal Code of Queensland, were introduced into Papua and, after 1921, into New Guinea along with a formal court system. The civil jurisdiction of these courts was taken up with the regulation of the commercial activities of the small European community. Serious criminal cases were heard by a single judge in the district or supreme courts. However, the main body of introduced law affecting local people was a comprehensive set of Native Regulations. These applied exclusively to indigenes and could be made in respect of any matter having a "bearing or affecting the good government and well being of natives" (Native Administration Ordinance, Section 4).[4] Many dealt with the punishment of minor crimes, while others ranged across such diverse matters as "sorcery, adultery, cruelty to animals, the obstruction of watercourses, taking part in the production of motion pictures, and the wearing of clothes" (Geeves, 1979, p. 56).

Whereas Australian criminal law was administered by professional judges or magistrates, the regulations were enforced through Courts of Native Affairs (New Guinea) and Courts of Native Matters (Papua) presided over by field officers. This dualistic system recognized the need to temper the strict application of law given the considerable gulf separating colonial and indigenous social orders. As noted by Downs, "Regulations for human conduct introduced the people to an alien society as well as to an alien judicial system. Administration and justice were intertwined" (1980, p. 148). The formal courts also applied more lenient penalties to indigenous offenders with a limited exposure to the colonial social order and whose criminal actions were deemed to have been influenced by customary beliefs (Dinnen, 1988).

Knowledge about local people and their cultures was viewed as an important condition for effective performance by field staff. Cadet patrol officers posted to New Guinea after 1926 returned to Sydney after two years' service. The School of Civil Affairs, renamed in 1947 the Australian School of Pacific Affairs, provided instruction in colonial administration, anthropology, law and order in PNG, practical administration, elementary medicine, tropical agriculture, geography, *Tok Pisin* and *Motu*, animal husbandry and entomology, and something called "the administration and administrative policy in New Guinea" (Kituai, 1998, p. 30).

In practice, the intensity of government by patrol varied considerably. For villages close to administrative centers it might mean a couple of visits a year, a single visit every one or two years for more distant communities, and even rarer in less accessible places. The *kiap*, assisted by village constables in Papua and *luluais* and *tultuls* in New Guinea,[5] would inspect the village, collect head taxes, complete the census form, and hear cases. Subject to qualifying examinations, field staff were appointed members of the Courts of Native Affairs or Native Matters in their second or third year of service. In this capacity, *kiaps* dealt with around 75% of all court cases heard in the colony (Downs,

1980, pp. 148–149). The *kiap* court would usually be held in the open, with the *kiap* seated at the front, facing the litigants or alleged offenders, and often with the entire village in attendance. He would listen to what everybody had to say, sum up the situation, then make a decision. Inputs from village leaders were critical in the resolution of most cases. Decisions were recorded and appeals could, in theory, be taken to the district courts. Although technically illegal, *kiaps* sometimes opted for out-of-court settlements in the interests of maintaining peace. Most were also aware that village officials and traditional leaders convened their own unofficial courts, and the *kiaps* often lent their tacit approval to these village fora (Downs, 1980, p. 150).

The active role of indigenous actors in the mediation of colonial power was an important reason for the relative success of the *kiapdom* (Gordon, 1983). *Pax Australiana* could not have been achieved without the acquiescence of most indigenous leaders and groups. The successful ending of intergroup warfare forced together groups that had previously existed in a state of mutual suspicion. In doing so, it generated new social and economic opportunities dramatically through expanding existing horizons. Ambitious individuals were not slow to recognize this potential and exploit its possibilities (Rowley, 1972).

The *kiap* system was successful in large part because it did not displace local power structures or dominate local politics. In the case of local dispute resolution mechanisms, "customary law held sway and only when it failed was the *kiap* involved" (Clifford, Morauta, & Stuart, 1984, p. 112). *Kiaps* tended to let local parties resolve disputes themselves. As Gordon put it, "[*Kiaps*] had a basic anthropological training; enough to realise that matters or disputes were more complex than they appear on the surface, and thus should be left alone" (1983, p. 210). In this pluralistic setting, *kiap* courts provided additional fora that could be incorporated into local political strategies. Decisions by unofficial mechanisms could be confirmed or contested in the new courts provided by the colonial state. Interactions between indigenous and colonial systems thereby served to strengthen each other. "Unofficial courts served to make kiap's 'law' 'strong' because of the nature of cooperation which existed between kiaps and unofficial 'magistrates'" (Gordon, 1983, p. 211).

It is also important to appreciate the critical role of the *kiap's* indigenous police and the manner in which their roles complemented each other. Working with the *kiap* brought considerable prestige to local police, while European *kiaps* depended on their subordinates for local knowledge and language skills. This dependence also rendered the *kiaps* susceptible to manipulation. As Waiko observes, "The colonial officers were not aware of the complexities of the relationships between clans and tribes; nor did they realise that in the early period of contact it was often the police who determined whether relations between groups were to be hostile or peaceful" (1989, p. 97).

Institutional Modernization and the Decline of the *Kiap*

Paul Hasluck—Australia's long-serving minister for external territories (1951–1963)—played a key role in transforming the framework of administration in PNG. From the outset he identified justice as a major target for reform. His broader project of institutional and political modernization aimed to replace the old colonial system of native administration with a system of modern bureaucratic government. Hasluck's approach fell squarely within the tenets of the prevailing modernization paradigm with its assumption as to the universal and linear direction of historical progress.

An early priority was to establish a separation of powers between judicial, administrative, and executive arms of government. This meant supplanting the administrative model of colonial control with an independent, institutionally differentiated, and professionally staffed system of justice. Hasluck wished to abolish the dualism that discriminated between indigenes and expatriates, and replace it with a unitary system of courts administering a single body of law (Hasluck, 1976, p. 348). The first stage was completed in 1957 with the establishment of a separate prisons branch under the Corrective Institutions Ordinance. He then set about the more challenging work of separating the police from the Department of Native Affairs and the control of the *kiap*. An Australian jurist, David Derham, was commissioned to undertake a comprehensive review of the administration of justice in PNG. Derham's report became the blueprint for the modern justice system inherited at independence (Derham, 1960). While recognizing the important work performed by the *kiap*, Derham viewed it as an idiosyncratic and essentially transitional institution—a preliminary stage on the way to establishing a fully modern system.

The establishment of centralized policing as part of the larger process of decolonization was not unique to PNG and occurred in most other former British colonies. As independence approached, colonial police forces become more paramilitary in character, developed centralized command systems and specialized units, and usually grew dramatically in size (Anderson & Killingray, 1992, p. ix). In 1961 the Papua and New Guinea police were separated from the Department of Native Affairs, and in 1966 they were removed from the control of the Public Service Commission in order to ensure their neutrality. These reforms resulted in a police force that was initially divided between an urban constabulary under the command of full-time police officers and a rural constabulary under the command of *kiaps*. The number of police stations increased dramatically during the decade before independence (Gordon & Meggitt, 1985, p. 84). With the expansion in size and operational scope of urban policing, tensions developed between the two branches. European police officers resented working under the authority of district officials (Downs, 1980, p. 155). *Kiaps* complained that regular constabulary sent to rural areas "rarely [left] the town in which [they] were stationed" and were commanded by "European officers with little knowledge of the country" (Oram, 1973, p. 12), while regular police were accused of reluctance to intervene in the intergroup warfare that began to reappear in parts of the Highlands from the late 1960s, as well as of incompetence when they did. Police mobile squads were formed after the police reorganization in 1966 and used for this and other public order purposes.

The courts also underwent significant change from the mid-1960s, with a shift away from the relatively informal *kiap* courts to more formal court procedures. Local courts were intended to replace the *kiap* courts. These would, in turn, be eventually replaced by district courts staffed by professional magistrates. Most of the Native Regulations were repealed in 1968 and replaced by summary offenses codified in criminal legislation.

These reforms had significant impacts at local levels. Under the old system, the dispute resolution powers of the *kiap* could be supplemented with powers issuing from his various agency functions (Gordon, 1983, p. 220). In addition to his penal powers, he could try and induce behavioral change by using his authority to provide roads and other services. The *kiap* had a wide range of sanctions to choose from, as well as the discretion to adapt these to different circumstances. Sanctions could be applied immediately, with minimal formality or delay. Through working with local leaders, the *kiap's* decisions were usually accorded a high level of legitimacy.

By contrast, the discretion of the professional magistrate was constrained by a multitude of substantive, evidential, and procedural rules. Professional justice took a long time. It entailed a cumbersome process conducted in an arcane foreign language that was incomprehensible to most Papua New Guineans. As well as weakening the local standing of the *kiap* by depriving him of his most potent powers, these changes contributed to growing levels of dissatisfaction with state regulation among indigenous parties. The new system was viewed by many as confusing, unpredictable, and unjust. Speaking of the Western Highlands, Strathern observed that

> the kiap's handling of trouble cases in the past combined both a concern for public order and a capacity to deal with minor offences. In fact, these derived from different aspects of his roles (administrator and magistrate), but it meant that he 'settled disputes' roughly along lines familiar to Hageners. The paradox is that although the modern official courts are ostensibly concerned with law and order, they fail in Hageners' eyes to take cognisance of matters directly related to both of these elements. (1972, p. 143)

The authority of the police was also diminished, with this formerly powerful and prestigious agency of pacification now subject to regular and humiliating defeats in court, often on obscure technical grounds.

The rapid localization that commenced during this period also had a weakening effect on state controls, not only because of the short-term effects of replacing experienced personnel with less seasoned ones, but also because of the effects of the erosion of the social delineation between colonial officials and their clientele. *Kiaps*, magistrates, and other expatriate officials exercised considerable autonomy in their dealings with local leaders precisely because they were foreigners. Their apparent lack of interest in competing with Melanesians by engaging in local politics and their immunity to the pressures of *wantokism*[6] contributed to an aura of independence and impartiality. However, the basis of these local perceptions was fundamentally challenged once Melanesians began occupying these positions. Irrespective of their individual integrity and professionalism, indigenous officials were immediately vulnerable to accusations of *wantokism* and to suspicions that they would become rivals in local political competition (Gordon, 1983, p. 215).

The Return of the *Kiap*

Many ex-*kiaps* were recruited by resource developers during the 1980s' minerals boom, often serving as community relations officers (Banks & Ballard, 1997). Much of their initial work involved the negotiation of land access and compensation issues, but this extended into other activities as individual projects matured. Their community liaison tasks are similar to those of the old *kiaps*. These include mediating disputes, overseeing compensation payments, determining land ownership and group membership, conducting censuses, as well as dealing with labor relations. An ability to access company resources means that like the old *kiaps*, they continue to be viewed as important gatekeepers to modernity and wealth. The continuing utility of the *kiap* model today highlights the importance of building and sustaining relationships with village people as a critical ingredient of successful administration in rural PNG. The returning *kiap* also has much higher levels of legitimacy among local people than do government officers, and these are mainly derived from the former's gatekeeper role. As Banks and Ballard argue, the link between providing development and legitimacy is critical in explaining the failure of government in contemporary PNG (1997, p. 163).

At the same time as PNG has seen this return of a new *kiap*, it has also seen a return of less paramilitary, less centrally administered police whose interactions with local communities are in some respects more akin to the old colonial system. Today these are community auxiliary police, who at least in parts of PNG, such as Bougainville, are respectfully connected to village people and their structures, which they seek to mobilize through a community policing philosophy. Unlike the RPNGC, who became progressively more urban based and focused on urban crime problems, the community auxiliary police, while under the control of the RPNGC, only served part-time as police and lived and worked in their village.

In the 1990s we also saw a return to some of the negotiated peacemak-ing that *kiaps* deployed in the pacification of rural intergroup warfare. These were the gang surrenders (mostly in urban settings) and peace settlements where the negotiators were not *kiaps*, but mostly officials and church lead-ers. Like the old intertribal pacification, this has had some success (Dinnen, 2001). Finally, we have seen a return to restorative justice, albeit with some modernist trimmings of training for facilitators, rights, and gender equal-ity concerns (Dinnen, 2006). There is not space here to describe and critique these adaptations of older approaches to contemporary settings. Our point is simply that a modernized, formal justice system run from the capital proved so incapable of dealing with such a great variety of problems that significant partial returns to village-based responsive and flexible governance of secu-rity became attractive and, in many cases, the only option available to rural dwellers.

While all of them can deliver some kinds of efficacy that urban-admin-istered Westernized justice cannot, all of them also threaten some of the genuine virtues of more formal rule of law. Here we think the restorative justice literature is informative on how new hybridities might save those rule of law virtues (Braithwaite, 2002). Patriarchy, or domination by big men, must be countered; new separations of powers must be infused into village justice that will work in a way that a man wearing a white wig in the capital may not. New human rights institutions that actually touch the traditional fabric of justice in villages where many people still live need to be, and can be, crafted. In this regard, Wardak (2004) provides some useful ideas on rights institutions that might check and balance the patriarchal domination of Afghan *jirgas*—*jirgas* that nevertheless deliver more practi-cal safety for villagers than paramilitary police and urban courts under the sway of warlords.

Conclusion: The Case for a Contemporary *Kiap*

In developed as well as developing societies, it is time rural communities got their fair share of the regulatory budget. Deputizing country police as multiskilled regulatory inspectors could be a useful piecemeal solution. If the money handed over by capital city regulatory agencies for this work increased the number of rural police by one-third, this could be good for rural crime control challenges that can be serious, especially in nations like Australia, where the outback has more poverty, more guns, higher concen-trations of displaced indigenous people, and more violence (especially fam-ily violence). Part of what is needed in a nation like Australia is for country police to do a better job at building relationships with the Aboriginal community. Providing some regulatory services that protect disadvantaged minorities from consumer rip-offs would not be a bad way of beginning to build that.

In the Solomon Islands, for example, the single most important issue for the future of villages is forests and logging. We have seen during our fieldwork the tragic sight of villagers asking the police for help in dealing with Asian logging companies, only to be told that that is the responsibility of the Forestry Department in the capital. Here is the nub of what concerns us in this chapter. The Forestry bureaucrats are in the capital (with minuscule travel budgets); the trees are out there among the villages. If we want to tackle this aspect of the global warming agenda, perhaps we need to think *kiap*, to think part-time village constables being responsible for forest enforcement, to consider reversing the Peelian revolution in its application to village societies.

There are more radical solutions still. One is to abolish the police budget in favor of a policing budget, and to do likewise with every kind of regulatory budget. Some Aboriginal communities in Australia might bid to do their own policing. Country towns could bid competitively to the state for a bundling of their share of the police and regulatory budgets into a multipurpose local policing/regulatory service. The policy detail would be difficult and inevitably vary between societies. But it might be a path to better justice and local democratic empowerment of rural communities. The idea of abolishing the police budget in favor of a contestable policing budget has been advanced by the Patten Commission into policing in Northern Ireland, and pushed in the scholarly writing of one of its members, Clifford Shearing, with co-author Philip Stenning (see Shearing, 1995). It is ironic that Ireland, birthplace of so much of the colonial policing doctrine of the British Empire, should be the site where the idea of regulatory hybridity through contestable policing budgets should now emerge. It is an idea worth considering for fostering the hybridity needed for the unique regulatory problems of both contemporary developed and developing societies. Even when nations have strong states that make policing work well in the city, those states are often weak and ineffective for rural citizens, especially disadvantaged ones.

Democratic experimentalism (Dorf & Sabel, 1998) and learning through doing are needed to develop these ideas. It is hard to envision the path such innovation might take, and the traps it might fall into. What is easier to see is the folly of transplanting Peel's basically sound policing innovation for London through security sector development assistance into village societies. It may be that these villages would be less well served by paramilitaries in expensive patrol cars than by *kiaps* on foot working with part-time community auxiliary police living in the village.

References

Anderson, D., & Killingray, D. (1992). *Policing and decolonisation: Politics, nationalism and the police.* Manchester: Manchester University Press.

Arnold, D. (1992). Police power and the demise of British rule in India, 1930–47. In D. Anderson & D. Killingray (Eds.), *Policing and decolonisation* (pp. 42–61). Manchester: Manchester University Press.

Banks, C. (1993). *Women in transition—Social control in Papua New Guinea.* Canberra: Australian Institute of Criminology.

Banks, G., & Ballard, C. (1997). The return of the Kiap: Recolonising rural Papua New Guinea. In D. Denoon (Ed.), *Emerging from empire? Decolonisation in the Pacific* (pp. 160–164). Canberra: Australian National University Press.

Blackstone, W. (1769). *Commentaries on the laws of England* (Vol. 4). London: Dawsons.

Braithwaite, J. (2002). *Restorative justice and responsive regulation.* New York: Oxford University Press.

Clifford, W., Morauta, L., & Stuart, B. (1984). *Law and order in Papua New Guinea* (Clifford Report). Port Moresby: Institute of National Affairs and Institute of Applied Social and Economic Research.

Derham, D. (1960). *Report on the system for the administration of justice in the territory of Papua New Guinea.* Canberra: Department of Territories.

Dinnen, S. (1988). Sentencing, custom and the rule of law in Papua New Guinea. *Journal of Legal Pluralism and Unofficial Law, 27,* 19–54.

Dinnen, S. (2001). *Law and order in a weak state: Crime and politics in Papua New Guinea.* Honolulu: University of Hawai'i Press.

Dinnen, S. (2006). Restorative justice and the governance of security in the Southwest Pacific. In D. Sullivan & L. Tifft (Eds.), *Handbook of restorative justice* (pp. 401–421). London: Routledge Press.

Dorf, M., & Sabel, C. (1998). A constitution of democratic experimentalism. *Columbia Law Review, 98,* 267–473.

Downs, I. (1980). *The Australian trusteeship: Papua New Guinea 1945–75.* Canberra: Government Publishing Service.

Garland, D. (2001). *The culture of control: Crime and social order in contemporary society.* Oxford: Oxford University Press.

Geeves, R. (1979). *The administration of justice and the European residents of Rabaul and the mandated territory of New Guinea, 1921–1942.* MA thesis, Australian National University.

Gordon, R. (1983). The decline of the kiapdom and the resurgence of "tribal fighting" in Enga. *Oceania, 53,* 205–223.

Gordon, R., & Meggitt, M. (1985). *Law and order in the New Guinea highlands.* Hanover: University Press of New England.

Griffin, J., Nelson, H., & Firth, S. (1979). *Papua New Guinea: A political history.* Melbourne: Heinemann Educational Australia.

Hasluck, P. (1976). *A time for building: Australian administration in Papua and New Guinea 1951–1963.* Melbourne: Melbourne University Press.

Kituai, A. (1998). *My gun, my brother. The world of the Papua New Guinea colonial police, 1920–1960.* Honolulu: University of Hawai'i Press.

McLeod, A., & Dinnen, S. (2007). Police building in the Southwest Pacific—New directions in Australian regional policing. In A. Goldsmith & J. Sheptycki (Eds.), *Crafting transnational policing: Police capacity-building and global policing reform* (pp. 295–328). Portland, OR: Hart Publishing.

Nelson, H. (1982). *Taim bilong masta—The Australian involvement with Papua New Guinea*. Sydney: ABC Books.

Neocleous, M. (1998). Policing and pin-making: Adam Smith, police and the state of prosperity. *Policing and Society, 8*, 425–29.

Oram, N. (1973, January). Law and order: Maximum participation at all levels. *New Guinea*, pp. 4–22.

Pasquino, P. (1991). Theatrum politicum: The genealogy of capital—Police and the state of prosperity. In G. Burchell, C. Gordon, & P. Miller (Eds.), *The Foucault effect: Studies in governmentality* (pp. 105–118). Hemel Hempstead, UK: Harvester Wheatsheaf.

Rowley, C. (1972). *The New Guinea villager: A retrospect from 1964*. Melbourne: Cheshire.

Royal Papua New Guinea Constabulary. (2004). *Administrative review committee (ARC)* (Draft report). PNG: Government Printer.

Shearing, C. (1995). Reinventing policing: Policing as governance. In F. Sack, M. Voss, D. Frehsee, A. Funk, & H. Reinke (Eds.), *Privatisierung staatlicher kontrolle: Befunde, konzepte, tendenzen* (pp. 70–87). Baden-Baden: Nomos Verlagsgesellschaft.

Sinclair, J. (1984). *Kiap—Australia's patrol officers in Papua New Guinea*. Bathurst, NSW: Robert Brown & Associates.

Smith, A. (1978). *Lectures on jurisprudence*. Oxford: Clarendon Press. (Original work published 1762–1764)

Strathern, M. (1972). *Official and unofficial courts: Legal assumptions and expectations in a highlands community* (Bulletin 47, pp. 1–166). Port Moresby: Australian National University, New Guinea Research Unit.

Waiko, J. (1989). Australian administration under the Binandere thumb. In S. Latufeku (Ed.), *Papua New Guinea: A century of colonial impact 1884–1984* (pp. 75–108). Port Moresby: National Research Institute.

Wardak, A. (2004). Building a post-war justice system in Afghanistan. *Crime Law & Social Change, 41*, 319–341.

Wolfers, E. (1975). *Race relations and colonial rule in Papua New Guinea*. Sydney: Australia and New Zealand Book Company.

Endnotes

1. Pasquino (1991, p. 112) reports a 1937 bibliography for German-speaking areas that lists 3,215 publications from 1600 to 1800 under the listing "science of police in the strict sense."
2. *Kastom* is the Melanesian *Pigin* term for culture or tradition.
3. The word *captain* was corrupted into *kiap* in New Guinea Pidgin (Nelson, 1982, p. 33).
4. The regulations applying in both territories were essentially the same in substance, although the New Guinea regulations tended to carry harsher penalties. After WWII they were gradually pruned, and some were abolished. See Wolfers (1975).
5. *Luluais* were village leaders appointed by the colonial authorities to represent the government at the village level. *Tultuls* were their interpreters.

6. The term *wantok* in Melanesian Pidgin means someone who speaks the same language (literally, "one talk") but is popularly used to describe relations of obligation and reciprocity binding relatives, members of the same clan or tribal group, and much looser forms of association. In the modern context, *wantokism* is often used in the negative sense of nepotism.

Policing in Cambodia
Legitimacy in the Making?

20

RODERIC BROADHURST
THIERRY BOUHOURS

Contents

Long-term Australian involvement in law enforcement capacity building in postconflict Cambodia provides an opportunity to assess the role of international aid in reforming policing practice. This article focuses on the community standing of police and the extent to which policing practices have achieved legitimacy in Cambodia. We draw on the significant decline in the level of crime as measured by national police statistics, press reports, and the United Nations International Crime Victim Surveys (UNICVS) conducted in 2001–2002 and repeated in 2006–2007. We suggest that the dramatic fall in the rates of street crime is the result of a nexus of factors that include modernization (i.e., marked socioeconomic improvement supported by international aid), relative political stability, and cultural resilience. However, regime capture, endemic corruption, especially in the criminal justice system, and lower tolerance to these burdens have limited the positive effect that increased security may bring to state legitimacy.

As both violent and property crimes have declined (the latter dramatically in rural areas), functionalist perspectives have some explanatory purchase

Adapted from Broadhurst, R. and Bouhours, T. (2008). Policing in Cambodia: Legitimacy in the making? *Policing and Society*, http://dx.doi.org/10.1080/10439460802187589

but do not account for the high levels of corruption, organized criminal activities (e.g., Global Witness, 2007), and consumer fraud that are still evident. Indeed, predatory crime by elites remains a significant and unresolved legacy of the transition to an "illiberal democracy" (Peou, 2000, 2006) and regime continuities with the People's Republic of Kampuchea (PRK) and State of Cambodia (SOC). The potential emergence of a "shadow" state and kleptocracy in the context of the rapid development of a market economy is also a significant constraint on the legitimacy of policing institutions. As the special representative of the UN Secretary General for Human Rights in Cambodia, Yash Ghai (2007) concluded in a recent report:

> The absence of effective institutions of government, basic laws, and an impartial judiciary, accompanied by continuing impunity and threats against those who criticize the status quo, increasing landlessness, and growing numbers of displaced persons all leave Cambodia's citizens insecure, vulnerable to systemic denial and violations of their rights, and exposed to well-established methods for maintaining the existing economic and political order. (p. 1)

The concepts of police and policing are not indigenous to Khmer, and the idea of the police is relatively novel. Official rates of crime are remarkably low and are not simply the result of underreporting and underrecording. Traditional concepts of order and authority are contextualized in patron-client relationships within a communitarian society governed by the ideals of Buddhist conduct. Peacekeeping and crime prevention are not usually externalized as activities of agencies such as the police, but remain, at least in rural areas, in the domain of village and commune chiefs. Social order and peacekeeping function through social gossip, natural surveillance, reciprocal relations based on kin and village, and long-standing practices of mediation and reparation. Only the most serious criminal matters gravitate to district and provincial centers, and therefore to outside scrutiny.

The extreme case of Cambodia offers a unique window on how modernization of both the state and economy modifies crime and violence (Arthur & Marenin, 1995; Johnson & Monkkonen, 1996). The Cambodian experience tests functionalist assumptions about how market development and state legitimacy suppress violence. Australia's 10-year-plus engagement through the Cambodian Criminal Justice Assistance Project (CCJAP) to strengthen the rule of law also provides a rare opportunity to evaluate police reform in a transitional state. Crime victim surveys, the monitoring of reported violence, and interviews with key players provide measures of change in the nature and prevalence of crime and lethal violence from which both the role of modernization in a "fragile state" (Anderson, 2005) and the impact of the CCJAP can be assessed.

Assistance to police in developing states has evolved as a response to international and regional cooperation aimed at suppressing cross-border crime and terrorism. Cambodia, due to its history and socioeconomic circumstances, poses such a risk, and Australia, with other countries, has provided both financial and technical assistance to support crime prevention. It has also been assumed that developing police professionalism would support adherence to the rule of law and respect for human rights. A key motivation for assistance is national self-interest and the need to strengthen countermeasures via bilateral and regional policing assistance. Thus, assistance is designed to strengthen the capacity of developing countries to combat transnational criminal networks and to avoid the creation of criminal safe havens (Broadhurst, 2003, 2006).

In 2003, Australia provided AUD39.6 million in aid to Cambodia (about 9% of the total East Asia aid budget and one of the highest per capita), and about 15% of this figure was earmarked for better governance programs. These funds also helped train and equip law enforcement for the challenges of local and global crime. Since 1997, the Australian government has provided CCJAP with AUD30.6 million* to strengthen the rule of law via police reform processes. A further AUD30 million is now being provided in Phase III (2007–2012) to support selected legal and judicial reforms consistent with priorities set by the Council of Legal and Judicial Reform in the light of the Royal Government of Cambodia's (RGC) National Strategic Development Plan (2006–2011). Priorities for aid are likely to be focused on juvenile crime, sustainable management of prisons, and corruption (AusAID, 2007a, 2007b). Reviews of earlier phases were critical of the effectiveness of the police training component and have not endorsed significant further effort in Phase III (AusAID, 2007b).

Overcoming problems in establishing effective policing in fragile states is a crucial factor in developing stable democratic governance (e.g., Donias, 2005, with respect to Haiti; Bertrand, 2004, for Indonesia). Measures of police performance and crime reduction (e.g., violence, fear of crime, and confidence in police) are used to assess the level of security and the legitimacy of RGC law enforcement. Evidence from the UNICVS, attitudes to corruption, official crime statistics, extrajudicial homicides, election violence, and interviews with Australian and Khmer participants are combined to assess the RGC's standing as a state of concern. This chapter therefore adds to the literature about the effectiveness of international policing assistance to post-conflict states and the nature of violent crime during state formation.

We track key indicators of crime and security in Cambodia over 15 years (1992–2007). Data from several sources are used to estimate changes

---

* For Phase I (1997–2002), AUD12.6 million was allocated, and for Phase II (2002–2007), AUD18 million.

in violence as measured by homicide incidents, other violent and property crime victimization, election violence and vigilantism, as well as attitudes toward crime and corruption. The prevalence of homicide and the severity of violence in Cambodia have been detailed, and a decline in homicide has been observed (Broadhurst, 2006). More recent data (as presented below) confirm this trend, which extends to crime in general. Why this has happened and what role the police have played in reducing crime is unclear. However, improvements in socioeconomic standing, reductions in the availability of small arms, and political stability are significant factors.

Both concepts of wealth and political stability are used here in a relative sense. In relation to socioeconomic improvements, GDP per capita has increased from approximately USD160 in 1992 to USD384 in 2006. General improvements in living standards have been observed. Infant and child mortality, illiteracy, and TB have declined. The education level of girls has improved, although universal primary education has not yet been achieved, and one-third of the population remains illiterate. Life expectancy is only 56.4 years; however, this is already an improvement on conditions in 1992, when life expectancy was estimated to be about 53 years. Some 35% of Cambodians were still under the national poverty line in 2004, but this was better than the estimated 47% in 1994 (Men et al., 2005; Murshid, 1998). Recent socioeconomic data show further improvements and significant uptake of modern media and communication. UNICVS data suggest that most respondents also note improvements in economic standing. Since 2000, economic growth has averaged over 7% per annum, and foreign direct investment has increased from USD129 million in 2000 to USD358 million in 2005. Recent economic indicators show a rapidly expanding economy that is forecast to grow at around 9% per annum (Asian Development Bank, 2007). However, the government is still aid dependent, relying on donor countries for approximately 50% of its revenue.

With the slow but final demise of organized armed struggle between 1993 and 1998, political stability and the reduction of electoral violence have also occurred. Forty years of conflict, including revolutionary genocide, Vietnamese occupation, and civil war, theoretically ended with the UN interventions of 1991–1993 and the first national elections. The subsequent forced alliance of Royalist democrats (Funcinpec) and the former State of Cambodia (SOC) Vietnamese-supported Cambodian People's Party (CPP) was inherently unstable and led to the 1997 *coup d'état* and political violence during the second national elections of 1998. However, the 1998 elections completed the demise of the Khmer Rouge already seriously weakened by defections to either the Royalists or CPP.

Regime stability was firmly established after the 2003 third national elections with the political alliance that arose in 2004 between the CPP and a greatly weakened Funcinpec. In effect, this was the eclipse of the discredited

Royalist alliance and heralded the complete political domination of the CPP. In turn, the CPP had itself become dominated by Prime Minister Hun Sen, supported by a formidable praetorian guard, and "power rather than the rule of law remain[ed] a reality" (Peou, 2006, p. 57). The dominance of the CPP was clear with the overwhelming support it won in the first commune elections of 2002, especially in the rural areas, where CPP activities had traditionally focused. The second commune elections in 2007 consolidated the position of the CPP even further and suggested that the 2008 national elections will continue to strengthen its political dominance. Once composed of former communists who are now unabashed modernists and capitalists, the CPP is set to remain the dominant power bloc for the foreseeable future.

Theories of Crime, Modernization, and Development

Functionalist theories of modernization suggest that development will reduce violent crime, while at the same time increasing property and other crimes (notably those against the state, e.g., regulatory offenses and corruption) as the rationalization of modern governance is achieved (Durkheim, 1950). Modernization requires a shift in economic modes of production from feudal/mercantilist to industrial forms, or from Asiatic command to market economies. This shift in productive forces produces greater individualism and a significant middle class, weakens communal regulation, changes the nature of relationships from hierarchical to exchange, and moves social control from informal to formal modes. Shifts from state command economies to free markets are also accompanied by higher risks of corruption and plunder.

In functionalist versions, modernization in its early phases increases differences between rural and urban life and generates acquisitive crime by weakening social control and unleashing expectations, but reduces violent crime. In late modernization, the gap between rural and urban life diminishes, but violence may increase as conflict reemerges due to rapidly changing modes of production and the fragmentation of postmodern identities. Modernization is usually measured by economic development and, following the European experience, the degree of urbanization. Research so far has not found a clear association between economic development and homicide, but has found a significant relationship between the latter and urbanization (Alvazzi del Frate, 1998; LaFree, 1999; Newman, 1999). As noted, Cambodia is one of the least economically developed and urbanized countries in the region. Thus, if functionalist theories about modernization in Cambodia apply, then in an early phase, violent crime should decline while property crime increases and differences between the countryside and town are accentuated.

Cultural integration or homogeneity, often associated with Durkheim's (1950) idea of organic solidarity and measured by fidelity to religious, linguistic, and customary beliefs, has also been hypothesized as a factor in societies enjoying low rates of violent crimes. However, studies of the relationship between culture and homicide, using measures of religious and ethnic homogeneity, have not found a consistent pattern (see, for instance, Neopolitan, 1997). Although significant numbers of Mhong, Cham, and ethnic Vietnamese reside in some locations, overall, with more than 94% Buddhist, Cambodia has a high degree of religious homogeneity, which could play a positive role in the changes to its rate of violent crime. Moreover, according to Elias (1994), the civilizing (or socializing) effects of modernization render violence more problematic, so that the latter is subjected to an intensified criminalization process combined with an increasing reliance on bureaucratic surveillance and special policing institutions.

The role of the rational state through its security management (i.e., monopolization of violence) and welfare functions is crucial in this civilizing process. By improving health services, livelihood security, and literacy, and suppressing crime, the state legitimates its governance. As a "reorganization episode," Cambodia offers an opportunity to observe the nature of crime following a state-induced collective disaster (Evans, Rueschemeyer, & Skocpol, 1985) and how, in the process of state formation, the establishment of a criminal justice system impacts on the prevalence of crime (notably homicide) and perceptions of security. For example, according to Archer and Gartner (1976), one of the effects of war is increased peacetime homicide arising from officially sanctioned wartime violence. Cambodia has been exposed to this legitimation of violence mechanism and had a high peacetime homicide rate, which, despite the absence of reliable data on prewar crime to confirm this hypothesis, might arguably have been the result of state-legitimated wartime violence carrying through into a higher homicide rate in peacetime.

Following decades of war, genocide, and civil dislocation, Cambodia has since undergone state formation and democratization, and experiences crime differently from that of established states. The political settlement that led to the re-creation of a constitutional monarchy in 1993 required the formation of a new state. However, the law and order institutions of this new state did not enjoy public support and legitimacy (Broadhurst, 2002; Peou, 2000, 2006). The absence of an established legal culture restricted the RGC's ability to assert a credible threat to crime and disorder.

Following other explanatory theories of cross-national differences in violence (such as opportunity/stress theories), crime and disorder in the new and fragile state of Cambodia might be the result of changes in the pool of potential offenders and opportunities for violence that vary according to economic and social hardships. Thus, the relative size of high-risk groups (young unemployed males), population density, household size, income inequality, unemployment, and infant mortality have all been employed with varying degrees of success as determinants of violence. Cambodia, with its exceptionally young population, acute levels of income inequality, and relatively high underemployment (reliable data on unemployment rates are unavailable), could also be vulnerable to higher risks of violence. Competition over scarce resources may be reflected in the high levels of robbery-murder (i.e., lethal robberies) that have been observed in Cambodia (Daly & Wilson, 1999).

Methodology and Results

Three main sources of crime data supplemented by in-depth interviews with CCJAP staff and key Khmer stakeholders, as well as socioeconomic trend data, have been used in this research. A major component of the study was a repeat of the UNICVS first conducted in 2001 in order to measure changes in the crime victimization experience, reasons for reporting or not reporting crime to police, fear of crime, attitudes to punishment, and trust of police and other government officials. The UNICVS does not include homicide events; therefore, additional sources (e.g., newspaper crime reports) as well as official statistics were used. The objective was to acquire multiple measures of the level of crime and insecurity in Cambodia for 1992–2007, with emphasis on the periods 1997–2001 and 2002–2007 that coincide with the two distinct funding phases of the CCJAP (AusAID, 2001). The latter period represents a concerted effort at developing district and provincial crime prevention programs, while the earlier period was an indirect phase focused on training, police reform, and infrastructure development. With such data, theory testing and an evaluation of the impact of criminal justice reforms and crime reduction programs in the context of economic and political development can be attempted.

Official Crime Reports

Crime recorded by the police from 1992 onward is reported in Table 20.1. The overall rates of recorded crime through 1992–2005 have varied between a low 30.3 (in 1994) and a high 58.5 (in 1998) per 100,000 population, and are low by comparison with developed states (see Broadhurst, 2002). Since 1998, crime rates have steadily decreased to only 32.4 per 100,000 in 2005. Estimates of homicide victims, including suspect death, grenade events, and common murder/manslaughter drawn from RGC judicial police and other sources from 1992–2005 (not reported in Table 20.1), show that suspect death and grenade events have become less frequent, while overall rates of homicide victims have fluctuated between a high 12.9 per 100,000 in 1993 and a low 3.8 per 100,000 in 2005. However, police statistics underreport crime (they measure police activity rather than criminal activity) and are often inaccurate and therefore supplemented by crime victim surveys and newspaper data.

Table 20.1   Crime Trends Recorded by Judicial Police, 1992–2005

	1992	1993	1994	1995	1996	1997	1998	1999	2000	2001	2002	2003	2004	2005
								Number of Recorded Crime Events						
Murder	429	599	303	397	542	317	793	581	571	407	425	509	511	448
Armed robbery	1,414	1,613	905	832	1,345	887	1,822	1,396	1,252	1,296[a]	1,419[a]	1,175	1,320	868
Grenade attack	40	157	79	27	54	46	68	42	39	21	10	23	33	20
Rape	106	43	39	84	122	46	130	165	209	218[a]	279[a]	331	281	254
Kidnap[a]	9	93	133	24	44	23	130	91	63	51	38	25	7	10
Poisons[b]	14	47	42	23	24	21	0	20	31	n/a	n/a	6	n/a	n/a
Patrimony[c]	8	6	20	12	6	n/a	n/a	2	4	n/a	n/a	n/a	n/a	3
Theft	1,420	792	835	896	1,471	868	1,871	1,789	1,827	1,854	1,846	1,741	1,503	1,458
Assault/disputes[d]	515	267	353	423	1,050	445	1,114	1,058	1,130	1,131	1,141	1,301	1,024	1,010
Fraud/pickpocket[e]	23	117	163	214	233	97	244	246	218	116[f]	202[f]	160[f]	113[f]	104[f]
Illegal weapon	136	514	235	310	79	n/a	n/a	n/a	96	67	76	64	43	43
Other offenses	n/a	n/a	20	n/a	668	208	905	639	387[g]	381[g]	309[g]	358[g]	161	256[g]
All crime	4,114	4,248	3,031	3,260	5,638[h]	2,958	7,077	6,029	5,827	5,542	5,745	5,693	4,996	4,474
Rate per 100,000	45.7	44.7	30.3	31.5	51.2	25.5	58.5	48.6	46.2	43.3	44.2	42.8	37.0	32.4
Population[i] (mil.)	9.0	9.5	10.0	10.5	11.0	11.6	12.1	12.4	12.6	12.8	13.0	13.3	13.5	13.8

Sources: 1998, 1999–2003, 2005 annual returns, MOI Judicial Police Centre; 1997 data incomplete.

Notes: n/a = not available.

a Also counts robbery and rape murder.
b Poisoning and kidnapping are presumed nonfatal.
c Theft of cultural heritage.
d Records only injurious assaults.
e Offenses combined in original source.
f Pickpocketing counted in theft from 2001.
g Attempted killing is included: 2000 = 51, 2001 = 153, 2002 = 102, 2003 = 87, 2005 = 69.
h Total includes 201 injuries associated with grenade attacks.
i Population estimates are derived from Asian Development Bank "Country Strategy and Program Update" and are approximate; all data revised December 2007.

Newspaper Crime Reports

From 1998 onward, crimes reported by Cambodian newspapers were also monitored, with special attention to vigilante and extrajudicial homicides. Changes in the type of crime reported by the press as well as a decline in vigilante and police killings were indicated. In 1998, 32% of homicides reported by the press involved police, military/militia, or vigilante action, but this had fallen to 8.8% in 2006. Such data measure police probity, and decreases in extrajudicial homicides may indicate a strengthening of the rule of law; however, newspaper reports of homicides and other fatalities may not be a reliable index of these events. Nevertheless, the proportion of homicides among crime stories had also reduced from that reported in 1998.

Estimates of political and election-related violence compiled by the UN and other human rights groups also show reductions. National elections in 1993 and 1998 were among the most violent, although this was not repeated in the 2003 elections. Hughes (2006) notes that the frequency of politically motivated killings has declined, but they remain potent symbols of the continued role of political violence. Data compiled from secondary sources (i.e., UN Office of Human Rights in Cambodia and local civil society nongovernmental organizations (NGOs)), police, and newspaper sources do suggest that some political violence occurred in 2004 and was associated with the post-2003 election stalemate that remained unresolved until mid-2004 (newspapers reports showed a peak in vigilante actions in 2004 compared to 1999–2003 and 2005–2006). National elections in 2008 will offer a further opportunity to observe shifts in presumed associations between violence and politics.

Crime Victim Surveys

The first Cambodian UNICVS was conducted in 2001 in Phnom Penh and five geographically representative provinces (Kampot, Kampong Cham, Kampong Spueu, Kandal, and Kampong Chhnang). The second survey was completed in two stages: first in Phnom Penh and Kandal in October 2006 and then, using the same procedure, in Kampong Cham in October-November 2007. It was administered as a face-to-face household survey (N = 2,300 in the first sweep* and N = 2,517 in the second). The crimes covered included car theft, theft from cars, car vandalism, bicycle and motorcycle theft, livestock theft, attempted and successful burglary, personal theft, consumer fraud, assault (including sexual assault), robbery, and corruption. A survey of mortality, including suicide and homicide incidents in every participating household (a total of 790 households and 4,683 individuals in

---

* With Kampot, Kampong Spueu, and Kampong Chhnang the total N was 3,062.

2007), was incorporated in the revised UNICVS protocol for the 2007 sweep of Kampong Cham. No suicide and two homicides were reported over the past five years. UNICVS also asked general questions about the reporting behavior of victims, fear of crime, satisfaction with police, and attitudes toward crime and punishment.

The annual prevalence of crime estimated from the first and second surveys showed significant declines in crime victimization across all offense categories, with declines in Kampong Cham the most dramatic. Small increases in robbery and bicycle theft were observed in Kandal, but these were the only exceptions (see Table 20.2). For example, motorcycle theft, burglary, and livestock theft all showed dramatic declines. The observed reductions in crime, while substantial, still revealed large gaps between the experience of victims and the records of police. Willingness to report crime to police showed some increase in motorcycle theft and rape, but in general victims remained reluctant to call on police.

However, field interviews with key commune officials (i.e., village heads, post police, commune chiefs, and clerks) revealed that citizens frequently report crime, especially in rural areas, to the village or commune chiefs in the first instance, but these are often not recorded by police at the district, provincial, or national level. Thus, like official police data, the UNICVS underestimate the reporting level of crime victims. Respondents often referred to the problems of reporting crime to the police in terms of the costs: police often demanded petrol money or other fees (i.e., bribes) before taking action. Questions about reporting behavior are especially useful in measuring confidence in the police and other criminal justice agencies, while questions about fear of crime gauge citizen's assessments of security (see below and Skogan, 2007).

The decline in violent victimization can be partly explained by the civilizing effect of modernization. For instance, the general improvement in the socioeconomic circumstances of many citizens (observed during the Kampong Cham UNICVS) has lessened the incidence of violent predatory crimes such as robbery motivated by extreme deprivation. However, the simultaneous decline in nonviolent property crime does not support the traditional functionalist hypothesis that with greater materialism and insatiable desire for possessions, modernization also brings a sharp rise in property crime. Here a cultural interpretation, which can also account for the low levels of reporting crime to the police and a general mistrust of state institutions, seems more appropriate. Strong Buddhist values and traditional forms of social control also help to inhibit criminal victimization. While regime capture and corruption are likely to generate distrust in state institutions, manifested, for instance, in the unwillingness to report crimes to the police, there is also an enduring culture of self-help that has seldom relied on the central state to manage conflicts.

Table 20.2 One-Year Victimization Estimates and Percent Reported to Police, in Phnom Penh, Kandal, and Kampong Cham, 2000, 2005–2006

| Crimes | Phnom Penh | | | | Kandal | | | | Kampong Cham | | | |
| | 2000 | | 2005 | | 2000 | | 2005 | | 2000 | | 2006 | |
	% Vic	% Rep	% Vic	% Rep	% Vic	% Rep	% Vic	% Rep	% Vic	% Rep	% Vic	% Rep
Car theft[a]	1.3	100.0	0.0	0.0	1.5	100.0	0.0	0.0	0.0	0.0	0.0	0.0
From car[a]	20.5	4.3	4.3	10.0	15.2	0.0	3.6	0.0	8.3	0.0	5.7	0.0
Car vandal[a]	2.6	0.0	1.7	0.0	1.5	0.0	3.6	33.3	0.0	0.0	0.0	0.0
Motorcycle theft[a]	7.7	61.5	2.4	69.6	4.5	46.7	4.2	66.7	5.4	46.7	1.0	50.0
Bicycle theft[a]	9.9	10.9	5.8	2.4	6.7	8.7	7.6	5.3	14.7	13.8	3.1	0.0
Livestock[a]	20.0	5.3	8.2	0.0	19.1	1.8	13.6	0.0	24.8	8.9	11.1	1.3
Burglary	16.2	16.2	7.5	18.3	10.5	10.0	6.1	15.4	12.7	11.4	2.2	0.0
Attempted burglary	7.8	31.5	2.7	6.9	5.2	20.0	3.5	18.2	7.6	45.2	1.6	15.4
Fraud	39.6	5.7	25.4	6.5	31.8	5.5	18.7	1.7	29.8	2.4	22.0	4.6
Corruption	27.8	1.2	18.2	1.0	18.5	1.9	18.3	3.4	15.6	1.2	12.9	5.9
Person theft	13.8	8.6	6.5	9.9	5.2	3.3	3.1	0.0	7.3	10.0	2.3	5.6
Robbery	1.9	45.5	1.5	62.5	0.3	100.0	0.6	50.0	0.9	100.0	0.1	0.0
Assault/threat	7.8	27.2	2.0	27.3	4.4	28.0	2.8	27.8	6.2	29.4	2.3	44.4
Sexual assault[b]	1.8	8.3	0.2	50.0	0.3	0.0	0.0	0.0	0.3	0.0	0.0	0.0

[a] Percent victimized calculated on number of owners.

[b] Percent victimized calculated on number of victims; % vic (percent victimized) based on one-year prevalence; % rep (percent reported) calculated on number of females. For Phnom Penh and Kandal UNICVS 2001 and 2006, one-year estimates respectively correspond to 2000 and 2005; for Kampong Cham UNICVS 2001 and 2007, one-year estimates respectively correspond to 2000 and 2006.

Fear of Crime

Over two-fifths of Phnom Penh respondents in our first and second sweeps felt unsafe or very unsafe "walking alone in [their] area after dark" (46.5% in 2001 and 41% in 2006). In Kandal fewer respondents felt unsafe (39.5% in 2001 and 33% 2006), and likewise in Kampong Cham (33.6% to 30.4%). Respondents also felt much safer "at home after dark," with 29.5% feeling unsafe or very unsafe in Phnom Penh in 2006 compared with 39.5% in 2001, while in Kandal the proportion fell from 34% to 25.5%, and in Kampong Cham from 27% to 22%. Overall, more respondents felt safe in 2006 compared to 2001. The decline in fear as well as in the perception of the risk of burglary may be associated with the decline in the risk of crime noted by the UNICVS. By controlling political violence, regime stability has played a role in lessening feelings of insecurity, but again, cultural factors also play a significant role. Communitarian attitudes generally prevail in Cambodia, and individualism is not privileged as in the West. For example, more than 95% of the UNICVS respondents declared that in their area "most people helped each other." Such perceptions are likely to help build confidence, self-help, and feelings of safety.

Public Perceptions of Police

In general, Cambodians are less satisfied with their police services than they were in 2001–2002. Police enjoy some degree of legitimacy—a legitimacy that is conditional on a modicum of service and an absence of rent seeking. Differences between the policing services are not measured, but in the case of rural villages, post police or local police are the usual focus of respondents. In our interviews with local village heads and commune officials, problems of underpolicing, poor equipment, and inadequate numbers were noted (e.g., one commune had a police establishment of nine officers but only three were posted to the commune). Often reinforcements were slow to arrive and offenders had eluded arrest. A key factor in the legitimacy of police is the very notion that, if the police are called, they will come and order and justice can be restored. If the citizen believes this to be the case, then the mere threat of calling the police amplifies the efficiency and efficacy of the police (Proenca & Muniz, 2006).

Many respondents, especially those in rural areas, commented on the limited response of both local and district police. Attitudes toward police have become more critical in respect to both controlling crime and helpfulness, with more people stating that police were doing a poor job. Nevertheless, about two-thirds of respondents felt police were helpful and doing a good job in Kampong Cham (compared to 70.5% in 2001), and over half remained positive to police in Phnom Penh and Kandal (compared to two-thirds in

2001). Despite the significant decline in criminal victimization, including police corruption and the moderation of the fear of crime, this was not matched by greater public confidence in the police. Other results from the UNICVS support the suggestion that citizens now expect more professional and community-oriented policing. Although Cambodians often have a more positive view of their police than many respondents from developed countries, the impact of modernization also renders them less tolerant of crime and more demanding of law enforcement agencies.

Corruption

The UNICVS also asked respondents about their experience with corruption and their perception of the likelihood of corruption. Most experience with corruption involved elected commune or municipal officials and police, but the pattern varied depending on the location. Significant declines in actual victimization were observed in Phnom Penh (from 27.8% in 2000 to 18.2% in 2005) and Kampong Cham (15.6% in 2000 to 12.9% in 2006) but not in Kandal (18.5% in 2000 to 18.3% in 2005). The actual experience of corruption had also decreased with respect to police (except in Kandal). In Phnom Penh, the proportion of victims of police corruption declined from 10.1% in 2000 to 5.7% in 2005 and represented 31.2% of all victims of corruption compared to 36.5% in 2000. In Kampong Cham the proportion reduced from 4.5% in 2000 to 2.5% in 2006 and represented 20.2% of all victims of corruption compared to 29.1% in 2000. In Kandal, however, the experience of corruption by police officers had increased, from 3.5% in 2000 to 4.4% in 2005, and represented 24.1% of all victims of corruption compared to 18.9% in 2000. In the three provinces the most frequently cited officials by victims of corruption in both the first and second sweeps were elected commune officials.

The perception that overall corruption by public officials was more likely increased in Kandal and Kampong Cham between 2001 and 2006–2007 (but not in Phnom Penh, where it significantly decreased). In the first UNICVS, Cambodians were more likely to consider teachers, doctors, and local officials as corrupt than local police; however, in the rural province of Kampong Cham this sentiment shifted by the second sweep, when elected and municipal officials, as well as court officials and police, were perceived as most likely to be corrupt.

Perception of corrupt conduct by police officers had significantly reduced in Phnom Penh, from 28.9% of respondents who felt police officers were likely to be corrupt in 2001, to 14% in 2006. However, in Kandal and Kampong Cham, respondents' negative perceptions about the conduct of police officers had increased from 16.7% in 2001 to 19.8% in 2006 in Kandal and from 31% to 60.6% in Kampong Cham.

Discussion

The data indicate a substantial decrease in both property and violent crimes. A significant decline in homicide (including extrajudicial homicide) has occurred. Such forms of homicide are indicative of weak formal social control but, with greater regime stability, are far less common in 2006 than in 1998. Given the appalling trauma of the recent past, political conflict, the scale of economic adversity, and the rapidity of urbanization and social changes induced by market development, the current level of homicide is consistent with expectations. More developed neighbors also appear to experience similar levels of homicide but do not share the degree of social desperation or deficits in human assets. Indeed, a rate somewhat lower than would be predicted by an integrated strain and cultural theory of violence may be indicated.

While political stability and disarmament have led to a decrease in group conflicts and war-legitimated lethal violence (Wille, 2006), such events only account for a declining fraction of homicide in Cambodia. The general decline in lethal violence may also reflect the substantial improvements in overall wealth (although the latter is associated with declines in equality per Gini levels, especially in the 1990s) and the steady economic growth that have contributed to a reduction in extreme competition over resources and improvements in some basic services.

Communal traditions, localism, and pro-social Buddhist values have prevailed as potent forms of collective protection and could be reinforced by effective governance. The decline in crime shown by the UNICVS also suggests a high degree of social resilience among Khmer, especially in rural areas. These shields may be fragile and are threatened by the tendency of modernity to privilege individuality and materialism. High unemployment among young rural males also appears to be a potential stimulus to crime and disorder and is the focus of concern for many village heads and commune chiefs.

Theoretical implications for crime in a developing economy such as Cambodia are framed by both functionalist and conflict or "world systems" accounts of crime. Functionalist accounts provide plausible explanations for the decline in violence, but are not consistent with the significant reduction in property crime and the apparent convergence between urban and rural areas. The new dynamics of modernization processes in late-20th-century contexts, including globalization and international aid mechanisms, may have cancelled or changed the effects of early modernization phases predicted by orthodox functionalism. This suggests that modernization theory itself needs to be modernized (or postmodernized) to better fit these new contexts and dynamics, and should give more prominence to the role of cultural influences. Conflict approaches help explain transnational and state crime—notably the entrenched forms of corruption associated with the plunder and rent seeking of government officials, including police, although the experience of street-level corruption in Cambodia has also abated.

This chapter provided some assessment of an earlier Australian forward strategy originally justified on humanitarian grounds but now redesigned to prevent, *inter alia*, a criminal safe haven scenario from arising in Cambodia. As Australia becomes increasingly engaged in overseas police assistance, it is useful to reassess what may be achieved. The CCJAP example offers such an opportunity because sufficient time has elapsed to observe meaningful change. The data on crime and victimization also enable reconsideration of the forms of engagement needed in fragile states (Anderson, 2005). These data suggest that assistance via a police reform strategy may provide limited benefits in improved professionalism, but that these gains may be compromised by the weakness of the court system and the absence of the political will to address corruption at all levels.

Police reform in fragile states has often failed, and policing institutions have become part of the problem rather than the solution—because they either have been captured by organized crime or have reverted to repressive-style regime policing. Although the risks remain significant in the case of Cambodia, the current evidence indicates that policing institutions have continued to struggle against organized crime and sought to legitimize themselves independent of regime politics. In this regard the results seem mixed: While reductions in police violence and actual police corruption are noted, Khmer are less positive and confident in police than in 2000–2001—when both crime and socioeconomic conditions were worse. There are also growing concerns about juvenile crime, which, unlike the general trend, appears to be rising. So possible changes to the fabric of informal social control, induced by modernization, are under way and create gaps that an under-resourced police force cannot address. Changing attitudes toward crime and higher expectations about what the state should deliver in response to new challenges to social control have also raised the standards expected of police, and accordingly public confidence in the police.

Rule of Law and the Cambodian State

The fragmentation of the original civil society by war and genocide has required a conscious effort to reinvent and reproduce the social and moral order of an ideal prewar Khmer nation. The 1991 Paris Accords reconstituted, under United Nations Transitional Authority Cambodian (UNTAC) supervision, the RGC as a pluralistic state made up of the former SOC, Khmer Rouge, and Royalists under the rubric of "nation, religion, king." The functioning of state institutions and their agents independent of CPP politics remains weak, with corruption and cronyism evident. The merging of CPP and the state now seems complete, and the regime exercises administration more in terms of traditional patron-client relations than rational allocation of resources.

The transformation of the governance of state security from a military to civil form was a key goal of the first national development plan along with improving food and personal security, human rights, health, education, and economic development. Under the 1993 UNTAC demobilization plan, large numbers of former soldiers were placed in policing roles on below subsistence wages. Consequently, the management and discipline of such a large body of armed and ill-trained police has been a major problem and source of impunity. The planned progressive reductions in the number of underemployed untrained police and military personnel required that by year 2001 their numbers fall from 137,000 to 67,000. In 2001 this had not occurred; there was doubt about the effectiveness of the demobilization plan, and misuse of funds was identified by donors such as the World Bank (Adams, 2001). Reductions in the size of the security forces and weapon availability had been hampered by factional differences in the key Ministries of the Interior (MOI) and Defense until 2003–2004, when CPP domination was completed. Although substantial progress has been made in the reduction of small arms, significant units of the Royal Cambodian Armed Forces (RCAF) remain beyond effective civil control or answer only to key officials. This appears to be the case with Brigade 70 and the prime minister's powerful bodyguard unit (Global Witness, 2007). Thus, the overall civilianizing process will continue to be complicated, and some units continue to pose formidable risks of violence.

However, while in 1995 the shift required from a military command economy to a market economy was burdened by the 62% of the RGC revenue absorbed by the security forces (Ministries of Interior and Defense), this had substantially decreased to 18.3% in 2006 (Asian Development Bank, 2007). In 1998, as little as 10% of meager revenues went to education, 6% to health, and 3% to agricultural development, but by 2006 budget expenditure on education had increased substantially to reach 19.2%, and 11.25% for health (Asian Development Bank, 2003, 2007; Konrad Adenauer Foundation, cited in *Phnom Penh Post*, 1998).

The RGC has operated in the context of a politically divided government of former antagonists—Royalists, revolutionaries, and socialists. Consequently, state institutions are complex and, until 2004, were open to factional conflicts, and an effective lawmaking consensual process has not been achieved. Historically, the kingdom had a weak indigenous bureaucracy based on a French and Vietnamese colonial legacy in which recourse to state and legal institutions was grossly underdeveloped. Traditionally, the Cambodian state was hierarchical, with the revered king, elite government officials, villagers, and Buddhist monks all in their place in the complex web of patronage and power. In crucial ways these traditional, often unmediated, hierarchical relations found their expression in the utopian self-sufficiency program of the revolutionary (Khmer Rouge, 1975–1979) and continue to shape Cambodian personal and social relationships (Chandler, 1992, pp. 53–54). The ceaseless cycles of rice growing that define Khmer village life impose a natural social order based on communal surveillance, which reduces the need for intervention by the state. Accordingly, the role of police in creating order is limited to the extent that national uniformity may be required in the context of a devoutly Buddhist society. Preexisting social identities and relationships account for the form of social order found in rural Cambodia.

The new penal code started in 1994 was not expected to pass the National Assembly until late 2007, and current laws are based on the 1992 UNTAC criminal code. In January 2002 this was augmented by amendments that strengthened the role of the MOI. The UNTAC code failed to provide a comprehensive ethical system or secure due process consistent with Khmer values, further eroding the legitimacy of law. Court procedural laws were eventually enacted in 2007; however, courts remain a concern and are widely considered unreliable. UN-sponsored efforts to rapidly develop a modern court and dispute settlement process included a judicial mentor program that relied on guidance by overseas judges. This attempt to provide training for court officials (most former SOC judges) faltered because the poorly paid judges were prone to corruption or intimidation, and access to courts was prohibitively expensive to all but the elite. A substantial number of offenses and disputes are resolved at the commune level without the involvement of provincial or national courts. Therefore, some serious crime and much petty crime and disorder, as everywhere, will be underreported. The UNICVS data also show that significant levels of crime, although reported, are not recorded.

Supported by international assistance, the RGC has promised to develop a state of rule of law through reforms of the policing institutions, but shortages of human and social capital tend to mobilize underpaid policing institutions according to market forces and not abstract notions of the rule of law. Low salaries, poor training, and patron-style leadership induce bribery and corruption, and provide the thread of impunity that enables predatory corruption to thrive and challenge or even capture key elements of the state. Widespread concern about elite corruption is not simply a product of lawless behavior but the absence of effective anti-corruption laws and agencies with the necessary political will to enforce them. The recent discovery of potentially large offshore reserves of oil and gas (on-stream by 2011) may be the key to the realization of the worthy goals of poverty reduction and national development, but the large revenues anticipated may also be at risk of misuse by weak institutions dominated by regime elites.

Conclusion

If the assumption that strong states are more effective at suppressing ordinary crime is valid, then the evidence presented here suggests that the steady assertion of CPP dominance over the security forces has led to a diminution of the more extreme examples of violence. It has reduced competition between faction warlords and insured greater control over the diverse independent elements that make up the policing apparatus whose loyalty is now associated with a CPP-dominated government. Thus, in seeking legitimacy, the RGC has been able to give priority to security while increasingly diverting resources to other pressing priorities. In this sense, policing in Cambodia may be characterized as regime dependent, and it seems unlikely that the new legislature and king can establish the kind of supra-loyalty among these forces that may serve to limit their predatory tendencies and those of the new business elites.

The plural democratic state envisaged by the 1991 Paris Accords, replete with checks and balances and respect for law and human rights, has yet to fully emerge, and elements of the state itself are immune from oversight. In this context, efforts at supporting police professionalism, while pivotal to the rule of law, may be counterproductive given ineffective courts and weak oversight of the executive by the democratically elected legislature.

References

Adams, B. (2001). Demobilizations' house of mirrors. *Phnom Penh Post, 10,* 14.

Alvazzi del Frate, A. (1998). *Preventing crime: Citizens' experience across the world* (Issues and Reports 9). Rome: UNICRI.

Anderson, I. (2005). *Fragile states: What is international experience telling us?* Canberra: AusAID. Retrieved March 28, 2006, from http://www.AusAID.gov.au/publications/pdf/fragile_states.pdf

Archer, D., & Gartner, R. (1976). Violent acts and violent times: A comparative approach to post-war homicide rates. *American Sociological Review, 41,* 937–963.

Arthur, J. A., & Marenin, O. (1995). Explaining crime in developing countries: The need for a case study approach. *Crime, Law and Social Change, 23,* 191–214.

Asian Development Bank. (2003). *Cambodia: Country strategy and program update 2004–06.* Manila: Asian Development Bank.

Asian Development Bank. (2007). *Asian development outlook.* Manila: Asian Development Bank. Retrieved May 17, 2007 from http://www.adb.org/Cambodia/default.asp

AusAID. (2001). *Cambodian criminal justice assistance project: Feasibility study phase II.* Unpublished report, Canberra.

AusAID. (2007a, July). *Independent completion report: Cambodia criminal justice assistance Project PCCJAP II.* Unpublished report, Phnom Penh/Canberra.

AusAID. (2007b, May). *Australia's assistance to criminal justice reform in Cambodia: Strategic framework document.* Unpublished report, Phnom Penh/Canberra.

Bertrand, R. (2004). Behave like enraged lions: Civil militias, the army and the criminalisation of politics in Indonesia. *Global Crime, 6*, 325–344.

Broadhurst, R. G. (2002). Lethal violence and state formation in Cambodia. *Australian & New Zealand Journal of Criminology, 35*, 1–26.

Broadhurst, R. G. (2003). Rapporteur's report. In R. G. Broadhurst (Ed.), *Bridging the GAP: A global alliance perspective on transnational organised crime* (pp. 1–25). Hong Kong: Hong Kong Government Printer/Hong Kong Police.

Broadhurst, R. G. (2006). Lethal violence, crime and political change in Cambodia. In A. Croissant, B. Martin, & S. Kneip (Eds.) *The Politics of Death: Political Violence in Southeast Asia.* (pp. 343–378). Hamburg: Lit Verlag.

Chandler, D. (1992). *A history of Cambodia.* Sydney, NSW: Allen and Unwin.

Daly, M., & Wilson, M. (1999). An evolutionary psychology perspective on homicide. In M. D. Smith & M. A. Zahn (Eds.), *Homicide: A sourcebook of social research* (pp. 58–71). London: Sage Publications.

Donias, T. (2005). Back to square one: The politics of police reform in Haiti. *Civil Wars, 7*, 270–287.

Durkheim, E. (1950). *The rules of sociological method.* Glencoe, IL: Free Press.

Elias, N. (1994). *The civilizing process.* Oxford: Blackwell.

Evans, P. B., Rueschemeyer, D., & Skocpol, T. (Eds.). (1985). *Bringing the state back.* New York: Cambridge University Press.

Ghai, Y. (2007). *Implementation of General Assembly Resolution 60/251 of 15 March 2006 entitled, "Human Rights Council."* Report of the Special Representative of the Secretary General for Human Rights in Cambodia, A/HRC/4/36.

Global Witness. (2007). *Cambodia's family trees: Illegal logging and the stripping of public assets by Cambodia's elite.* Washington, DC: Global Witness.

Hughes, C. (2006). Violence and voting in post-1993 Cambodia. In A. Croissant, B. Martin, & S. Kneip (Eds.), *The politics of death: Political violence in Southeast Asia* (pp. 319–342). Muenster: Lit Verlag.

Johnson, E. A., & Monkkonen, E. H. (Eds.). (1996). *The civilization of crime: Violence in town and country since the Middle Ages.* Chicago: University of Illinois Press.

LaFree, G. A. (1999). Summary and review of cross-national comparative studies of homicide. In M. D. Smith & M.A. Zahn (Eds.), *Homicide: A sourcebook of social research* (pp. 125–145). London: Sage.

Men, B., Grundy, J., Cane, J., Ramsey, L., An, N. S., Soeung, S. C. et al. (2005). Key issues relating to decentralization at the provincial level of health management in Cambodia. *International Journal of Health and Management, 20*, 3–19.

Murshid, K. (1998). *Food security in an Asian transitional economy—The Cambodian experience* (Working Paper VI). Phnom Penh: Cambodian Development Resource Centre.

Neopolitan, J. (1997). Homicides in developing nations: Results of research using a large and representative sample. *International Journal of Offender Therapy and Comparative Criminology, 41*, 358–374.

Newman, G. (1999). *Global report on crime and justice.* New York: UN Office of Drug Control & Crime.

Peou, S. (2000). *Change and regime change in Cambodia: Toward democracy?* London: St. Martin's Press.

Peou, S. (2006). Consolidation or crisis of democracy? Cambodia's parliamentary election in 2003 and beyond. In A. Croissant, B. Martin, and S. Kneip (Eds.), *Between consolidation and crisis* (pp. 41–84). Hamburg: Lit Verlag.

Phnom Penh Post. (1998–2006). Police blotter. *Phnom Penh Post*, Vols. 7–16 (weekly).

Proenca, D., Jr., & Muniz, J. (2006). Stop or I will call the police: The idea of police, or the effects of police encounters over time. *British Journal of Criminology, 46*, 234–257.

Skogan, W. (2007). Survey assessments of police performance. In M. Hough & M. Maxfield (Eds.), *Surveying crime in the 21st century* (pp. 165–182). Cullompton, UK: Willan.

Wille, C. (2006). Finding the evidence: The links between weapon collection programmes, gun use and homicide. *African Security News, 15*, 59–70.

Index

A Call for Authors

Introducing a New Book Series from CRC Press

Advances in Police Theory and Practice

AIMS AND SCOPE:

This cutting-edge series is designed to promote publication of books on contemporary advances in police theory and practice. We are especially interested in volumes that focus on the nexus between research and practice, with the end goal of disseminating innovations in policing. We will consider collections of expert contributions as well as individually authored works. Books in this series will be marketed internationally to both academic and professional audiences. This series also seeks to —

- Bridge the gap in knowledge about advances in theory and practice regarding who the police are, what they do, and how they maintain order, administer laws, and serve their communities

- Improve cooperation between those who are active in the field and those who are involved in academic research so as to facilitate the application of innovative advances in theory and practice

The series especially encourages the contribution of works coauthored by police practitioners and researchers. We are also interested in works comparing policing approaches and methods globally, examining such areas as the policing of transitional states, democratic policing, policing and minorities, preventive policing, investigation, patrolling and response, terrorism, organized crime, and drug enforcement. In fact, every aspect of policing, public safety, and security, as well as public order is relevant for the series. Manuscripts should be between 300 and 600 printed pages. If you have a proposal for an original work or for a contributed volume, please be in touch.

Series Editor
Dilip Das, Ph.D.
Ph: 802-598-3680 E-mail: dilipkd@aol.com

Dr. Das is a professor of criminal justice and Human Rights Consultant to the United Nations. He is a former chief of police and founding president of the International Police Executive Symposium, IPES, www.ipes.info. He is also the founding editor-in-chief of *Police Practice and Research: An International Journal* (PPR), (Routledge/Taylor & Francis), www.tandf.co.uk/journals. In addition to editing the *World Police Encyclopedia* (Taylor & Francis, 2006), Dr. Das has published numerous books and articles during his many years of involvement in police practice, research, writing, and education.

Proposals for the series may be submitted to the series editor or directly to –

Carolyn Spence
Acquisitions Editor • CRC Press / Taylor & Francis Group
561-998-2515 • 561-997-7249 (fax)
carolyn.spence@taylorandfrancis.com • www.crcpress.com
6000 Broken Sound Parkway NW, Suite 300, Boca Raton, FL 33487

CRC Press
Taylor & Francis Group